PRETTY KITTY HERRICK

THE HORSEBREAKER

A

ROMANCE OF LOVE AND SPORT

BY

MRS. EDWARD KENNARD

AUTHOR OF "THE GIRL IN THE BROWN HABIT"; "KILLED IN THE OPEN"; "MATRON OR MAID"; "A REAL GOOD THING," ETC.

NEW YORK
JOHN A. TAYLOR AND COMPANY

COPYRIGHT, 1891, BY
JOHN A. TAYLOR AND COMPANY

CONTENTS.

PRETTY KITTY HERRICK.

CHAPTER I.

GOING CUB-HUNTING.

"Papa, are you ready? We shall be late for the meet if you don't make haste. Gretton Grange is quite ten miles from here, and the Duke of Furrowdale does not give one much law this time of year. We really ought to be off," said Kitty Herrick, a trifle impatiently, addressing her father, who was sitting opposite at the breakfast-table.

They were both dressed in riding apparel, and were making a hasty meal before going cub-hunting. Miss Kitty's appetite had not taken so long to appease as the worthy Squire's, and it seemed to her that he would never finish eating.

"All right, little woman," he replied, heroically gulping down a cup of boiling tea. "I wont keep you waiting much longer. That's the worst of the cub-hunting season; one has to start so infernally early, and although I don't much mind getting up myself, it's next door to an impossibility to prevail upon one's servants to be punctual. I told Barlow to call me at six, and it must have been nearly half-past before he brought my hot water. However," he added, pulling out his watch, "I make it only a quarter to eight now."

"And they meet sharp at nine," said Kitty, with a touch of severity. "We are running it very fine."

"I'm coming, my dear—coming." So saying, Squire

Herrick rose reluctantly from the table, and was preparing to move towards the door when a copy of an evening newspaper happened to catch his eye. Although he had already read its contents, he could not resist the temptation of having another look at them—or at least at that portion in which he was most vitally interested. A shadow passed over his daughter's bright young face as she observed the action. Experience had taught her that unless she interfered he would soon be absorbed in the doings of the money market, oblivious of everything else.

"Papa," she said, in her clear voice, determined to prevent him from falling into a brown-study which only had the effect of depressing his spirits, "the pony chaise is at the door, and if we don't make haste Templar will kick the cart to pieces. You know how he hates being kept waiting, and I can see him from the window rounding his back and fighting with John, as much as to say he wont stand it much longer."

The Squire threw down the newspaper with a sigh, and strode off to buckle on his spurs and get into his heavy box-cloth driving coat. In spite of the impatience which she had previously exhibited, Kitty stayed behind for a moment. She was a true daughter of Eve, and possessed her sex's proverbial curiosity. Her quick eye travelled over the columns that were wont to engage her father's attention so deeply. She could not understand wherein their charm consisted.

"Ugh!" she exclaimed aloud. "Stocks and shares, as usual! Horrible things! I hate them. They seem to spoil even the very nicest men. As for papa, since he took to bothering his head about Great Easterns, Egyptians, Mexican Bonds, and similar rubbish, he is not half as cheerful as he used to be. In fact, my belief is they are making him quite ill. Two years ago he was ever so much keener about hunting than he is now, and I attribute the change entirely to that odious Stock Exchange. I hope to goodness Cyril never will have anything to do with it." Upon which, Kitty crumpled

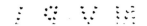

up the newspaper resentfully and gave it an indignant kick with her pretty little foot. She was only nineteen, and had the spirits of a child.

Five minutes later the redoubtable Templar was bowling father and daughter along at a rattling pace. He was an old hunter, and had not been in harness more than some half-dozen times. Consequently, he proved decidedly skittish, and required a skilful charioteer. The Herricks, however, came of a fearless family, and were constitutionally brave; therefore, when more than once Templar's heels rattled against the splashboard of the two-wheeled cart, its occupants' serenity did not appear disturbed in the smallest degree. On the contrary, they looked at each other and smiled, as if to say, "This is rather fun than otherwise."

Squire Herrick belonged to the good old-fashioned class of sporting gentlemen. From his earliest childhood he had been accustomed to horses and hounds, and in the whole county there was not a better judge of equine and canine worth. For many years he had himself carried the horn, and only relinquished it owing to advancing age, increasing size, and a wave of agricultural depression which threw several of his principal farms on his hands, necessitating a large outlay in the shape of stock. Within a radius of twenty miles no man was more popular than he. The younger generation looked up to him as an authority on sport, and in matters connected with the noble pursuit of fox-hunting his word was considered final. Whenever any knotty point arose he was invariably appealed to by those in office. It proved a general surprise to his friends when, comparatively late in life, he entered the holy bonds of matrimony. Rumor whispered that they did not suit him, but the truth on this head was never known, since a year after his marriage his wife died, leaving an only daughter behind her.

Miss Katherine Herrick, familiarly known as Kitty, was a fortunate young woman. Her father adored her; she could do what she liked with him, and was complete mistress of his establishment. Hardly a girl in the county but who envied her her freedom and position. Kitty might go hunting whilst they had to stop at home and mope; she had no one but herself to consult, whilst they were always being ordered about by their papas and mammas. They would willingly have changed places. Under the circumstances, it was greatly to Kitty's credit that she fully shared the popularity enjoyed by her father. She had hardly an enemy in the world. The gentlemen were unanimous in the opinion that she was "a good sort—no better," and the ladies condescendingly called her "a nice, unaffected little thing, much to be pitied for not having a mother to look after her."

Kitty was full of tact—a heaven-born gift. She never lost an opportunity of conciliating her own sex, and so they forgave her for being admired by the other. A critic no doubt would have averred that she possessed but few claims to positive beauty. Well, perhaps not. Her soft, kittenish face was too round, its outlines too undefined to please a classical eye; but the brown eyes were singularly clear, the dark hair very luxuriant, and the complexion as fresh and wholesome and rosy as a sun-kissed apple. In short, she had what was better than beauty—charm—and looked thoroughly healthy and honest. A girl who would scorn to tell a lie, who had not an artificial thing about her, and who, if she once loved a man, would stick to him through thick and thin. Such girls are getting rare. Their fashionable sisters, up to every dodge of advancement and self-improvement, in the egotistical sense of the word, may contemptuously dub them "country bumpkins." But for all this, when men make their acquaintance, they still have the good sense to appreciate such girls. Wise men know that they will prove truer and tenderer wives than the vapid young women with whom they flirt, but seldom marry.

When it is said that Kitty was believed in the county to be her father's sole heiress, and that Squire Herrick was reputed wealthy, it seems almost superfluous to state she did not want for admirers. As a matter of fact, she possessed two very devoted ones. With the usual contrariness of the female sex, she preferred the least eligible. Being, as before mentioned, entirely her own mistress, Miss Kitty had been having a very delightful time of it lately. Fathers are proverbially blind, and either Squire Herrick did not see what was going on, or else he considered it wiser not to interfere. During the last month he and Kitty had gone out cub-hunting whenever the hounds met anywhere within reach. Somebody whom the girl liked very much, and whom, in her secret heart, she considered handsomer— that, of course, came first—and nicer and cleverer than any one she had ever met, had paid her a great deal of attention. Without undue vanity, she could not help perceiving that Cyril Mordaunt's good-looking face brightened up very perceptibly whenever she appeared, and that he never lost an opportunity of riding by her side. Hunting and love-making were pleasant work.

Until the present season she had always thought the two did not go together, and could not possibly be combined. She had entertained a lofty contempt for coffee-housing, and considered flirtation and the pursuit of a man very poor fun in comparison with the pursuit of a fox. But of late her opinions had become modified. It seemed to her now that paradise itself could contain no more perfect happiness than fell to her share on these bright October mornings, when she stood at the covert-side listening with one ear to the merry music of the hounds as they rattled the cubs up and down, and with the other to the softly spoken utterances of a congenial companion. The air felt so fresh, the sky looked so blue, the sun shone with such clear golden rays. Surely there was something peculiar in the season. All the years that she had hunted, never could she remember such perfect mornings. They sunk into her spirit and made an indelible impression.

Ah! *it was good to be young and to love; better even*

than hunting, which hitherto she had always regarded as the height of human enjoyment. Nevertheless, she rejoiced that Cyril was a keen sportsman, and rode so well to hounds. She should not have liked him so much had he "funked." It was downright splendid to see him cross a country, except that sometimes she could not help feeling afraid when he charged a huge, stiff fence first. She venerated him for his courage, especially when he got safely over; since in the hunting field, as everywhere else, failure never appears as admirable as success. If a man negotiates an almost unjumpable place satisfactorily, he is termed a fine fellow; but if he falls, he is dubbed a fool for his pains.

Each time Kitty met Cyril Mordaunt, her heart fluttered more and more wildly, for a conviction was gradually springing up within her breast that before long he would inevitably propose. And when he did, she knew quite well what her answer would be. The fascinating young guardsman, with his smart clothes and smart figure, his blue eyes and lovely little auburn mustache, had put poor Lord Algy Loddington into the shade altogether.

Lord Algy was thirty-two—almost middle-aged, according to Kitty's ideas; and although not ugly, could not compare with Cyril. Certainly he rode straight enough on occasions, but he prided himself on never jumping a fence unless absolutely necessary. In short, he had not a particle of Cyril's dash, and when she thought of him at all, she thought of him as "A good old Thing." One may like "good old Things," very much in a friendly way, but one does not feel any particular inclination to marry them. They inspire a kind of sisterly affection, which possesses no disturbing elements. They are always there when they are wanted; and can be dismissed when they are not. To sum up, one treats them as brothers. These were precisely Kitty's sentiments with reference to admirer No. 2. She liked him; she felt extremely safe and comfortable *with him*, but nothing more. He had not the power, like Cyril, to make the blood in her veins glow, or quicken the beatings of her heart. In Cyril's presence she experienced a perfectly insane desire to appear at her best. She didn't care twopence how she looked in Lord Algy's, or whether she had on her oldest habit, patched at the knee, or her least becoming waistcoat. It was all the same to him what she wore, for he was not the kind of man to notice such details. Cyril, however, had the eyes of a hawk, and besides, he was so beautifully turned out himself. His boots were so glossy, his leathers so white, and his coat fitted so faultlessly, that she could not have endured him to think her shabby. To-day, therefore, although the glass was going down rapidly, and heavy rain-laden clouds were rising from the horizon, threatening to obscure the sun, foolish little Kitty had arrayed herself in a brand-new Busvine habit, with a pale-blue double-breasted waistcoat, and a soft white washing-silk tie. In short, she was in the height of fashion, and certainly looked as pretty an Amazon as one could wish to see. Her eyes sparkled like two stars from beneath the rim of her natty "pot" hat. Her thick brown hair was coiled at the back of her shapely little head in smooth shining plaits, and the quick drive to covert through the fresh morning air lent to her cheeks a delicate peach-like bloom.

Thanks to Templar's long, swinging trot, they arrived at Gretton Grange a couple of minutes before the hounds moved off. Squire Herrick's groom was in attendance with the horses, and Kitty lost no time in mounting. She was riding her favorite hunter, an animal who went by the euphonious name of Tiny Tim. Her father had picked him up as a four-year-old for a mere song, his breeder declaring that without exception he was the most obstinate, ill-tempered brute he had ever had to do with. For this reason he was ready to throw him away and incur any loss rather than keep him in the stable. Tempted by the lowness of the price, and by Tiny Tim's good looks, the Squire bought the horse and put one of his stablemen up in order to ascertain if his evil reputation were really deserved. Tiny Tim's first performance was to kick the man off; then he proceeded to " savage " him whilst he lay on the ground. After this Mr. Herrick declared that the brute should be sent to the kennels; but Kitty intervened, and begged hard to be allowed to try her hand at taming the new purchase. " I don't believe he's as bad as he's painted," she said. " At all events, let me see if I can do anything with him."

In a few weeks she succeeded in completely subjugating Tiny Tim. Kindness and sugar worked wonders, and it transpired that the poor animal's character had been much maligned, since in his former home he had had a drunken groom, who had done his very best to spoil a temper naturally good, but rendered sullen and suspicious by ill-usage. As soon as Tiny Tim found that Kitty did not want to hit or abuse him, it was wonderful how much more amiable he became. She rode him about during the summer, so that when the cubbing season came round they were on thoroughly good terms with each other, and before long she began to suspect that she possessed a treasure. Tiny Tim took to hunting in a most extraordinary manner. He was a fine, big, natural jumper, and required next to no teaching. A couple of winters' practice developed him into a perfect performer. All he wanted was to be with hounds, and as Kitty's wishes coincided with his own in this respect, the pair never fell out.

CHAPTER II.

DRAWING THE GRETTON GRANGE LAURELS.

IF Tiny Tim had had a nervous rider on his back, it is quite possible that he might have continued to show temper, but Kitty was a magnificent horsewoman, and no animal could have carried her more brilliantly than he did. Throughout the county he had earned a great reputation. Although he only stood fifteen one and a half, he was a big little one, and, in spite of his small size, well up to thirteen stone. He could show a clean pedigree both on the dam's and the sire's side. In color a bright bay with black points, his coat shone like satin. He had a well-shaped, intelligent head, with a prominent blue eye, an elegant neck, whose symmetrical outlines were clearly defined by a hogged mane, grand shoulders and loins, great wide hips, muscular thighs, and clean strong hocks. No day was too long for him. He could gallop and stay until hounds returned to their kennel, and, last but not least, was a rare "doer." The severest run never put him off his feed. The moment he came home he would plunge his nose into the manger and gobble up its contents.

Kitty was passionately fond of the little horse, and prided herself with justice on having made him what he was. He looked a perfect picture as he stood tossing up his head and pawing impatiently at the ground, whilst the sun caused his sleek sides to shine like burnished gold. After his summer's rest he was full of ardor, and beside himself with delight at again seeing hounds. As Kitty gently took up the reins he gave a squeal of pleasure, and bounded high into the air. She sat as firm *as a rock*. It would have taken a good deal to unseat *her*. She merely gripped the saddle a shade tighter, and, leaning forward, patted her favorite on the neck.

"Good morning, Miss Herrick," said a masculine voice close by. "I hope I see you well."

All of a sudden the blood rushed up to her cheeks, and lifting a pair of shy, glad eyes, her glance encountered that of the young gentleman who just now occupied so large a share of her thoughts.

"Good morning, Captain Mordaunt," she said playfully. "You don't generally appear till much later on in the day. How is it you have managed to get up so early?"

"Can't you guess?" he responded in a confidential tone, which showed that they were on tolerably intimate terms. "For the pleasure of seeing you and enjoying an extra hour of your society. The charms of bed are nowhere in comparison."

She blushed and looked at him very kindly and encouragingly, but a forward movement among the hounds prevented her from making any answer. Perhaps she felt that his speech required none. Just then, too, Lord Algy rode up and made some commonplace remark about the weather.

"Is our noble master out to-day?" she inquired, thinking how broad his back was and how loosely his clothes hung when compared with Cyril's, and wondering why he did not take pains to smarten himself up a little more, instead of going about like an old farmer rather than the second son of the duke. "I have not seen him."

"No," replied Lord Algy. "My father had to go to London on business, so I am head lad for to-day."

"What do you intend drawing?"

"The spinneys round Gretton Grange first. I believe there is a litter of cubs there, and afterwards I propose going to Carshalton Wood. It is swarming with foxes, and we have only given the varmints a shaking up once this season."

"Very likely we shall get on to the line of an old dog fox if we apply to Carshalton," said Kitty smilingly.

"Well! if so, all the better."

"You mean that you will let the hounds go, Lord Algy?"

He laughed at the pleading intonation of her voice.

"I mean that it is some time since we had a gallop, and I shant stop them if I can help it."

"Hooray!" exclaimed Kitty.   Then turning to Captain Mordaunt, she said with playful levity, "Do you hear what his lordship says?   I should advise you not to go in for too much coffee-housing this morning.   We mean business."

"And so do I," he answered, in a tone meant only for her ears.   "But in another direction."

Again the hot blood dyed her fair face crimson, but Lord Algy's presence relieved the necessity of a reply.

"Have you heard that Gretton Grange is let at last?" she said, turning to that gentleman in order to hide her confusion.

"No!   Who has taken it?"

"Some people called Van Agnew, I believe.   They are an enormously rich brother and sister of Jewish-Dutch extraction who have become smitten with a love of sport.   It is said that Miss Van Agnew has twenty thousand a year, and is the biggest heiress in England." Then she glanced mischievously at Cyril, and added, "A chance for you, Captain Mordaunt."

"Ha, ha!" laughed Lord Algy, thoroughly appreciating the joke.   "A capital one.   I should advise you to be on the lookout, my dear boy."

Cyril drew himself up with an air of displeasure.

"Thanks," he said stiffly.   "You are very kind; but really I quite fail to see why it should be more a chance for me than for anybody else.   Besides, I prefer my own compatriots."

"Twenty thousand a year is not to be despised," said Kitty demurely, toying with her reins as she spoke.

"Then," he said shortly, "I should recommend you

to turn your attention in the direction of **Mr. Van Agnew**. No doubt he is quite as great a catch as his sister."

"I am humble-minded," she responded, still in the same tone of light banter, "and don't aspire to great wealth."

Gretton Grange, whose new tenants had given rise to the discussion, was an old-fashioned country place, enclosed in park-like grounds. The laurel shrubberies close to the house frequently held a fox, and on the present occasion hounds had hardly begun to scatter through them, pushing their way amid the dry stems and shining leaves, before old Milkmaid threw her tongue and proclaimed a find. The puppies, attracted by her cry, took up the chorus, and soon the air rang with their eager, high-pitched notes. Every now and then a white stern gleamed aloft, waving above the glossy bank of green, whilst the quick, excited breathing of its owner could be distinctly heard amid the crackling of twigs and the pattering of feet. Before long, Pug began to find the place too hot for him, and a ruddy-coated cub stole out, and made his way across the park, intending to gain the shelter of a friendly plantation close by. But in this intention he was baulked: for the first whip happened to spy him, and gave a loud "view holloa," which quickly brought both pack and huntsman at his heels. Although a novice at the game, it did not take him long to understand that it had its serious side, and unless well played was very apt to end disastrously. Fortunately for himself, he inherited the cunning of his ancestors. It came naturally to him to twist and turn and have recourse to subterfuge. Despite his tender age, so crafty a customer did he prove that, after being rattled round and round for over an hour without showing any disposition to face the open, he eventually baffled his pursuers by taking refuge in a drain running between the kitchen garden and the stables. It was useless trying to dislodge him, so the chase had to be abandoned.

The short gallops, first in one direction, then in another, had put the horses on their mettle. They snorted and blew, pranced and pawed, in a perfect fever for a run. Meanwhile, Master Reynard's brethren had evidently taken themselves off, for on proceeding to draw the remainder of the Gretton Grange spinneys no fox was forthcoming. It was now close upon eleven o'clock, and after a short consultation with the huntsman Lord Algy decided to trot straight off to Carshalton Wood without losing any more time. It meant a three miles' jog, and the sun was gaining power and fast drying up the dew. There was a small field out. Many of the regular *habitués* were still away, and the procession when formed could not have numbered more than forty or fifty souls all told. As usual, Cyril Mordaunt edged his way to Kitty's side. In his breast coat-pocket he carried a letter from his mother, which he had received the previous day, It had made a considerable impression on him, and he was prepared to act on the advice contained therein. Lady Mordaunt wrote as follows:—

My dear Boy,—Colonel Brabazon came to see me yesterday. He told me that he had been staying with the Duke of Furrowdale, and had met you several times out cubhunting. I gathered from his remarks, as also from the tone of your recent letters, that you are very much *épris* with one Miss Katherine Herrick. As your mother, I have always considered it my duty to impress the fact upon you that you are bound to marry money. We are not well off, and it was only by great sacrifices on my part that you were enabled to join the Guards. I did not regret them. I would make them again to-morrow for your sake and to insure your having a good position in society. At the same time, I must very clearly bring before your notice that nowadays none but rich men can afford to indulge in the luxury of proposing to a girl without a penny. You may call it mercenary if you like. I call it common sense to look at things as they are. Your income is much smaller than people imagine, and in addition you are very extravagant. You want the best of everything, without possessing the legitimate means of gratifying your wishes. On the other hand, you are extremely handsome and taking, and have every right to look forward to making a good marriage. Under the circumstances, I need hardly say that I received Colonel Brabazon's news with considerable anxiety. Fortunately, I have a friend who knows the Herricks intimately, and I lost not a moment in applying to her for accurate information regarding Miss Herrick's financial position. My dearest Cyril, I congratulate you on the wisdom of your choice, though it was foolish of me ever to doubt it, for you are your mother's own son, and a true chip of the old block. It appears that by the provisions of the late Mrs. Herrick's will the young lady is entitled on her twenty-first birthday to a lump sum of twenty-five thousand pounds. Her father is the sole trustee, and she comes into undisputed possession, quite independently of any allowance which Mr. Herrick may see fit to make on his daughter's marriage. She will, I am assured, inherit his entire fortune, which my friend believes represents at least five or six thousand a year. This I think is good enough, and my advice is, strike while the iron is hot. Let me know as soon as you have proposed to the dear girl, and bring her to see me *at once*. I am dying to welcome her as my future daughter-in-law. You might send a telegram directly the affair is settled. It will relieve my maternal anxiety. There is not the least doubt about her accepting you, I suppose. By-the-by I heard to-day that those rich Van Agnews have taken a place somewhere in your part of the world. It almost makes me wish you had not been quite in such a hurry. They say their wealth is fabulous. Ever my dear boy, your affectionate mother,

CHARLOTTE MORDAUNT.

Cyril was a good son, and had a great regard for his mother's opinion. He knew he should never have occupied his present position had it not been for her maternal solicitude and ceaseless desire for his social advancement. The receipt of this letter confirmed him in a resolution which he had almost arrived at previously. Now, he determined to act without loss of time on Lady Mordaunt's advice. She was a clever woman, and although Lord Algy Loddington might not be particularly smart or captivating, he quite saw that his title and family connection rendered him a very formidable rival. True, up to the present, Kitty appeared to have had the good taste to prefer himself, but if he shilly-shallied too long the prize might easily be snatched from under his nose. He had known her now for nearly three weeks; that was quite enough time for a man to find out if he liked a girl or not. And he did like her. She was a "ripping" sort, a magnificent rider, and a good sportswoman all round. These qualifications endeared her to him highly. It did just flash across his brain that after they were married it might perhaps prove a bore having to mount her as well as himself, but by a generous effort he dismissed the thought as premature. These things had a satisfactory way of arranging themselves very often. In short, should an opportunity arise, he had made up his mind to propose this very day, and to put an end to his suspense.

But with Kitty mounted on a mad-fresh animal who did nothing but whinny and kick, and with his own steed almost equally as gay, Cyril found it simply impossible to relieve his overcharged heart on the way to Carshalton Wood. Moreover, people kept continually riding by and interrupting their *tête-à-tête*. He managed, however, to convey to the young lady that he had something very particular to say to her whenever he got the chance, and no doubt she had a tolerably good inkling what that something was. Anyhow, her pretty brown eyes shone with a soft expectant light every time he opened his lips, and her round rosy face literally rippled over with smiles. Yes, Kitty knew well enough what was coming, and she felt wildly, idiotically happy. She looked up to and trusted him implicitly. In her sight he was absolute perfection, and so superior as to be hardly human.

She had never forgiven Lord Algy for having incautiously termed Captain Mordaunt a toady in her presence. The remark produced an irritation and sense of resentment which she had not yet succeeded in overcoming, and which *ever since* its utterance rendered her manner

towards his lordship decidedly more distant.   The only
way she could account for so absurd and ill-natured an
observation was, that he felt jealous of Captain Mordaunt's greater attractions, which were of course patent
to the whole world.   She took good care to let him see
that he gained nothing by making such speeches to her.
They did not ingratiate him; quite the contrary.   Jealousy was contemptible enough in a woman, but it was
a thousand times more so in a great, strong, healthy
man.   She treated his criticism with the scorn it
deserved, and took every opportunity of showing him
that it did not influence her opinions in the slightest
degree.   He might call Captain Mordaunt a toady a
thousand times over, for all she cared.   Only it was
annoying.   She kept puzzling her brain to arrive at an
exact definition of the obnoxious word, and caught herself watching Cyril more narrowly than hitherto.   But
as long as he remained her devoted slave she could find
no fault with his behavior.   What woman would?

CHAPTER III.

IN revenge for the uneasiness he had given rise to, Kitty snubbed Lord Algy unmercifully, but he was one of those good-natured or impervious—she never could quite make out which—people who refuse to be suppressed, and who reappear smiling after every rebuff. At the precise moment when Cyril's conversation was getting most interesting, he had a knack of turning up and volunteering some ordinary remark about the weather or the hunting. Although she was sometimes almost rude, he never seemed to see that he was not wanted. On the other hand, if she ever got into difficulties, had a toss and required friendly assistance, there he always was, ready to perform her slightest bidding. Last season he lost his place in a very good run simply because she happened to drop her crop in a gateway. He stopped behind to pick it up whilst she went careering on. Numerous similar acts of kindness prevented her from disliking him wholly, in spite of the "toady" episode; but, all the same, when she particularly wanted to talk to Cyril, he bored her very much indeed.

"I used not to think him stupid," she said to herself, "but he must be frightfully blind not to perceive that two are company and three is none. Somehow or other he either can't or wont understand that Cyril and I don't derive any pleasure from his society."

On the present occasion, Lord Algy seemed denser even than usual. He would not leave the lovers alone, but took up a position on Kitty's other side, and remained there pertinaciously until they arrived at Carshalton

Wood. He did not take the slightest notice either of
her indifferent answers or of Cyril's black looks, but
chatted away with an apparent cheerfulness and monotonous fluency which had an exasperating effect upon
the girl's nerves.

"You seem in remarkably good spirits this morning,
Lord Algy," she observed, a trifle sarcastically.

He looked away. A covey of partridges rising in a
stubble-field hard by engaged his attention for a few
moments. When the birds had flown out of sight—he
had watched their disappearance with a keen, sports-
man-like eye—he answered quietly:

"Do you think so, Miss Herrick? I am not aware
that I have any particular cause for cheerfulness; rather
the reverse."

Some indescribable inflection in the tone of his voice
occasioned a sense of embarrassment. It contained an
underlying current of sadness which affected her painfully. She had known him all her life. In the olden
days, when she had been a child, and he a tall young
stripling, they had called each other by their Christian
names. It was only lately that the more formal appel-
lations of Miss Herrick and Lord Algy cropped up.
And perhaps in her secret consciousness she realized
that he had liked her always, and was a little sorry for
him. It did seem rather hard that a comparative
stranger should have supplanted the friend and companion of her youth so entirely. Once upon a time,
and not so very long ago either, he had occupied a tolerably prominent position when she built her castles in
the air.

"There is the hunting," she said, seeking to give a
different turn to the conversation. "One always feels
lively at the beginning of the season. I know I do.
It is so delightful to get out again. The very horses
are of the same opinion."

"Yes," objected Lord Algy, "but hunting is not
everything."

"You say that because you don't care much for it."

"I beg pardon, Miss Herrick.   I care a great deal for
it; but I care for other things as well."

"Oh! of course," she said lightly.   "So does everybody.   Hunting is not the be-all and end-all of existence.   Fond as I am of the noble sport, I am quite
willing to admit that."

Squire Herrick now joined the party, and the talk
became general, greatly to Kitty's relief.   Seeing that
the fates were not propitious, Captain Mordaunt gave
the girl a supplicating glance which seemed to say,
"Follow me, there's a darling," and plunged into Carshalton Wood after the huntsman.   The rides were
extremely deep and holding, nevertheless Kitty was on
the point of imitating his example when her father
intervened.   He usually seemed to know by instinct
where to stand in order to secure a good start.

"Don't go in there," he said.   "We are far better
outside to-day.   The wind is all our way, and if we stay
where we are the odds are in favor of our seeing the
fox break covert.   Those boggy rides play old Harry
with the horse's joints, and it is always better to avoid
them when one can."

Kitty had not the courage to disobey her father openly.
Besides, she was too good a sportswoman not to be aware
that he was right in what he said.   So she reined back
Tiny Tim with a suppressed sigh of impatience.   The
truth was she could not bear to lose sight of Cyril.
After the hint he had let fall she suffered from a feverish expectation which kept her on tenter-hooks.   Every
minute spent apart from him seemed a waste of time.
In fact, she was very much in love, and would have followed him to the end of the world.   Five minutes later,
however, she was destined to bless the parental inter-
ference which had prevented her from diving into the
recesses of Carshalton Wood.   A fine old dog fox crept
cautiously out, within thirty yards of where they were
standing.   He looked around him, then seeing that the
coast was fairly clear, began gliding over the green grass
at a swinging stealthy trot.

The Squire raised his hand with a repressive gesture. "Hist!" he said, in warning accents. "Don't make a noise. They may not mean going after him; but, at any rate, let him get well away first."

All doubt as to the intention of pursuing was speedily set at rest by the hounds themselves, for suddenly the woodland echoes resounded with murderous canine voices clamoring after the quarry, whose fresh, hot scent came borne to·their nostrils in fragrant whiffs. Every leaf, every nettle, seemed to hold it this morning. There was no question as to which road Pug had taken. One by one out leaped the hounds; the matrons first, the younger generation following close in their footsteps; and in less time than it takes to tell they were flinging forward on the line with a dash and a vigor not to be denied. The whole pack were animated by a unanimous spirit. Useless now to try and stop them. All the thongs in the world would not have succeeded in the attempt. They meant business whether their human masters did or not. It was a glorious sight to see them stream out of covert and race over the springy turf, their beautifully marked bodies accentuated by the greenness of the far-stretching pastures. A sight to rejoice the eye of men and horses, and set every nerve quivering.

The Squire's face kindled. It lost the look of care which for some months past had been its principal characteristic, and shone rosy and smiling, as in the good old days when he did not trouble himself about the doings of the money-market. His blue eye flashed, his form became erect, and instinct with vigor. Up till this moment he had kept his companions in check, but directly the hounds were a clear couple of hundred yards ahead he stood up in his stirrups, and in a mellow; ringing voice gave a loud "Gane forrard aw-a-ay!" Then he set spurs to his horse and proceeded to make the best of an excellent start, which, thanks to not having gone inside the wood, he had been fortunate enough to secure.

Kitty, Lord Algy, and some half a dozen others were equally lucky. For the first three fields the Squire led his division gallantly through a line of gates. The country was still horribly blind, and no one felt particularly anxious to jump unless absolutely obliged. The gates happened to be handy, and they saved casualties. But after five minutes' hard galloping it became evident to the pursuers that they were in for a run, and if they would keep within measurable distance of the hounds the time had now come when it was incumbent on them to throw caution aside, or else fall hopelessly in the rear. The choice suddenly presented itself of sticking to a nice, safe road which led straight to the point for which the fox was apparently making, or of jumping a nasty fence out of the highway, with an extremely blind ditch on the take-off side, and overgrown with weeds and eddish to such an extent that it required sharp eyes to see it at all.

"Forrard!" rang out the Squire, who knew every inch of the country, and could not resist the temptation of riding cunning. "He's bound for Copple Clump. The macadam's the best for a 'monkey.' Come on, Kitty," and he galloped ahead as fast as his stout roan cob could carry him, followed by a few keen but equally prudent Nimrods.

The girl took a comprehensive view around, and made up her mind in an instant. Sixty is more cautious than nineteen, and has a decidedly greater dread of risking its bones by a fall. She saw Lord Algy flounder into the ditch, go through the hedge, carrying its top-binder away, and narrowly escape a roll. That decided her to turn a dumb ear to the admonitions of her sire. Lord Algy never jumped an unnecessary fence, and rarely led the way, unless hounds were running very hard. Then, in all Midlandshire there was no better man across country; but he was not one of your flashy, spurty riders, who go larking about all over the place. He had too much regard for his own neck and his horse's limbs to court danger heedlessly. Captain Mordaunt had once or twice deprecated his performances, but Kitty had quickly put him right on this score. When in the proper mood, Lord Algy was undeniably bad to beat, in spite of his quiet, placid manner and apparent want of hurry. He had two things in his favor: he always kept his head, and he was never in a bustle.

So when Kitty saw him valiantly charging the fence out of the road, she felt that she must follow suit. She whipped round, therefore, without a second's hesitation, and set Tiny Tim at the obstacle. One of his peculiarities was, that he resented having his mouth interfered with: consequently, as she neared the grass-grown ditch she dropped her hands in the last stride until the reins hung quite loose on his glossy neck. But in order to warn him to be extra careful, she pressed her left heel against his side. He knew the danger signal. The good little horse lowered his head, gave one fearless look, then taking off, with quite a foot to spare, bounded over the fence without touching a twig. Nothing could have been more beautifully done. Immediately afterwards Kitty heard a tremendous crash, and looking back saw one of the foremost riders of the hunt bite the dust. Although the gentleman's pluck was undeniable, he had heavy hands, and they served him badly on this occasion. It is an ill wind, however, that blows nobody good, and his downfall cleared the way, and enabled his successors to negotiate the fence—or rather what there was left of it—in safety.

The huntsman had evidently got an indifferent start, for he now came galloping up in hot haste, but Kitty could not see Cyril anywhere. It was becoming difficult to give the absent more than a passing thought, since her energies were rapidly getting concentrated elsewhere. She settled her hat more firmly on her head, shortened her reins, and sat down to ride, letting Tiny Tim stride along over the undulating ridge and furrow at his topmost speed. He sprung from one grassy crest to the other with the lightness of a fawn, never once

pitching and rolling in the distressing manner so common to some otherwise really good hunters.

Meanwhile the hounds were rioting ahead, their sleek
white-and-tan coats flashing every now and then like a
crystal stream when the sun's rays happened to catch
them. They were almost mute. The scent was too
good for much music, but their silence was, if possible,
even more deadly than their previous rhapsody. It
contained an inexpressibly bloodthirsty element. The
pace, the elasticity of the sound old turf, and above all,
the elbow-room, were delightful. The blood in Kitty's
veins began to glow. Her soft, pink cheeks took on a
deeper hue; a look of determination stole into her fair,
girlish face. What mattered the blindness of the country now? Who, any longer, gave it a thought? Fear
had vanished before the warm, intoxicating rush of
physical pleasure, which for the time being dwarfed
every other sensation. Later on, one might marvel at
one's rashness, but as long as the run lasted one was
prepared to die rather than be left behind. With such
a fox in front, and such a scent, there could be no question of funking! As a matter of fact, they had not time
to look and crane, even had they felt the inclination.
The huntsman, having once regained his place, charged
fence after fence in his horse's stride without turning
a hair's-breadth either to the right or to the left. It
was a brave sight to see him just shake up his good
hunter and ride at the great leafy hedges which now
looked so much more formidable than when stripped
bare by frost and snow. Both man and beast required
a stout heart. The gallant gray he bestrode never once
checked nor faltered, but jumped with a freedom and
will which carried him safely over everything.

Lord Algy lay close behind, on a bold young four-
year-old, who, after his blunder out of the road, had
seemingly learned wisdom by experience, and was now
taking off a yard before he came to each ditch. A little
in his lordship's rear rode Kitty, guiding Tiny Tim
quietly and artistically, and with the exquisitely light

hands which that high mettled but perfect hunter would alone tolerate.

In all, a dozen men comprised the field. Some, like Cyril Mordaunt, had been unfortunate at the start; others had followed Squire Herrick down the road and made for Copple Clump; whilst yet another division had remained stationary on the wrong side of Carshalton Wood, and did not awake to the fact that the hounds were running like storm until they were at least a couple of miles away.

These are the vicissitudes of the chase. But for the lucky few does any subsequent run ever quite come up to the first good gallop of the season. We are not yet *blasé*, and bring to it such freshness of sensation. We feel so thoroughly happy at the prospect of resuming our favorite sport, with five long—for they always seem long in October, however short they may be to look back upon when we are surrounded by April buds and spring lambkins—and enjoyable months before us. When the mornings are just beginning to sharpen with a touch of frost, when the yellow leaves flutter gently from the tree-tops, and half our boon companions have not yet appeared on the scene of action, a good burst over grass produces an impression not quickly effaced. One looks back on the amusements of London, of foreign watering-places, of grouse-shooting, and even of salmon fishing, and says, "Bah! You are not to be compared with this. Fox-hunting is and always will remain the king of sports with those who are fortunate enough to possess the health and nerve to ride,"

CHAPTER IV.

A KILL IN THE OPEN.

SOME such thoughts as these flashed across Kitty's brain as she became more and more inoculated with the delirious delight of galloping over grass field after grass field, and successfully clearing a number of charming flying fences at steeplechase speed. Up till now the fox had taken a perfectly straight line. No doubt his original point had been Copple Clump, but the hounds were so close at his brush, almost from the moment he broke covert, that he found himself forced to alter his intentions. Hitherto not a single check had served the laggards and stragglers. They might as well have remained at home, for all they had seen of the run; and disconsolate sportsmen were wandering about the country in every direction, putting the dejected query, " Have you seen the hounds?"

Grief had been plentiful, as is always the case early in the season. The fortunate minority who survived might be counted on the fingers of one's hand. The huntsman and Lord Algy still retained their position as leaders, but the latter's young horse had shot his bolt, and chanced the last fence or two in a far from agreeable or reassuring manner. His rider was thankful when at this juncture a flock of sheep foiled the line, and for the first time caused the hounds to scatter and stoop their proud heads.

Their hesitation, however, was only brief. It was clear they were close upon their fox, and after feathering for a couple of minutes they once more flung themselves forwards. Suddenly two men on a hill-top close by were heard shouting, " Tally-ho, tally-ho!" Charlton cheered on the pack, who, with bristles up, hanging tongues, and gleaming eyes, now filled the air with their murderous notes. The sobbing horses pricked their ears in response to the inspiriting music, and strained every nerve to keep pace with their canine friends. Over a newly plashed stake and bound fence they flew, forgetting their fatigue in their excitement. Crawling down an opposite hedgerow, the huntsman's sharp eyes spied a spent and bedraggled red object, wearily trailing a heavy, white-tagged brush behind him. No sentiment of compassion entered into this vulpine butcher's breast. He waged war against the whole species, respecting only an expectant mother. The instinct of hunting was stronger than that of mercy. He never troubled his head about the sensations of the poor, exhausted, goaded creatures during their last bitter moments of life; yet agonizing they must indeed have been, for few endings are more conceivably painful than to be hunted to one's death.

"Forrard, my beauties, forrard on!" cried Charlton, in tones of wild excitement. "Yonder he goes. 'Leu leu,' on to him."

The words still lingered on his lips when the foremost hound sprung at the fox and bowled him handsomely over in the open. His struggles, if sharp, were short. Charlton jumped from his horse and triumphantly sounded the "who-oop!" Then he seized Reynard's dead body, and waved it aloft in a transport of elation, whilst the hounds leaped and clamored about him, like so many mad things. At last, with a ringing cheer, he threw the fast-stiffening carcass in their midst, when hundreds of sharp teeth at once tore it to pieces. A few minutes ago it had been instinct with life, like themselves. Its limbs had been strong and fleet, the blood coursed warmly through its veins, it was susceptible to heat and cold, hunger and thirst. Now it was reduced to a "hundred tatters of brown," and soon nothing would show that it had ever existed save a gory mask hanging from the huntsman's saddle.

Kitty looked steadfastly in another direction. She never enjoyed the obsequies of the chase, and always felt much happier when the fox escaped. The better the run, the more fervently did she hope that the end might not mean slaughter. It always seemed to her that a good, straight-necked animal deserved his brush, and if he ran to ground or managed to elude his pursuers she secretly rejoiced at the fact. Besides, she had an innate aversion to taking life. It is so easy to destroy, yet so impossible to restore, that it inspired her with a kind of reverence. Of her own free will she would not have harmed a fly. Her sympathies, therefore, were all with the fox, and she never liked the hounds so little as when they were snarling and quarrelling over his remains. Lord Algy knew her sentiments, and to a great extent shared them. He pulled up alongside of her.

"By Jove!" he exclaimed, consulting his watch, "we've been running for three-and-thirty minutes. No wonder the horses are done. It's the best and smartest thing we've had this season. The hounds fairly smothered their fox, and there was such a screaming scent from start to finish Charlton had not occasion to lift them once."

"And if it hadn't been for your gallant lead out of the road," said Kitty, her whole face aglow with pleasurable excitement, "I should have found myself left miles behind. Papa shouted to me to go on to Copple Clump with him. Luckily, I caught sight of you at that critical moment, and I made up my mind to reject his advice."

"One can't always be right, not even the Squire," responded Lord Algy. "No doubt Copple Clump was the fox's original point, but being too hard pressed to pick and choose, he was forced to alter his intentions. Well, we have to thank those poor shreds," and he indicated a sinewy morsel over which a couple of hounds were growling, "for a very enjoyable gallop."

"It was *glorious*," she rejoined enthusiastically.

"My only regret is that it should have come to an end so soon."

"The horses are not of the same way of thinking. Most of them have had enough," he observed, glancing at his four-year-old's panting sides and quivering tail. "It's early in the season yet, and they are not very forward in condition. Nothing ever seems to affect that wonderful little animal of yours, however," he continued. "He looks as fresh as if he had only been out for an exercise gallop, and has hardly turned a hair."

There was no surer way to Kitty's good graces than praising Tiny Tim. It is just possible that Lord Algy was aware of this fact. She smiled at him in quite a friendly manner, ignoring for the moment all previous causes of offence.

"He has not forgotten to jump since last season, has he?" she said, stroking her favorite's silky mane. "The country rode very blind—more so than usual, I thought, but he never put a foot wrong."

"There's no better hunter for his size in this county," returned Lord Algy. "All the same, he's not everybody's horse."

"What do you mean?" she said, bridling up.

"Only that if you were to put a bad rider on his back, who hauled and tugged at his mouth, I believe he'd be simply a demon. Without undue flattery, Miss Kitty, a good deal of Tiny Tim's success is due to your steering."

Her countenance relaxed, and immediately became illuminated by a bright smile.

"We understand each other's little ways," she said. "That makes a wonderful difference."

"It does indeed. Horses resemble people. They are not all to be treated alike, just as if they were turned out from the same mould. Each one is a study in himself, and the rider who most carefully considers the peculiar temperament of his animal is bound to get more out of him than he who treats the poor brute merely as a machine."

"I quite agree with you," she said, "and it always seems to me that the great majority of hunting men are singularly indifferent to the idiosyncrasies of their steeds, and do not take half enough trouble to understand them. So much can be done by kindness and patience, and so little comparatively by blows; if they would only take that fact to heart. For my own part, I never could like a man who ill-used his horse. However nice he might appear, I should always have a feeling that there was something radically wrong about his composition, and that he was a cur and a bully at bottom."

"In other words, you think he would make his wife's life miserable," laughed Lord Algy. "Well, perhaps you are not far wrong. I have often had occasion to remark, Miss Kitty, that your powers of observation are excessively keen, and that if some of your criticisms are sweeping, they generally possess a solid sub-stratum of truth."

"Shall I tell you an observation I made to-day?" she said gayly.

"Yes, if you will be so good." And he glanced at her happy young face, and thought to himself how fair and innocent it looked, as the fluctuating brilliancy of the sun peeping out from behind a cloud rested upon it, and lit up her clear, shining eyes, her definite arched eyebrows, and her pink-and-white complexion.

"I came to the conclusion, Lord Algy, that often as I have seen you go well to hounds, I never saw you go more brilliantly than to-day. Desperate was the only word for the way you were charging the fences on a raw, young four-year-old. May I ask if you are particularly anxious to break your neck, and desire to depart this world?"

He gazed at her so significantly that suddenly and against her will she could feel the color rushing to her cheeks, and immediately regretted having put the question, no matter how jestingly. Then slowly he averted his gaze, and began to loosen the girths of his saddle,

an operation which effectually prevented her from seeing the expression of his face.

"I think I do feel a little more desperate than usual,"
he said, in a curiously subdued voice which, steady it
as he might, betrayed a hidden force of emotion. "I
shouldn't so much mind if I did get a bad fall, and
were laid up for a while."

"Why?" she queried uneasily, disapproving of the
sentiment, and shocked to hear him express it so
grimly and determinedly. Yielding to a sudden
impulse, he lifted his head from the flap of the saddle,
and looked at her with such a direct glance that there
was no avoiding it. Her confusion increased.

"Kitty," he said, in his excitement forgetting the formal prefix, "you and I are old friends. Not so very
long ago we were *good* friends into the bargain——"

"We are good friends still," she interrupted hastily.
"At least, I hope so."

"Oh! yes, in a way; but it is useless to deny that a
feeling of constraint has sprung up between us lately."

"Really, Lord Algy, you exaggerate matters. I am
not aware of any difference."

"No, because you don't care enough about me to
notice it. But," he went on moodily, "I should be a
blind owl did I shut my eyes to its cause. My impressions are very sensitive where you are concerned, and
seldom play me false."

She stooped down to arrange her habit. The effort
brought a rush of blood to her face.

"I am at a total loss to understand your meaning.
You speak in enigmas." But the vibrating tones of her
voice belied the words, and he knew well enough that
she was equivocating, and trying hard to prevent him
from saying more. The knowledge had an exasperating
effect.

"If I were an unselfish person," he resumed, endeavoring to maintain his self-control, "no doubt I should
enjoy coming out and seeing you flirting on every
possible occasion with another man. Unfortunately, I

possess my fair share of egotism, and perhaps I have dreamed foolish dreams. Anyhow, I have never hated anything so much in my life as I have hated this cursed cub-hunting season."

"It is such a nice one," she interposed.

"You may think so; I don't. It wouldn't be my idea of enjoyment to have a dressed-up young jackanapes always riding in one's pocket. However, there's no accounting for taste. Evidently yours and mine don't agree."

Her eyes flashed fire. She drew herself up with an offended air. Until to-day, whatever Lord Algy's faults might be, she had looked upon him as a gentleman. Now, for the first time during all the years she had known him, she saw cause to alter her opinion. It was not often she lost her temper, but he had provoked and insulted her beyond reasonable limits.

"No, thank goodness," she exclaimed indignantly. "And, what's more, our tastes are never likely to agree. May I venture to inquire by what right you find fault with mine?"

He looked at her sadly. Angry as she was, the dumb yearning expression of his countenance sent a queer, uncomfortable little thrill through her frame.

"By no right," he said. "I am but too well aware of that."

"Your behavior is quite at variance with the admission," she returned haughtily. "I would not stand such language from my own father, much less from you. He might have some excuse; but you—you (suddenly breaking down) have none. I shall never forgive you—never. I used to like you, but I don't now—not one bit."

"Don't say that," he pleaded humbly, aghast at the storm he had raised. "It will break my heart."

"I don't care if it does. You have wounded my pride in the most gross and cruel manner. What girl could bear to be told that she spent all her time out hunting in flirting with a man who, for all she knows, may not even care about her? It's not particularly nice to be accused of riding in people's pockets. I wonder you don't say I run after *you*. I suppose that will be the next thing." And she laughed hysterically.

"There's no fear of that," he said sorrowfully. "I only wish to goodness there were."

"Oh! indeed. You relieve my feelings vastly. I rejoice that where your lordship is concerned you acquit me of such unmaidenly conduct. That is an immense consolation to my feelings. You don't really think I have systematically made up to you, then?"

He could not bear her sarcastic tone. It wounded him to the quick. He put out his hand, and before she knew what he was about he was wringing hers hard, with a vice-like pressure that nearly brought the tears to her eyes.

"Forgive me!" he said penitently. "I had no earthly business to speak as I did. If you like Captain Mordaunt better than you do me, and he has it in his power to make you happy, it's all right. God bless you, Kitty dear, whatever happens. You are angry with me now, and deservedly so, but perhaps by and by, when things turn out according to your wishes, you will come to see that when a fellow is very wretched he does not always pause to choose his words." So saying, he hurried away, leaving her full of vague regret that she should have occasioned so much pain to one whom she liked very well in his way, yet unable to see how it could have been prevented.

CHAPTER V.

LOVE-MAKING.

A SLIGHT mist obscured Kitty's vision as she watched her late companion go up to Charlton and enter into conversation with him.

"Poor old Algy," she soliloquized. "Why wouldn't he take a hint and hold his tongue. Men are so stupid; and yet I'm awfully sorry for him. He's such a good soul, and I believe he's genuinely fond of me. Papa likes him, too, and in some ways it's unfortunate that I can't return his affection; but I can't, especially since I've known Cyril, so it's no use thinking about it. Now, I suppose things will be more uncomfortable between us than ever. He'll get to calling me Miss Herrick next. Heigh, ho! It's a sad pity he wont content himself with our relations being friendly and nothing more. One can't marry everybody in this world, even if one wanted to. I wonder where Cyril is all this time. I hope to goodness he has not had a bad fall and broken his bones. I'm always afraid of some accident happening to him. He does ride so hard, and even recklessly, that I often wish he had just a trifle of Lord Algy's judgment."

People were now beginning to arrive from various directions, and at length, to her great joy, she perceived the object of her thoughts coming cantering along with a very black face and a very muddy coat, plastered over with Midlandshire clay.

She went up to him at once, unable to conceal her anxiety, in spite of the sting implanted by Lord Algy's remarks.

"Oh, Captain Mordaunt," she exclaimed, "I am grieved beyond measure to see you in this plight, and do hope you are not hurt."

"Thanks," he replied. "I'm all right, bar a little dirt and a bruise or two on my left leg."

"How did you fall?"

"My brute of a horse," striking the poor animal a blow on the head with the butt-end of his hunting-crop, an action which caused Kitty to wince, "turned clean head over heels whilst I was galloping after Charlton down one of those confounded rides in Carshalton Wood. He went such a complete somer-sault that I lost hold of the reins, and he got loose, leaving me to pursue in a pair of new and conse-quently tight boots. Just see the state they are in." And he lifted his feet for her inspection with a shudder of disgust.

She looked at them commiseratingly, remarking, "It was awfully bad luck. We have had such a splen-did run."

"I know that," he returned, tearing savagely at his mustache, and gnawing the ends with vexation. "You may spare yourself the trouble of dinning the fact into my ears. I have not met a single soul who has not already done so, and I am tired of hearing about the good gallop I have lost. My mortification is complete, I can assure you, without listening to further panegyrics." His tone was rough, not to say rude; but she was accustomed to the growlings of disappointed sportsmen, and took no notice of it.

"Accidents will happen sometimes," she said, sooth-ingly. "I suppose you were never quite able to catch us up?"

"No, I've been riding a stern chase all the way. Hounds went at such an infernal pace that I could not succeed in making up lost ground, and was at least half a dozen fields behind the leading division. Have you any idea what they are going to do next?"

"Nothing, I fancy," she responded. "Time is getting on, and I heard Lord Algy give the order for home a few minutes ago."

"It's quite early yet," objected Cyril, anxious to atone for his defeat.

"Yes, but both he and Charlton seem to think that horses and hounds have done enough for to-day. The whips are only mounted on cub-hunters, and as the duke's sale is next Tuesday I expect they don't want to give them too much of a gruelling. One never quite knows the wheels within wheels. Anyhow, home, sweet home, is the order of the day, to which *nolens-volens* we must submit."

"Lord Algy is such a deuced careful fellow," observed Cyril sneeringly. "The old duke has a thousand times more 'go' in him."

"I don't think you quite do Lord Algy justice," she said. "He is very quiet, and strangers sometimes mistake him for a slow-coach, but he is far from being one in reality. He rode splendidly to-day—almost as well as you could have done yourself, which is saying a good deal."

"Oh! of course," he retorted brusquely. "You stick up for him. That's quite natural. A title invariably has its attractions."

This time she was roused by the irritability—not to say uncivility—of his address, and looked at him with reproachful severity.

"I do not think you are in a position to make that remark to me, Captain Mordaunt. It is ungenerous, if nothing more, and I did not give you credit for any lack of generosity. I am sorry to be undeceived."

Her words struck home. He began to feel ashamed of his ill-humor, and especially of venting it upon her. A flush rose to his face. "Where is your father?" he inquired, seeking to change the conversation. "Was he thrown out also?"

"Yes, I fancy so. Papa went on to Copple Clump, and he has not turned up since. I have been expecting him every minute."

Cyril gave his horse a touch of the spur, and came close alongside of Tiny Tim, who laid back his ears as if resenting such close proximity.

"Shall we ride home together?" he said, lowering his voice. "It's not much use standing about here any longer, letting the 'gees' catch cold; and unless my bump of locality plays me false our road is the same for the first part of the way."

A thrill shot through her frame. She had a presentiment of what was coming, and why he was so anxious to secure a *tête-à-tête*.

"If you like," she responded, almost inaudibly, turning Tiny Tim's head in the desired direction. "Every one will be going soon."

Lord Algy, although he appeared so interested in what Charlton was saying, saw them move off, and a shadow passed over his placid, good-humored face. He smothered a sigh, and, turning on his heel, remounted the gallant young horse which had carried him so well through the run.

"It's not the least use my proposing," he soliloquized bitterly. "I would in a minute if I thought I had a chance; but I haven't—not the ghost of one. Since that confounded young puppy appeared on the scenes he has quite cut me out. She used to like me well enough once, but now it's all over, and the game is lost, or as good as lost. I wonder what she sees in him—I wonder how the dickens he has managed to get round her in the way he has. Here have I been trying for years to make her care for me, and no sooner does he turn up than she falls head over ears in love with him. Bah! I wish Mordaunt would propose and have done with it; then perhaps I should not feel as restless and miserable and unsettled as I do now. She'd take him, I feel sure, though according to my way of thinking he's very far from being a good chap."

Thus meditating, he turned resolutely away, so as no

longer to torture himself by the sight of those two fine, straight young figures riding side by side.

"They'll make a handsome couple," he mused, with a pang of envy. "To give him his due, the fellow is uncommonly good-looking in the curled and scented barber's block style. I don't admire it; but evidently the girls do. Miss Merton is quite wild about him also, and ready to tear Kitty's eyes out for being first favorite. I wonder what there is about a guardsman which always takes with the women."

Meanwhile, the objects of his thoughts were calmly pursuing their homeward way. Their hearts were full, and a magnetic consciousness existed between them which proved an effective hinderance to fluent speech. An onlooker might easily have mistaken them for a very dull couple with nothing, or next to nothing, to say to each other. That he would have been mistaken, we know; for their silence did not proceed from stupidity, but rather from an inward happiness which made them speculate as to whether any spoken words could add to it. Rightly or wrongly, Kitty said to herself that she could have been content to remain forever in this blissful stage. The expectancy of love is often sweeter to a woman than the love itself. Her fancy builds up such beautiful illusions. She weaves around it so many tender ideals drawn from the pure recesses of her imagination; yet even while she does so, an uneasy, vague presentiment whispers that the holy bonds of matrimony may never succeed in realizing them. And so she would fain rest on the threshold and bask in the sunshine of courtship, not anxious to precipitate an event which will surely bring serious cares and increased anxiety.

, But the man is differently constituted. After he has looked at the fruit for a short time he wants to taste it, and covets possession, even although he may weary of the object of his desires directly it is attained. Love is not so sacred to him as to the woman. It is merely an incident *in his life*; an event in hers on which

all her future happiness depends. She approaches it,
therefore, with a deeper and more reverent feeling.

Meanwhile, our riders reached a nice, well-kept road
with a wide margin of smooth turf on either side.
Nature had already painted the hedge-rows with bold
autumnal colors. Her liberal hand had dashed in reds,
and yellows, and browns in a harmonious mingling of
tints which no human draughtsman can aspire to imi-
tate. Here and there, amidst the general signs of de-
cay, a cluster of leaves retained their summer hue, and
shone out brilliantly green. The long grasses waved
their russet tufts and took on a dusky shade as the fresh
morning breeze swept over them, causing them to rustle
and sigh. The trees overhead were shedding their foli-
age, carpeting the ground, and leaving bough and bole
to stand out black against the cloudy sky, through which
the sun broke at irregular intervals. A patch of light
fell on Kitty's chestnut-brown hair, and irradiated it
with a borrowed glory. It lit up the smooth contour
of her cheek, revealing the fineness and softness of its
texture. A gleam of tawny orange shot from the
depths of her dark eyes, lending them fire and force.
All of a sudden Cyril felt that the moment had come,
and the strings of his tongue became unloosed. Her
lithe, swaying form, filling the saddle so gracefully;
the delicate poise of her head, carried alert on her fine
white neck; and the shadowy sweep of her long eyelashes, inspired him with a determination there and
then to put an end to the situation. She had everything that he desired to meet with in a wife. Wealth,
youth, beauty—where could he hope to find a better
bride? And he had not so very much to offer on his side
to make him look higher. Only a loving heart and a
wardrobe full of smart clothes, most of which were not
paid for. Five-and-twenty thousand pounds down in a
couple of years, with excellent prospects and a nice girl
into the bargain, were not to be despised. Arguing
thus—for his love was not of that uncomfortable, overpowering kind which defies reason—he cleared his

throat, and said, "I wanted to tell you that I heard from my mother yesterday on a subject which concerns me very nearly."

"Indeed," responded Kitty, with a pretty show of interest. "What was her news?"

"She wants me to come and see her as soon as possible, and "—pausing to ascertain what effect the words would produce—"bring you."

"Bring me! That is very kind of Lady Mordaunt. Some time or other I should extremely like to make your mother's acquaintance," for she felt a reverent regard for the woman who had been the means of bringing so perfect a son into the world.

"It seems," he continued, gazing at her steadily, "that the old lady has been hearing some reports about you and me. People do talk so infernally."

A vivid blush dyed Kitty's face crimson. He smiled triumphantly at the sight. It made him feel more than ever sure of her.

"I—I—hope Lady Mordaunt is not angry," she stammered confusedly, finding he waited for a reply, and at a loss what to say.

"Angry," he laughed. "Why should she be?"

"I—I—don't know."

"On the contrary," he resumed, "my mother is most anxious for me to write and let her know if she may welcome you as her daughter-in-law."

Total silence succeeded this speech, somewhat to his amazement. He had expected an immediate answer, and was a trifle disconcerted.

"May she, Kitty?" he said persuasively, after a slight pause. And reining in his horse to a standstill, he placed a detaining hand on Tiny Tim's mane.

The first shock over, she was both too honest and too much in earnest to conceal her feelings or to practise the least coquetry. She turned a happy face towards him, and with eyes smiling, yet withal bashful, and lips parted in a tender curve, said frankly:

"Oh! Cyril, you know that you may. What must you have thought of me to doubt my reply?"

In spite of Tiny Tim's evident disapproval, he managed to put his arm round her waist, and to steal a kiss which left her all rosy and confused.

"Kitty," he said presently, "you have made me so happy. I don't think there ever was a much happier man than I am at this moment. All the last week I have been longing to tell you how dearly I loved you, and to-day I made up my mind to know my fate. The suspense was getting unbearable." And again he would have attempted an embrace had not Tiny Tim defeated his intention.

"How long is it since you first began to like me?" she asked, her face one sparkle of a smile.

"I don't think I ever *began* at all. As far as I was concerned, it was an instantaneous affair—a regular case of love at first sight. Do you remember the morning the hounds met at Bosquet Grove? Well, I was struck all of a heap, and could not rest until I found Colonel Brabazon, whom I had seen speaking to you a short time previously, and got him to introduce me."

She laughed, a satisfied laugh.

"And what did you think of me, Cyril? I should like to hear."

"I thought you, without exception, the very prettiest and nicest girl I had ever set eyes on."

"But you must have seen so many nice-looking girls, especially in London. Guardsmen get invited to all the best houses, and they are proverbially popular. Are you quite, quite sure, sir, that you never lost your heart before? It seems incredible."

He stroked his mustache complacently.

"I have seen any number of girls," he said, "but not one to compare with you." And he glanced at her with genuine admiration.

CHAPTER VI.

A SUITOR OF THE PERIOD.

THEORETICALLY she was aware that men are deceivers, but she believed him a complete exception to the rule, and as much to be admired for his moral as he was for his personal qualities. Therefore, she sighed softly, and drank in his words with delight. At nineteen one is credulous enough.

"Is it possible that you really like me so much?" she said, with a charming dimple showing in either cheek.

"Yes, quite possible," he responded. "And now, Miss Kitty, I think I have a right to hear what were *your* first impressions."

"Is it necessary to state them? After what has passed it seems so utterly superfluous. You must know, surely."

"I have satisfied your vanity, or curiosity—whichever you like to call it. I think you might appease mine." And he smiled brightly.

She averted her head, and gazed at a bold bullfinch trying to poise his fat little body on a slender sapling growing out of the hedge-row.

"It is so hard to explain what I felt," she said shyly, "especially as I had never previously experienced any similar sensations. From the moment you were introduced I thought you quite different from every man of my acquaintance. You stood on a pinnacle by yourself."

His light-blue eyes gave forth a satisfied gleam. He found it very pleasant being worshipped by a pretty girl who had not an atom of humbug in her whole

45

composition. It raised him in his own self-esteem, and put him on wonderfully good terms with himself.

"In what way did you consider me different?" he inquired, trying to lead her on to say more in the same agreeable strain.

"Oh! nicer, and better-looking, and cleverer, and—and"—breaking off short, and looking at him with an infinitely loving expression, which said more than any number of words—"you know."

"Yes," he said, "I do know. I know that you are a real darling, and that I am an uncommonly lucky fellow to have taken your fancy. I wonder what his priggish lordship will say when he hears the news and learns he is out of the running. He'll be a bit disappointed, I take it, eh?"

"Poor Algy," she said pityingly. "I am sorry on his account. Although you and he don't hit it off, he is such a genuine, well-meaning fellow."

"Very likely, but he has the manners of a bear—at least, where you are concerned. However, I suppose people don't appear to the best advantage when they are riding a losing race. It's not every one who can stand being beaten. Are you sure, though, Kitty, that you have no regrets? It would be a fine thing for you to be 'my lady,' and it is not too late yet to change your mind if you have any hankerings that way."

She raised her luminous eyes to his. They were so wondrously clear, that he could almost see his own reflection mirrored in their large pupils.

"No," she said simply, "I have no regrets. How could I have any when I look upon myself as the most fortunate girl in the United Kingdom. My only fear is, Cyril, that I am not half good enough for you. You see, I have lived in the country all my life, and am not used to town ways. When you come to introduce me to your fine London friends, very likely they may turn up their noses at me, and call me a hoyden." She hesitated, blushed, then, not liking to conceal anything from him, added, "Some people do even here. That hard-riding woman, Mrs. Bagot, told papa the other day that I was no better than a tomboy, and wanted a lot of toning down. What do you suppose she meant by toning down? Am I really very slangy, or fast, or what? I wish you would tell me, Cyril. You needn't be afraid of hurting my feelings."

"Did Mrs. Bagot say that?" he exclaimed indignantly. "What a nasty, spiteful old cat she is, to be sure! I strongly advise you not to trouble your head about her petty speeches, Kitty dear. She makes them because she is jealous of not being able to hold a candle to you with the hounds."

"But," objected the girl, "I sadly fear there is some truth in what she says. The fact is, I have not received the same education as other young women. My mother died at my birth, and papa was so good to his one ewe lamb that he never kept her in proper subjection. I have been allowed to have my own way in everything, and to do just as I like, and so, although my life has always been a very happy one, it is just possible that I may have had more liberty than is usual with girls of my age. Of course," she concluded, apologetically, "one can't help taking it when one gets the chance. But I begin to realize the result. I am not what I ought to be. I am not conventional; and in the eyes of my own sex, and probably in yours also, that is an unpardonable sin. Women are bound to run in grooves. The least deviation, and they fall out with Mother Grundy."

"Fudge!" he ejaculated contemptuously. "As if you were not a thousand times better than the stereotyped society Miss one meets by the score."

"There are lots of people who disapprove of hunting women," she resumed gravely, "and who think that because a girl rides, and is fond of horses and hounds, she must necessarily be fast, and red-faced, and coarse, both in mind and conversation."

"Nonsense," he interrupted. "Those old-fashioned ideas have long ago gone to the wall. Why, every young lady who can manage to stick upon a horse, and has an old crock to ride, comes out hunting nowadays. If she doesn't care for the actual sport, she cares very much for the opportunities of seeing plenty of men and getting on friendly terms with them."

Kitty laughed in spite of herself. Although the observation was not exactly flattering to her sex, she knew there was a good deal of truth in it.

"That may be," she rejoined. "Nevertheless, it does not do to ignore other people's opinions, even when they don't agree with one's own, for the simple reason that they are generally based on some foundation. There is nothing like cultivating an impartial mind."

"And what does all this discourse tend to prove?" he inquired a trifle impatiently.

She glanced at him with sweet humility. Evidently he did not understand.

"Only that as I said before, I am not nearly—*not nearly*—good enough for you; and I would rather let you know most of my defects before marriage than that you should discover them of your own accord afterwards. It seems fairer and more honest."

"My darling," he said, touched at last by the sweetness and depth of her love, and perhaps conscious that he was not worthy to adorn the exalted pedestal on which she had raised him. "Let us cease this foolish talk. I would not have a single thing about you changed—not even if a conjurer's wand were placed in my hand and I could metamorphose you at will."

Wait a bit, though; he forgot. He might just as well turn the five-and-twenty thousand into half a million. That would give them a nice little income to live upon which would enable him to race, bet, and gamble at will. Yes, it was a pity she had not Miss Agnew's fortune.

Kitty's face, which just before had been a little downcast, brightened instantaneously. His praise was as sweet music in her ears.

"Are you sure you mean it, Cyril? I would not take you in for worlds."

"Of course I mean it. I should be a born idiot if I didn't. There is no one in the whole world to compare with you."

She heaved a sigh of content. The assurance was infinitely comforting, and there is seldom much difficulty about believing what we wish to believe.

"Do you think that your mother will like me?" she inquired, after a moment's pause. "I am so afraid that she may not."

"Little goose! Yes, of course. It is I, not you, who should feel nervous, for I can't disguise from myself that Mr. Herrick's wishes lie in another quarter. However, I trust his paternal affection may prove stronger than his ambition. Between you and me, Kitty, I expect we shall have some trouble to get his consent. The Squire has never looked with much favor on my suit."

She reddened consciously. Although the subject had not been mentioned between them, she knew instinctively that her father had his own views on the matrimonial question, and that they were not likely to coincide with hers. But he had never denied her anything, and she trusted much to her powers of persuasion.

"I am not quite sure how papa may take the news," she said, a little uneasily; "but this I do know, he is certain to give in in the end, for he is the best and kindest father that ever girl had. I think I had better tell him at once. It will be more comfortable to have no concealments."

"By all means," said Cyril. "By the way, Kitty," he added abruptly, as if the thought had only just occurred to him, "do you know that I am, comparatively speaking, a poor man?"

"Are you?" she returned, with serene indifference. "Nice men always are; therefore, I took it for granted."

"I have not even expectations worth talking about," he resumed. "Of course I shall get something more

4

at my mother's death, but nothing worth mentioning. And then she is not very old, and may live for a long while; so that it would not do for us to count upon any immediate increase of fortune on my side. At the present moment eight hundred a year represents my income, and the regimental expenses come very heavy. They swallow up ever so much.

"Never mind," she said. "It does not make any difference. I should like you just the same if you had not a penny."

"But will Mr. Herrick?" he inquired anxiously. "You are sweetness and kindness itself; but I have my doubts of him."

She pursed up her pretty red mouth, and looked down meditatively at Tiny Tim's hard crest and fine, arched neck.

"Papa may object just at first, Cyril; you must not be disappointed if he does; but he wont oppose me when he finds my heart is set on our engagement. Even if the worst comes to the worst, we need only wait a couple of years. I have got twenty-five thousand pounds of my own, as you know,"—he bowed his head—"and when I come of age I am entitled to it. You are not extravagant; we can live quite well upon that."

"Yes," he said, not very responsively. "I suppose we can. But it's surprising how money runs away nowadays. It costs such a lot going about, and married people are paupers on anything under three thousand a year."

She swung the lash of her hunting crop to its full length, and then catching it dexterously, curled it twice round her hand.

"Does not that depend a little on whether they possess simple or luxurious tastes?"

"Naturally. Unfortunately, everybody in one's own set seems endowed with a love of luxury, and unless a fellow does pretty much as his neighbors do he soon gets left out in the cold. No one is prepared to make more sacrifices for love's sake than I, but I have seen enough to know that in our class of life a cottage is not its proper dwelling-place. Hold up, you brute," he concluded, as his horse, which happened to have lost a shoe, made a bad peck over some stones. "Why the —— don't you look where you are going?"

A shadow passed over Kitty's face, and its expression became unusually serious.

"You don't think, then," she asked, "that a man and a woman can live happily together on a comparatively small income without troubling themselves much as to the outside world? It's not always necessary to be going about, surely?"

"On the other hand," he protested, "it is very dull sticking at home. One gets rusty, and illiberal, and narrow-minded, if one leads a Darby and Joan existence from one year's end to another. Variety is good for everybody, but variety means outlay."

"Unless we can make up three thousand a year you consider that we ought not to think of getting married, then?"

There was a directness about this question which he found extremely embarrassing. He took refuge in equivocation.

"I was speaking generally," he responded. "I only meant to convey that it is difficult to live on small means, especially for two people like you and me, who have been accustomed to ride good horses, and enjoy themselves. Have you never noticed in your own experience that directly the shoe pinches a fond couple are very apt to get discontented and to allude to what each has had to give up for the sake of the other."

She looked away, gazing with unseeing eyes at the wide, undulating pastures and the billows of green grass that rolled on all sides to the horizon.

"I suppose you are right," she said, smothering a sigh. "Anyhow, you must know better than I; but it seems to me all wrong for us to be such slaves to our comforts and amusements that we are unable to exist without so large an expenditure. Look at people in a humbler position. They get on very comfortably, even although they may not have a great deal of money. I do not know a happier pair anywhere than our stud groom and his wife. They have six children, all well educated and nicely brought up. They are the most cheerful and united family I ever came across, and yet Johnson has only seven-and-twenty shillings a week. It shows that wealth is not everything, after all."

"Dear little woman," he said lightly. "Don't moralize. Believe me, it is a mistake. Besides, there is no occasion for us at present to look solely on the gloomy side of things. What you have got to do is to talk papa into a good humor."

His flippant tone jarred upon her susceptibilities. She was vaguely conscious that they were not so much in sympathy with one another now as they had been a few minutes ago. Cyril's arguments had a decidedly worldly flavor about them.

"I will speak to my father directly I see him," she said, in accents of gentle dignity. "As for 'talking papa into a good humor,' it is quite a work of supererogation, for he has never uttered a single harsh or unkind word to me in his life. You do not know him, or you would not deem it necessary to tender such advice." And she smoothed back a rebellious lock from her temple. Cyril bit his nether lip. Intentionally or otherwise, she had administered a reproof which he had the sense to feel was not wholly undeserved.

"Well," he said, in a milder and more conciliatory tone, "let us hope for the best, at any rate. With your permission, Kitty, I will call to-morrow, in order to hear Mr. Herrick's verdict. What hour are you likely to be at home?"

"You had better come to lunch, Cyril, then you are sure to find us, and can have a long, quiet talk *with papa.*"

"So be it," he answered. "And now, sweetheart, I must wish you good by, for I settled to run over to Berrington by an afternoon train to look at a young horse belonging to a farmer who lives in the neighborhood. I want another badly. You wont mind going the rest of the way alone, will you?" And so saying, he blew her a kiss from the tips of his fingers, Tiny Tim's eagerness to return to his stable rendering the repetition of an embrace impossible, and cantered rapidly away.

Kitty stood and looked after his retreating figure with a full heart.

"Oh, God!" she murmured, "I thank thee for my happiness; only it makes me tremble, for it seems too great to last, and I have done so little to deserve it. Ah! how good life is. How can any one ever wish for death?"

She had been so absorbed in Cyril that she had not noticed how the cloud-shadows were spreading over the green fields, swallowing up all the light, and reducing them to a gray uniform hue. The wind began to rustle right royally through the tree-tops, causing them to toss to and fro with creaky, rebellious motion. Dark, rain-laden clouds closed in upon the sun, and quenched its fitful brightness. The whole fair and open landscape underwent a transformation. Kitty shivered. By some mysterious affinity with nature, the gladness died out of her spirit, even as the golden sunshine disappeared from the face of the earth. She gathered her reins up short and set off at a brisk trot.

"It is going to rain hard," she said to herself. "And I may as well save a wet jacket, especially as I have got my best things on."

CHAPTER VII.

KITTY had not gone more than about a quarter of a mile before she spied a well-known figure ahead, mounted on a substantial roan cob, whose round quarters were exceedingly familiar. It belonged to Squire Herrick, who was walking leisurely home. Increasing her speed, she soon ranged alongside of him.

"Halloo! papa," she exclaimed playfully, "where do you hail from? We don't often part company so completely as we have done to-day. I looked everywhere for you at the finish."

Now, our good friend the Squire was not much better pleased than Cyril Mordaunt at having lost the run. Few keen sportsmen possess such an equable temper as to be absolutely impervious to so great a misfortune. If not actually cross, like the spoiled young guardsman, Mr. Herrick felt decidedly depressed and despondent. His daughter's badinage did not strike him, therefore, as being quite as delicate as usual. When people are crushed they object to being triumphed over, even in jest. His head was sunk on his chest, the reins hung loose on the mare's neck, and he was allowing her to crawl along at her own lazy will, munching at an occasional inviting-looking tuft of grass, or making a sudden snatch at some bunch of extra-succulent leaves. The rider sat limp and nerveless on her broad back, apparently plunged in thought. Man and beast brightened up simultaneously directly they were restored to the company of their kind. The roan pricked her long lop ears, champed at the bridle, and walked with more willing gait; whilst at the sound of Kitty's cheerful young voice Squire Herrick drew himself up in the saddle, and his countenance assumed a brighter expression. His was a very kindly face—not strong, perhaps, nor intellectual, but with a hearty good-humored expression which was infinitely attractive, and made its owner beloved by young and old.

"It is not often I make a bad turn," he responded, in answer to his daughter's inquiry, "but somehow or other to-day I was quite out of luck. I went straight for Copple Clump, thinking that was sure to be our fox's point. Needless to say, when I got there I saw no signs of the hounds, so after riding about in various directions without falling in with them I finally determined to come home. That is the full, true, and unvarnished account of my morning's fiasco, and for all the pleasure I have derived from it I might just as well have stayed in my bed. And now let me hear how you fared, Kitty, though I need scarcely ask. Your face shows plainly enough that you were not among the poor wretches left out in the cold."

"No," she said; "I was very fortunate, and had the good luck to be with them from start to finish." Whereupon she proceeded to give her father a circumstantial account of the run. It did not tend to diminish his regrets, as may be conceived by all true lovers of the chase.

"So our friend Algy was well in it," he observed, when she had pretty well come to the end of her narrative. "He may not be exactly brilliant according to the new-fangled sense of the word, "but he's a very sure, steady man to hounds, and knows more about hunting than all the young division put together. Most of them nowadays think only of jumping, and don't care a hang what the pack are about. And pray, where was Captain Mordaunt? I look upon him as a regular spurter."

Kitty felt herself growing hot with indignation at this unjust criticism, but she thought it best to take no notice, and answered quietly, though not without constraint:

"His horse fell in Carshalton Wood while galloping down a muddy ride, and he never saw a yard of the run. He was, in fact, very much annoyed and put out, and I question whether he enjoyed himself more than you. At any rate, he takes his misfortunes less philosophically."

The squire chuckled. He felt a certain antipathy for Cyril, which, although he could not have defined, was none the less real and hard to overcome.

· "I can imagine his being awfully savage," he said. "Nature has not blessed him with the best of tempers. Every now and then it peeps through the veneer of his company manners."

Kitty reddened and cleared her throat.

"Papa," she said, "I would rather, please, that you did not talk like that."

The Squire looked at her in astonishment. Perhaps the tell-tale color which mounted to her face gave him a suspicion of what was coming.

"Bless my heart alive!" he exclaimed sharply. "Why not? Do you mean to tell me that I haven't a right to my own opinions? Hoity-toity. What next, I wonder?"

"I—I think you ought to know that I rode back with Captain Mordaunt, papa. In fact, we have only just parted company."

The Squire's countenance clouded, and into his bright gray eyes there stole a careworn look. Evidently Cyril was no favorite of his.

"Captain Mordaunt—always Captain Mordaunt," he ejaculated, with a petulance most unusual. "I am sick of the fellow's name. It seems to me that you and he are almost inseparable."

He paused, hoping for an indignant disclaimer; then finding that none came, although the color burned brighter and brighter in her smooth cheeks, he resumed seriously—

"I am not at all straitlaced or pig-headed about these things, Kitty, as you ought to know by this time; but really if you continue to associate so much with that young man people will begin to talk, and in my experience, when a girl's name gets bandied about from one to the other she seldom gains much by the proceeding. Once set female tongues a-wagging and there's no stopping them. The only plan is not to give them an opening."

Kitty's white eyelids closed over her full eyes. A demure smile caused her lips to curl and to show two rows of little, even, white teeth.

"There are certain cases," she said, "where it is almost impossible to prevent people making remarks. They will always talk about something or other. That is the only part of hunting I dislike. Everybody takes such a vital interest in everybody else's affairs, and gossips about them just as if they were of the deepest importance. 'Have you noticed how attentive Mr. A. is to Mrs. B. ?' 'Have you heard that C.'s butler has run off with his wife's lady's-maid?' That's the way they go on. One's most private concerns are made public."

"What you say is true enough, my dear child. Nevertheless, a pretty girl like yourself can't go about much in the company of a young man without giving rise to remark. I don't for a moment mean to insinuate that your conduct has been imprudent; but at the same time I consider it my duty to warn you what the result will be if you and Captain Mordaunt continue to be seen together so much. And you have been together a great deal this cub-hunting season, Kitty," he concluded anxiously. "You can't deny that."

For a moment she was silent; then she raised her clear brown eyes to his, and with characteristic honesty and directness, said:

"I quite understand your meaning, papa, and should consider you perfectly right in warning me as to my position were I amusing myself by a mere vulgar flirtation. *Let me assure* you solemnly and distinctly,

however, that such is not the case. The truth is," and
with a sudden sense of maidenly embarrassment she
began toying with her reins, "I—I have something
very important to tell you. Can't you guess what it
is?" casting a swift, shy glance at him.

"Something to tell me!" he echoed, his rosy face
turning suddenly pale. "Good gracious! Kitty, what's
up now?"

"Only," she said, in a sweet, ringing voice, "that
Captain Mordaunt proposed to me this morning, and
I—I accepted him."

A long pause succeeded this announcement. The
troubles of a father were upon the Squire now with a
vengeance, and he felt overwhelmed by the intelligence.
He had looked forward to Kitty marrying some day,
of course, but in contemplating the event he had invariably selected a son-in-law of his own choosing,
and not hers. The intimation that she had taken the
matter into her own hands, and found a husband for
herself, proved a bitter pill to swallow. Astonished at
her father's silence, Kitty looked at him fixedly. To
her surprise, she saw that he was trembling all over,
and that the muscles round his mouth and eyes
were quivering in a most distressing fashion. It was
plain that the news afforded no pleasure, but the reverse.
Her heart sank. Mr. Herrick's emotion proved com-
municative.

"Papa," she called out in alarm, "why do you look
like that? Why don't you say anything? Are you
ill?"

He gathered himself together with an effort, and
sought to conceal his agitation. The attempt was very
pitiful, and she asked herself what she had done that
was wrong. Surely it could not be wicked to love.
He had loved and married, himself, once upon a time.
He must have foreseen that sooner or later this would
happen.

"Papa," she said again, "are you angry with me?
You know that I would not vex you willingly."

He gave a start, and in a curiously troubled voice which filled her with vague uneasiness said:

"Child, are you in earnest? Answer me truthfully. Do you really—*really*—care for this Captain·Mordaunt, or is it nothing but a passing fancy such as young girls often take?"

"I care for him very much indeed," she said; "so much that I feel prepared to make almost any sacrifice for his sake."

"Don't think me mercenary, Kitty, but I have one very important question to put. Have you any idea what his fortune is?"

"I don't know the precise sum, but I know it is not large. In fact, Cyril told me himself that he was afraid you would very likely object to our engagement on account of his being a poor man. But," she added, "if I don't mind I don't see why any one else need."

The Squire sighed heavily and shook his head.

"My dear," he said, "I will not disguise from you that this is a terrible disappointment to me. I had hoped—especially of late years—that your heart might have been given in another direction. I think you were aware of my wishes?"

"Yes," she answered. "I will not pretend the contrary; but, alas! I cannot accede to them."

"Why not, Kitty—why not?" And his voice sounded hoarse and eager.

"How can I give a reason? There are some things which defy definition. I like Lord Algy extremely. I have the greatest respect and regard for him. He is kind-hearted, generous, full of excellent qualities. If I were in trouble, there is no one to whom I would sooner apply for assistance; but," shrugging her shoulders, "I do not love him. That explains everything."

"You are young, child. There is no hurry. Let it be for a bit. You might get to care for him in time."

"No; it is useless to deceive either you or myself. I don't believe my sentiments would ever change. As matters stand at present, I can't either think of, or talk to, Lord Algy when Cyril is by. He engrosses me so completely."

"It would have been such a good match," murmured the Squire, regretfully. "Daleford can't possibly live more than a couple of years. All the doctors say that that spinal complaint must kill the poor fellow, and then Algy will be heir to the dukedom. Besides which, I have known and liked him ever since he was a boy in jackets, and quite apart from his rank, there is no one in whom I have more confidence, or to whom I would sooner intrust the happiness of my only daughter."

Kitty felt painfully affected by the expression of her father's desires and her own total inability to comply with them. She loved him very dearly, and was prepared to do everything she could to please him. But her heart grew cold at the thought of giving up Cyril. The warmth of this new affection caused all others to appear pale and shadowy in comparison.

"I wish it could have been," she said sorrowfully. "I can't bear the thought that I am disappointing you; but, papa dear, you know people cannot help these affairs. If they always did what was wise and best for themselves from a mere worldly point of view, I suppose there would be no such thing as love. At all events, it would generally go smooth."

"It's you sentimental girls who make it go wrong," growled the Squire. "The men aint such fools, and once they've turned twenty don't feel inclined to give up all their comforts, unless they get some substantial equivalent in the way of settlements in return. Most of 'em have their weather eye open nowadays, for the youth of the period are not given to proposing to penniless young women."

"Papa," said Kitty, "shall I tell you a secret? Knowing what your wishes were, I tried—yes, I honestly did try—to care for Lord Algy other than in a friendly manner, but when Cyril appeared on the scene it was all up with me." And she blushed a vivid crimson.

"—— him," murmured the Squire through his set

teeth. "I wish to Heaven he had never taken it into that conceited empty head of his to hunt in this part of the world. Some day all would have been well, I verily do believe." Then, turning to his daughter, he said aloud, "And supposing I find, on going into the matter, that Captain Mordaunt can't afford to keep a wife, how can I give my consent?"

In his innermost consciousness, Mr. Herrick knew that he would have been only too glad of any loophole of escape which might prevent the marriage, yet not let it appear as if he were dealing harshly towards his daughter.

She hesitated a moment before replying.

"There is my own money, papa. If you can't afford to give us an allowance, we can wait until we get that."

"Oh, of course," he said shortly. "I am quite aware that you are entitled to do as you please when you come of age. I shant for a moment expect to have any control over your actions *then*. Money makes young ladies wonderfully independent of the parental yoke."

She was infinitely distressed by her father's tone, which was quite new, and also by the conviction of having excited his deepest displeasure. According to her idea, the cause appeared inadequate to the offence, and she could not help feeling that there was something in the whole matter which she did not understand. But to quarrel was dreadful. *That* she could not bear.

"Papa," she said, with the tears springing to her eyes, "what must you think of me to speak in such a way? Surely you ought to know that I would never do anything without your consent. Rather than go against your wishes, I—I," breaking down a little, "would remain as I am, and give up all thought of getting married until you came round. Only don't ask me to forget Cyril entirely. I will be very patient. I will wait as long as you like; but whilst my heart is as full of him as it is, I can't care for any other man. It is better that you should know the true state of the case."

The Squire's bark was much worse than his bite.

He began to feel an uncomfortable lump rising in his throat, which refused to be coughed down. A softer-hearted man never lived, and he idolized this only daughter of his. He could not persist in giving her pain. So he brought out his big pocket-handkerchief with a flourish, blew his nose with uncommon emphasis, and said:

"Well, well! We will see what can be done. Perhaps the young man has more means than you imagine. He can't be so very badly off if he can afford to hunt and keep five or six horses. Anyhow, I had better hear what he has got to say for himself."

Kitty's face became illumined with smiles.

"Oh, papa!" she exclaimed. "How good of you! Now you are just like your dear old darling self again."

He looked away. He did not care for her to see how watery his eyes had grown all of a sudden.

CHAPTER VIII.

A MYSTERIOUS TELEGRAM.

"MIND you, though," resumed the Squire, after a brief silence, "I don't make any rash promises. If Captain Mordaunt can prove to me that he is in receipt of a sufficient income on which to maintain a wife, then it will be time enough to talk of a hard-and-fast engagement. Do you hear, Kitty?"

"Yes," she answered. "I quite understand. By the way, Cyril is coming to call to-morrow."

"Oh! is he? It strikes me he might have waited till he was asked. These young men have cheek enough for anything."

"*I* asked him, papa," she confessed, with the warm color mantling in her cheek. "It seems Cyril wanted to write and tell his mother as soon as our little affair was settled, and so I said that if he wished to catch you he had better look in at luncheon time."

"I am sorry you fixed to-morrow," said the Squire, "for I've got Patterson coming to see me about taking one of those confounded farms off my hands. If only I could let the Hermitage it would be an immense relief, for I've quite come to the conclusion that gentleman-farming is the most expensive luxury a man in my position can indulge in. There's simply no end to the outlay, and it requires a very clever fellow to make it pay. I know I can't, for one." And he heaved a deep sigh.

"Times are bad," she said sympathetically. "The worst of it is, they always are. I wish things would begin to look up a bit by way of a change, but perhaps they may if Patterson takes the Hermitage. What with

repairs, draining, stocking it, and one thing and another,
it has cost more than all the other farms put together."

"It has indeed, and if Patterson and I can only come
to terms it will be all the better for this gay lover of
yours, Kitty. That reminds me, do you happen to
know who or what his people are? Although we have
met pretty often out hunting, as far as I am concerned
we are next door to strangers; but I suppose you are
acquainted with his family history."

"Cyril's father is dead," she replied. "He was in
the City, and got knighted during the Shah's first visit
to England; at least, so I believe. Mr. Mordaunt speculated a great deal on the Stock Exchange, and a short
time before he died lost more than half his fortune.
Otherwise his son and widow would have been better
off than they are."

"Humph! Not a very clean record. Now you come
to speak of it, I do remember some fellow called Mordaunt being mixed up in a discreditable transaction
connected with the buying and selling of shares. He
did not get off without a black mark against his name,
if it is the same man I mean, although his friends managed to hush up the affair. I have a kind of an idea
that he was self-made, and had not any pretensions to
be styled a gentleman. If he was really Captain Mordaunt's father, Kitty, you wont be marrying into much
of a family." And the Squire shook his clean-shaven
chin in a disapproving fashion.

She bit her lip with vexation. These reminiscences
of the dead and gone were just a trifle trying to her
patience. Cyril's father might have been a bushranger,
for all she cared. It was Cyril himself whom she loved,
and his ancestors could in no way weaken her affection.
She could not, however, hear them attacked without
attempting some defence, so she said, with a certain
amount of warmth:

"Country folk as a rule think a great deal too much
about blue blood, old families, and all that kind of nonsense. They live in such a little gossipy circle that

they can't help getting narrow-minded, and attaching undue importance to questions of pedigree. What on earth does it matter whether your father was a knight or a baronet? For my part, I can't see any difference. One person is as good as another, every bit, and what spoils England is these absurd social distinctions, which render it imperative to know who everybody is, and whether they belong to the right sort or the wrong sort. One set looks down on the other set, and considers it not good enough to associate with, until you do away with all free and pleasant intercourse. This is what society means nowadays. There is a great deal of philanthropy and humanitarianism preached, but it is wonderful how little is practised amongst the so-called upper classes. Why should you and I despise a self-made man? Is it not to Mr. Mordaunt's honor if he rose from the ranks? and yet you speak of it as if it were a disgrace——" She stopped short, afraid of being carried away by her feelings, and saying more than was prudent. To her relief, her father burst out laughing, and appeared highly diverted by the theories which she had propounded.

"You terrible little Radical," he exclaimed playfully. "Goodness only knows where you get your ideas from. No one would ever imagine you to be the daughter of a sound old-fashioned Conservative. But whatever her faults, England is a good enough country for me to live in. And now, what do you say to a jog? The weather is getting nasty."

As he finished speaking it began to rain in earnest. Great stinging drops came pelting down from the purple clouds overhead, causing the horses to shake their lively ears with disgust, and sidle away from the cold, driving wind which now blew fiercely over the uplands. It effectually put a stop to further conversation, and with one accord Squire Herrick and Kitty started off at a hand gallop, and never drew rein until they pulled up in the stable-yard of Herrington Hall. The stud groom

and his satellites rushed to receive them at the first
sound of hoofs clattering in the flagged yard.

"Has 'ee carried you well, miss?" inquired the facto-
tum who presided over the equine department, as he
lifted his mistress from the saddle with a care which
showed how much pride he took in her riding. "I see
by the looks of 'im," eying Tiny Tim critically, "that
you've 'ad a gallop, and I'm glad of it. It will do the
'oss good, he's so uncommon fresh."

"We have had a first-rate run," she answered, bestow-
ing a parting caress on her favorite hunter, "and I was
never better carried in my life."

"That's capital," said Johnson, leading Tiny Tim
into his box, which was piled up with yellow straw, and
at once busying himself about the preparation of warm
gruel. "I was afraid 'ee might pull you a bit until 'ee
settled down; but there, I really do believe 'ee goes
kinder with you than with any one else. 'Osses is that
sensible, they knows quite well them as likes 'em, and
them as don't. The secret is, never lose your temper
with dumb creatures. It don't pay." Uttering which
sentiment Johnson bustled across the yard to the wash-
house.

Wet to the skin, but as fresh and blooming as a rose,
Kitty preceded her father into the house. On the hall
table lay a yellow envelope, which at once caught her
eye.

"Here is a telegram for you, papa," she said, handing
the despatch to him. "Let us hope it contains some
good news, and that stocks have rushed up."

She spoke lightly, and without giving the matter
much thought. Squire Herrick tore open the envelope
and glanced hurriedly at its contents. A ghastly change
came over his face. All of a sudden it turned ashen
white, and he leaned up against the wall for support.
His breath came fast and slow, as if the air passed with
difficulty to and from his lungs. Kitty noticed that his
eyes shone with a strange, fixed light, and their pupils
were hard, bright, and unnaturally dilated.

"Papa!" she cried. "Oh, papa! what is wrong?"

He did not seem to hear her demand. He stood there like one stunned by some unexpected blow which temporarily suspends every faculty. The fingers of his right hand had closed round the telegram in a rigid grasp. She looked with feminine curiosity at the pink paper, and longed to read the words written thereon, but she did not dare extricate it from his firm grasp. Something in the expression of his countenance checked further query, and made her realize instinctively that whatever the trouble might be which had fallen upon him, he intended, at all events for the present, to bear it alone. Anxious and disturbed, yet not quite knowing what to do, she rang for the butler, and waited silently by her father's side until he appeared in answer to the summons.

"Is there a fire in your master's room?" she inquired.

"Yes, miss," he answered. "It has been lit some time."

"That's right, Barlow. You had better go upstairs with Mr. Herrick at once, and help him off with his wet things. I am afraid he has caught a chill and is not feeling very well."

The sound of his daughter's well-known voice at length pierced the stony impenetrability which seemed to have enveloped the Squire's senses. Gradually his fixed, unseeing stare gave place to a look of infinite pain, which, if less alarming to Kitty, was vastly more pathetic. She made a movement as if to assist him, but he waved her back-and also the butler. He was a man of simple tastes, who had a profound dislike to being valeted, and dressed and undressed like a doll. In this respect he differed from the younger generation.

"No," he said, speaking in a strange, hoarse voice which she scarcely recognized. "I prefer to go alone. When I want Barlow I will ring for him." And so saying, slowly and feebly, as if in ten seconds he had aged ten years, he dragged himself up the polished oaken stairs, *still grasping* the mysterious telegram in

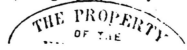

his right hand. Kitty looked after him uneasily; then stooping, picked up the envelope which had fallen to the ground. "Herrick, Herrington, Midlandshire." That conveyed no information whatever. With an icy stricture at her heart, not wholly attributable to wet clothes, she followed the Squire's example, and retired to her room to undress.

"What can have upset papa so?" she mused uneasily. "I expect it's some bad news from that horrid City, as usual. He's always getting telegrams about those abominable shares. When he talks of being hard-up, I don't believe the farms have anything to do with it. In my opinion it's speculating that is at the bottom of the mischief. He pretends that he doesn't, but I know better. Really I shall have to give him a lecture, for I feel quite sure that the little he makes is not worth all the anxiety of mind he has to go through. Every one says how much he has altered in the last year or two, and although he is always the dearest, kindest father that ever lived, he is not half as cheery as he used to be. Well, well! I must see what I can do to wean him from the City, for I am perfectly certain that horses and hounds are not only much nicer, but far less expensive in the long run."

Thus meditating, she made haste to discard her heavy habit, and, attiring herself in a neat, tailor-made gown, ran swiftly downstairs, expecting to find her father already there. The squire was usually a quick dresser, but to her surprise, she beat him for once, and he had not yet appeared. It was now close upon three o'clock, and what with an early breakfast, the long ride, and the keen morning air, she felt most desperately hungry. Thinking that her father was certain to join her in a minute or two, she went into the dining-room, where the table was laid with cold comestibles. The sight proved so tempting that she began to eat with a real, hearty appetite which would have provoked the contempt of a town-bred young woman. But when the first pangs of hunger were appeased she grew more

ánd more uneasy at her father's continued absence.
After a while, she rang the bell, and told the butler to
go up to her father's room and see why he did not come
down. Barlow returned shortly, saying that he thought
Mr. Herrick must be taking a nap, since his door was
locked, and that when he knocked he received no
answer.

The Squire was not in the habit of going to sleep
after hunting; but Kitty thought something had happened to upset him, and he wanted to be alone. Therefore she dismissed her anxiety as groundless, or, at any
rate, sought to do so, and sitting down in a big arm-
chair, toasted her feet before the fire, and gave herself
over to the pleasing occupation of thinking of Cyril.
How handsome and happy he looked when she had confessed her love. He was indeed a lover to be proud of.
The clock on the mantel-piece struck four before it once
more occurred to her that there was something strange
about the total reversal of her father's customary habits. Never had she known him sleep through an afternoon in this fashion, especially when fasting. Jumping
up from her seat, she murmured, "I hope to goodness
he has not been taken ill. I will go myself and see if
anything is the matter. He is sure to let me in."

Thus determining, she ran quickly upstairs, and tap-
ping at Mr. Herrick's door, called out, "Papa, are you
there? What have you been doing all this time? It is I,
Kitty. I want to speak to you." She waited a moment
or two, confidently expecting an answer; but, to her
astonishment, none came. Then, with a vague feeling
of fear stealing into her heart, she turned the handle
vigorously, both to the right and to the left. In vain.
The door was locked from the inside securely enough.
There could be no doubt about it, and the inference
was plain. Her father had not left his room since his
return home. If he were really asleep, he must be sleep-
ing uncommonly soundly.

"Papa," she cried again, this time more loudly and
imploringly. "Please wake up. You must be so hun-

gry and cold, and we shall soon have tea in the study.
There is such a glorious fire there, and I'm so dull all
by myself. Come down and be sociable—do, there's a
dear, darling papa. If anything *has* gone wrong, it is
much better for you and me to talk it over together."

She put her ear to the keyhole, and waited breathless-
ly for an answer; but not a sound could be heard in reply to her appeal. A deathlike silence prevailed within
the chamber. It was so unlike the Squire to remain insensible to his daughter's demands that her apprehen-
sions became confirmed. There was nothing for it,
however, but to wait; so she crept back to the study and
tried to derive comfort from the glowing fire. But even
the recollection of Cyril could not succeed in quieting
her anxiety now. Five, ten, minutes passed in ever-
increasing suspense and expectation. Whenever the
logs on the hearth cracked, she started and looked nervously round. The tension was rapidly becoming
unbearable, when to her great relief Barlow entered,
bearing the tea-tray. He was an old confidential servant, who had been in the family many years. She
turned to him instinctively for advice and consolation.

"You have not seen your master, by any chance,
since he came in?" she inquired of the faithful old man.
"His bell has not gone, has it?"

"No, miss," he responded, in a solemnly mysterious
voice, which did nothing to decrease her alarm. "It's
very strange, but I've tapped at Mr. Herrick's room
three times and can't get any answer. He has not had
his hot water nor anything. I've never known him refuse to let me in before, although he don't like any
one fiddling about when he's dressing."

And Barlow looked so aggrieved, and intimated so
plainly that his dignity was hurt, that Kitty could not
repress a faint smile. Nevertheless, she felt in no
mood for merriment, and looked at him with troubled
eyes. By some mesmeric affinity, she was certain the
same thought had occurred to his mind as to hers.

"Something must have gone wrong," she said unsteadily. "My father seemed very much disturbed when he read that telegram, and did not look like himself afterwards. I shouldn't be at all surprised if he were ill. Don't you"—hesitating—"don't you think, Barlow, that we ought to force open the door? He can only scold us at the worst."

Barlow's eyes, which had been roving restlessly from the fire to the tea-table, became stationary, and encountered those of his young mistress in a fixed glance. There was an expression in them which, according to Kitty's now thoroughly excited imagination, foreboded evil. She could not shake off a sense of impending misfortune.

"I never likes when people takes to locking themselves up in their rooms," said Barlow oracularly. "And what makes it seem all the stranger is that it aint the Squire's practice. He aint one of the sort who goes in for barring and bolting of doors. He's much too careless and open in his ways. It's the first time in five-and-twenty years that ever he's denied me an entry, and I shouldn't be speaking the truth, Miss Kitty, if I didn't tell you that I don't like the look of things at all. Depend upon it, the master's ill."

This was precisely the girl's own opinion. Uppermost in her mind was the thought that her father had had a fit, or seizure of some kind. She was haunted by the recollection of his blanched face on perusal of the telegram. Whatever calamity had happened, she held that unwelcome pink paper responsible.

"Do you think you could manage to open the door, Barlow, without making a fuss or letting the other servants know," she inquired.

"Yes, miss, if I fetch a chisel and one or two tools out of my tool-box," he replied.

"Make haste, then, and I will go upstairs and wait outside on the landing until you come."

Her heart was beating fast, and a painful sense of expectation had fastened upon her spirit. By a vague yet irresistible presentiment, she was prepared to encounter evil in some shape or form, and suffered now from a feverish longing to ascertain its extent. She felt convinced that something unusual must have befallen her father to induce him to depart so completely from his customary habits. It seemed an age before Barlow returned, creaking with heavy but cautious tread up the polished stairs. The tools were in his hand, and he looked to her for the signal to commence operations.

"Let us knock once more," she said. "It is just possible we are frightening ourselves unnecessarily, and he may be awake by now."

So saying, she tapped briskly, and listened eagerly for a response. But no sound broke the silence reigning within the closed chamber.

"The sooner you begin, Barlow, the better," she said, her face white and grave. "There is evidently nothing for it but to force the door."

Barlow nodded his head, and applied himself to his task with such energy that in a very few minutes the lock was wrenched from its hold. Kitty gave the door a determined push and walked in.

Ah! what a relief! What a blissful answer to her nameless fears! Her father was quietly sitting with his back towards her, in his old leather arm-chair, which was drawn close up to the table. She laughed for joy.

CHAPTER IX.

"OH! KITTY, KITTY, PITY ME."

THE Squire's bedroom was a very large, old-fashioned apartment, furnished partly as a sitting-room. The blinds were half drawn, a huge log of wood hissed and sputtered on the hearth, its centre burned and falling into white ash, and a suit of dry clothes was spread to air on a wicker chair before the fire. At first sight everything wore a comfortable, familiar, and reposeful air. Kitty advanced with restored confidence, and approaching her father from behind, laid her hand caressingly on his shoulder.

"You naughty, foolish, dear old papa," she exclaimed in accents of loving reproof. "What on earth do you mean by going to sleep in your wet clothes and giving Barlow and me such a fright? If you don't catch your death of cold you really deserve to for being so imprudent. I can't allow you to take liberties with your constitution."

He did not utter a single syllable in response to her words. Only his gray head fell sideways on to his shoulder with a jerk. Why was he so quiet, so cold and rigid? With a single rapid stride she moved forward to where she could see his face, and all at once a piercing scream rang through the room. Oh! merciful Heaven, what was this? There was a blue mark on his right temple from which drops of blood were slowly oozing and staining his white neckcloth, and—and—oh! horror, on the floor at his feet lay a revolver and an empty cartridge-case.

In an agony of terror she seized his hand, crying out, "Father, father, speak to me! Just one word—only one."

Alas! there no longer was any warmth in the con-
tact of those massive fingers. They sent an icy chill
travelling through her veins, which gave birth to an
overwhelming dread. With wild, despairing eyes she
looked round at Barlow, who had followed her into the
room, and who stood close by, his face wearing a dazed
and awe-stricken expression.

"Oh! Barlow," she said tremulously, "you know better about these things than I do. Perhaps you can tell
me what is the matter."

Trembling like an aspen leaf, the old servant knelt
down by the side of his master and shook him gently.
The only result was that the Squire's big burly form,
which had been supported in a natural attitude by the
back of the chair, slipped helplessly down over the right
arm, whilst the blood, encouraged by the downward
position of his head, dripped drop after drop on the
carpet. The sight was more than poor Barlow could
stand. He burst into tears, and wept like a child,
whilst Kitty, who felt as if suddenly turned to stone,
stood motionless and dry-eyed.

"Barlow," she said again, in a hollow voice, "what *is*
the matter? Surely you must know."

"God help us, Miss Kitty, dear," he sobbed. "The
Squire is dead. Lord have mercy upon his soul! He
has shot himself by his own hand." And Barlow's
grief broke forth anew. At this awful confirmation of
her worst fears, she seemed to lose consciousness. The
room spun round and round, her heart ceased beating,
a loud singing deafened her ears. Like one felled by
a mortal blow, her limbs gave way, and she sunk to the
ground by the dead man's side and hid her face on his
knees. She was so stunned and prostrated by the shock
that for several minutes she was absolutely incapable
of thought. A kind of numbness descended upon her
senses which at first paralyzed all pain. But it did
not last. The respite from suffering was short-lived.
Little by little the full horror of the situation forced
itself upon her comprehension, and she envied Barlow

his tears. Comparatively, they were an easy method of expressing grief. Her father, whom she had so loved and respected, to take his own life violently! She could not believe it, even with the terrible evidence before her eyes. She must be dreaming—a false, cruel, horrible dream, suggested to her imagination by the anxiety which she had lately felt on his account. She would wake up by and by and find everything as usual.

Hoping against hope, she staggered to her feet and looked again at the familiar figure, now lying so still and passive in the cold embrace of death. For once, its contemplation brought no comfort. The dear, kind face wore a suffering expression. The eyes, already glazing fast, were fixed and dilated, whilst the good-humored, well-modelled lips, which during life had rarely uttered a harsh or disagreeable word, were compressed in a resolute line that betrayed the determination of despair. The awful quietude turned her heart to stone. She felt as if it were constricted by a band of iron. To lose him in the ordinary course of nature would have been painful enough; but to lose him thus, with a slur forever cast on his beloved memory, was intolerable anguish. Of all the men she had ever known, he was the last of whom it might have been predicted that he would commit suicide.

Suicide! How she winced at the word! What a pang of mingled sorrow and shame it created! For the worst of it was, she could not hold him blameless. In her eyes it was a cowardly thing for a man to take his own life, and that her father should have done so was simply incomprehensible. She knew of no motive which could have prompted the act. That it was not premeditated, she felt certain, for she remembered the plans formed for the morrow, and how hopefully he had looked forward to seeing Mr. Patterson and letting the Hermitage Farm. Some sudden misfortune which had temporarily upset his reason must be at the bottom of the business. She could account for it in no other way. He had succumbed in a moment of weakness, and yielded to a fatal impulse that his common sense would have deplored had he but given himself time.

"He must have gone mad—he must have gone mad," she mused. "He never would have done it otherwise."

And then her thoughts reverted to the telegram which he had received on his return from hunting. Crushed between the strong fingers of his left hand, the pink paper still peeped out. Mechanically she extricated it from his detaining grasp, smoothed the sheets, and read these words: "Panic on Stock Exchange. Great Northern and nitrates dropped ten. Further losses impending. Better sell at all costs. Bowyer, London." Bowyer was the name of her father's broker—the man whose messages for months past she had learned to dread. It was as she suspected. The squire had evidently been speculating largely and lost. In a fit of despair he had put an end to his existence, refusing, in his trouble, to take counsel even with those nearest and dearest.

She could not help thinking with a shudder what a crushing load of misery might have been spared her had he but communicated the contents of the fateful telegram at the moment when he and she stood in the hall together. Ah, why had he withheld his confidence? What were poverty, reverses, ruin, compared with the bitter pain of losing him, and in such a manner? He could not have had much trust in her love if he believed her so little capable of sacrifice. She would have given up her home, her hunting—ay, even Cyril—just to have him back again. They two might have lived in a garret, no matter where, so long as they were together. And now to think that they were parted—that in all the long, long years to come she should never hear the sound of his voice nor be gladdened by his kind, bright smile. The thought was exquisite sorrow. She could not realize her life without him. He was so much a part and parcel of it.

"Miss Kitty, Miss Kitty," said Barlow's tremulous voice, "for God's sake, don't take on so. We may be wrong. There is perhaps a chance yet. One never knows. Don't you think we ought to send for a doctor?"

She shook her head and smiled—a faint, wan smile, more expressive of unutterable woe than floods of tears.

Her heart told her there was no hope, and she knew that the dead cannot be brought back; but she said: "You may send for one if you like. I wish to Heaven it could do any good; but it wont. You are as well aware of that, Barlow, as I."

"Still, we should have professional advice." And turning, he was about to leave the room, when she called him back.

"Don't tell any of the other servants at present," she said, imploringly. "They will only tattle, and the quieter we can keep it the better. I think I shall die if every one all over the country is to know how he met his death. It is our duty, Barlow, to spare his memory as much as possible from—disgrace." Her face quivered as she uttered the concluding word, and its expression was very piteous to behold. The tears rolled unrestrained down Barlow's cheeks. As yet, she had not shed a single one.

"I will go and fetch Doctor Mackinnon myself," he said, "without letting a soul guess what my errand is; only I can't bear to leave you all alone by yourself, Miss Kitty."

"Don't think about me," she answered. "Do whatever seems to you best in the circumstances. I will stay with my father"—lowering her voice—"whilst you are gone. It is important that nothing should be touched in the room. I expect there—there will have to be an inquest, wont there, Barlow?"

"I expect so, miss." The sight of her pale features twitching with suppressed grief was more than he could endure. He hurried away and left her without another word.

Into the darkened room crept the gray twilight, weird and mysterious, stealing round the dead man and cast-

ing a softening mantle over the vivid crimson of his
hunting-coat and the whiteness of his snowy leathers,
for the Squire would never condescend to "mufti." He
lay there chill and cold, with the blood that had trickled
from the bullet wound congealing on his once ruddy
cheek, and the film of an eternal sleep clouding the
brightness of his formerly vivacious eyes. Now and
again a flickering tongue of flame shot up from the
dying embers and cast fantastic shadows on the wall.
Out-of-doors the wind blew and the rain descended,
coursing in swift rivulets down the window panes, and
pattering from the eaves and shrubberies with steady,
iterative sound. Ah! What a change a few hours
had produced! Only that morning Kitty had gone
forth gay and unthinking, with hardly a care in the
world; and now, here she was, crushed to the very
ground by a burden of grief, rendered doubly heavy by
the element of disgrace it contained.

Such are the vicissitudes of life. The Reaper swings
his scythe, and no one knows on what loved head it may
descend.

After Barlow had been gone a few minutes the girl's
thoughts gradually grew clearer. Her first act was to
throw a fresh log of wood on the fire, and to light a
candle. She intended to search the room thoroughly,
in the hope of finding some further clew which would
explain the commission of her father's deed. Barlow's
absence proved a relief. In the poignancy of her grief
she experienced a craving for absolute solitude. If
only she could stay in the room always, and never be
forced to go out into the world again, or face a crowd
of well-meaning but unsympathetic acquaintances, she
might perhaps have fortitude to bear the cruel blow
with which it had pleased God to visit her. Even
although the dead man could not return her fond
glances, or give a single sign of life, he did not appear
so far away, nor so utterly removed as long as she could
look at him. It seemed very hard that the four walls
of his bed-chamber could not shelter them for ever—

that she must go forth to take up the thread of life just as if it had not been snapped asunder; whilst he—he would be under the earth, hidden away, and left to the tender mercies of loathsome crawling creatures. The mere idea of his beloved form slowly decaying beneath the sods was horrible. The common lot of humanity, viewed from this aspect, caused a shudder of irrepressible disgust to run through her veins. Youth fears death as a grim ravager, and cannot realize how welcome its advent often proves to the spent and the weary.

After a while Kitty gathered sufficient strength to walk towards the writing-table and examine the different papers strewn about on its surface. Suddenly she gave a start and uttered a low cry. On the first page of the blotting-book lay a square white envelope, addressed to Miss Herrick, in the well-known handwriting. He had left her a message, after all. With a thrill, almost akin to joy, and which penetrated to the innermost depths of her being, she thanked God that in his last moments he had not forgotten her. Then the short-lived feeling of elation passed away, leaving her sadder even than before; for all at once the thought flashed through her brain that never again would he put pen to paper. With trembling fingers she tore open the envelope, and read its contents. They ran as follows:

Kitty, my darling Kitty, whether I live or whether I die, it is impossible for you ever to forgive me. I am ashamed—yes, positively ashamed—to look you in the face. Such a wretch as I has no right to continue in this world; for, oh! my child, my dear little ewe lamb, I have not only ruined myself but also you. It is a long story. I have not time to tell you all the ins and outs, so must cut it short.

Some two or three years ago, when those cursed farms were thrown upon my hands, I was forced to borrow money so as to stock them. In order to pay off the debt, I took to speculating, and from that time to this I have never known a happy moment. Everything I touched went wrong, until at last my ill-luck became proverbial on the Stock Exchange. It *seemed as if I* could not succeed. Hoping to

atone for previous losses, like a fool I went in for fresh
ventures, and on a larger scale, but always with a similar
result.

About a month or six weeks ago I found myself threatened
with bankruptcy and exposure unless I could pay off a sum
amounting in all to five-and-twenty thousand pounds.
Would to God I had told you the whole wretched history
then, and trusted to your generosity to help me out of the
situation; but although it was on the tip of my tongue over
and over again to do so, my courage always failed me when
it came to the point. Pride stood in the way, and I could
not bear to lower myself in your eyes. Ah! how short-
sighted we mortals are!

However, to go on with my tale. I did not possess the
money, and it was quite impossible for me to raise so large
a sum at such short notice. Kitty, darling, I blush as I
write these lines. I, your guardian and trustee, the person
who of all others should most carefully have guarded your
interests, took the fortune which belonged to my child, in
order to shield my name and pay the debts I had so foolishly
incurred. I do not attempt to defend the action. My conscience tells me it is inexcusable; but, as there is a God
above, in whose presence I shall shortly stand, I swear to
you that I only meant it as a loan. If the stocks in which
I had speculated had risen ever so slightly I should have
been in a position to pay back every penny. My dear one,
badly as you must think of me when you read this letter,
you will not think so badly, will you, as to believe that I
was a big enough brute to rob deliberately?

Until to-day, I confidently looked forward to repaying
every farthing, with interest at five per cent. Nevertheless,
when you told me on our homeward ride that you were in
love with Captain Mordaunt, and wished to marry him, I
saw breakers ahead. Had the object of your choice been
Lord Algy Loddington, a young man whom I like and
respect, and who is full of sympathy for the faults and
frailties of human nature, when the crash came I think I
could have confessed all my weakness to him. But to a
stranger—no. Therefore, when I received a telegram from
Bowyer this afternoon stating that the money-market was
in a state of panic, and I became aware that I had not only
ruined you financially, but also in all probability wrecked
your girlish dreams of love and happiness, I felt too great a

beast to live. How could I go to Captain Mordaunt and tell him that I had made away with your fortune? If it had been Lord Algy, it would have been different. He loves you for your own sake, and I have reason to know would marry you if you had not a brass farthing.

But it is useless talking of what might have happened. We have to do with what is. I feel as if I were going mad. The blood rushes to my head in a hot wave which makes my temples throb and my senses reel. The strain has been so great of late that my nerve is shaken. Good by, Kitty, my child, my dear, *dear* girl. I love you well, even though I have treated you shamefully—so shamefully that it seems to me now the only way in which I can possibly serve you is to rid you of my presence. If your lover cares for you as a man should care for the woman with whom he proposes to spend his days, he will stick to you through thick and thin, and forgive the sins of the father for the sake of the daughter. My prayer is that you may be happy. And so—farewell—farewell! Think of me as kindly as you can. Ever your loving, but distracted father.

Then, in a postscript, he had evidently added as an afterthought:

You will probably want a friend to help you through this business. If so, send at once for Lord Algy. You can safely trust him. With the exception of Bowyer and my solicitor, he knows more of my affairs than any man living. He will stand by you in case of need. Pray Heaven, however, it may not arise. Oh! Kitty, Kitty, pity me, and when you go to bed to-night offer up a prayer to the Almighty for my soul,

6

CHAPTER X.

Kitty read her father's letter three times over, until at length every sentence was indelibly branded on her memory. After perusing it her, anguish was if anything augmented; for indirectly it appeared she had been instrumental in bringing about the awful deed. In black and white it was written by the dear departed that hàd she only chosen Lord Algy instead of Captain Mordaunt he would not have withheld his confidence. She felt like his murderess, and remorse was added to her sorrow. How clearly she could see the struggles, the regret and penitence, of that tender nature. What did she care about the loss of the money in comparison with losing him? Ah! Why had he not spoken? Why had he not spoken?

With an exceeding bitter cry, she flung her arms round the Squire's neck, and for the first time slow, difficult tears forced their way to her burning eyes. There they remained locked in a close embrace—the dead man and the living girl, the one almost as pale and cold as the other—and there Barlow found them when, about half an hour later, he returned with Dr. Mackinnon. A short examination soon proved that the Squire was past medical aid, and indeed must have been dead some time before he was found. The doctor could do nothing but express his extreme sympathy for the bereaved daughter, and after a while he took his departure, leaving behind him a certificate of death.

Left once more to her own resources, Kitty sat down at her father's writing table, and taking a sheet of paper, wrote hurriedly on it to Lord Algy: "Please come to me at once. I am in dreadful trouble. Barlow will explain." Strangely enough, in this supreme crisis of her life her natural impulse was to apply to him. She turned instinctively to the friend of her youth rather than to the lover of an hour. The latter all at once was reduced to the position of a comparative stranger, seeing that he knew nothing, or next to nothing, of her dear father and his concerns. It was impossible for Cyril to realize the extent of her loss. Lord Algy, on the other hand, had been on terms of intimacy with them for years. He had seen her grow from a child to a woman, and was aware how happily she and her father had always lived together, and how devoted they were to one another. Yes, he would feel for her in her present distress, and do everything in his power to alleviate it. Although she did not love him, she trusted him implicitly, and had a respect for his judgment.

Therefore, she sealed and directed the note, and begged Barlow to drive over with it at once to Furrowdale Castle, and wait for an answer.

And now she again remained a prey to her own sad and miserable thoughts. For a while she experienced no fear at being closeted in the chamber of the dead; but as the hour grew later and later, the silence more and more absolute and impressive, and the immovable figure in the chair became stiffer, and consequently less lifelike, a nameless dread stole over her being. She sat there spellbound, afraid to stir, whilst her excited imagination conjured up a whole host of weird and horrible pictures. How slowly the hours crept on! Would life always seem so interminable in future? She wondered what Barlow could be about. Furrowdale Castle was not more than four miles distant from Herrington. He had had plenty of time to go and return. If he stayed much longer she *would have* to call the housemaid or some one. That awful Thing in the arm-chair was acquiring complete ascendency over her nerves. Its glassy eye haunted her, no matter which way she turned, or how much she sought to avoid it. And the poor pale face, with its ashen cheeks, marble brow, and purple lips stained with bloody froth—she should go mad if she were shut up with it all night.

Little by little she discarded the notion of being able. to preserve complete secrecy. The impossibility of maintaining it became patent; and if the whole county must know that the Squire had died a violent death by his own hands, it was comparatively a matter of small importance whether the evil news spread sooner or later. On one point only she saw her way clear. The world must be made to believe that his reason had been seriously impaired prior to the fatal act. But when she remembered how many of his friends had seen · and conversed with him only that very morning in the hunting field, her heart sunk with a sense of difficulty. It would be no easy matter to keep his fair name untarnished. Nevertheless, what energy and vitality were still left to her she determined to devote entirely to the task. A host of vain regrets surged up into her brain, and its unspoken cry all the time was, "Oh! if I had but known; if I had but known."

She could not help being conscious of the fact that, strongly as Cyril Mordaunt's personality had attracted her from the moment of their first acquaintance, she might have stood proof against his fascinations had she but been aware of the vital issues at stake.

"I could have struggled with my love, and prevented it from gaining power, instead of abandoning myself to it as I did," she mused bitterly. "I was so happy that it never even occurred to me I might be building up fresh difficulties for papa. And now no sacrifice will avail to save him. Henceforth I shall always think that I could have spared his life and *didn't.* I shall never know another peaceful moment—

never. I have been so full of my own concerns during the last few weeks that I scarcely gave any heed to his, or noticed his different moods. And now this is the result. No doubt he saw how pre-occupied I was, and unconsciously I repulsed the poor dear's confidence. Oh, papa, papa, why did you not trust me? It would have saved us both so much wretchedness."

Her whole nervous system was thrown out of gear by the shock it had sustained, and the prolonged solitude, by rousing her mind into abnormal activity without affording any bodily occupation to relieve the tension, served but to increase the morbidness of her reflections. As we have already seen, they were of the most sombre hue. It is a common enough habit of the living to blame themselves for their shortcomings towards the dead. Very few of us live in such perfect amity with our fellow-creatures that we cannot recall some sins of omission or commission once they are gone, and no doubt we should often shape our conduct very differently if we thought their last moments were near at hand. It is human nature to feel remorse for the incurable, and to delay whilst the remedy is still available. A thousand hitherto unconsidered actions crowded upon Kitty's recollection, and she blamed herself for not having been more uniformly loving and unselfish.

Nine o'clock struck, sharp, clear, and distinct. She longed now, with a fierce, feverish longing, for some break to this awful quietude, and for the comforting sound of a human voice—no matter whose. The great immediate need of solitude, which is the first instinct of every sorely stricken soul, was passing away as the demarkations between Life and Death grew sharper, and by a gradual revulsion of feeling she experienced an intense yearning for the protecting presence of a companion. She was so helpless and lonely, and there was so much to be done, that her spirit quailed at the prospect.

Two *years ago,* her father's last surviving sister had

died, leaving them without a relative in the world. She had no aunts or cousins for whom she could telegraph. Until to-day she had never realized the forlornness of her position, but now its terrible isolation became borne in upon her. Strange, that in this first great trouble of her young life the truest friend she possessed should happen to be of the opposite sex—a man, not old, who had asked her, or as good as asked her, to be his wife.

She told herself she must contrive to let Lord Algy know at the first opportunity that she was engaged to Cyril Mordaunt. Otherwise the fact of her applying to him for assistance might give rise to false hope and render the situation embarrassing. A melancholy smile played about the corners of her lips as she recalled her love-passages of the morning. Looking back upon them, she could hardly believe that she was the same Katherine Herrick who had listened with such secret exultation to Cyril's professions of affection. A black gulf of distance seemed to stretch between them now, and she felt changed from an unthinking girl to a grave and earnest woman. For nothing sobers so quickly as sorrow, or leaves such an indelible impression of the Pain of Life.

At length, to the girl's inexpressible relief, she heard wheels coming up the drive, and shortly afterwards subdued voices were audible in the hall. She opened the door a little way and peeped expectantly through it, until, by and by, she saw Lord Algy ascending the staircase, stepping softly and cautiously. Then she shrunk back, shivering from top to toe, and succumbing to a rush of sorrow and shame which rendered her scarcely mistress of her actions. But he had caught sight of the pretty rounded figure, whose symmetrical outlines he had so often admired in the saddle, and almost before she knew what she was about she found her two burning little hands firmly clasped in his strong, cool ones. He tried to speak, but could not. For several seconds they stood quite silent; he, rendered speechless through an overpowering sympathy; she, by excess

of grief. At length she summoned up sufficient courage
to look into his face, and then she saw that it was working desperately, and that two big tears stood in his eyes.
Somehow, the sight made him feel very near to her, and
she was drawn towards him by an irresistible impulse.

"It is good of you to—to come," she faltered. "I
knew th-that you would—be—sorry."

"Sorry!" he exclaimed brokenly. "My poor Kitty,
I wish to God I could give my life for his, and restore
him to you. Willingly, willingly would I lie there in
his stead."

His unfeigned sorrow comforted her more than any
number of set, formal speeches. She felt that his words
came from the heart.

"You always liked him, Algy, didn't you?" she said,
with tremulous intonation, and a pathetic droop of the
upper lip. In her emotion she unconsciously dropped
all ceremony, and called him by his Christian name.

He noticed the omission of the formal prefix which
of late she had studiously employed, and his heart gave
a great, sudden bound. Then, with a deep ring in his
manly voice, he answered, "Yes, always; I can't tell
you how inexpressibly shocked and distressed I was
when Barlow came over and fetched me. I should
have been here sooner, but as bad luck would have it, I
happened to be dining out at the Markhams, and Barlow had to drive the three extra miles. You could
have knocked me down with a feather. Poor old Squire!
A better fellow never wore shoe-leather." And he
cast a reverential glance at the arm-chair, not free from
awe; for solemn as death always is, it appears doubly
so when self-invoked and brought about by an act of
personal violence.

Kitty's eyes followed the direction of his.

"I wish to goodness I were dead," she said, with a
sudden burst of misery. "You don't know, Algy; but
it is I who killed him."

"Nonsense. What are you talking about? Have
you taken *leave of your* senses?" he said.

"Almost, I verily do believe." Then she drew a step nearer, and fixing her sorrowful gaze on him, said, "You have always been his friend. In this letter which I hold in my hand, my father recommends me to ask your advice and assistance. It was his wish that you should know the whole truth of this miserable business. May I confide in you, and rely on your honor never to reveal what I am going to tell you to a living soul? We must shield his memory at all costs."

He wrung her hand hard—so hard that she drew in her breath, whilst the moisture glistened bright in his honest eyes.

"Kitty," he said, "you may trust me as you would yourself. You know what my hope has always been, and, although this is no time to talk of it, I have loved your father as if he were my own, ever thinking that some day we might be related. There is nothing in the whole world I would not do for you, if only you would let me."

She shook her head slowly and sadly. For a moment it flashed across her mind that possibly she had grasped at a shadow and thrown away the substance in her selection of a husband; but she dismissed the thought almost as soon as it arose as ungenerous and disloyal to Cyril. Hitherto the comparisons which she had made between the two men had invariably ended in his favor. It was only that Algy was so kind and sympathetic, whilst her present distress rendered her peculiarly sensitive to kindness and sympathy. But she must tell him of her engagement at once. It was not fair to keep him in ignorance of it.

"If you are to be my friend—really my friend," she said, with a hot flush, "you can only be so on one condition."

"What is that, Kitty?"

"You must give up talking to me of—love." And she looked away.

"Your father wished it," he said. "Not that I would

urge his wishes upon you, especially at such a moment, but he would have given us his consent."

"I know. This letter tells me so in plain language, and that makes it all much harder to bear."

"Why harder? It ought to make it easier. A sorrow shared is never so bad as when it must be borne alone."

"You don't understand. If my father had only informed me of the embarrassed state of his finances, and I had been educated in the belief that it was important I should marry a rich man"—Lord Algy winced—"no doubt I should have made up my mind to the situation like a sensible and dutiful young woman. As it was, I had not the slightest idea of the involved condition of papa's affairs. I thought I was free to choose as I pleased, and so—and so," she concluded, the color deepening in her polished cheek, "I accepted Cyril——"

"You have accepted Captain Mordaunt?" broke in Lord Algy, his voice hoarse with agitation.

"Yes, he proposed to me this morning as we rode home together. Later on I overtook papa, and told him of Cyril's proposal."

"And what did the Squire say?" inquired her companion. His face had grown suddenly white, his manner constrained.

"At first my father did not seem pleased. In fact, he was very much put out. But by degrees he appeared to grow accustomed to the notion, and after some discussion ended by saying he would see Cyril to-morrow."

"He did make plans, then, for the future? That looks as if the deed were not premeditated."

"Yes," she said. "I am positive that *it* "— lowering her voice—"was not in his mind then. He could not have spoken as he did."

"Go on," said Lord Algy. "Tell me what took place next. Had you any quarrel over this engagement of yours?"

"Quarrel! No, certainly not. Papa was vexed because *he had hoped* I would marry somebody else."

The blood showed red beneath her transparent skin. "But when he saw that I was in earnest, and that it was no mere childish fancy on my side, he gave in. The latter part of the way it came on to rain very hard, so we rode home as fast as we could, and had not much opportunity of continuing the conversation. But papa was quite cheerful and like himself—at least," modifying the statement, "as cheerful as he has been for some time past. When we entered the house I handed him a telegram which was lying on the hall table. Directly he opened it he seemed struck as by a mortal blow. He tottered against the wall, his limbs trembling, his eyes staring and unseeing, and looking so like as if he were going to have a fit, that, frightened out of my life, I rang for Barlow."

CHAPTER XI.

"OUGHT I TO GIVE HIM UP?"

"AND then?" inquired Lord Algy, who listened to the above narrative with profound interest.

"And then," she continued, "my father went upstairs and I never saw him again alive. I waited and waited for ever so long. Finally we made up our minds to force open the door, and"—with a sudden break in her voice—"we found him like this."

"It is too shocking for words," said Lord Algy. "He must have been mad, surely."

She caught eagerly at the suggestion.

"Yes, he must have been mad—that's just what I say. He never would have done it had he been responsible for his actions. There were heavy losses on the Stock Exchange. I don't know their full extent, but they appear to have driven him to despair. He was threatened with bankruptcy, and to avoid it he very properly borrowed my money. It was his—his. He was welcome to every penny of it. I would willingly have given it to him as a free gift had he told me of the straits he was in. But he elected to keep his own counsel, and things went wrong."

"And your fortune?" inquired Lord Algy.

"My fortune was swept away; but that is a matter of no consequence. My poor father, however, tormented himself with vain regrets with reference to his share in the business. He never had a secret from me before."

"Would to God that he had not kept this one from you!"

"He says in his letter, Algy, that—that he could have made a clean breast of the whole affair to you; if—if I had *but acted in* accordance with his wishes, he would

not have been lying there now. But I knew nothing,
and the last straw broke the camel's back. When I
told him about Cyril, and the telegram came right on
the top of that piece of news, without taking time to
reflect, he shut himself up in his room, and there and
then must have put an end to his troubles."

Lord Algy had grown very pale whilst he listened
to Kitty's words, and his nether lip trembled; nevertheless, he managed to say with a fair show of composure:

"Hush, Kitty, don't blame yourself. You were in
total ignorance of the state of affairs, and consequently
it was not in human nature that you should go against
the dictates of your heart."

She looked at him in astonishment.

"Do you really mean what you say, Algy?"

"Yes, certainly, I mean it. I can't see that you have
anything to reproach yourself with."

"Ah! if I only thought that——" Her voice gave way,
and she did not finish the sentence.

"It is your duty to think it; not only because it is
the truth, but also because no good can be gained by
torturing yourself unnecessarily."

"And Cyril?" she faltered shyly. "What of him?
Ought I to give him up?"

Lord Algy's face changed. All of a sudden a terrible
temptation seized him. Some instinct warned him that
she was prepared to abide by his advice, and he realized
that his future happiness depended upon the answer he
gave to this question. But as he looked at her sorrowful countenance, with its sad eyes and woe-begone
expression, his better angel triumphed, and he also
realized that the happiness of the girl whom he loved
ought to be and should be of higher importance. If
self were allowed to weigh down the scales, then what
he called his love was worth nothing, absolutely nothing.
Kitty saw the irresolution depicted on his features, and
repeated the demand, vaguely conscious of its cruelty,
yet too bruised and shaken herself to be as considerate
of his feelings as on an ordinary occasion.

"Algy," she said, "tell me.   You know better than
I.   Ought I to give up Cyril?"

He looked away.   The direct questioning of her
glance was more than he could endure.   And then he
spoke.

"No, certainly not.   Besides, what good would it do?
Neither you nor I can recall the past, and no sacrifice
on your part will avail to restore the dead."   So saying,
he walked to the mantel-piece and stood with his back
against it, whilst the leaping flames illumined the outlines of his strong shoulders and spare, sinewy form.

Curious thoughts flit across a person's brain, even in
seasons of the deepest and most genuine distress.   It
occurred to Kitty that he looked like a man, and in spite
of a certain homeliness of feature, she appreciated the
pose of his muscular neck and the erect way it supported
its owner's head.

She sighed heavily, feeling inwardly comforted by
his words, yet making a show of resistance to them.

"I feel so wretched—so guilty.   It no longer seems
to me right to think of Cyril.   And yet his image
continually rises up before me."

"Your hesitations will grow weaker after a time, and
finally they will disappear altogether."   Then he laid
his hand on her shoulder, as if he were her brother, and
she a dearly loved sister, and in his deep voice said,
"Promise me one thing, Kitty."

"What is it?" she asked faintly, and with a feeling
of distrust springing up within her bosom.   The next
moment she was heartily ashamed of it, and of her own
suspicious nature, which, on the slightest provocation,
made her ready to doubt her best friend.

"Henceforth," he said, "don't be afraid of me, or of
what I may say——"

"I'm not afraid, Algy," she interrupted, though the
rose in her cheeks denied the assertion.

"Yes, yes, you are.   I know better.   But you need
not be.   In future, I want you to forget any foolish
words of love that I may ever have spoken, and to let

me be your friend, and only your friend. In this way
I can serve you best; for, oh! my dear, my poor dear!
you will want some one to stand by you now, and an
old playfellow may surely be allowed to take part of
the burden off the shoulders of the girl he has known
since she was a little thing in short frocks."

The kind manner of the man, his largeness of view
and nobility of soul, touched her to the very quick, and
opened the flood-gates which until now had remained
obstinately closed. All at once the hardness and bitterness of her grief melted away, and moistening tears
rushed to her dry eyes. They relieved both heart and
brain, making the one feel less cold and stony, the
other calmer and more tranquil. She seized her companion's hand, and by a swift impulse of gratitude and
admiration pressed it to her lips, crying, "Oh! Algy,
you are very good to me—far too good, for I have
treated you but badly, and don't deserve that you should
show me any kindness."

The blood leaped in his veins. For a moment it
seemed as if he were about to forget all his fraternal
resolutions. The next—he drew away his hand gently,
but determinedly, and said, "We have agreed never to
talk of that any more. I deny that you have treated
me badly, and I am the last man in the world to wish
to force a young girl's inclinations. Trust me, Kitty—
trust me. I ask no other boon. Let me help you, and
be of use to you. And now, dear, wont you go to your
room and rest a little? I will stay here for the present,
and make all necessary arrangements for to-night.
Mother Grundy wont allow me to sleep under the same
roof as yourself, I suppose, but I will drive over again
the first thing to-morrow morning. If you could only
doze for two or three hours I should feel easier in my
mind regarding you."

She suffered him to lead her away like a little child,
for, truth to tell, she was thoroughly worn out, and later
on swallowed a cupful of beef tea at his bidding. It
was eleven o'clock before he left the house. He came

and stood outside the door of her room for a minute, and said very softly, "Kitty, are you asleep?" And she answered, "No." For how was it possible to sleep on such a wretched, wretched evening? And then he said, "Good night, Kitty dear. God bless you." And shortly afterwards she heard his dogcart rolling off down the drive.

His presence had soothed and consoled her wondrously, and she no longer felt utterly alone and forsaken. Somehow he seemed so strong to bear, so capable and unselfish, that she found herself thinking of him in a totally new light.

The commonplace events of every-day life weave a curious crust round a man's real nature, which only some very unexpected or tragical event breaks down. Sometimes the crust becomes so hard that nothing will break it, but such was not the case with Lord Algy. His big tender heart refused to be trammelled or silenced, and a woman in distress appealed to it powerfully. He had been accustomed to a laughing, rosy, coquettish, and provoking Kitty. The sight of a Kitty with pale cheeks, quivering lips, and wet eyes filled him with huge compassion. He felt capable of any sacrifice if only he could restore her to her pretty smiling self again—the self that was printed so sharply and clearly on the tablets of his memory.

As she lay in the darkness Kitty's thoughts dwelt almost unconsciously on her late visitor. "Poor, dear old Algy," she mused. "How well he took it when I told him about Cyril. There is not one man in a hundred who, under the circumstances, would have taken it so well. I wonder why I don't care for him in the way that he wanted and papa wanted. It seems strange, especially when he is such a dear. The girl who marries him will be very lucky; but of course I am luckier— a hundred thousand times luckier with Cyril."

After a while she cried herself into a restless, uneasy sleep, from which she awoke unrefreshed, and dressing automatically, went languidly downstairs. But here a fresh shock awaited her; for the familiar rooms looked so dark and silent and dreary, with the blinds funereally drawn, and bearing no signs of occupation, that she could not rest in them, but wandered from one to another, not knowing where to take up her quarters. The dining-room and study were both too full of reminiscences. Their associations were exquisitely painful, for they were the apartments which her father and herself had usually occupied when alone. She walked through them, feeling as if a sharp knife were being run into her heart, and fled to the large drawing-room beyond, which they had only used on state occasions, few and far between, especially of late. It was formal and ceremonious, and the Squire had never patronized it. Here she pitched her tent after a while, and rang the bell for Barlow.

"I suppose the servants all know by this time what has taken place?" she asked drearily of the faithful old man.

"I couldn't help it, Miss Kitty," he responded in a tone of self-exculpation. "I swear to you I haven't told one of 'em. But you know what servants are. It is impossible to keep anything from 'em for long. They're that prying and inquisitive."

"Never mind, Barlow. Everybody must know before the day is out."

"They *will* talk in the 'all, miss, and no matter how I tell 'em to hold their tongues, I can't prevent people from making their hobservations."

"What you say is true, Barlow. I have been thinking things over during the night. No one knows the exact truth except you and me, the doctor, and Lord Algernon Loddington. Now, what I want you to do is this: I want you to give out that my—my father died through the effects of an accident. Do you understand?"

A look of intelligence and relief stole over Barlow's face.

"Yes, yes, Miss Kitty—that's it. A haccident. Oh! *my good* master," lifting his eyes to the ceiling until their whites glistened. "I've served you true and faithful for five-and-twenty years, and nobody will ever find me saying a word against you."

A few minutes later Lord Algy arrived, according to his promise, and Barlow bustled out of the room.

Lord Algy was shocked beyond measure at Kitty's appearance. The girl's face looked pale and drawn, there were great purple rings round her eyes, and the eyes themselves were rendered heavy and lustreless by an expression of acute suffering. The full lids seemed as if they could hardly support their own weight, and the muscles round the corners of her mouth were agitated by a nervous twitch. She greeted him with a faint smile as he entered the room, and said apologetically and with a feeble assumption of her ordinary tone, "Good morning. I am ashamed to give you so much trouble."

"Trouble!" he exclaimed. "It went to my heart to leave you last night as I did. I could not sleep for thinking of you left all alone in this house of mourning. Did you get any rest?"

She shook her head.

"Not much. I fancy I must have dozed a little towards morning, but my brain was full of chaotic thought, which kept me awake."

"Have you no friend for whom you could send to keep you company?"

"I have plenty of friends of a sort, but none," lifting her eyes to his, "whom I would care to see at a time like this, except yourself."

Again a thrill of pleasure shot through his frame, and he had to control himself before replying.

"Does—does Captain Mordaunt know what has happened?" he inquired.

"No, not yet. He was to have come to-day. I forgot all about it, but I suppose now I had better write and put him off."

"Why? His presence would comfort you, Kitty. If

7

you like, I will go to his lodgings, and, provided he has not heard the news already, break it to him."

Her face brightened visibly for a moment. Then it relapsed into melancholy. She loved Cyril with all her heart, but she was not sure of him. She had not known him long enough to tell in what way he would receive the intelligence.

"Well?" said Algy. "Shall I go?"

Then she summoned up courage to speak the doubt that was in her mind.

CHAPTER XII.

A TRUE FRIEND.

"ALGY," she said, "you will think my hesitation strange, but may I tell you what accounts for it?"

"Why, surely," he replied.

"It has occurred to me that when Cyril learns I have lost my fortune, and instead of coming to him fairly dowered, he finds I am but a penniless bride, he may cease to care for me, and regret his share of the bargain. Many men would do so in his place."

"Tut, tut, Kitty. You must have a very poor opinion of Captain Mordaunt if you believe him capable of such an act of meanness."

"You *would* call it meanness, then?" she asked, relieved by the summary way in which he dismissed the supposition as impossible to the code of honor of a gentleman. "All people's ideas are not as strict as your own on these points, and Cyril is poor, remember."

"I don't care. If he were to throw you over now, just at the very moment when you most require his sympathy and support, I should call it as caddish and low a thing as a man could well do." Lord Algy looked so fierce that she could not help smiling.

Her fears were set at rest, for of course her Cyril would never be guilty of a low and caddish action. He was one of those rare personages, nature's noblemen.

"I ought to tell him at once," she said. "It would not be right for me to conceal from him that I am ruined and no longer possess any fortune."

Her companion pondered for a moment.

"Ultimately, of course, you must tell Captain Mordaunt," he said; "but at present I can see no necessity for such *desperate haste.*"

99

"Why, Algy, surely you would not have me deceive Cyril? I could not have believed that you would give me such counsel."

"There is a great difference between deception and premature confidences calculated to mislead. If I were in your place I should say nothing about your financial position for a few days."

"And pray, why not? It seems to me that I should be acting very wrongly indeed if I attempted to conceal anything from Cyril."

"On the other hand, your father's difficulties may not prove as great as he imagined. Men who suffer from sudden losses often take an exaggerated view of their affairs. It may prove so in the present case."

"But even then——" she objected.

"My advice is, wait for a day or two until you know exactly how you are situated. The money may not be all gone. With a little care and patience we may find it possible to recover some portion, if not the entire bulk of your fortune. Things very seldom prove quite as bad as they appear at the first blush—at least, that is my experience. Anyhow, a few days' delay can do no harm. I have telegraphed for your father's lawyer, and expect him to-morrow. No doubt he will throw some light on the situation. Until then, as I said before, I strongly advise you to keep quiet as regards the money question."

Kitty perceived the force of this reasoning. There was too much truth in Lord Algy's remarks for her to remain insensible to them.

"Yes," she said thoughtfully. "I suppose you are right, only I can't bear the idea of accepting Cyril's love on false pretences."

Lord Algy caught the right end of his mustache between his strong teeth, and gnawed at it viciously, whilst his breath came fast and slow.

"If it *be* love," he said impressively, "it wont allow itself to be influenced by a mere question of pounds, *shillings*, and pence, and if it is not——"

"Ah!" she exclaimed, her whole frame quivering with emotion. "If it is not——"

"Then, dear," he said very gently, "it may be better for you to learn the truth now, rather than when the knowledge might come too late. The pain would be insignificant in comparison. But this is gloomy talk, and there is no occasion to prophesy evil."

"Evil comes, though, all the same. Yesterday morning, only yesterday morning, see how happy I was, and look at me now."

"Some day, please God, you will be happy again."

"If I am, it will never be in the same way. Papa is dead. Something has been taken out of my life which cannot be restored. A child who has lost his ball does not always feel comforted because a top is offered in its stead. I am like that child. Even Cyril, much as I love him, can never take the place of my own dear father. Until quite lately we were everything to one another."

"And yet, the little happy bird that was so well off and cared for could not rest content in the parent nest, but wanted to fly away out into the great world, with all its cares, and strife and sorrow, and build a home for itself with a comparatively unknown mate."

She hung her head, and he smiled a smile devoid of merriment, and full of irrepressible sadness.

"It is human nature," he said. "One sees it everywhere going on. The old birds centre their affection in their young, and would fain keep them if they could. They toil and slave, they shower favors upon them, but in vain. The young birds *must* learn to fly on their own account, no matter how often they fall to the ground. Life, life, experience, urge them on. Yes, it is everywhere the same. No one is quite satisfied with what he has. Everybody wants something more. But again our talk is running into solemn grooves."

"I like it, Algy. It suits me. Go on philosophizing, please."

"*Philosophy is as useless as everything else.* When

you have come to my age, Kitty, you will realize that
all things in this world are phantasmagorical, and but
the outcome of the human fancy.   Our philosophy!
What is it?   On what is it founded?   On nothing save
the imaginings of the individual brain.   Each person's
definition of the world varies, and yet we call philosophy
a fixed, grand principle."

"Algy, you are bitter.   What is the matter with you
to-day?   I have never heard you talk like this before."

"The ravings of my individual brain," he said with
a forced laugh.   "Forgive me, Kitty.   I was forgetting
you, and thinking only of myself.   You were right to
pull me up.   There was something I wanted to ask you.
Let me see now—what was it?"   And he put his hand
to his forehead, and thought for a moment or two.
"Ah! yes, I remember.   Captain Mordaunt has a
mother living in town, has he not?"

"Yes," answered Kitty.   "Lady Mordaunt lives in
Sloane Street, and is there now."

"I—I have been thinking that you—you will want a
change after the—the funeral.   What do you say to staying with your future mother-in-law for a bit?   It would
be the best and most natural arrangement in the circumstances, and of course the visit need only be a
temporary one.   In fact," he added brusquely, "as soon
as a decent interval has elapsed, the sooner you are
married the better."

"You seem in a desperate hurry to get rid of me,"
she said, and there was a ring of pique in her tone.

"It is not that.   But you can't live alone.   A girl of
nineteen or twenty must have a settled home."

"But," she objected, "I can scarcely offer myself on
a visit to Lady Mordaunt.   I have not yet made her
acquaintance, and she may not ask me."

"If she does, would you be prepared to go?"   And
Lord Algy looked inquiringly at his companion.

"Yes; that is to say, if Cyril wishes it."

"Cyril—always Cyril," he murmured, under his
breath.   Then aloud, "He shall wish it.   I will take

care of that. By the by, Kitty, my father and mother
send you no end of kind messages. Indeed, they would
like you to come to Furrowdale Castle, but," and he
flushed a dull red, "I knew you would not care about
that as long as I happened to be there."

"Thank you," she said. "The duke and duchess
are very kind, but," and her eyes sought the carpet,
"since you seem to say that I must leave my own
home, it may, perhaps, be better for me to go to
town, always provided I receive Lady Mordaunt's invitation."

"I thought you would prefer to go there. I told the
Governor so, but if at any time you want a home,
remember Furrowdale Castle is always open to you.
No, Kitty," he added quickly, "I do not mean in the
way that I can see you are thinking of. My father and
mother have a sincere regard for you.. They like you
for your own sake, and if you were to drop me a line
beforehand, I could easily contrive to be out of the way,
you know, without their suspecting that anything was
wrong."

The delicacy of mind which prompted this speech
produced a deep impression on her. She stretched out
her hands, but finding he made no corresponding sign,
drew them back quickly, with a mingled feeling of
embarrassment and guilt.

"Oh! Algy," she exclaimed warmly, "what must you
think of me, if you actually believe that I would drive
you from your own house?"

He looked at her in an uncertain manner, as if it
were on the tip of his tongue to make some eloquent
but imprudent answer. Then he walked to the window,
and taking up the tassel of the blind, drew it restlessly
backwards and forwards through his fingers.

"You know what I think of you," he said after
a while. "Nothing will ever alter my opinion; but
henceforth I shall never give expression to it, unless,"
and he laughed a short laugh, "something very unlikely
occurs."

"What is that, Algy? I don't understand you. You talk so strangely."

"Unless you give me encouragement to speak. And as that is not likely, I shall keep my sentiments to myself."

She made no answer, for the very good reason that she could not find a single word, either kindly, witty, or sarcastic to say. He had succeeded most effectually in rendering her dumb, and she found herself watching his movements involuntarily and with a certain discomfort. For she did not feel at ease. Nothing could be more admirable than Lord Algy's conduct. Try as she might, she could not find a fault with it, and yet, in her innermost consciousness, a little voice whispered that she was gradually letting herself drift into a new and unintended channel. Luckily for her, he was very good and honorable. He was evidently prepared to adhere strictly to their compact of friendship, and did not offer to take advantage of any temporary weakness on her part. But that that weakness should exist at all was disquieting, and seemed like treason to Cyril. In short, her sensations were so mixed that she did not care to analyze them, and took comfort in the belief that the touch of Cyril's lips, the clasp of Cyril's arms, would immediately banish every disloyal thought.

Yes, even although it was very wicked, with her poor, dear father lying dead overhead, and the time was not one for thinking of marriage and giving in marriage, she longed for his presence. Lord Algy had divined the most secret yearning of her being when he had suggested that Cyril's company would probably console her more than that of any one else. If only she could lay her head on his shoulder and sob her heart out there, whilst his enfolding arms held her safely protected in a loving embrace—if he did but kiss away the salt tears as they rose to her eyes, she told herself that in spite of the great and terrible loss she had sustained, after a long, long time life might still prove worth living. Cyril's love would brighten her days and soothe her grief, until little by little the love that was lost and gone forever would be replaced by an affection as true and tender. Her drooping spirits revived, and as she mapped out the future it no longer seemed utterly dark. Far off a light shone in the horizon which promised to develop into a glorious sun. In spite of all that had been taken from her, she was not wholly unhappy, since Hope and Faith were left.

For several seconds Lord Algy stood and watched the girl whilst these thoughts were passing through her mind. Then he turned on his heel and said:

"All right, Kitty. I see how it is. I will go and fetch Captain Mordaunt at once."

At that her fortitude gave way altogether, and with a pathetic quaver in her voice, she cried, "Thank you, Algy—oh, thank you. Don't think me ungrateful or insensible to your kindness, but I do want him so badly. I feel as if I could not rest until he came."

Their eyes met, and something in the dumb, patient expression of his aroused a sudden sense of shame in her breast.

"Oh," she exclaimed impulsively, "I'm so sorry. Somehow or other I'm always forgetting. Sorrow has rendered me not only selfish, but cruel."

"Neither selfish nor cruel," he answered bravely. "Your wish to have Captain Mordaunt by your side at such a time as this is both natural and legitimate. Dear friend," he went on, holding out his hand, whilst a mournful smile flitted across his features, "don't be too sensitive about my feelings—I mean, don't let them worry you. I am a big, rough fellow, used to being knocked about in the world, and can take uncommon good care of myself. From this day forth, never allow a thought of me to trouble your memory." And so saying, he took up his hat and stick and went off to fetch the man who had supplanted him in the affections of the girl whom he had loved ever since she was a wild slip of a thing, with tangled hair falling in disorderly waves around her shoulders. There was a constriction at his heart, but he did not flinch in his purpose.

"After all," he muttered to himself as he passed out, "it matters very little about me. The great thing is to secure her happiness. If the poor old Squire had lived, and I had had him on my side, I might have made a better fight of it, but as it is, she ought to be my first consideration." Then he clinched his strong right hand, and added, "And by Heaven she shall be. If this fellow, Mordaunt, sticks to her, well and good. But if he doesn't, if he proves himself to be a mere mercenary money-seeker, bent on his own advancement, and who looks upon a wife as a stepping-stone whose gold enables him to rise, then I will show her that a man's love is not all made up of selfishness and passion, as she once jestingly asserted. So help me God." He set his jaw, as he did when he was going at a big fence, and his good-humored lips became compressed in a resolute straight line. He was prepared to prove to all the world that the confidence of his dear old friend, Squire Herrick, had not been misplaced.

CHAPTER XIII.

DOING A DEAL.

CYRIL MORDAUNT occupied some comfortable little lodgings in the market town of Furrowdale, which was situated about two miles distant from the ducal abode. On this particular morning he happened to be in an especially good humor. Every now and then—though usually at rare intervals—there are certain phases in one's life when for a brief period everything seems to go right. For some time past all his affairs had prospered. He had won a sufficient sum of money over the big autumn handicaps to pay off his most pressing creditors and keep him comfortably going through the winter without having recourse to his friend, Mr. Solomon Isaacs, of Milford Lane, Strand. He had succeeded in selling a hunter—afflicted with fever in the feet, and an incipient roarer—to a brother officer for twice what the animal was worth, and he had his eye on a young 'un, belonging to a sporting farmer, which he believed could be purchased for eighty guineas, and which, if decently fed and ridden during the hunting season, ought to realize the best part of two hundred guineas at the sale he contemplated holding at Tattersall's in the spring. In addition to all these causes of satisfaction, he had proposed to and been accepted by the nicest girl in the county—a girl who, even if she had not had a sixpence to her name, would still have proved attractive. Needless to say, a fortune of five-and-twenty thousand pounds, besides excellent prospects and expectations, helped to make her still more captivating. When Cyril thought of Kitty's money, and of dear Kitty herself, he felt that, all things considered, he had done very well indeed. No wonder he was in a satisfied frame of mind.

He had risen early, and walked to the post-office before breakfast in order to telegraph the good news to his mother. An hour or two later came an answering message: "My congratulations. Bring the dear girl to see me as soon as possible. Can put you both up." Cyril read the telegram, and shoved it into his breast coat-pocket, meaning to show it to Kitty when he went over to lunch at Herrington Hall.

"H'm!" he soliloquized. "Rather a bore just now, and I don't suppose Kitty will care about leaving the hunting any more than I. However, we shall have to run up to town for a day or two, some day or other, and we may as well get the visit over. I'm bound to appease the mater's curiosity, and let her form a personal opinion of her new daughter-in-law. Still, it's a nuisance." Thus thinking, he walked to the mantel-piece and took up a printed card of that week's fixtures. "I wonder where the meets are likely to be. If we could hit off a couple of days when they are a long way off, we might manage to put in a little trip to London without losing any sport. I'll consult Kitty, and hear what her views on the subject are." He undid his tie— the bow was not quite to his mind—and did it up carefully before the glass. The reflection presented by the mirror was evidently pleasing, for he smiled placidly and contentedly, turning his head first to one side, then to the other, as much as to say, "I'm a very good-looking boy indeed." He would not have liked to be caught thus employed, but when entirely alone it did not much signify, and he could not help knowing that he was an uncommonly smart, well-set-up fellow. He had read approval in the ladies' eyes much too often not to find commendation in his own. After all, there is a great pleasure in being the possessor of a nice straight figure, surmounted by a handsome face. People may say what they like about the worthlessness of *looks* in comparison with virtue, but they count for a great deal in a world where appearances are considered far before merit. Presently, as he continued to gaze, Cyril's thoughts took a different direction. Even admiration of self palls after a time, and a frown caused a perpendicular line to appear in his smooth brow, making the fair eyebrows almost meet.

"I wonder what the old Squire will say to our engagement," he muttered impatiently, striving to suppress a certain feeling of anxiety. "I bet a pony he'll raise objections. He has never taken to me, and is all in favor of Loddington. I can tell that by his manner. Luckily, Kitty is pretty far gone, and she wont throw me over in a hurry. That's one mercy. If the girl is all right and means business, one can generally snap one's finger at the papa, especially when the money is independent."

His meditations were here disturbed by the entrance of the landlady, who came to say that Mr. Brown was waiting to see him down below. Brown was the name of the young farmer whose horse he wished to buy. On hearing this information, Cyril put on his hat and went into the street immediately. On the previous afternoon he and Mr. Brown had not succeeded in coming to terms. Brown had asked a hundred and fifteen guineas, and Cyril would not offer more than eighty. The fact was, he happened to know that the owner of the horse wanted money badly, and therefore felt pretty sure of his man. Consequently, he refused to give a farthing more, and his last words had been:

"All right, my good friend. Don't let me spoil your sale. If you can get a higher price for the nag, do so, by all means. But if you find by any chance that you can't, why, then—remember my offer. Eighty guineas, and you shall have the check the very day you bring the horse over to me. I can't speak fairer than that."

But Mr. Brown vowed nothing would induce him to part with Springbok at so ruinous a price. He declared that, without exception, he was the finest hunter and biggest fencer he had ever ridden to hounds, that he was dirt cheap, and worth double the sum asked. All of which Cyril knew quite well. Nevertheless, he remained obdurate to poor Brown's entreaties that they should split the difference. At length, in despair, that individual reduced his terms to a hundred. But still Cyril stood firm, and declined to make any concession. Many a horse-coper before now had found him hard to deal with.

He shook his head in reply, and said, "No, Brown, I've made my offer, and I stick to it. To tell you the truth, I'm not over and above keen. There are half a dozen fellows at the present moment all wanting me to buy their horses, and I got a letter from a friend only this morning saying he was going abroad, and offering me a rattling good hunter for his keep. If I had not happened to see you out last week it would never have occurred to me to look at your chestnut. Good-by, Brown, good-by. If you care to reconsider the question of price, let me know." And with that Cyril galloped off, feeling tolerably certain that the transfer of the fine up-standing chestnut gelding from Mr. Brown's stables to his own was merely an affair of time. But he had sacrcely expected so speedy a surrender, and was pleased at the swift result of his predictions. He descended the stairs cheerfully, whistling a popular air. His tones were peculiarly fluty and bird-like. At the sight of young Brown mounted on Springbok he exhibited a well-simulated surprise, slightly dashed with a mixture of contemptuous patronage.

"Halloo! Brown," he exclaimed, "you here! This is an unexpected pleasure. Come into market, I suppose, and thought you'd give the chestnut a little exercising trot, eh?"

"No, sir," answered Brown, wofully, fumbling at the reins and looking down in evident embarrassment. Then he cleared his throat, and added with an effort, "Fact is, sir, I received a very unpleasant letter this morning—a very unpleasant letter indeed."

"Really! I am sorry to hear that. We are all of us subject to them at times."

"The truth is, Captain Mordaunt," and Brown's tone became preternaturally grave, "it was a *summons.*"

Cyril laughed.

"Oh! Was that all? I thought you were going to tell me of something serious."

"I have heard as how you gentlemen gets so many that you takes no notice of 'em and just pitches 'em into the waste-paper basket," answered Brown guilelessly. "But it's a very serious affair to me, and I don't half like it."

"Quite right, Brown—quite right. The honesty of your sentiments does you credit. How your creditors must admire it."

"There's a matter of forty-five pound nine shilling and twopence," continued the other, "which I've been owing to a man for very nigh a twelvemonth. I allers told him as how I meant to pay fair and square, if only he'd give me time. And he promised he would, but he hasn't. This paper," pulling a blue, official-looking document from his pocket, "came upon me like a thunderbolt. It's the first summons as ever I had in my life, and I don't like it—no, that I don't. And I can't abear the sight of the thing. And so," concluded Brown, "although you're pressing me very 'ard—very 'ard indeed, Captain Mordaunt—and a few pounds more or less will make a long sight bigger difference to a needy man like me than they will to a rich man like yourself, sir, I've "—and the poor fellow's intonation became decidedly unsteady—"I've made up my mind to part with Springbok at a sacrifice."

"I'm delighted to hear it," said Cyril, showing his fine teeth in a friendly smile.

"Nothing but necessity has druv me to it, Captain Mordaunt, and I trust to you to treat me handsome."

"Business is business," observed that young gentleman dryly. "You're not the only person who receives summonses. If you think you are, you're very much mistaken. Nowadays a summons does not entitle one to much compassion."

Brown sighed.

"Perhaps when you're in the habit of receiving 'em it's different. You get 'ardened, so to speak. But when you're a plain working-man, who never has had anything to do with the law, this here bit of paper comes as a shock. It gave me a reg'lar turn, it did, and when I clapped eyes on it I could not rest until I had put the saddle and bridle on Springbok. As long as I've got this thing hanging over my 'ead I don't feel like an honest man, nohow."

"You are too sensitive, my friend—too sensitive by half. So you really wish to part with Springbok, eh?"

"Yes, sir, I must," answered Brown, wiping his dolorous countenance with a fancy cotton pocket-handkerchief. "There's no help for it. He'll be six next grass, and a better 'orse never looked through a bridle. Any one will tell you in the field how well he carried me last winter. He knows his business, and is the cleverest and boldest young 'un as ever I sat on." And so saying, Springbok's owner swung himself from the saddle to the ground, and laid his coarse but kindly hand on the animal's arching neck.

"I shall require a trial," said Cyril, who was old in the ways of the world, and knew that when a man wants to sell it is folly to believe a word he says, or to rely on anything save your own personal judgment and experience. "There are some meadows at the back of the house where, if you have no objection, I could see how he gallops, and pop him over a jump or two."

"You can do what you like with him," said Mr. Brown, conscious that Springbok was a good, sound, genuine horse. "I ain't afraid of *his* legs cracking. You don't often meet with such legs as those. Just feel them, Captain Mordaunt."

Cyril passed his hand down the chestnut's flat, cool members, and expressed his approval of their condition.

"Yes," he said, "he's clean enough on his pins. There's a slight splint on the near fore, but it does not seem to interfere with the sinew, and, as far as I can tell, is nothing very serious.'"

"He had that splint when he was a two-year-old," said Brown, in reply, "but it has never grown any bigger, and I should recommend you to leave it alone. A light blistering, no doubt, would take it away altogether, only the 'orse is so sound and well, it seems a pity to mess him about."

"I am inclined to think you're right," said Cyril, lengthening the stirrups previous to mounting, whilst Brown stood at the chestnut's head, eying him with mournful pride. "In cases of this sort blistering very often does more harm than good." So saying, he sprung lightly into the saddle, and walked off towards the meadows, Brown marching with long, swinging strides by the animal's side, and occasionally smoothing Springbok's silky mane.

The town of Furrowdale lay imbedded in a sea of grass, and was surrounded in all directions by undulating billows of ridge and furrow. They soon reached the outskirts, and stopping before a five-barred gate, unlatched it after some little difficulty, and entered a large, flat field. This field was bounded by a high and stiff fence, with a deeply cut ditch on the take-off side. Directly Springbok felt the elastic turf beneath his hoofs, and the cool, green grass greeted his eyes in place of the hard macadam, he cocked his small, spirited ears, and inhaled the fresh air with a series of little playful snorts. Cyril allowed him to break into a trot, and then, when he had ascertained that Springbok's action was true and springy, he increased the pace to a canter, and so on until at last the horse was fairly extended. Twice, thrice, he raced him round the field at topmost speed, until the good steed's veins began to swell on his glossy neck, the linings of his clear-cut nostrils showed red, and great white flakes of foam flew by from *his sensitive* mouth. Mr. Brown stood in the cen-

8

tre of the field and watched Springbok's movements anxiously. There was no fault to be found with them. The horse bounded smoothly and lightly from one ridge to the other, and galloped close to the ground in a racer-like fashion which proclaimed that he owned a fair turn of speed. It did not take Cyril long to discover that he was fast enough to live with any hounds, but he was careful not to allow his satisfaction to appear, and said little in answer to the proprietor's enthusiastic observations.

"May I put him over that fence?" he asked, curtly, cutting Brown's eulogy short.

It was by no means a nice place to ride a horse at in cold blood, and the better the hunter, as a rule, the greater objection he has to being barked. Young Brown, however, was a desperately hard man, and he and the gallant Springbok were accustomed to perform feats of valor. It took a good deal to stop them. They were notoriously bad to beat when it came to stiff fencing.

CHAPTER XIV.

RIVAL SUITORS.

Brown nodded his head in answer to Cyril's query, and said, " Do what you like with him, sir. You'll find I am not telling you false. A freer animal never was foaled, and he'll jump anything in reason."

Upon this Cyril shortened his reins, and set Springbok resolutely at the fence. The courageous horse quickened his stride directly he made sure of his rider's intention, and showed no symptoms of refusing. When he neared the ditch, and perceived how big and deep it was, he dropped his head and took a careful look at it. Then, measuring the distance like a practised hunter who knew exactly what was required of him, he sprung over with the ease and agility of a deer, and alighted safely on both hind legs.

Cyril was more than ever pleased, for the style in which the horse jumped left no doubt whatever as to his being a finished performer, and he made up his mind to buy him, even if he had to spring a little more. To test Springbok's powers still further, he galloped him round the next field, and this time came swooping down upon the fence the reverse way, and the ditch being now on the off side, he put on considerably more impetus. But it made no difference to the gallant chestnut. He pricked his ears and jumped so enormously big that Cyril experienced considerable difficulty in retaining his seat.

Whereupon Mr. Brown, with the innate politeness of his class, remarked sympathetically, " He's powerful strong behind, sir, and many's the time I've had 'ard work to sit him myself. He do jump so uncommon clean. There's never a thorn to be picked out of his legs, no

matter how long or severe the run.   He tops the binders
just as well at the end as at the beginning of the day."

"That's the sort," said Cyril, carelessly flinging the
reins on Springbok's neck, and dismounting whilst the
horse stood catching at his breath.

"He's a good honest animal, I really believe, and if
you are willing, I'll take him at the price mentioned."

"Make it ninety-five guineas, Captain Mordaunt, and
he shall be yours," pleaded poor young Brown.   "Nothing but necessity induces me to part with such a horse
at the commencement of the season.   It goes to my
heart to sell him at all, but poverty is a hard task-mis-
tress, as I hope you may never live to discover, sir."
And he sighed heavily.

The sun was shining very brightly right in Mr.
Brown's eyes as he spoke, and it made them glisten.
He turned abruptly away so as to avoid the golden rays
which interfered with his vision.   He was in a despondent mood.   The thought of having nothing but a raw
young three-year-old to carry him to hounds made his
spirits sink to zero.   Cyril, on the other hand, felt unusually elated, and his warm, flushed face wore a benig-
nant expression.   He was fully conscious that he had
all the best of the bargain, and that Springbok was a
much more valuable animal than his humble owner was
aware of.   So he gave another of his cold, radiant
smiles, twisted the ends of his mustache between his
fingers, and said with wonderful grace, as if he were
granting an immense boon, "Il'l tell you what I'll do,
Brown, I'll make it eighty-five guineas, and if you
will walk back with me to my lodgings we'll have a
drink just to clinch the bargain, and you can go home
happily, with a check in your pocket.   Bother! who's
this?" he exclaimed, as a black figure on foot was seen
rapidly advancing towards them.   "There always seems
a Fate against doing a deal in peace.   Somebody or
other invariably interrupts you.   Why, it's Lord Algy
Loddington, I declare.   Now, what the devil can he
want?" So saying, Cyril went to meet him, by no means

pleased at his lordship's unexpected advent on the
scene. There was little love lost between the two men.
There existed on either side one of those antipathies
which, although very real, are not always easy to account for. They shook hands with formal ceremony,
neither party exhibiting much cordiality. Lord Algy
took in Cyril's occupation at a glance, and at once
jumped at the conclusion that he still remained in ignorance of Mr. Herrick's death.

"Ahem!" he said, giving a preliminary cough. "You
have not, then, heard the news?"

"News, no. What news?" answered Cyril, somewhat astonished by the extreme gravity of Lord Algy's
manner.

"Our poor old friend, Mr. Herrick, is dead."

"You don't say so! Are you sure? Why, the old boy
was alive and kicking four-and-twenty hours ago."

"Yes; it seems that when he came in from hunting
yesterday he went upstairs and took his revolver,
intending to clean it, or something of that sort. There
must have been an accident. Probably the thing went
off unintentionally. Anyhow, when his daughter and
servant, becoming alarmed, went to his room and opened
the door, life was extinct."

"By Jove!" exclaimed Cyril. "Looks rather like as
if he had shot himself, doesn't it? These accidents are
always suspicious, to my mind." As he uttered these
words, quite independent of any effort of will, a thought
flashed across his mind of which a moment afterwards
he felt heartily ashamed. And that thought was, "Kitty
will come into her kingdom now. Herrington Hall
will belong to us—to her and to me—and we shall be
rich—rich—rich. How true is the saying 'that it's an
ill wind that blows nobody any good.'"

"Poor old Squire," said Lord Algy, in a muffled voice.
"He was so popular, and we all liked him so much.
Kit—I mean Miss Herrick—is almost prostrated. The
shock was terrible, and its absolute suddenness rendered it harder than ever to bear."

"Yes, yes ; of course. That goes without saying. How is Kitty? Feeling tolerably well?"

Lord Algy's perceptions were very quick—almost as quick as a woman's, and he knew by intuition that Cyril's sorrow was not genuine, but only of that assumed kind which tries hard to conform to the conventionalities of grief, and asks itself all the time, "Now, am I doing what is right? Is my face sorrowful enough, does my speech sound properly sympathetic, am I acting my part sufficiently well to deceive people, and especially the friends and relatives of the deceased? I don't want to appear wanting, although it is absurd to expect I should be much cut up. Still, it is bad form not to show a decent amount of feelings on these occasions."

"The brute!" murmured Lord Algy, between his teeth, "I don't believe he's a bit sorry for poor, darling little Kitty. As if she could be well at such a time as this." He dug the end of his stick into the ground, and made several vicious holes in the grass. Then he said aloud, and with a quiet dignity which exasperated Cyril intensely, since it made him realize that his acting was of no use here, "Miss Herrick is in a sad state— the sort of state in which any man who loves a girl should at once fly to her assistance and do all in his power to offer comfort and consolation." He looked so significantly at Cyril that a hot flush rose to that young gentleman's face. He had an uneasy sensation that his lordship was rating him, and taking it upon himself to point out his shortcomings.

"May I inquire if that was the reason why *you* were so prompt in your attentions?" he asked, with a sneer.

"Look here, Mordaunt," said Lord Algy, "it's no good my pretending not to know what has taken place between you and Miss Herrick. She herself told me of your engagement, and distinctly stated that you had proposed and been accepted."

"May I conclude that your hopes are at an end?" inquired Cyril haughtily.

Lord Algy turned with a gesture full of strength and

manliness, and fixed a pair of flashing eyes upon him. Cyril's drooped insensibly.

"Whatever my hopes may have been, Captain Mordaunt, I fail to see how they can concern you. As a friend of the Squire, he begged me to look after his daughter's interests. At the present moment I have but one object in view—namely, if possible, to ease Miss Herrick's suffering, without regard to any personal feeling. You can believe me or not, as you like."

The sincerity with which the words were spoken touched Cyril, and made him repent his ungenerous jeer. He held out his hand, but Lord Algy looked away and pretended not to see it. Strive as he might, his heart was wroth against the man who had robbed him of his love, and who furthermore had the bad taste to triumph in an ungentlemanly and obtrusive manner over the discomfiture of an adversary.

"Do you—do you think that Miss Herrick would see me?" inquired Cyril, rather awkwardly, for he was conscious of a rebuff.

"Yes, I am sure she would. In fact, I came here to fetch you. I have reason to believe that your presence would be a great comfort to her just now. She is so young and so lonely, and," concluded Lord Algy with a painful effort, "she loves you."

This admission, coming from the lips of one who had been his rival, affected Cyril not a little. His nature was not perhaps very deep, nor yet very tender; but it succumbed easily to transient impressions. Then, too, he was really fond of Kitty, and thought her the brightest, pluckiest, jolliest girl he had ever come across. Naturally, she would rather have him to help her than Lord Algy.

Thus thinking, he said, "I will come at once. I would have gone sooner had I known how things were. Good morning, Brown. I am called away on urgent business, but we may as well consider the matter settled."

"And my check, sir," said Brown. "It would be a great convenience if I could have it to-day."

"All right. I'll send it by post this afternoon. Take the horse back to the town, and tell my groom to put him in the spare box."

When these details were settled, Lord Algy said, rather impatiently, "My dogcart is waiting in the road. If you like, I can drive you straight to Herrington, without returning to Furrowdale. She is anxiously expecting you, and begged me to lose no time."

"Thanks. I am quite ready to make a start whenever you please. Do you happen to know that horse of Brown's," pointing to Springbok, as the owner led him off. "He's the best young 'un I've sat on for ages. He'll make a grand hunter by another year."

"Very likely!" responded Lord Algy, who felt too upset to take any interest even in matters connected with horseflesh, and on whose memory was indelibly branded the recollection of Kitty, sitting forlorn and alone in the great state drawing-room. "Come, let's be going."

The two men mounted into the dogcart, and as they bowled along at a rapid trot Lord Algy gave his companion further details of the catastrophe that had taken place overnight. Cyril listened, but beyond a few exclamations of horror and sympathy he did not say much. Truth to tell, he was beginning to entertain a wholesome dread of his lordship. Their natures were not congenial, and for the life of him he could not see why such a fuss should be made over one old man's death. That Kitty should feel upset was only what might be expected under the circumstances, but for a great hulking fellow like Lord Algy to be on the point of blubbering every time he mentioned Squire Herrick's name struck him as being too absurd. So after a while they relapsed into silence, which was not broken until they came to the lodge of Herrington Hall, and passed under the tall old elms, whose rapidly thinning branches formed an archway overhead. Then Lord Algy sat up

very straight on the box seat, cleared his throat resolutely, and said:

"By the way, has it ever occurred to you that it wont
do for Miss Herrick to remain here by herself? As
soon as the funeral is over, the will read, etc., she ought
to go away to some place where she will be kindly
tended and cared for. She has received a fearful shock,
and it must necessarily take a long time before she
regains her usual frame of mind and accustomed
spirits."

"Oh! Ah! Yes, I suppose so," assented Cyril.
"Nevertheless, it's wonderful how soon people get over
these sort of things."

"Some do and some don't. It depends entirely upon
the person. For my own part, I believe Miss Herrick
to be capable of true and lasting affection. But that is
neither here nor there. Don't you think "—he glanced
tentatively at his companion's handsome profile—"that
it would be a good thing if she were to go and stay with
your mother for a while? Of course, this is only a
suggestion."

"I dare say it might be managed," responded Cyril,
rather lukewarmly, for he foresaw that such an arrangement would interfere very considerably with his hunting, and entail a great deal of going backwards and forwards. "I don't suppose my mother would object."

"If you were to make the proposition," said Lord
Algy, staring hard at the horse's ears, whilst his face
took on a strangely impassive expression, "I fancy
she would think a lot more of the invitation coming
from you than from any one else."

"Very likely," remarked Cyril, with a conscious smile.
As regarded Lady Mordaunt, he did not anticipate the
slightest difficulty, for he remembered the words of her
letter, "Bring the dear girl to see me at once"; but he
could not help giving a thought to his own convenience.
If Kitty wanted him to stay in town with her, and he
wanted to hunt from Furrowdale, complications would
certainly arise. "Did I understand you to say that Mr.

Herrick's will would be read immediately after the funeral?" he asked.

"Yes," answered Lord Algy curtly.   "I believe so."

"The old chap had no relations, had he?"

"No, not that I am aware of.   When his sister died he was very much cut up, because he said that he and she were the last of the family."

"H'm," thought Cyril.   "If Kitty and I were to be married tolerably soon we could spend the winter at Herrington, and it need not interfere much with my season's hunting, especially if we took advantage of the first frost.   She, of course, would not be able to hunt, but I might exercise her horses and keep them in condition."

Lord Algy sat straighter than ever on the box seat, and did not say another word.   Only, as they entered the house he cast a contemptuous glance at his companion.   That glance said as clearly as any speech, "Oh! you brute, you!   I know quite well what you're thinking about, and nothing would give me greater pleasure than to punch that sleek, well-scented head of yours."

CHAPTER XV.

" DUST TO DUST: ASHES TO ASHES."

THE two young men were shown into the drawing-room by Barlow. Cyril caught sight of a slender figure dressed all in black, and of a pretty, well-shaped chestnut head outlined against the window-panes, and suddenly he felt his heart grow soft. He had flirted with many other girls, but Kitty Herrick was the only one for whom he cared the least little bit, and she inspired a hitherto unaccustomed sense of respect and affection. As far as he was capable of loving truly and well, he loved her; but his rearing had been of that kind which teaches a young man to consider himself and his own interests before everything else. For the first time since hearing of the Squire's death, he was genuinely affected, and realized that sincere regret for the dead is possible to some natures.

"Kitty, my poor Kitty!" he cried, holding out his arms.

She rose hurriedly from her seat, looked straight into his eyes for the space of a few seconds, then flying towards him, hid her face on his breast, sobbing meanwhile very pitifully. He pressed her close to his heart, and kissed away the hot, salt tears as they rolled down her cheeks. His kisses comforted her greatly, and yet just at first they only caused her to sob the more. She could not help remembering that she had only him left now—only him. But her grief was shorn of its bitterness, and those smarting drops were a much more natural expression of sorrow than the stony misery which had preceded them.

Looking on, Lord Algy realized that the crisis was

over so far as she was concerned. Provided the man of her choice did not fail her, or rob her too swiftly of the girlish illusions by which she idealized him, from this day forth she would recover, until in time the. wound inflicted by her father's tragic ending would heal. As in a mirror, he saw, or thought he could see, the future reflected. A happy home ordered by a charming woman, sweet-voiced children, Peace and Content. He had dreamed of these things in the by-gone days, but they were not for him. Another had snatched from its stem the fresh and fragrant bud of maidenhood which he so coveted. He had done all he could for Kitty for the present, and she did not want him now. Indeed, the lovers seemed hardly aware of his presence. As he recognized this fact a hard lump rose in his throat which refused to be swallowed down, try as he might. A feeling of unutterable despondency and isolation took possession of him. He was nothing— nobody. He did not count. It signified little what *he* suffered. As long as they were together, the whole world might slide. Well, well, he need not feel so sick and sore. It was but human nature, and doubtless they intended no unkindness. But he could not endure the pain of standing idly by—a passive spectator—and watching them. He could bear a good deal, but he could not bear *that*. With a dull ache at his heart, he crept softly out of the room. The air seemed lighter when he found himself alone. He drew a deep breath, such as a strong man breathes who has just been exposed to great torture. His brow was damp with moisture.

"Only until the day of the funeral," he murmured. "It wont last long. I must stand it until then, and perhaps when she comes back I may feel better."

Even the holiest love contains an element of selfish-ness, and Lord Algy's surmises were correct. Neither Kitty nor Cyril gave him a thought. He was as much a cipher as if he had never existed, and this was the reward for all his loving care. Yet they meant no dis-courtesy; only the ways of lovers are not sociable, and forcibly illustrate the proverb that "Two is company and three is none."

What Captain Mordaunt and Miss Herrick said to each other, it is needless to repeat. At first their talk was hushed and subdued, as befitted the sad circumstances in which they met; but gradually it developed into that tender kind ordinarily prevalent amongst engaged couples. Looks, smiles, and caresses did the work of speech, and apparently much more satisfactorily. Anyhow, when Lord Algy re-entered the room after an absence which had seemed to him interminable, he found Kitty looking decidedly brighter. He experienced a strong feeling of relief when Kitty informed him that it was definitely settled she should leave Herrington Hall immediately after the funeral. To stand quietly by and look on at the courtship, was trying his powers of endurance too high. He felt that he could not support the tension much longer, and turning abruptly on his heel, left the room without wishing its mistress farewell.

Lord Algy did not see Kitty again until the funeral. On the day of that mournful ceremony he and the duke drove over to attend it. His Grace had always entertained a very real friendship and regard for Mr. Herrick, and although suffering from a bad cold, he insisted on being present at the final obsequies.

Of course, by this time the real nature of the genial old Squire's death was pretty widely known; and it may be taken as a tolerable proof of his popularity that, instead of severe censure, the universal feeling in the county was one of sincere regret and commiseration. High and low united in deploring his loss. Kitty received numerous invitations to stay with her various friends. The Duke of Furrowdale was particularly pressing that she should make his house her home for a while, and although she had no intention of doing so, she could not help feeling deeply touched by his kindness. He arrived early, before the other guests, and when he saw her he kissed her on the forehead, just as if he had been her father. He was a tall, fine-looking man, with noble features and a fresh, clear countenance, set in a frame of silvery hair. Until to-day, she had always felt just a little afraid of him. He was such a great personage in the hunting field, and wherever he went people treated him with such distinction that unconsciously she had formed an idea he could not be made of quite the same flesh and blood as ordinary mortals. But as his lips touched her brow in the most paternal and sympathetic of embraces, it suddenly became borne in upon her that in spite of his title and position he was both very human and very kind. Nothing could be gentler than his manner, and yet she had heard folk call it stern. She was sure she could never feel any constraint in his presence again. Born as he had been with a golden spoon in his mouth, he possessed a true and tender heart. As he took her hand in his, and held it in a soft pressure, she liked him once and forever. There was a polish and a chivalry about his bearing which she did not fail to appreciate.

"My dear," he said, "I am not going to say much, because I know on these sad occasions how little speech can avail; but I was your father's friend, and I hope that henceforth you will let me be yours. Don't hesitate to apply to me, if at any time I have it in my power to render you the slightest assistance. Before I started this morning the duchess begged me to say that she quite shares my sentiments; and we both hope that on your return from town you will come and pay us a long visit. You shall be as quiet as you like, and we will do our best to make you comfortable."

The tears rose to Kitty's eyes. At the present moment she was unusually sensitive to kindness.

"Thank you very much indeed," she said. But even as she sought to express her thanks she was conscious of a certain embarrassment, which she felt persuaded must make her manner appear awkward and ungracious. As a matter of fact, she did not know whether the Duke and Duchess of Furrowdale were aware of her engagement to Cyril or not; and the uncertainty regarding this point created considerable perplexity, for in her heart of hearts a secret voice whispered that they might not have been quite so cordial had they known that she had refused, or as good as refused, their darling son Algy.   They were anxious for him to marry and settle down, and she had a sort of an idea that they were prepared to welcome her as their daughter-in-law.   And as she had no intention of becoming Lady Algernon Loddington, the mere suspicion of sailing under false colors occasioned a sense of constraint which she regretted but was unable to conquer.   The hour was unsuitable for confidences, else once or twice it was on the tip of her tongue to tell the duke how affairs stood between her and Cyril.

That was a terribly trying day to poor Kitty. Had it not been for the solace derived from her betrothed's society, she hardly knew how she could have gone through with it. · When she saw the mournful procession leave the house and watched the black hearse and carriages disappear down the avenue in solemn line, her wretchedness reached a culminating point.   Even then she could scarcely believe that it was not all a bad dream.   Once or twice she looked around, half expecting to see her father's well-remembered figure occupying its accustomed seat in the study.   It was almost impossible to realize that she had just beheld the last of his earthly remains, and that henceforth he was as complete a cipher in the world's daily round of toil and amusement as if he had never existed.   The thought was fraught with exquisite pain, and she asked herself what was the good of living at all, since the end was always Death.. "Not to be" seemed so much best. It saved so many heart-aches, and such an infinity of strife and struggle.   Her soul cried out, *Cui bono?* If the choice might have been hers at that moment she would gladly have followed her beloved father to the grave, and so have shirked the burden imposed upon her by continued life. Until recently she had thought life so bright, so happy. Many and many a time she had thanked God on her knees for it, and now, without having committed any special sin that deserved punishment, the lightness was turned to darkness, and everything was changed— cruelly changed.

When Captain Mordaunt returned from the church-yard he was surprised and secretly relieved to find how rationally and quietly Kitty comported herself. He had feared a scene, and perhaps hysterics. His mother was subject to the latter, and there were few things which he dreaded more.

"I predicted that she would very soon get over it," he mused complacently, "and, by Jove, she is doing so already. Sensible girl that—very. Knows exactly what the circumstances demand. Nothing could be more admirable than her behavior. It is quite perfect."

But Lord Algy, who watched her closely, with the eyes of an absorbing if unreturned passion, knew better. He could see that behind her outwardly stoical and impassive demeanor she suffered terribly, and that her heart was bleeding from a wound which, heal as it might, would leave an indelible scar behind. Once he managed to draw near her, and murmur a word of sympathy in her ear. She looked at him in a strange, unseeing way, as if she heard but did not understand what he said. Her pretty fresh face was quite drawn and white. Its expression was full of woe.

After a while, the company assembled in the big drawing-room in order to hear the reading of the will. As yet the secret had been well kept; and with the exception of two or three present none suspected Mr. Herrick's financial difficulties. The popular belief inclined to the opinion that he had succumbed to some sudden and unaccountable fit of mental aberration.

Mr. Morgan, the family solicitor, now put on his spectacles, cleared his throat fussily and in a manner calculated to command attention, and then proceeded to read out the will. Its contents were what every one expected. In the case of the deceased there were no

tribes of relatives hanging open-mouthed on its deposi-
tions like a shoal of sharks round a well-provisioned ship.
The will was dated some eight years previous to the
Squire's death, and with the exception of a few legacies
to old and valued servants, everything was left, without reserve or condition, to "My beloved daughter,
Katherine."

Cyril tried hard to conceal his satisfaction at this
announcement, but nevertheless a complacent smile
curled his lip for a moment. Suddenly he looked up
with a flush of vexation. He had become conscious
that somebody was watching him steadily, and his eyes
encountered Lord Algy's. For a moment, the glances
of the two men met. The one expressed annoyance
and confusion at having been surprised, the other contempt and dislike. In these silent passages of arms, it
is wonderful what clear expression can be given to the
feelings. Language could not have more distinctly
stated what was passing in their minds. Cyril reddened
consciously, and turned away so as to avoid his lordship's searching gaze. The feeling of being read and
understood was not altogether comfortable. Some of
his thoughts produced a transient shame, and it was
highly disagreeable to find that they were patent to
another.

After the reading had come to an end the company
began to disperse. At christenings and weddings, provided there is plenty of good cheer, folk will dally, but
they invariably make haste to get away from funerals.
It is not pleasant to see a friend's body shut up in an
oaken box, lowered into the ground, and covered over
with shovelfuls of earth. People don't like to think
that their turn may come next, and that it does not take
much to cause men and women to shuffle off this mortal coil. A funeral makes death seem very real and
very near, and induces gloomy thoughts as to the
shortness and insecurity of life.

In spite of the depressing nature of the ceremony,
however, Cyril's spirits were unusually buoyant. He

totted up what Herrington Hall might be worth, and the result of his mental arithmetic appeared highly satisfactory, for when most of the company had gone he crossed over to the retired corner where Kitty, thankful beyond measure that the proceedings were coming to an end, had taken up her station.

CHAPTER XVI.

THE FIRST TIFF.

"My darling," said Cyril, in an extra-tender voice, "I hope you are not very tired. If I consulted my own inclinations I should like to spend the evening with you, but I must go back to my lodgings and make ready for to-morrow's start. By the way, don't forget that our train goes at ten-fifty-four. I shall be looking out for you at the station, and will get the guard to keep us a carriage to ourselves."

"How thoughtful of you to think of that," Kitty said gratefully. "It seems to me you think of everything, and I am sure I never should have got through this dreadful day but for you. And yet, Cyril, do you know, I begin to feel so nervous."

"Nervous, Kitty! What about?"

"I am so terribly afraid that your mother will not like me. With such a fine, handsome son, she may consider he ought to do better than marry a simple country girl with no particular means or looks. I should, in her place. The Queen of England herself would not be good enough for my boy if I owned one like Captain Cyril Mordaunt."

Her artless flattery was infinitely agreeable to him. Few sensations are more pleasant to a man than being admired by a pretty woman. He very seldom asks himself if he is worthy of the affection it has been his good luck to inspire, but accepts such adoration as a fitting tribute to merit. Is he not the superior animal, and she the weaker? It is but right and natural that she should look up to him as to a demi-god. If she fail to do so—if she see flaws in her masculine idol—the fault is hers, not his. By the right of might and of his

131

own ruling he sits on high, whilst her duty is to sit at
his feet and endow him with every good quality under
the sun. No matter whether he possess them or not,
it is her place to think so. Oh, fortunate men, who
have so many good gifts freely offered for your accept-
ance! Why do you abuse them so often, and break
the tender hearts that love you so much better than you
deserve? Cyril placed his forefinger playfully on Kitty's
lips, and exclaimed:

"Silly child! Your eyes are blinded to your own
charms. My mother is not as formidable a personage
as you appear to imagine, and I have told you before
that she is sure to like you." And he twisted the ends
of his mustache into a point.

"But she may not approve of me, Cyril, when she
hears——" Then remembering the caution she had received, Kitty stopped short.

Cyril's curiosity, however, was aroused. "Hears
what?" he inquired.

Her eyes travelled in the direction of Lord Algy,
who, although conversing earnestly with Mr. Morgan,
had evidently overheard the remark, for he frowned
slightly and in a warning manner which seemed to say,
"Don't be in such a desperate hurry. Wait for a day
or two longer."

She interpreted his glance aright, and answered
abruptly, "Nothing—at least, nothing that wont keep.
I'll tell you all about it when we are in town."

"Why not now? There is no time like the present,"
urged Cyril.

"I can't very well, although it is something most
serious and important."

"Which concerns me?"

"Yes, which concerns us both."

"Secrets!" he exclaimed irritably. "And secrets
from me, of all people in the world. Surely, Kitty,
this is not right."

"No," she answered humbly. "But I promised to
keep silent for two or three days."

"And pray, whom did you promise, if it is not an impertinent question?"

"I promised Lord Algy Loddington."

Cyril's face suddenly grew dark.

"Oh, indeed! May I ask what he has got to do with our affairs—for since they are yours I presume they are mine also?"

His tone was so cross that it aroused a sense of resentment in Kitty. She was not accustomed to being spoken to angrily, and on the present occasion she felt that Cyril's wrath was quite undeserved. She had done nothing to provoke it.

"My dear father thought very highly of Lord Algy— of his business capacity, I mean," she added quickly, seeing his countenance grow yet more black, "and in his last letter he begged me to consult him in the event of any difficulties arising."

"Do you mean in reference to the property?"

"Yes, with reference to his affairs generally. We have reason to believe that the estate is embarrassed, and Lord Algy has kindly undertaken, in connection with Mr. Morgan, to sift the matter thoroughly. Cyril, you must be content with this explanation. In a few days' time I hope to be in a position to give you fuller particulars."

"I don't see what Lord Algy has to do with it," he retorted. "If Mr. Morgan has need of a colleague I am the person to whom he ought to apply."

"My father was not aware of our engagement until the day of his death; besides which, he had extraordinary confidence in Lord Algy," she returned.

"Oh, very likely; but let me tell you of this, Kitty. I wont have him interfering in our affairs. He's a great deal too fond of having his fingers in everybody's pie. Perhaps you think I can't see how he is always hanging about after you, and inventing excuses to call. Now, I am not the least bit jealous. Please understand that once for all. There never was a man less jealous than I. It's not in my nature. But there are some things which naturally put a fellow's back up, and the long and the short of it is, I wont stand any nonsense between you and him. Do you hear?"

She looked at him for a long time before replying, as if her ears refused to credit what he was saying. That slow, steady gaze produced a feeling of discomfiture which after a few seconds caused him to lower his eyes. A prolonged pause ensued. He feared he had gone too far, and longed for her to break it.

"Yes," she said presently, "I hear. But you forget that Lord Algy is an old friend. He has been very kind to me, and I—I have known him all my life."

"I don't care. He wants to marry you, and is as savage as a bear because you prefer me to him. You can't deny it."

"Since you have worsted him, surely you can afford to be generous."

"No, that's just where I differ. Women always cherish a sneaking regard for an old admirer. I've seen a good deal of the world, Kitty, and I don't believe in your platonic friendships between two people of the opposite sexes. Mind you, I don't say that there must necessarily be harm in them. Indeed, I have known instances where there was none. Nevertheless, one thing may invariably be taken for granted. In every case, whether innocent or the reverse, the male and female friends are attracted by each other. If they are not very near, they would like to be so did the circumstances permit. Now, I don't choose that Lord Algy should attract you, though I can quite understand the fascination which you exercise over him." Cyril had talked himself into a heat, and when he came to a conclusion his face was quite flushed, and his eyes glittered with a metallic brightness.

Again there was a silence, during which Kitty said nothing. His words created a very painful impression, all the more so, perhaps, because she was conscious that although they grated harshly on her sensibilities, they were not without a species of rude, coarse truth that rendered it impossible to rebut them in the indignant manner which had been her first and natural instinct. She was vainly conscious that Lord Algy would never have spoken to her like this, or have wounded her pride so cruelly. She remembered the evening of her father's death, and how in her sore need and distress he had come to Herrington and sat with her in the darkening room. And she remembered also, with a feeling almost akin to guilt, how close to each other they had seemed on that occasion. Had there been no Cyril, and had he asked her to be his wife then, she could not have refused him. Realizing this, she sought to master her anger, and would not speak until she had her temper well under control. Then she said, in a constrained voice:

"It is possible that you may be right—at all events, in a measure."

"I am sure of it," he retorted triumphantly. "I have a pair of good eyes in my head, and know how to use them to advantage."

"All the same," she continued thoughtfully, "it seems to me that it depends entirely upon people's minds whether they are disposed to look at matters from a pure or impure point of view. You can see harm in everything, if you choose, and if you persist in dwelling on the bad rather than on the good side." And as she spoke she crossed her little white hands on her lap, whilst the shadow from her long eyelashes rested on her smooth cheek.

"I suppose you mean to suggest that *my* mind is impure," he said, with the uneasy personal consciousness which sooner than anything else makes an argument degenerate into a squabble.

"I hope it is not, Cyril," she said earnestly. "I hope it is not, both for your sake and my own. But why do you ask me to give up an old friend?"

"Because I believe you prefer him to me."

"You know that I don't."

"I can't think what you see in the fellow, Kitty.

The most that one can say for him is that he is a good-natured bore."

"I see," she retorted with spirit, "that he is honest, and straight and true; and although I do not love him, I like him very much indeed for his good qualities."

"Are you so sure of the state of your heart?" he asked ironically.

The hot blood rushed in a quick wave to her face.

"You have no right to put the question. My choice is made. I do not repent it. Cyril, why are you so doubtful and suspicious? Believe me, you have nothing to fear. When you talk like this, it makes me think that your love cannot be very genuine, since it is devoid of all element of trust."

He looked away, feeling rebuked by her words. Then his better nature asserted itself, and broke through the husk of worldly wisdom by which it was enveloped.

"You are right, Kitty," he said. "Pray forgive me. Henceforth I leave the matter in your hands. But you know my wishes. It may prove difficult for you to drop Lord Algy now without any apparent reason; still, these things are easily managed, and after we are married we can contrive to let his lordship see that he is not absolutely indispensable to our happiness. Eh! what do you say?" And he gave one of his cold smiles. It did not, however, succeed in conjuring up a brighter expression to Kitty's face. On the contrary, she looked more serious than ever, and an air of determination stole over her features.

"I shall always entertain a very real liking and respect for Lord Algy," she said impressively. "Even to please you, I cannot alter my opinion."

"Well, well," he exclaimed impatiently. "Let us drop the subject, and talk of something more agreeable. I am sick of it, even if you are not."

Kitty lifted her eyes with a flash. Then, after examining him narrowly, a demure curve caused her lips to part ever so slightly.

"I am glad you told me that it was not in your nature

to be jealous, Cyril," she observed, with veiled sarcasm, "since but for that assertion I could have sworn you were a victim to the 'green-eyed monster.'" So saying, the cloud cleared from her countenance. If her suppositions were correct, she could forgive him a few rough and tactless words. Every woman does under the circumstances. It flatters her vanity to imagine that her lover is jealous of another man, and before marriage such an exhibition of temper or feeling does not displease.

"Pooh! Nonsense," said Cyril. But the idea was so distinctly agreeable to Kitty that, in spite of their little fracas they parted quite good friends, intending to meet on the morrow. When he had gone, Lord Algy crossed the room and occupied the place left vacant by his successful rival.

"I have come to say good-by," he said. "In all probability I shall not see you again for a long time, and I hope you will be happy where you are going."

"Thank you," she said, feeling her throat begin to swell as she met the gaze of his kind eyes. "By the by, I wanted to ask you something. When may I tell Lady Mordaunt and Cyril of the disastrous state of my father's affairs?"

"I have just been speaking to Morgan, and we have arranged to go over Mr. Herrick's papers to-morrow morning. In a couple of days from now I hope to be able to let you know exactly how you stand."

"Thanks. I shall be glad if you will do so as soon as possible. I can't bear the feeling of meeting Lady Mordaunt under false pretences. She imagines I am an heiress."

"You have hinted at this before. It is clear to my mind that your future mother-in-law inspires considerable awe."

"It is true. I can't tell you exactly why, but from little things Cyril has let drop at odd times I am persuaded that she belongs to the class of pushing, worldly women for whom I entertain a natural antipathy.

When she finds I have lost my money she may show me the door. I should not be surprised."

"What nonsense! You attach far too much importance to Lady Mordaunt's opinions. How can she possibly harm you, as long as matters are all right between you and her son? That is the main thing."

"I should not like to go into a family where I was not wanted, and where people looked upon me as a pauper," objected Kitty proudly. "I have heard Cyril say that a wife should contribute towards the maintenance of the household. Most young men think so nowadays."

"Come, come," he said, trying to cheer her up, "you must not give way to such gloomy thoughts. You are tired and out of sorts. Go to bed, get a good night's rest, and depend upon it, by to-morrow a great many of your doubts will have disappeared." ("Mercenary wretch!" he muttered inwardly.)

"I hope so," she returned, but he could not help noticing that her tone was not very confident. Indeed, she felt strangely depressed. Now that it had come to the point, she shrunk from leaving her own quiet home and going forth amongst strangers of whom she knew nothing. Lord Algy seemed to know by intuition what was passing in her mind.

"If the worst comes to the worst," he said, "and you do not like being in town, you can always return."

Her face brightened. "You think so? There wont be anything to prevent me?"

"What should prevent you, Kitty?"

"I don't quite know. Only it has struck me that if things are really as bad as papa believed it might be necessary to sell Herrington."

Lord Algy gave a long, low whistle. Such a contingency had not as yet presented itself to his mind.

"If I had to leave Herrington," she resumed in a minor key," and the dear old place passed into the hands of some rich tradesman, I believe it would break my heart."

"Are you so fond of it as all that, Kitty?"

"Yes, every tree, every bush, every stone, is dear to me. And now more than ever, on account of the associations; for," and her voice broke, "papa and I were so happy here together."

Lord Algy coughed to hide his emotion. The least reference to the Squire sufficed to upset him. This great, big man was as tender-hearted as a child.

"I do not know how things may be until I go thoroughly into them," he said, "but you may take my word for it, if it should prove necessary to sell Herrington I pledge myself not to let it pass into the hands of strangers. And now, Kitty, I must go. Good by dear. God bless you." So saying, he grasped her hand in a strong pressure and withdrew.

On the way home he was very silent, so silent that the old duke said, "Algy, my boy, what ails you?" Then he lifted his head and looked out of the brougham window at the rapidly thinning hedge-rows.

"Nothing," he answered. "It has been a sad, dreary day, and I don't feel in spirits."

The duke sighed.

"Poor old Herrick," he exclaimed. "When we were out hunting together last Friday who would have thought that in less than one short week he would be lying cold and stark under the ground."

"It is a strange, unsatisfactory world," said Lord Algy in reply.

The duke looked sharply at him with his clear, penetrating eyes, but he said nothing. He only shook his white hair to and fro, and sighed again.

CHAPTER XVII.

A SOCIETY WOMAN.

LADY MORDAUNT was one of those would-be society women whose numbers seem annually to increase. Her love of titles was only equalled by her love of money, and her great idea in life was to get on. Now, "getting on" is a most laudable ambition when it means improving the mind generally, fostering high aims and ideals, and progressing steadily towards a praiseworthy object; but when it merely signifies pushing and shoving so as to mount a step or two on the social ladder, cutting old friends for the sake of new, and looking down on your relations, then "getting on" degenerates not only into folly, but vulgarity of the worst kind. So many men and women in this world are snobs at heart that every grade of society is surrounded by a swarm of parasites.

There are certain signs by which the female sycophant is easily known. To begin with, she has a hard, roving eye, never at rest. Then, if you have the misfortune to be a nobody (and we can't all be somebodies), her answers are distinguished by their curtness and brevity. They are not always to the point. The fact is, she pays very little attention to your remarks, and indirectly gives you to understand that she does not care to waste her time upon you. Why should she? You do not entertain, you don't belong to any particular set, you have not even a house of your own in town, but pick one up cheap for six weeks in the height of the season, or else go to poky lodgings. Greatest sin of all, you have hardly a single member of the aristocracy on your visiting-list. In short, you are not worth the trouble of cultivating, and she lets you see it in a manner that would be considered downright rude had she not the advantage of mixing in polite society. Polite society is privileged, however, and it is astonishing how discourteously its members can behave to one another.

The woman who wants to "get on" thinks nothing of staring her friend and neighbor out of countenance. That is part of the process. Moreover, she will appraise every single article of wearing apparel the country cousin happens to have on, and comment disparagingly upon its cut. Audible asides are shafts which she freely uses. She has two modes of treatment. She either sneers at you or she ignores you. The one is as galling as the other. At the same time, nobody is more agreeable, more adaptable and compliant, than the female parasite when she has anything to gain. Her manner is quite perfect when she makes up to some old, titled dowager who knows plenty of smart people and gives good parties. She picks up her fan and her gloves, listens to the prosiest story with a smile, chimes in approval, astonishment, or indignation as the occasion demands, and in her inordinate desire to please entirely subordinates self. No wonder if casual acquaintances unite in dubbing her "A charming person."

It is easy enough to be a charming person when you are utterly unscrupulous and unsensitive, possess the nature of a chameleon, and are all things to all men. It is neither necessary nor desirable to have any fixed principles. They are out of date. What you want is to float uppermost on the stream, no matter where it takes you so long as you are in good company.

It doesn't answer nowadays to get left behind in the social race. It is a desperate struggle, like any other. Whether the prize be worth winning is a matter of opinion. Lady Mordaunt belonged to the number who thought it was. Ever since her husband's death she had been hard at work "getting on." Strangers as a rule liked her, but the people who knew her intimately shook their heads, and said among themselves, "What a humbug Charlotte is. One never can believe her, she is so terribly insincere." Her old father and mother, who lived humbly in a country village, said with a simple pathos, when asked after their daughter's welfare, "We hope she is well, but we don't hear very often. Charlotte is too fine for us. She has got to be a great lady."

A great lady indeed!—who neglected the parents to whom she owed her being, and in her secret heart was ashamed of them. Is not the simplest peasant girl better than some of our great ladies, who are hard and hollow, frivolous and artificial? Let no one envy them or take them as models. They may be rich, they may be beautiful, courted, and admired, but their lives are selfish and bad.

But to return to Lady Mordaunt. By dint of going through a great deal of dirt, and eating a very considerable number of humble pies, she had managed to attain the fringe of London society. That is to say, every now and again she was asked to a party, well advertised beforehand in the "Morning Post," and where a proportion of the *élite* were to be met. Looking back on the past, she felt that she had achieved much. Nevertheless, as long as the doors of Marlborough House remained closed, she could not rest on her laurels. Marlborough House represented —as it does to so many other ladies—the height of her secret desires. Unfortunately, she had not much chance of getting there. In her innermost conscience she reluctantly admitted this fact. Her best day was over.

She was no longer very young nor very handsome, and she had passed her forty-eighth birthday. Until recently she had made up remarkably well at night, and no one would have suspected her age; but she herself was cruelly aware of it. She was fast approaching the period when a woman has to become resigned to the disagreeable fact of getting old. For the last ten or twelve years she had helped nature a little—not much—but just a very little—which she imagined no one knew save herself. At first she took to pulling out

the gray hairs as they appeared, and spent hours thus
unpleasantly engaged, but very soon these natural ene-
mies of her sex multiplied to such an alarming extent
that, despite every care, they showed quite conspicu-
ously—or would have done so had she allowed them.
Upon this, she expended a small fortune in dyes and
washes and lotions. Alas! the results in each case
proved delusive, and did not justify the expenditure.
In despair, she put herself into Messrs. Truefit's hands,
and from that date went through inconceivable inconvenience. It is no exaggeration to say that she became
a martyr to her head. Every three weeks it was
necessary to repeat the mysterious process, and she dared
not leave the metropolis for a longer period, for fear of
being publicly branded as an impostor. Pay her visits
as stealthily as she might, her friends accounted it
strange that she should always be wanting to run up to
town to shop when London was comparatively empty
and every one was thankful to get out of it. They
might have pitied her, had they known the anxiety and
discomfort which those beautiful bronze-gold locks
entailed.

For years Lady Mordaunt struggled valiantly with
Old Time, and fought him inch by inch. It was a
combat à outrance. But finally a day came when, do
what she would, he gained the victory. Then she folded
her hands with a sense of utter despair and defeat, and
said: "It is no good going on pretending to be young
any more. I am past subterfuges, and can't keep my
age from showing. In future, whether I like it or not,
I must just let myself go and grow old with grace."

The consequence of this remarkable resolve, forced
on her by stern necessity, was that Lady Mordaunt's
hair began to grizzle rather quickly, whilst her pencilled
eyebrows became a shade less dark and clearly defined.
Her complexion, however, retained its delicate peach-
like bloom.

"One must have color," she murmured. "Nothing
is so hideous as white hair and a yellow skin, whereas

if one has nice rosy cheeks the contrast is charming, and adds greatly to one's personal appearance."

So she did not let herself go altogether. She found it too hard when it came to the point. From a good-looking young woman, however, she became metamorphosed into a good-looking middle-aged one of the stately, statuesque type which wears well, principally because it defies emotion and is incapable of much sympathy for the sorrows of others. She inhabited a small old-fashioned house in Sloane Street, which looked all the more modest when contrasted with its huge, new red-brick neighbors. But though the rooms were excessively tiny, she had contrived to make them extremely pretty in the draped, stuffy style so much in vogue. Everything was covered with bunches, bows, and loops of Indian muslin. Mirrors, chairs, tables, even the very footstools, were decorated. As for the windows, they had so many different sets of curtains that you could not see out of them. But that did not matter. Good taste and high art demanded the sacrifice, and consequently it was cheerfully made.

Lady Mordaunt was a shrewd and clever, rather than an intellectual, woman. She was imitative and adaptive in an unusual degree. Hence the success which in her own particular line she had managed to achieve. To give her her due, she had done wonders for her son. Left a widow with moderate means, she nevertheless contrived to send him to Eton, at which fashionable public school he made a good many desirable acquaintances, and received a highly defective education, which, however, glazed him over with the outward veneer of a gentleman. It taught him to be careful as to his clothes and appearance, to take a bath and keep his nails fairly clean, to have a mighty regard for every description of sport, and a corresponding contempt for book learning; and last but not least—to spend money. When Cyril Mordaunt left Eton, his fond mother put him into the Guards. Moreover, she did not rest content until he had acquired the art of waltzing in all its perfection. That was an indispensable accomplishment, calculated to further his interests more than any amount of knowledge. After this, she opined that he ought to be able to make his own way in the world. She had given him a good start in life, and it was for him to take advantage of it.

She possessed a great deal of hard common sense, which never allowed itself to be upset by such a poor, weak thing as sympathy. For years past she had urged upon Cyril the necessity of his marrying an heiress. A less reasonable woman might have expected him to secure an income of several thousands; but she was sensible enough to perceive that such fortunes are not easy to obtain without some corresponding equivalent in the way of rank, and she very wisely declared that whenever her boy fell in love—she always made a point of calling it "falling in love," it sounded so much better—she should be quite satisfied with a sufficiency.

Five-and-twenty thousand pounds down and excellent expectations appeared highly desirable, and upon the receipt of Cyril's telegram she lost not a moment in wiring back her maternal approval and congratulations. Since then, she had been further rejoiced by the intelligence of Mr. Herrick's death, which rendered the match brilliant in all respects. She was prepared to receive her son and his betrothed with every mark of outward content. Cyril's engagement was a great relief. For a long time past he had proved a considerable drain on her resources, which as we know were limited. He was inclined to be reprehensibly extravagant, and when hard set for money made frequent demands on her purse. Her son was the one person on earth who occupied a corner in her not over-tender heart, and for his sake she had at various times made a good many sacrifices; but all the same she felt that it would be extremely desirable for somebody else to have the pleasure and privilege of paying his bills. He was

10

quite old enough to be self-supporting, and to make some return for what he had hitherto cost. She could live very comfortably upon the small income she possessed, but it was not sufficient for two, especially when one of those two was a fashionable young man who wanted the best of everything.

So, when the engaged couple arrived, somewhere about one o'clock, she welcomed Kitty with the utmost cordiality.

"My darling girl!" she exclaimed, kissing her effusively on both cheeks, "I am delighted to see you. Let me have a look at you. Why, how pretty you are! As fresh as a rosebud. One can see at a glance that you come from the country. Ha, ha!" and she gave a satisfied laugh, which somehow jarred on Kitty's nervous system as a discordant note. "Master Cyril has shown good taste in his selection of a bride."

Kitty blushed up to the eyes, though not from pure pleasure. She had a kind of feeling that she was being valued like a bale of goods, and the conviction robbed her tone of warmth.

"I am so pleased you think so," she said. "I was afraid you might not consider me good enough for Cyril."

Lady Mordaunt arched her eyebrows playfully. She approved of the sentiment. It sounded very right and proper in her ears.

"You know what mothers are, my dear. They are given to thinking their geese swans. It is a pardonable delusion. But let me assure you once for all that I am quite satisfied with Cyril's choice. Yes," taking a comprehensive look at her future daughter-in-law's honest, open face, "quite satisfied."

"A nice little countrified thing without any guile," she muttered to herself. "Not bad-looking in the milk-maid line, but no style, none whatever. I foresee that I shall be able to do what I like with her, and manage the pair of them. Well, so much the better. I expect I've got the best head of the three, and Cyril is apt to be a little foolish and kick over the traces at times. If his wife turns out a dummy, I don't think I shall object. He is one of those men who require a pretty steady whip-hand over them to keep them up to the mark, and we are accustomed to each other's ways. That amiable ɂonentity would never manage him."

CHAPTER XVIII.

"HE LOVES ME FOR MYSELF."

First impressions are not invariably correct, and because Kitty was a little nervous and deferential to her *fiancée's* mother, that lady made a great mistake in the girl's character, which she was destined to find out ere long. Meanwhile, she showed Kitty to a pretty little bedroom perched high up on an upper story, and left her to her own devices for a few minutes.

Kitty heaved a sigh of relief.

"Thank goodness the introduction is over," she soliloquized. "After all, it was not nearly as bad as I expected. Lady Mordaunt welcomed me very cordially, and I am quite sure she means to be kind. And yet I wonder why I don't like her better than I do. It seems positively ungrateful. I ought to love Cyril's relations as if they were my own, especially his mother. He and she are curiously alike, too. The resemblance is striking, only her face is harder and sterner, and the expression more artificial. Her eyes are like bits of glass, so clear and stony, and they remind me of a cat. There is something feline also about her manner. Even her caresses inspire a feeling of distrust." Then Kitty took off her black crape hat, and gloves, and with a sudden reaction exclaimed aloud, "Ugh! what a horrid girl I am to have such detestable thoughts. Lady Mordaunt has received me with open arms, and appears delighted at the match altogether. I have no right to dislike her without cause, and what's more," pursing up her lips, "I wont."

Thus determining, she went downstairs, and during luncheon did her very best to make herself agreeable. Just at first she could tell, in spite of his assurances to the contrary, that Cyril was a little anxious as to the impression she was likely to make, but his countenance cleared when he perceived how well his betrothed seemed to get on with his mother, and he made a remarkably hearty meal. Almost immediately afterwards it came on to rain very hard, and in spite of the charms of Kitty's society, he began to feel bored and cramped for room in the tiny house, which, in truth, was scarcely large enough to contain him. About four o'clock he said rather awkwardly, as if he were making a proposal sure to be indignantly vetoed:

"I've half a mind to drive down to my club to see if there are any letters, and play a game of billiards. That is to say, if you don't mind."

Lady Mordaunt hailed with delight the opportunity of having a little private conversation with Kitty, and to Cyril's no small astonishment, but very decided relief, gave an unqualified approval to the suggestion.

"Yes, do, dear," she said. "Dinner is not until eight, and there will be plenty of time. It is unfortunate the weather being so bad, else you and Kitty might have gone for a walk together. But I dare say she will be good-natured, and put up with my company for an hour or two. Besides, it will give us a chance of becoming better acquainted."

Although Kitty inwardly shrunk from the idea of being shut up alone with Lady Mordaunt for the rest of the afternoon, she was bound to agree, and not to let any misgivings which she might entertain appear. So Cyril jumped into a hansom, thankful to make his escape, and left the two ladies together. As he drove off they stood at the drawing-room window and kissed their finger-tips to him. He might have been going to the end of the world, instead of to Pall Mall; but that is the way with women. They are such fond, foolish creatures, and when they care for a man do spoil him so dreadfully.

Kitty felt quite a sinking of the heart as she watched the cab drive away. The streets looked very dirty and wet. The stems of the poor stunted trees in the gardens opposite were grimed with black. The air felt heavy, the rooms oppressive. Every drop of blood in her body seemed to rush to her head. The impure atmosphere clogged her nostrils, and after the spacious apartments at Herrington, she experienced a sensation of being able neither to breathe nor move. She wondered how people could live in such little, dark, cramped boxes of houses, and keep their windows hermetically sealed. She longed to open Lady Mordaunt's, but did not dare, and sunk limply back on the nearest chair and the one furthest away from the fire.

"Wont you be cold there, my dear?" inquired Lady Mordaunt.

"No, thank you," she replied. "It is so much warmer in town than in the country. I feel quite hot."

"I dare say you are tired, too, after the journey," returned the elder lady. "It is always a bustle getting away by an early train. I hope you did not mind my sending Cyril off. An idle man about the house, even though he be one's own son, is always an infliction. They want room to stretch their legs in, and if one gets rid of them for an hour or two they come back to dinner ever so much better-tempered. There is no greater mistake than letting them smell the cabbage cooking beforehand. When you are married, Kitty, remember that; especially," she added, with a sigh, "as cabbages *will* smell, take what precautions you like."

"Cyril is very good," said Kitty. "He always seems able to accommodate himself to circumstances, and he is never in the way. Of course, it might be advisable to pack him off if he were like most men; but then he's not, he's quite different."

Lady Mordaunt looked at her sharply for a moment, then the hard lines of her face relaxed into a smile.

"You consider him perfect, evidently. Well, well, never mind," as the girl colored. "That's all as it should be." Then with a change of tone, "You wont think me selfish, will you, dear? but I'm so glad to get you all to myself. It's impossible to say a word when Cyril is by. He is so dreadfully spooney that I don't have a chance. Tell me exactly how long you have known each other."

"About four or five weeks," answered Kitty, blushing rosy red. "We used to meet out cub-hunting."

"Oh! I hear all the young ladies are taking to the hunting field nowadays. They say it is the only place where they come across eligible men, and I dare say there is a great deal of truth in it. Did you ever meet Bella Crompton, Lady Martinet's daughter?" Kitty shook her head.

"Well! would you believe it," continued Lady Mordaunt, "she was over thirty and had never sat on a saddle in her life. She had had thirteen London seasons. One day she said to her mother, 'Mother, we're doing no good. I may hang on forever in this weary sort of way. I've made up my mind that we must go to the shires and take a hunting-box next winter.'

"'A what?' shouted poor old Lady Martinet, in amazement.

"'A hunting-box,' repeated Bella, quite composedly. 'It's our last resource.'

"'And, in the name of goodness,' said her mother, 'what are we to do when we get there?'

"'Get a husband,' replied Bella. And sure enough they did. True, he was not much to look at, and was in the upholstery line, but he had a magnificent place somewhere near Birmingham, and ten thousand a year. Bella is a fine lady now. She has a house in Grosvenor Square, and no one's parties are more sought after than Mrs. Higginbotham's. It is not a highly aristocratic name, but then one can't have everything."

"No, I suppose not," assented Kitty. "But if you will forgive me for saying so, it seems funny to people who have hunted all their lives to go out hunting with the aim you describe."

Lady Mordaunt laughed. Her laugh was singularly metallic, like the glitter of her cold, colorless eyes.

"A man or a fox, what's the odds? I can quite fancy the chase of the former proving the most attractive of the two."

"I hope you don't think *I* chased Cyril," said Kitty, with maidenly dignity.

"You foolish child! of course not. I'm speaking generally. Besides, I quite understand that yours was a case of mutual attraction."

"Yes," said the girl. "At least, I know it was so on my side."

"And on Cyril's also. But, Kitty dear, is it not a stroke of good fortune everything being so nice and smooth?"

"In what way do you mean, Lady Mordaunt?"

"Oh, when two young people fall in love generally there are such a lot of bothers. Either papa refuses—forgive me, I was forgetting your recent loss—or else mamma puts her foot down and makes a fuss. As a rule, too, there is nearly always a hitch about money matters. Many loving couples have been parted forever on account of insufficiency of means."

"Yes," said Kitty, suppressing a sigh, "that is but too true."

"In your case, however," resumed Lady Mordaunt, with increased animation, "there seem to be no impediments whatever, and I am the more rejoiced because Cyril could not possibly have afforded to marry except under favorable conditions. I hope you wont think me worldly or mercenary, my dear, for alluding so openly to the fact. But love in a cottage is an exploded idea nowadays, and in this nineteenth century of ours sensible people don't become man and wife unless they possess a fair income between them. Monsieur wants his horses, his wines, and cigars; Madame, her fine frocks, her lady's-maid, and amusements. All these things cost money and require a good long purse."

"But one can do without them," objected Kitty. "If people are really fond of each other they are prepared to make some small sacrifices."

"Mighty few when it comes to the point. Men are selfish creatures at best. Dock them of their comforts and their passion soon cools. Believe me, I know the world, and egotism and luxury are the most striking characteristics of the age."

"That may be," returned the girl, "but Cyril——"

"Cyril is no exception to the rule," broke in Lady Mordaunt impatiently. "Undeceive yourself on that point once for all. He is good-looking, cheerful, and pleasant-mannered, but he has both the faults and the qualities of his generation, and is not any better than his neighbors. He would not make a pattern husband to a poor woman. That is why I am so thankful you and he have hit it off; for if he had been a hundred times in love he could not have afforded to marry a penniless girl, possessing the tastes and inclinations that he does."

Kitty changed countenance.

"Am I to understand," she said, and her voice shook a little, "that if I had no money the engagement would have to be broken off, however fond we might be of one another?"

Lady Mordaunt hesitated. Then she shrugged her shoulders with a gesture which implied a dismissal of the question as unworthy of an answer.

"What nonsense we are talking. You need not make yourself uneasy by any such foolish suppositions, my dear Kitty. Yours and Cyril's is undoubtedly a love-match. Any one can see that at a glance, and I was only commenting upon our good fortune in having no drawbacks to contend with."

"I trust it may prove the case," stammered the girl, with an almost insupportable feeling of embarrassment. Oh! how she hoped Lord Algy would write soon and tell her if she were really a pauper or not. This deception would kill her if it went on much longer.

"It may! It must," retorted the elder lady energetically. "You have five-and-twenty thousand pounds of your own, and Cyril tells me your father has left you

all he possessed   Why, my dear, you are quite an
heiress."

"I—I don't know," faltered poor Kitty.   Then, with
a sudden impulse, she added, "Please, Lady Mordaunt,
do let us talk of something else."

Her ladyship frowned, and looked at her for a moment
in surprise.   Her face soon cleared, however, and she
said, with a mixture of patronage and contempt:

"Well, well, never mind.   I suppose you are too
young to understand about business matters; but it's
all right, depend upon it.   I hear that you have a
charming place in the country, and no doubt there will
be plenty of money to keep it up.   Cyril is a good boy.
As his mother, I have hardly any cause to complain;
but he has one fault."

"What is that, Lady Mordaunt?   I have not discovered
it up till now."

"He is inclined to spend rather too fast.   It wont
signify when he has the means, and you can always
exercise a certain wifely supervision over the exchequer;
but I don't mind confessing to you that there have been
times when his extravagance has occasioned me very
considerable anxiety.   It is such a mercy to think that
you will be comfortably off.   Had he lost his heart to a
penniless bride, there would have been no end of complications.   But, as I said before, everything is now
fair sailing, and with his fortune and yours combined I
shouldn't wonder if you mustered an income of three or
four thousand a year, eh?"

This was a delicate way of saying, "How much have
you got?   I want to be told the exact figure."   Kitty
interpreted the speech aright, and writhed under the
penetrating gaze of her future mother-in-law's mesmeric
eyes.   It rendered her intensely uncomfortable, and
she moved uneasily on her seat.   If it had not been for
Lord Algy's counsel she must have revealed what she
believed to be the impoverished state of her father's
affairs.   All this worldly, mercenary talk, which counted
Love as nothing, Wealth as everything, stabbed her to

the heart, and was directly opposed to her own private convictions. She felt that she could not argue with her hostess; but the conversation had a distinctly disturbing effect.

"God help me if I am really ruined," she murmured inwardly. "I need not look for much sympathy or support from Lady Mordaunt—that is very clear. But I can't—I wont believe that Cyril is as mean as his mother. He loves me for myself, not for my money, I feel sure."

CHAPTER XIX.

BAD NEWS.

UNABLE to endure the situation any longer, Kitty suddenly rose from her chair and walked towards the door, bent on effecting her escape.

"Where are you going to?" asked Lady Mordaunt sharply, resenting this termination of their *tête-à-tête*.

"Upstairs," answered Kitty. "I am not yet accustomed to London air, and my head aches rather badly; so if you will excuse me I think I'll go and lie down for an hour or two in order to be fresh by the time Cyril comes back."

"Oh, certainly," said Lady Mordaunt sarcastically. "I was afraid you would find my society rather dull in comparison with his."

"It is not that," said Kitty, fearful of giving offence. "But—but," she continued, with a quick wave of emotion, "my poor father was only buried yesterday, and it seems so soon to be thinking of marrying and money and all that sort of thing. Of course, it is different for you who never knew him. But it gives me such a horrible feeling, just as if I were disloyal to his memory." And she marched out of the room.

"Little fool!" exclaimed Lady Mordaunt, *sotto voce*, when the door closed upon Kitty's retreating figure. "She aggravates me with her prim, goody-goody notions. Cyril and I will have to sharpen her up between us, else she'll turn out a very dead-alive piece of goods. Luckily the majority of men prefer stupid women with less brains than themselves. They can suppress them more easily than clever ones, and perhaps on the whole she may suit Cyril better than if she were brighter and smarter. Anyhow, she has got money, and that's the main thing. The rest is his affair, though I can't say Miss Katherine Herrick would have been my choice, even with the dollars."

There is no doubt the two women were antipathetic to each other. Lady Mordaunt's hard, pushing, slightly vulgar nature was not in unison with Kitty's simple, straightforward character. There was a lack of sympathy between them, which no amount of intimacy could bridge over. On the contrary, a further acquaintance was only likely to widen the gulf. Kitty was instinctively aware of this fact, and her heart filled to bursting. The old memories came crowding into her mind. She thought of the happy days that never could repeat themselves—of her father, of the rides and talks they had had together, of Tiny Tim, and a thousand dear, homelike things. When she contrasted them with Lady Mordaunt, a sudden thrill of indignation, grief, and loneliness travelled through her veins.

"I hate her," she soliloquized passionately. 'She is cold, and hard, and selfish. I don't believe she is capable of caring for a person for his or her real self. It is all what they have got. Oh! I hope—I *do* hope—that Cyril will never grow to be like his mother in disposition."

Having relieved her feelings by this outburst, she gradually grew calmer, and little by little her thoughts once more reverted to her beloved father and to Herrington. She had not much worldly wisdom, but she had what often stands in better stead—namely, an honest, upright spirit which recoiled from all things evil. She knew by intuition that the atmosphere of the house she had come to was many degrees less pure than the one she had left. In the company of a society woman like Lady Mordaunt she did not feel at ease, and was conscious that the influence Cyril's mother exercised cast a dark shadow on her soul's serenity. Country people might be a bit duller and slower than these fast, fashionable London ones, but at all events they were infinitely more restful and sincere. They did not jeer at everything you had been taught to believe was right, profess a supreme disdain for Love, and turn your ideas topsy-turvy. So reasoned the little country-bred mouse who longed already for the open green fields and fresh pure air which she had so recently quitted.

The next day passed without any particular *contretemps*. Cyril was very kind and attentive. In the forenoon he took Kitty out for a walk in Hyde Park. They discussed their future plans in the most orthodox, lover-like fashion. True, Kitty felt that their card-castles were built on a very unstable foundation, and might topple to the ground at any minute. Still, it was pleasant work, and Cyril looked so comely and handsome as the sun every now and then broke through its yellow haze of fog and shone down on his fair, close-cropped head that imperceptibly her spirits rose.

After luncheon, Lady Mordaunt announced that she had to attend a tea party, from which Kitty's mourning would of course preclude her, so the engaged couple spent another hour or two together, during which the girl felt happier than she had done since her father's death. Any doubts which she might have entertained of Cyril entirely disappeared. Unless he were the biggest humbug upon earth, she could swear he was fond of her for herself, apart from any question of money. And thus believing, her thoughts assumed a more cheerful tone.

"He has eight hundred a year," she mused. "If the worst comes to the worst we could live upon that. I am quite willing to make the experiment and put up with some privations, if Cyril is of the same way of thinking. I don't believe he is nearly as extravagant as his mother made out. Anyhow, men can often be led where they wont be driven, and if Cyril is not happy it wont be for want of trying on my part."

She was a good girl, was Kitty, and as honest as the day. In her company Cyril's better nature asserted itself. She made him feel ashamed of the egotistical self-indulgent sentiments which, in his case, were partly hereditary, partly the result of his bringing up and of having no real employment. Idling about town, going out to parties, drinking, dancing, flirting, and lying in bed until twelve o'clock the next morning are not exactly calculated to develop a young fellow's most manly attributes. To begin with, he sees too many women of the wrong sort. He starts by fancying himself in love with all, and ends by having no respect or chivalry for any. And this latter phase has a distinctly bad effect upon his character. He gets into the way of coarse jokes and *risqué* stories, and then makes the mistake of imagining that every woman he comes across must necessarily like that style. Once, Cyril had ventured upon an equivocal *double-entendre* in Kitty's presence, but the look of indignation which it had evoked warned him never to repeat the experiment. He liked her all the better in consequence, for the fastest men are generally those who, in their heart of hearts, most appreciate female purity and refinement. Since then he had placed a studious guard over his tongue. He saw that it was a mistake to shock her innocence, and that choice anecdotes of an improper nature were entirely thrown away upon her. London girls might like them, but she did not.

Had Cyril Mordaunt received a Spartan education, and been forced to work for his living, instead of possessing that small, fatal competence which is the ruin of so many promising youngsters, he might have been a very different individual. His misfortune consisted in having just enough money to deter him from any profitable occupation, yet not sufficient to gratify all his tastes and desires. There was but one easy way open to him of acquiring a fortune—a method that entailed comparatively little trouble, and was derogatory neither to his dignity nor position. In securing the hand of an heiress he achieved a good home and every comfort indispensable to his class. He thought it no disgrace to live on a wife's money and accept luxuries from her purse. As long as he got all he wanted, he did not much care how he came by it. There are thousands like him, who ask for nothing better than to have their cake without the bother of baking it.

And yet, he was vaguely conscious that he had greater causes for congratulation. As he sat by Kitty's side, listened to her innocent girlish talk, and felt the real affection which shone from her eyes every time she lifted them to his, he realized that she was a pearl of great price—a girl who would be as true as steel to the man she loved, and prove a helpmate in the best and highest sense of the word. Years afterwards he looked back upon that day spent almost entirely in her society and subject to her pure influence as the happiest of his life. On the tablets of his memory it shone out like a bright star on a moonlit night.

When his mother returned from her tea party, full of chatter as to how Lady X. was dressed in a beautiful new gown from Worth that had cost eighty guineas; and how Miss Esmeralda Sinclair, one of the belles of the last London season, had quite spoiled herself by dressing her hair in a new and unbecoming style, etc., it all seemed to him so frivolous and superficial that he could scarcely bring himself to listen civilly to the twaddle, and contrasted her conversation with Kitty's, much to his mother's disadvantage. Wonderful to relate, he did not even want to go to his club, but sat quite contentedly, after dinner, smoking a cigar, and when the ladies retired to rest he shortly followed their example, feeling very good indeed, and determined, moreover, to be good in the future.

The next morning, when Kitty was dressing, the housemaid tapped at her door and handed her in a letter. One glance at the superscription showed that it came from Lord Algy. She knew those big, firm characters well, and the sight of them produced a mingled feeling of fear and expectancy. Her heart beat so fast that a minute elapsed before she could steady herself sufficiently to break open the envelope.

"Just to think," she mused, "that all my future hap-

piness may depend upon this one little letter. I declare
I am afraid to read it." By and by, however, she took
courage, and sitting down on the edge of the bed, set
to work to master its contents. After she had perused
the first few lines her face suddenly changed and grew
· deadly pale. Then, unconsciously, a low sob escaped
from her. This was what Lord Algy wrote:—

My dear Kitty,—I hasten to write to you, according to the
promise given before you left home. To-morrow you will
in all probability receive a formal communication from Mr.
Morgan, but I am already in a position to anticipate the bulk
of his intelligence.

We spent the greater part of yesterday in going over your
poor father's papers. I hardly know how to break the result.
Alas! it is worse even than we feared. Not only has your
entire fortune been lost in speculation, but by the time Mr.
Herrick's principal creditors are paid there will be absolutely nothing remaining from his estate. Herrington will
have to be sold. There is no help for it, but the promise
made you is sacred. It shall not pass into strange hands,
and its doors shall always be open to her who is its rightful
mistress.

It grieves me to the heart to have to write you this distressing news. Would that I could have sent you a more
cheerful report, or held out some prospect of hope in the
future. But, Kitty, I know your character, and feel sure you
would rather hear the worst, however bad it may be, than
have it withheld from your knowledge. It all comes to this,
then, my poor dear friend. Instead of coming into about
seventy or eighty thousand pounds, as you had every right
to expect, when the numerous claims are paid off you will
not possess a penny in the world. Lucky it is that you have
your future husband's home to fall back on, for I know how
independent you are, and how difficult it would prove to
persuade you to accept assistance, even from those who
like you best and feel the most for your misfortunes. I
wish I could see any chance of saving something out of the
wreck. At present there seems none.

How the Squire got his affairs into such a terrible muddle
is a mystery both to Morgan and myself; but the Stock Exchange is at the bottom of the business. Had he left that
alone, he would have pulled round in time. But it is no use

II

talking. You and I know that he would sooner have cut off his right hand than deliberately rob his only child. Yet that is what it amounts to. Unfortunately, the past cannot be rectified, and he leaves you penniless. Trusting that the bad news conveyed in this letter may make no material change in your happiness, believe me, always your sincere friend,   ALGERNON LODDINGTON.

The letter dropped from Kitty's hands. An icy band seemed suddenly to constrict her heart and still its beatings. She sat quite cold and passive. When her thoughts had dwelt on poverty they had never pictured such utter ruin as this. She had always imagined there would be something left her—if not a large fortune, at any rate enough to subsist upon and render her independent. But now it appeared that if Cyril were to throw her over she might be forced to work—ay, positively work—for her living. Yet why should she doubt him, why place such small confidence in his love? He had done nothing to inspire the distrust which despite herself she experienced. If Lord Algy had been her lover would she have felt so uncertain as to his fidelity? The answer was no, ten thousand times, no! He would have stuck to her through thick and thin. But then he had money of his own, and was differently situated. He could afford to marry a poor girl, whereas Cyril couldn't. Lady Mordaunt had repeatedly told her so, and she was a formidable opponent. From the first moment that she knew for certain of her loss of fortune, Kitty was convinced all Lady Mordaunt's influence would be thrown into the scale against her. And would Cyril prove strong enough to resist his mother? This was the point which created so much misgiving in the girl's mind. Even now she refused to harbor a single resentful or ungenerous thought in connection with her father. Had it not been for her love she could have borne her reverses stoically. But it did seem hard now to part, especially when Cyril possessed the means to make her his wife if he chose to turn a deaf ear to his mother's mercenary arguments. She

knew enough of the real position of affairs to be aware
of that fact. If he liked her better than his horses and
his hunting, his good dinners and his amusements, and
would be content to settle down quietly in some cheap
little country place, then they might easily be married.
She was willing enough to face poverty for his sake.
The question was, was he?

She was proud—proud as Lucifer—however, and as
she sat there gradually taking in the situation, she
determined not to hamper his choice by a single word
of persuasion. He should be left free, absolutely free,
to cling to her or to forsake her, according to the
strength of the sentiment she inspired.

CHAPTER XX.

MONEY IS NOT EVERYTHING.

KITTY told herself that if Cyril refused to give her up, and in spite of his mother decided on marrying her, she would repay him by a lifelong devotion; and if not—but here she broke down, and could not summon up sufficient courage to face the alternative. One thing, however, was perfectly clear. She must communicate the contents of Lord Algy's letter without loss of time to both him and Lady Mordaunt. She had stayed too long in that house under false pretences, stifled by a sense of hypocrisy whenever her hostess talked of her wealth, and alluded to her being an heiress. Lady Mordaunt must be undeceived.

Thus determining, Kitty buttoned up her dress with trembling fingers and went downstairs. When she opened the dining-room door she found her lover and his mother already seated at table. They had just begun breakfast, but Cyril jumped up to meet her, and with a smile of greeting exclaimed:

"Halloo, Kitty, you're a bit late this morning. I hope you'll forgive us making a start." Then all at once he noticed how pale and discomposed she looked, and saw that instead of smiling back at him in her usual way her eyes were sad and serious. "Good heavens, child!" he ejaculated, in an altered tone. "What on earth is the matter? Has anything gone wrong?"

She put out her hand, and steadied herself against the back of a chair.

"I have had bad news," she said tremulously. "And it is my duty to tell you of it without delay."

"Bad news!" cried mother and son simultaneously, without, however, a suspicion of the truth.

"Yes," said Kitty. So saying, she drew Lord Algy's letter from her pocket, and made an attempt to read it out aloud; but a sudden swelling in her throat choked her voice and prevented it from rising above a whisper.

"Take it," she said nervously, thrusting the note into Cyril's hands. "Read it for me. I—I can't."

He unfolded the letter, and did as desired. During the perusal of its contents Kitty watched Lady Mordaunt's countenance with pitiful anxiety. If she saw one kindly gleam in those cold eyes, or the least sign of relaxing in her stern, strongly marked features, then she might hope. She felt like a prisoner at the bar hanging breathless on the judge's sentence. The moment was fateful, and it seemed to her that the whole of her life's happiness depended on it. Cyril read on to the end without coming to a halt. Then he gave a long, low whistle, which somehow sounded ominous in Kitty's ears. Instinctively his eyes sought his mother's. Lady Mordaunt was sitting very bolt upright, with her back to the light. Her lips were tightly compressed in a straight, hard line. It was difficult to say what was passing in her mind. She showed no emotion, and preserved an absolute frigidity of demeanor. One might almost have thought that she did not grasp the full significance of the news. Nevertheless, Kitty's heart sunk as she gazed on her cold, impassive countenance. A long silence ensued. You could have heard a pin drop inside the room in spite of the roar of traffic out-of-doors. To Kitty, it was intolerable. Neither Cyril nor his mother uttered a syllable. She looked imploringly, first at one, then the other. Did they intend to drive her mad? Would they never speak? Surely they must know how matters stood with her, and how anxiously she longed for a kind word. It wasn't her fault losing the money. It had been none of her doing. Why must she pay such a bitter penalty?

"Well," she said at last, in desperation, stealing timidly up to Lady Mordaunt's side, "have you nothing to say to me?"

That lady raised her cup to her mouth and sipped its contents with cruel deliberation. "What can I say to you," she answered, in a distinct voice, "which, after our conversation of the day before yesterday, you do not know already?"

"Do you—do you mean that the engagement between me and Cyril must be broken off?" asked the girl faintly.

During those few moments of seeming inaction Lady Mordaunt's mind had been busily at work, and it had already grasped all the bearings of the situation. She realized that Kitty was suddenly converted from an heiress to a pauper, and consequently, instead of the match turning out a good one for her son, as hitherto they had had reason to believe, it would now prove the very reverse. Such being the case, she decided there and then on the line of conduct to adopt, and was determined by hook or by crook to prevent the marriage. Having favored it so much was a little awkward, but she would not shirk her duty on that account, and in unpleasant matters of this sort the grand rule to remember was, that no good ever came of temporizing. A bold, straightforward policy was the best, and saved a lot of trouble in the long run. After all, there was not much harm done; Cyril and Kitty had only been engaged a few days, and as luck would have it, she had not yet sent any formal announcement to the society journals. The pair could part without anybody being the wiser, and go their different ways. As for wounded feelings, they were soon cured. Love was a very skin-deep affair nowadays. She was sorry for the girl, of course; but as Cyril's mother it was her duty to study his interests before everything else, and an imprudent marriage was just about the worst folly he could possibly commit. In her world, a man who did not better himself by matrimony was looked down upon; whereas he who secured a rich wife was considered an extremely clever fellow. So in answer to Kitty's piteous query she said very calmly, but decidedly:

"I do not wish to hurt your feelings, my dear, but I should have thought your own good sense would tell you that you and Cyril must part. Circumstances render it wiser to break off the engagement quietly and by mutual consent."

Kitty trembled as she listened to this ultimatum. A sudden haze obscured her vision. Only by a tremendous effort did she manage to falter, "It—it—is not—a necessity."

"What do you mean?" said Lady Mordaunt acridly.

"Cyril has a small fortune of his own." And Kitty glanced appealingly at her betrothed, who sat irresolute, but seemed about to make some reply when his mother intervened.

"You talk like a child," she said impatiently, "and after knowing Cyril for five weeks need not fancy that you understand him as well as I. I tell you he would be simply miserable if he had to live for the rest of his days in a hugger-mugger fashion, screwing and pinching, and considering every sixpence he spends. If you want to make him downright wretched, that is the way to do it."

"Speak, Cyril," said Kitty. "Is this true what your mother is saying?"

"Not altogether," he aswered lamely. "Of course, it's a great bore being poor, and not able to go about and enjoy yourself like other people, and the misfortune is, one can't live decently in England without a certain amount of money. There is no gainsaying that fact. On the other hand, I'm just as fond of you as ever. I've never seen any one a patch on you, and nothing can make the least difference in my feelings; but with the best will in the world I don't quite see how we should manage on twopence-halfpenny a year."

She took heart at this speech, vacillating as it was. He had alluded to his affection, and declared it to be unalterable.

"We might emigrate," she said sanguinely. "America, Australia, and even Africa, are open to us. I shouldn't mind where I went, if you did not. After all, money is not everything. People can be very happy and contented without it when they are fond of each other and make up their minds to give up a few luxuries for the sake of being together. It is wonderful, when one comes to think of it, how many things are superfluous and not really a necessity. If 'one's wants were fewer, and one's tastes simpler, riches would not seem nearly as important. England is not the only country in the world. There are plenty of others open to a young couple willing to work and possessed of a small capital to start with. I have often heard Mr. Vandevaid say—you know, Cyril, that nice old man who comes out hunting—that when he went to Australia he had just two-and-sixpence in his pocket after being landed in Melbourne. Now he is a millionaire. Some people can earn money, and why shouldn't we?"

She spoke quietly, but there was a wonderful fire in her eyes which roused his spirit, and made him ask himself for a moment "Why not? Why not, indeed?" The unconscious appeal of her voice and manner touched him not a little. Perhaps he knew that her words contained a considerable element of truth, and that there was more genuine happiness to be gained from the love of a pure, innocent girl like Kitty than from the purse of some rich woman wedded solely for her wealth. It is just possible that had he and she been alone together his better nature might have gained a decided victory over every sordid consideration; for although selfish, his youth was in his favor, and the thoughts and habits which had grown upon him since his boyhood were not yet so fixed as to be incapable of change. Neither was he entirely callous to elevating influences. But before he could answer his mother burst out laughing. It was a harsh, vibrant laugh which rang through the room.

"America, Australia, or even Africa!" she echoed sarcastically. "What nonsense you are talking, Kitty. It strikes me you have the Stanleyphobia, like all the rest of the world. Pray, may I ask what an educated

English gentleman is to do in those benighted parts? Get bitten by snakes, knocked down by elephants, and shot at with poisoned arrows, I suppose, or else make love to the black women whilst his wife is left at some coast station. Why should Cyril unclass himself, and give up home, country, and profession? If you were really as fond of him as you pretend you would not ask him to make such sacrifices on your account. You would think more of him and less of yourself. Why is he to be dragged down and prevented from getting on? It is all very fine to sneer at money, but it is the starting-point of everything. Success, fame, comfort—all depend upon it—ay, and love, too, for affection soon goes when people take to squabbling over the butcher's and baker's bill. Do you suppose that a man worthy of the name would be content to bury himself in the backwoods with some little country chit, and spend all his time in billing and cooing? They soon get tired of domestic bliss, as you would find out to your cost, and begin to look out for a fitting object on which to expend their energies."

"They can work," said Kitty stoutly. "Honest work is never derogatory, even to an English gentleman."

"Fiddle-de-dee. There's no end of nonsense talked about hones work. What does honest work mean? It means delving the soil with a spade until your hands are black and not fit to be seen, and turning yourself into an agricultural laborer at a pound a week. No, no, my dear young lady; I flatter myself Cyril is a cut above that. As I have told you from the first, he must marry a girl with money who can back him up and give him the position to which he is entitled by his manners and appearance. He may go into Parliament after a bit, distinguish himself as an orator, and end by being a Cabinet Minister. Who knows? That is a worthy ambition, if you like; but not pigging it in the Antipodes——"

"Hush, mother!" interrupted Cyril. "You are letting yourself get carried away, and should not talk like that. Kitty quite understands all you mean, no doubt, and there is not the slightest occasion to hurt her feelings unnecessarily."

Kitty's lip quivered. She had grown deadly pale during Lady Mordaunt's speech. But she drew herself up with a proud gesture which became her well, and looked unflinchingly at her companions.

"Your mother may be right, Cyril," she said. "I have had little or no experience, and don't pretend to set my judgment up against hers. I only go by the instincts of my heart, and in doing so it is possible that I have been selfishly short-sighted, and seen matters solely from my own point of view. I beg your pardon."

"Kitty, Kitty dear, I have nothing to forgive. Don't think that for one minute," he said, with real distress.

She shot a grateful glance at him, but went on more steadily and in a firmer tone. "If, unwillingly, I have done you wrong, I am willing to make atonement; for," and her whole face softened, "you are the last person on this earth I would wish to injure. Weigh the matter well. If you prefer worldly advancement, material ease and comfort, to me, you have but to say the word. The choice lies with yourself. 'A little country chit' can scarcely presume to compensate a man for such advantages, especially when she has nothing but her love to offer as an equivalent. I shall never reproach you, Cyril; but I think I have a right to ask this: Let your decision be uninfluenced by either your mother's remarks or mine. If, on reflection, you find it will serve your interests better to be quit of me altogether, say so honestly. We will part friends, without malice or ill-will on either side. But if"—and her tone became strangely tender—"you should find that I am dearer to you than the things Lady Mordaunt has pictured, and you believe that you are happier with me than in possessing them, then, by the strength of our mutual love, I maintain that no one has a right to come between us. I give you until to-morrow to decide. Then I either leave this house as your affianced bride or else to earn my own livelihood. Under no conditions whatever," and she held her pretty chestnut head erect, whilst her eyes shone like two stars, " will I consent to stay longer under this roof; for no matter how you choose, my presence will be equally unwelcome to your mother. Though I am poor, I still have some pride left, and nothing would induce me to inflict my company where it is not wanted."

Before Lady Mordaunt or Cyril could recover from the surprise occasioned by this bold address, she marched out of the room. She might be a poor, jilted, deserted, and neglected girl, but she nevertheless knew how to make her adversaries feel small, and to carry off the honors of war.

CHAPTER XXI.

LADY MORDAUNT was the first to recover her self-possession. That it should desert her even for an instant was rare.

"Well, I never!" she exclaimed. "Was there ever such impudence? The idea of a bit of a girl like that laying down the law and as good as telling me to my face that I am worldly and mercenary. What next, I wonder?"

"I don't think Kitty quite meant that, mother," said Cyril, smiling in spite of himself.

"Yes, she did; nasty little minx. What a temper she has got, to be sure! How she flared up when she talked all that romantic rubbish about love and sacrifice! As things have turned out, I congratulate you, Cyril. You are well rid of her." And she looked across the table at her son.

The expression of his face did not altogether reassure her, however. There was an indecision about it which created secret anxiety in the maternal mind. What if he were to prove obstinate and refuse to be guided by her advice? She could recall one or two instances—not many, but still one or two—when he had chosen to take his own way and turned a deaf ear to wise admonition. Surely he would not be so foolish, so mad, as to stick to the girl now she had lost her fortune and had no longer anything to recommend her. He might as well tie a halter round his neck at once. Cyril stared moodily down into his cup and stirred the dregs with a teaspoon.

"Your congratulations are rather premature," he said.

"I have not at all made up my mind that I shall chuck Kitty over."

"You haven't made up your mind!" fairly screamed his mother in reply. "May I ask you if you have taken leave of your senses?"

"No, but the long and the short of it is this—I'm very fond of Kitty."

"Pshaw!"

"You may not think so," he responded warmly, for the sneering nature of the ejaculation nettled him, "but I am nevertheless."

"Nonsense, Cyril. Do you mean to tell me that you are fonder of her than you are of your hunters, your sport, and your amusements? Answer me this question: Are you prepared to give them up, and ever so many things besides, for the sake of Miss Katherine Herrick? If so, you're a bigger fool than I imagined."

"I might manage to keep a screw or two," he answered doubtfully, not relishing the turn the conversation had taken.

"Don't bolster yourself up with any such vain hope," she said. "Kitty is just the sort of girl to have an enormous family. Instead of horses to ride, you'd find it uncommonly hard work to feed and clothe, let alone educate, the little ones, and keep the wolf from the door. I declare, Cyril, I thought you were more sensible."

"It looks so awful bad to throw a girl over the very moment she has lost her money," he observed moodily. "You may like to do those sort of things, and are not troubled by a conscience, but I am differently constituted."

"Since when have you become so wise?" she sneered, the color deepening in her cheek; for she could not bear that he should think ill of her. Then, controlling her anger, she added in a calmer tone, "Besides, if it came to that, you might bring about the rupture by degrees, although in my opinion it would be infinitely wiser to put an end to the affair at once"

"I don't see why we shouldn't wait," he said sullenly. "There is no such desperate hurry, and something may turn up."

"May I inquire if you have any expectations?" she asked, with exasperating irony.

"No. You know that I have not."

"Am I right in presuming that Miss Herrick has not either?"

"She has none that I am aware of," he answered reluctantly.

"Precisely. Under these circumstances, what good is to be derived from delay? You only get drawn tighter into a hopeless entanglement, and one from which, unless you exercise prudence, you may eventually find it difficult to escape."

"But I don't particularly want to escape, mother. That's just the knotty point."

"Yes, you do, Cyril. You are young and impulsive, and at the present moment are deceiving yourself. The girl is clever enough in her way. She talked very magniloquently about not using persuasion, and leaving your choice entirely free, but she knew how to influence your decision, nevertheless. Her sentimental nonsense has made a considerable impression upon you. But mark my words: as surely as you and I sit here, when it wears off, and the suggestions put into your mind by her vanish, you will come to see things with my eyes. Of course, she would like to marry you. That's natural enough. A young woman without a brass farthing in the world is wise to prefer a safe and comfortable home to going out as a governess. I don't wonder she clings to you like a limpet. I should do the same, in her place. But don't mistake it for affection alone. There's a good deal of self-interest mixed up with her love."

"If Kitty don't care for me, as you assert, at all events I care for her," he answered doggedly.

His mother looked at him steadily, and under her penetrating gaze he could feel himself coloring. She smiled contemptuously.

"Look here, Cyril," she said. "Drop that rubbish. I have seen two or three cases of real love in my life, and although I do not pretend to say that I have experienced the 'divine folly' in my own person, I yet know enough of the outward and visible signs to feel convinced that yours is not a *grande passion*. I predict that you will very soon recover from this affair, and before a year has gone by thank me for rescuing you from a life of wretchedness and poverty."

"Kitty is a charming girl," he replied. "There is something so fresh and honest about her. She gives one the feeling of being better than one's-self."

"That is all very well before marriage," rejoined Lady Mordaunt, who had an answer for every objection, "but it is not quite so pleasant after. I can't imagine its being particularly agreeable for a man spending his days with a woman who inspires a sense of personal inferiority. However, there is no accounting for taste."

"I did not exactly say that," said Cyril irritably. "You seem to take a delight in misconstruing all my words."

"What did you say, then?"

"You don't understand, mother. You don't happen to possess any sentiment yourself, and therefore are unable to sympathize with other people. It is a grave defect in your character. What I meant to convey was that Kitty's notions about things are generally right."

"And I contend that nothing aggravates an unfortunate husband so much as a wife who is so perfect as to be perpetually putting him in the wrong and making him appear a demon by contrast. Not one man in a thousand can stand it, and I'm certain you couldn't. These beautiful moral theories sound remarkably elevating and ennobling, and produce a great effect on weak minds, but in practice they nearly always break down. The angel who talks so glibly about work, and emigration, and sacrifice, doesn't relish being turned into a general servant a bit better than any one else

when it comes to the test.   She has her little humors,
just like other people.   No, no, depend upon it, it is
one thing to talk; another thing to live your life day
after day, year after year, cut off from all your old
friends and associations."

"There have been men before now," he argued, "who
went into exile for the sake of a woman."

"Who can count upon the female sex?   It is running
too great a risk to stake your all on such changeable,
capricious creatures.   Because the angel is an angel
now, there is no guarantee that she should remain one
six months hence.   After all, she is but human, and
her temper is apt to become impaired.   Imagine yourself in a foreign land.   Just at first your wife is amused
by the change, but very soon she begins to find it dull.
The same little round of household duties grows monotonous.   Her Harry is no longer as attentive as he
used to be.   After dinner, instead of making love and
adoring her as a goddess, he smokes a nasty pipe or
else falls asleep.   By imperceptible degrees she comes
to realize that love is a delusion—a mere effect of the
imagination which vanishes directly the mind once
more assumes its normal healthy condition.   He arrives
at the same conclusion, and before very long they wake
up to find that they have made egregious fools of themselves.   They do not communicate the discovery to each
other just at first.   They are too fearful of hurting one
another's feelings; but that stage is an inevitable outcome of the previous one, and the mask once dropped,
they end by mutual reproaches and recriminations, and
declare that never was there a more unsuitable couple."
Lady Mordaunt gave a hard laugh, and in conclusion
added, "Unfortunately, the matrimonial knot is tied and
can't be untied.   The angel is unable to take wings
and fly back to heaven: neither can the wretched hero
be restored to the pedestal from which he is dethroned."

Cyril made no immediate answer to this speech.   Its
shrewd common sense and pitiless reasoning were difficult to refute.   They impressed him uncomfortably.

His mother had drawn such a vivid picture of married life under unfavorable conditions that he could almost see it in his mind's eye. He could fancy himself in some remote spot, shut out from people of his own class, yet too proud to associate with those belonging to a lower, thoroughly discontented and dissatisfied and bored to death. In process of time he would get rough and coarse and common—a regular backwoodsman. He should have to wear ill-fitting, country-made clothes, get his head cropped by a village barber, and degenerate into a dull, uncouth Yahoo, without a word to say for himself—not that that would so much signify, there would be no one to say it to. And Kitty, pretty Kitty, would lose her good looks, become stout, slovenly, and matronly, with a crowd of children of all sizes and ages hanging round her skirts, rendering her sharp-tongued and careworn. Their sons and daughters must necessarily descend the ladder a few steps lower than their parents had done before them, and might consider themselves lucky if they attained to the station and position of respectable tradesmen.

It was not exactly a pretty picture, but that was what the *famille* Mordaunt would come to. He saw it all quite plainly, and gave an inward groan over the wreck. Given a certain amount of money, however, and the wretched, colorless daub, painted in such gray pigments, immediately became a glorious work of Art. Were a sweet pair of hazel eyes, a rosebud mouth, and a charming face—that would fade—worth paying so high a price for? There was the Future to consider as well as the Present. His mother was a clever woman. He had a great respect for her opinion. Could it be true that he was not really so very much in love with Kitty, but only taken by her appearance? He was unable to decide, ponder the question as he might. When he listened to the girl's stirring words they found an echo in his heart, and he believed what she said to be true. But when his mother preached a totally different theme, he perceived that she also had reason on her

12

side, and could not gainsay her statements.   They contained an equal amount of truth.

"It seems almost impossible for one to come to a decision when the pros and cons are so nicely balanced," he said uneasily.

"Quite true," assented Lady Mordaunt.   "But what you have got to do is to ascertain which scale contains the best weight.   Now, I contend that if you marry Kitty Herrick on eight hundred a year you will very soon find out your mistake.   Even as it is, nothing can keep you from horses and betting.   You would run into debt, be warned off the Turf, and probably end by having to abscond.   That is what happens when people plunge who have not capital enough to stand a run of bad luck.   On the other hand, if you were to turn your attention to Miss Van Agnew, for instance, you could indulge every fancy."

"She might not tumble to me," he said, with a modesty which did him credit.

"That is for you to find out.   They say," and Lady Mordaunt rose from her seat, and laid her hand on his shoulder, "that that girl has got no less than twenty thousand a year; and she is going to hunt in your part of the world all the winter.   There's a chance, if only you knew how to avail yourself of it.   Cyril," she continued earnestly, "promise me—promise me, there's a dear boy—to break off with Kitty."

He shook her off, but so gently that she experienced but little discouragement from the action.

"Look here, mother," he said, "you'd better leave me alone for a bit.   I know you mean well and have my interests at heart, but I want to think this matter over carefully."

"That's right," she said.   "I don't ask you to do anything else.   Reflection will soon show the wise and proper course to pursue."

"But mind you," he resumed, "I do not feel disposed to make any definite promise at present, one way or the other.   The fact is, I haven't settled as yet what I shall or shant do. So don't bother me—there's a dear, good mother." So saying, he drew down her hand, and lightly brushed his lips against it.

"All right," she answered briskly, "I wont." And, what's more, she kept her word. She was a very sensible person, was Lady Mordaunt, and understood that there is more sometimes to be gained by silence than by speech; especially when you have already had your say, and further discussion only means repeating yourself. She knew that she had skilfully implanted the "rift within the lute," and unless Cyril were more seriously *épris* with Kitty Herrick than she believed, he would shortly put an end to the engagement. Anyhow, there was nothing for it but to leave him to his own reflections. Once a young man is grown up he likes to consider himself free of maternal guidance, even if he may not be so in reality, and in nine cases out of ten the lighter the bridle with which he is bitted the more kindly does he go. Lady Mordaunt had long ago recognized this fact, and now she left the room, if not altogether content, yet not wholly dissatisfied with the result of their conversation. She felt that she could afford to wait, and trusted to time as her best ally. Nature was given to change, and she had a firm belief that men and women were subject to the same law, talk as they might about eternal constancy.

CHAPTER XXII.

A LOVER OF TO-DAY.

DIRECTLY she left Lady Mordaunt's presence, Kitty put on her walking things and went round to the nearest post-office. Taking a telegraph form and a pencil, she wrote the following message to Lord Algy. "Can I return to Herrington for a day or two? Wire reply." She prepaid the answer, at once walked back to Sloane Street, and set to work packing up her box with feverish energy. She was quite resolved, whatever happened, to leave on the following morning. Her surroundings were uncongenial, and she longed to escape from them. Although she would not have admitted it, she was glad of an excuse to cut her visit short.

"I have only been here two days," she said to herself, "and I have already seen what comes of living on other people's charity. They think it gives them a right to insult you and to reproach you with your poverty. Even if Cyril does remain true to me, we could not possibly be married for some little time. I should not like to show any disrespect to papa's memory. However, there is always a moral to be gained from one's reverses. If Lady Mordaunt has taught me nothing else, she has taught me a good lesson by which I intend to profit. Thanks to her, I have learned that it is infinitely better to work than to beg, to earn your daily bread, no matter how, rather than accept it from friends, since nothing cools their friendship so quickly as putting it to the test."

A couple of hours later an answer came to Kitty's message. It was brief, but characteristic of the sender, and contained only the two words, "Of course." She *felt better and less* raw after receiving it.

The idea of going home, even for a short period, was infinitely comforting. She required time to think over matters and settle her plans. They needed a good deal of consideration, for she quite realized how difficult a thing it was for a girl in her position, suddenly thrown entirely on her own resources, to earn a livelihood. Young ladies, as a rule, who had the misfortune to be similarly situated fell back upon being governesses. She saw, however, that she had little or no chance of success in the scholastic line. To begin with, the market was terribly overstocked, and the supply greatly exceeded the demand. Secondly, the requirements of the age were all for certificated teachers, past their first youth, and not likely to inflict damage on the susceptible hearts of husbands and sons. They must have been educated at Cambridge or some well-known college. These were the governesses who alone commanded high salaries. The majority were little better paid than an upper housemaid, and a great deal worse than any decent cook.

Kitty possessed one very valuable faculty, not always to be met with in youth. She had the gift of seeing things as they actually were, stripped of tinsel, and she recognized that she should never get on as a governess. She was too young, too ignorant, and it was not her vocation. She could play a little, sing a little, dance as well as most girls, and ride a good deal better. That comprised the list of her accomplishments. They seemed pitifully small when she came to review them, and to ask herself what their money value represented. She did, perhaps, know enough to hammer the alphabet into the heads of very young children, but that only meant about ten shillings a week. And even if she put up with the drudgery, it was impossible to subsist in any decency or comfort on so insignificant a sum. Dressmaking occurred to her as a profitable profession, and one become quite fashionable for ladies in reduced circumstances; but then she was not naturally fond of sewing, and hated a confined life, which necessitated being shut up within four walls all and every day, Sunday alone excepted. Almost every respectable trade was already blocked, and not by young, inexperienced people like herself, but by ones specially educated. What chance had she against these?

The outlook was anything but promising; nevertheless, Kitty did not despair.

"Where there's a will, there's a way," she mused, "and I'll support myself somehow until Cyril is ready to marry me."

To tell the truth, she had an idea in that active little brain of hers, but she did not intend to communicate it to a soul until she knew whether it were feasible or not. The day wore away slowly. She sent word to Lady Mordaunt that she had a headache, and luncheon consequently was served to her in her room. She stayed there until about half-past three o'clock, when the brougham came round to the door, and, greatly to her relief, she saw Lady Mordaunt step into it and drive away

Now was her opportunity. She stole downstairs, taking care to cough rather loudly as she went, and took up her station in the drawing-room. She had a kind of feeling that Cyril would find her out before long. Neither was she mistaken in her surmise, for five minutes had scarcely elapsed before she heard his step on the landing. Up to this moment she had retained her self-possession in a marked degree, but at prospect of the coming interview her bosom heaved, and for a few seconds her breath came fast and slow. The mere consciousness of his presence sufficed to affect her, but she did not choose that he should perceive the fact, and sat quite still and motionless. Cyril opened the door, peeped in, closed it carefully, and entered the room. She watched every movement from under her long eyelashes, but otherwise she made no sign, and did not utter a word. She had delivered her protocol, and it was for him to make the first advances. He *appeared embarrassed* by this behavior, for he did not venture to sit down on the sofa by her side, but walked to the mantel-piece, and stood with his back turned towards the fire. He cast a sidelong glance at her, but though she was perfectly aware that his eyes sought hers, she obstinately refused to raise her own. These tactics proved disconcerting in the extreme. He cleared his throat three or four times, and at length summoned up courage to say:

"You are not really going to leave us to-morrow, are you, Kitty?"

"Yes," she answered, with forced composure. "According to my present intentions, I most certainly am."

"You must not pay too much attention to what my mother says," he returned. "Her tongue is a bit sharp at times, but she means well."

"Very likely," said Kitty spiritedly. "People generally *do* mean well when they insult you to your face, and say the most biting, bitter things possible to conceive of—at least, so you are told. I fail to see that that is any balm to your wounded feelings."

"My mother was put out," he said, apologetically, kicking up the end of the hearthrug with the toe of his boot.

"Well, I am put out too, to the extent that I decline to trespass any longer on her hospitality. Once let me see I'm not wanted and I act on the hint. Would you not do the same?" And she folded her hands with an air of quiet resolution.

"But, Kitty," he said uneasily, "think how queer it will look you running back to Herrington in such a hurry, when every one knows you left it meaning to pay us a long visit of weeks, if not months."

"I really do not see why folk should think it queer," she rejoined. "The matter is self-evident. I hear that I am ruined, and that Herrington is about to be sold." A large tear fell with a splash on the back of her hand, but she brushed it away hastily, and continued in a firmer tone, "What more natural than that

I should return for a few days to pack up my individual belongings?"

"That's right enough as far as it goes," he said, not wholly satisfied with this reasoning. "But afterwards?"

Then for the first time she raised her eyes, and they challenged his with a singular directness which held him in thrall.

"Afterwards depends on yourself," she said slowly and impressively.

As she spoke a soft pink blush suffused her cheek, and colored all its smooth texture. The extreme clearness of her complexion was rendered more striking by the deep mourning that she wore. It set off her fair and delicate face, and certainly enhanced its beauty. Her pencilled eyebrows showed dark against the arch of her polished brow, which was framed by a crop of chestnut ringlets, curling round it like the tendrils of a vine. Here and there a few hairs shone out distinct from the mass, like threads of ruddy gold, and formed a kind of aureola to her finely shaped head as she sat with her back to the light. Cyril thought he had never seen her looking so pretty.

"Oh! Kitty!" he cried, with a burst of self-pity at the Fate which doomed him either to lose her or give up his pleasures—a Fate calculated to leave him miserable either way. "I am so wretched. You have no idea how wretched I am."

"Are you, dear?" she said, her voice quite soft and tender, and every vestige of sharpness gone from it. "I am very, very sorry."

"You heard what my mother said," he went on excitedly. "I declare I feel perfectly distracted. If I refuse to give you up as she wishes, then I must be prepared to face the alternative of quarrelling with her. And she is not a pleasant person to quarrel with."

"Pray don't do so on my account," said Kitty, with a quick gesture of pride. "I would not come between you for worlds."

"*One's mother* is one's mother," he continued.

" Mine has been very good to me at different times, and it vexes me to run counter to her wishes."

" If you prefer her to me, Cyril, you are quite right to consider her feelings before mine."

" But I don't, Kitty. That's just the knotty point. Look here, I've been thinking the matter over since this morning, and I can't for the life of me see why we should not just let things remain as they are for a bit, and wait on the chance of something turning up."

Kitty's eyes grew very bright. A wonderful light illumined them, and her whole face suddenly became radiant. She gave a kind of gasp.

" Oh! Cyril," she cried, " do you mean it? Are you really willing to wait—actually *wait* for me in spite of my being poor?"

Her joy was so spontaneous and sincere, her affection so evident, that they gratified him. And yet, he could not help feeling somewhat of a traitor at heart. Was he dealing altogether fairly with her? Would it not be better to act on his mother's advice, and part now, rather than run the risk of inflicting terrible pain hereafter? His inward monitor said yes, but he lacked the moral courage. She was too pretty, too fond, and she fascinated his senses. Moreover, he had not been accustomed to deny himself any toy which he might happen to covet.

" We should have to wait until the spring, at all events," he said rather lukewarmly. " We could not well be married sooner, and that would give us time to look round, and see how things are likely to shape."

Even as he spoke, he knew his reasoning to be false; but she was easily satisfied, so long as she did not lose him entirely, and it rendered her content.

" You have made me so happy, Cyril," she said softly and gratefully. " I was so dreadfully afraid you would not care for me when you found that my money was gone. Forgive the doubt, darling. Wait, indeed! Why, I would wait until the end of time for you." So saying, she rose from her seat, and putting her arms round his neck, kissed him all uninvited. Ten minutes ago, it would have seemed to her an unmaidenly thing to do, but now her emotion overcame her girlish modesty, and she was not ashamed to let him see how dearly she loved him. "Oh! Cyril," she whispered, "my own, my beloved, it grieves me to think how much you are giving up for my sake, and yet in my selfishness I cannot refuse to accept the sacrifice. I believe I ought to, but I can't, and that's just the truth. Henceforth the one endeavor of my life shall be to atone to you for what you have lost through marrying me."

"Pooh! pooh! Kitty," he said, lamely enough, "I am no hero."

"Yes, you are. The biggest hero that ever lived. And even if you weren't, you would always be mine; for oh! dear love," and she drew his face down to a level with her own and gazed at it tenderly, "you are good and noble and true—in short, all that a man should be."

Her praise was a little exaggerated. However exalted an opinion he might entertain of himself, he could not help feeling that. To do Cyril justice, he quite appreciated the situation. If there had been no such thing as £ s. d. in the world it would have been simply delightful. Even as matters were, it was impossible for him to remain like a marble statue whilst a sweetly pretty girl, instinct with life and vitality, was showering every term of endearment upon him. He could but follow suit. He told himself that any other fellow would have done the same in his place. The temptation of the moment was too strong for flesh and blood to withstand. Looking back upon their *tête-à-tête*, it seemed to him that somehow or other she had settled the matter before he realized all it involved. At least, as he subsequently explained to his mother, it was entirely Kitty's doing, not his. She led him astray by the warmth of her affection. In short, the old, old story, so typical of man's strength and generosity, repeated *itself.* "The woman gave me and I did eat." It did

not occur to him to say, "Yes, it was a very good apple,
and had a sweet, nice taste which we both enjoyed.
She took one half and I the other. We are equal cul-
prits." No, the manly, honorable course was to declare, "She is alone to blame, for if she had not put the
cursed fruit in my way I never should have thought
anything about it."

So Cyril returned to the sofa at last and pulled Kitty
down on to his knee, put his arm round her waist, and
spent a very agreeable half hour. After all, the present
is one's own. Why not make the most of it? We miss
so many golden moments just because of a few tiresome
scruples, and because we are weak enough to listen to
the whisperings of that ridiculous thing called conscience, which when you come to analyze it is neither
more nor less than a slowly evolved production of civil-
ization. Thus Cyril reasoned, but all the time, deep in
his heart, he knew that such reasoning was nothing
but mischievous sophistry, opposed to right, truth, and
chivalry, and to the higher teachings of humanity.
When Kitty gave him that first kiss she surrendered
him everything. And what did he offer in return for
her pure, innocent love? Only a mock passion, whirled
here and there like a dead leaf by the wind, on the
turgid tide of self-interest.

CHAPTER XXIII.

KITTY RETURNS TO HERRINGTON.

Thought after thought revolved in Cyril's mind, even whilst engaged in the pleasing occupation of courting Kitty. After a while he said:

"I think we had better keep our engagement dark. Under the circumstances, it may be wiser, and it seems a pity to irritate my mother needlessly."

"But, Cyril," remonstrated Kitty, "you will have to tell her, wont you?"

"Yes, something; but there is no necessity to tell her all. She may as well cool down first."

The girl looked serious, and not altogether satisfied.

"I am so sorry about Lady Mordaunt," she said penitently. "I wish I had not spoken my mind quite so freely."

"It would not have made much difference even had you kept silent," he returned. "The fact is, she was regularly disappointed about the money."

"Yes, so I suppose; but it seems very mean of me to clear out to-morrow morning and leave you to bear the brunt of the battle."

He laughed—a forced laugh, devoid of mirth.

"I intend to follow your example, and beat a timely retreat very shortly. I hate town out of the season, and the horses are eating their heads off. There's no earthly reason why I should not hunt as long as I can," and from consideration to his listener's feelings he smothered a sigh.

"Then I shall see you sometimes," she said cheerfully. "At least, I hope so."

"Yes," he replied, "if you stay in the country. I suppose," he added jealously, "that you will go to

Furrowdale for the winter? I heard the old duke begging you to make the castle your home."

"He was very kind," she said quietly, "but I shall not avail myself of his hospitality if I can help it. I wish to be independent, and have other plans."

"What are they, Kitty? It seems to me you are wrong. The duke and duchess are good people for us to know, and you would be in clover there."

"Yes, no doubt; but I have arrived at the conclusion that there is no greater mistake than living on your friends. You only expose yourself to insult. The mere fact of being penniless, too, takes away immensely from their affection."

Cyril reddened at this speech. It struck home.

"Come, come," he said, "it is a mistake to look at matters too seriously. You and my mother had a bit of a breeze, but it is bound to blow over before long. You must make allowances, Kitty, and forgive the maternal, even if she *is* a trifle angry and sore. In the years to come, if you have an only son, perhaps you also may indulge in magnificent expectations where he is concerned, and be hard to please in the selection of a daughter-in-law."

The girl's face softened.

"Yes, Cyril," she said, "you are right. As soon as your mother can forgive me for loving you as I do, then, believe me, I will meet her more than half-way. And now, dear, I think I hear wheels, and had better not risk another encounter. Say good-by nicely, for we are not likely to have the chance of a quiet talk tomorrow. I leave by the 8.45 train."

"Good-by, Kitty. It is not for long. I shall see you again in a day or two. The hounds meet at Morriston Dale, close to Gretton Grange, on Thursday next, and if all goes well I shall be there. Drop me a line as to your movements, there's a dear, and send it to my club."

Once more he took her in his arms, and would have been quite happy had he not been disturbed by a secret conviction that he was throwing away his chances and making a fool of himself. Strange! Why did the casual mention of Gretton Grange bring up a crowd of images to his mind which had the effect of cooling his embraces? Kitty, with her quick feminine perceptions, was at once aware of the difference. She looked up in alarm.

"Is anything the matter, Cyril?" she inquired uneasily.

"No, nothing," he responded. Then she heard the front door shut to with a bang, and afraid of being caught by Lady Mordaunt, ran quickly upstairs. She was happy—very happy. Her lover had remained true, and yet in her cup of joy she already tasted a drop of bitterness, which caused her to reproach herself when alone for having departed from her resolution and influenced his decision, even though almost unconsciously.

"I broke down in my part," she mused. "Do what I would, I could not help letting him see how much I loved him, and how miserable I should have been had he settled to break off our engagement. Dear Cyril, I wonder why he looked so gloomy when he said good by. I hope—I do hope—he is not already beginning to repent, If I thought that, I would—yes," and a shadow passed over her face, "I would—give—him—up."

On the following morning she rose early and breakfasted in her room. She fully expected to see Cyril before leaving, and put off her departure until the last moment; but as he did not appear she was reluctantly forced to step into the cab, which had already been waiting ten minutes at the door. Just as it was on the point of driving away, the housemaid came rushing downstairs with a note.

"This is for you, miss, please. Captain Mordaunt wished me to give it you," she gasped, quite out of breath.

Kitty seized the precious letter, and proceeded to read its contents while the cabman whipped up his horse. They were short enough, and contained only the following words: "Awfully sorry not to see you off. I quite meant to, but like an idiot managed to oversleep myself." She was much disappointed at going from the house without another sight of him, and could not help asking herself if *he* had been leaving whether *she* should have slumbered quite so peacefully. The pang was somewhat sharp while it lasted, but she endeavored to dismiss her regrets as selfish and exacting.

After Cyril's noble conduct, she registered a vow not to let the slightest doubt of him cast a shadow over her love. Yet the strange thing was, strive as she might, she could not dismiss certain anxieties and fears. She had seen enough to realize that his mother possessed a very considerable influence over him. During her short stay in Sloane Street, she had not failed to discern on what lines the household was conducted, and perceived that in order to maintain the outward show deemed essential it was necessary to effect a great many internal economies. The fires were kept very low, and at regular intervals the respectable man-servant appeared in order to rake the ashes carefully over them. The gas was never turned up to its full pitch, and wherever it was possible, one burner was made to do the duty of two. The helpings at meals were curiously small, and distributed in mathematical proportions. The hostess drank water, and the glasses of those who took wine were only three parts filled. The servants were perpetually giving warning, and three months was the longest period a cook had ever been known to stay.

Kitty knew these signs. She had but too good cause to be aware that they meant a scanty purse. Often and often at Herrington, during the last two years, she had piled the cinders up herself, so as to make the coals last longer. She could feel for Lady Mordaunt; but this very fact caused her to dread her the more, since she admitted that the arguments her adversary was likely to employ against her were weighted with truth. No doubt it would be better for Cyril to marry a rich wife. But she judged his love by her own, and knowing that she would willingly give up everything for his sake, imagined him to be equally ready.

When she stepped out on to the platform of Herrington station it was about twenty minutes past eleven. The first thing she saw was a big, straight figure, clad in a checked shooting suit, whose owner immediately advanced towards her.

"Why, Kitty!" exclaimed Lord Algy—for it was he— holding out both hands. "Travelling third class! This is something quite new."

"Don't acknowledge me if you are ashamed," she returned, with a heightened color. "I am trying to accustom myself to my altered circumstances, and thought the sooner I began the better."

"Poor dear!" he murmured under his breath.

"It's really wonderful how comfortable one is, and what nice people one meets," she rattled on, with forced gayety.

"I dare say," he answered. "The whole question is entirely a matter of false pride."

"I had a charming young couple for travelling companions," she continued, in a more natural tone. "Don't laugh, Algy."

"I'm not laughing, Kitty. I don't see that there is anything to laugh at."

"Well, then, I repeat the word charming. I suppose they were poor, for like myself they must evidently have seen better days; but I assure you it quite did me good to watch them. Third-class people are more human and infinitely more affectionate. It was quite beautiful to see the way in which that young man and woman behaved, and how they took the baby in turns, so as to rest each other's arms, and dandled her, and cooed to her, and rocked her to sleep. What patrician father would have done such a thing, or mother either, for the matter of that? You see," she concluded cheerfully, "even if I had to put my dignity in my pocket, the moral lesson derived was certainly better than if I had been shut up in a first-class compartment, with some . luxurious, somnolent old couple, their rugs tucked well round their fat legs, and who only spoke to make an occasional observation *sotto voce* of a fault-finding nature."

This time Lord Algy laughed genuinely. He was delighted to find she had come back more like her old self.

"What a real little Radical you are," he exclaimed jestingly. "I believe you love the people."

"Yes, of course I do. I have the greatest respect and admiration for their many virtues. I often ask myself if we should be half as good, as patient, and long-suffering in their place."

"We wont argue that point," he said, "for I think we are pretty well agreed. I wanted to talk over one or two matters, Kitty, and so thought I would come to the station and meet you." And he flushed up under the brim of his brown pot hat.

"Thanks," she said gratefully, "you are always much kinder to me than I deserve."

"My trap is here," he continued, "and if you have no objection I propose driving you over to the Hall. By the bye," turning furiously red, "I wanted to ask you something: I hope you wont think the question impertinent."

"What is it, Algy?"

"Have you—have you money enough to carry on with? I am in a position to furnish some if you are at all hard up."

"Impertinent!" she exclaimed, thinking how kind and considerate he was, and what a pleasant feeling of being thoroughly protected and cared for she always experienced in his society. "On the contrary, I greatly appreciate the delicacy which prompts the inquiry, and will answer it quite frankly. I have enough money by me to last for ten days, or even a fortnight with economy. Long before then I hope to have found something to do. I don't eat very much when I am by myself," she added pathetically enough. "Tea and

13

toast go a long way when you are alone, and luckily they are cheap."

"What a thorough woman's speech," he exclaimed, with a jocularity intented to hide the emotion occasioned by her words.

It was so pleasant, however, to see her again—to hear the sweet ring of her fresh young voice in his ears, and above all, to have her seated by his side whilst they bowled along the country lanes behind a good, quick-trotting horse — that imperceptibly his spirits rose. Kitty was awfully nice to him, too. She really seemed pleased to see him. He was very curious to learn what had brought her back in such a hurry, and inwardly wished she would broach the subject. At length he could contain himself no longer, and after a pause in the conversation, said interrogatively:

"Well, and how have things gone with you since the receipt of my letter? It made me feel such a brute to have to write it." She knew what he wanted to hear, and she had so much trust and confidence in him that she poured forth the whole story of her quarrel with Lady Mordaunt and Cyril's subsequent resolution. She never told him of his note, in which he begged pardon for having overslept himself. It was a strange thing to make a confidant of a man she had refused, and confess her anxieties regarding an accepted lover to a rejected one. She was vaguely aware of the fact, but it was a relief to unburden herself to somebody; and then, he was not like other people. At last she came to an end of her narrative, and looked at her companion questioningly.

"What do *you* think of it?" she said. "I should like to hear your opinion."

A somewhat dogged expression stole over his face. He had his own ideas on the subject, but knew better than to mention them.

"I would rather not give an opinion," he replied, flicking a fly from Titan's back with the end of the whip.

"Why not?" she asked persistently.

He was silent for a moment, then he turned and looked her straight in the eyes.

"Because I am not an impartial critic. Surely you must know that, Kitty. I don't wish to say anything against Captain Mordaunt. If I did," and he gave a short laugh, "I should only expose myself to the charge of jealousy. On the other hand, I am not sufficiently magnanimous to laud a successful rival to the skies. Consequently, I prefer to hold my tongue."

CHAPTER XXIV.

TINY TIM.

"But, Algy," Kitty expostulated, wishing to demonstrate the exceeding unamiability of his refusal to comply with her request.

"Pardon me," he said, very stiffly and sternly. "You must allow me to hold my own views on the subject. I am only too happy to manage all your *other* affairs for you, but those of the heart you can surely conduct for yourself. If you are convinced of Captain Mordaunt's sincerity, well and good. I congratulate you on having gained the affections of an honest, single-minded man. Time will prove whether he is one or not. There is nothing more to be said."

Why could she not answer him indignantly and stick up for Cyril? for say what he might, his words implied a doubt. Why did those foolish tears come welling up into her eyes instead, and a longing seize her to be good friends again? That stern, decided tone of voice was so new. She had heard it occasionally when others had done wrong, but never before had it been applied to herself.

"Algy," she said penitently, "I beg your pardon. It was stupid of me to ask your advice. I ought to have known better; but you are so clever and so sensible that somehow or other I always come to you in a difficulty. I promise, however, not to do so again. I will try and keep my worries to myself. You—you are not angry with me, are you?" And she turned a pair of glistening eyes to his.

He had felt that she was hardly fair to him—that she *asked too much* of his discretion and endurance; but at the first symptom of regret on her part his smouldering wrath subsided, dispersing like smoke in an airy sky.

"All right," he said, in his usual cheery voice. "Don't let us say any more about it. We will change the subject. I can't help being rather short sometimes, Kitty. I haven't felt particularly amiable of late, but I dare say my temper will improve after a bit."

She made no reply. It was not easy, since she knew to what cause the deterioration was due.

"Here we are at the poor old place," said Lord Algy presently, as he pulled Titan up short before the lodge gates of Herrington Hall. "By the by," he added carelessly, "I have arranged with Morgan that you are to have everything that belongs to you or that you may happen to fancy—your father's picture, which was presented to him when he gave up the hounds, for instance. I thought you would like that."

She put out her hands, and pressed his in token of gratitude. He seemed to read her most secret wishes.

"Are—are all papa's presents which he gave to me at different times mine?" she asked uncertainly.

"Yes, of course."

"Tiny Tim and little Pattercake?"

"Most decidedly."

"To do what I choose with?"

"Yes, to do exactly what you choose with." She heaved a sigh of relief.

"Thanks, Algy. It was important that I should know this point."

The dogcart halted before the front door. Lord Algy jumped out and rang the bell, and a woman-servant answered it.

"Where is Barlow?" she asked in surprise.

"Barlow has gone home," he said apologetically. "I didn't think you were coming back so soon, so I paid off all the servants except this one housemaid. It had to be; and, as I said before, not expecting you, it seemed to me the sooner the better." He did not add *that the money* had come out of his own pocket, and that he had met all the most pressing expenses. There was no need to trouble her with such details. She had enough to worry her as it was.

"Oh! of course," sad Kitty, hurriedly

And then, as she looked round the empty, desolate house, which was home and yet not home, she suddenly burst into a flood of tears. The sight quite overcame her, recalling as it did all she had lost.

Lord Algy was infinitely distressed. He longed to take her in his arms, and whisper words of comfort and endearment; but as this was out of the question he stood by, looking very awkward and very miserable, until the first passion of her grief had spent itself. Then she dried her eyes and said:

"Forgive me. I—I am better now. It was only just at first that it all seemed so strange. I do mean to be brave, and not to bother other people with my troubles. Indeed—indeed I do. You were quite right when you said that just now. I have no business to expect that strangers should interest themselves in my affairs."

"Hush, Kitty," he said. "I was a brute to say what I did. And if you begin to look upon me as a stranger, I shall never forgive myself. Why," and he forced a brave smile to his face, "we are just like brother and sister."

"Yes," she said, in rather a subdued voice, "just like brother and sister. I expect that is why we fall out occasionally."

"Time is precious, and we can't afford to quarrel at present," he said, pulling out his watch. "There are ever so many business things I want to consult you about, and I promised to meet my father at the kennels at one o'clock sharp. He has just bought three couples of Lord Porterridge's hounds with the celebrated Reefer blood in them, and is anxious to inspect his purchases."

After some further conversation, they went round the house together, and Lord Algy insisted on putting a private mark on every kind of article which he thought was endeared to Kitty by association. Her father's arm-chair, the bureau at which he used to write his letters, his favorite books and pictures, and her own pet piano and knickknacks—he seemed to know them all, just as well as if he had been one of the family, and picked out the very things which she felt most loath to lose. His selections became so numerous that at length she interfered.

"Really, Algy," she said, "it is extremely kind of you to wish to me to appropriate all this furniture—to which, by the way, I don't suppose I possess the slightest right, and in carrying it away should be defrauding the creditors. But even if this were not the case, you quite forget that I am not likely henceforth to live in a palace, and have nowhere to house so many things."

"I'll make it all right with the creditors," he answered. "You need not bother about them. I'm answerable, and as for the furniture," his brow contracting, "it will come in useful when—when you are married. I'll stow the stuff away and see that it comes to no harm."

"But, Algy," she began, "I can't accept——"

"Now don't make me unhappy by standing on your dignity," he interrupted hastily. "It's pure selfishness on my part. I would not have that piano sold at auction for anything in the world. Why, Kitty, don't you remember, when you were quite a little thing of about twelve, how you used to sit on my knee, strum away with your forefinger and sing 'Auld Lang Syne,' in your pretty, childish voice? By Jove! I've never heard a song to equal it ever since." And he began softly whistling the familiar air.

It was useless to argue the point. He was evidently set on her retaining all her own and the Squire's private belongings. Seeing this, she became quite passive, and stood mutely by whilst he went from one room to another. It was sad work at best, and she did not venture to say much for fear of breaking down. His silent sympathy and consideration were infinitely touching, and she could not help wondering how it was she had failed to appreciate him hitherto at his full value, and had thought him a bit heavy and slow-going.

Time passed quickly, and when Lord Algy again consulted his watch, he found he should have to drive at Titan's best pace in order to keep his appointment. He shook hands with Kitty hurriedly, and as he jumped up into the dog cart, called out:

"Good-by, Kitty. Be sure and send a post-card if you happen to want me for anything. If I don't hear, I shall look round in the course of a day or two, just to see how you are getting on."

When he had gone she felt curiously restless and lonely, and inclined to sit down and have another good cry. Fortunately, at this juncture the maid created a diversion by bringing in luncheon on a tray. Kitty revived after having had something to eat, and, going round to the stables, ordered Pattercake to be put into her little pony trap. She intended to drive over to Belfield, a village about four miles distant from Herrington, where resided one Mr. Peter Ruddle, a well-known horse-dealer. Pattercake was the smartest fourteen-hand cob in the county, bar none. He could trot twelve miles in an hour without an effort, and was a perfect beauty to look at. He stood next to Tiny Tim in Kitty's affections. When she went up to him in his stall, and patted his firm neck, strong as a miniature dray-horse's, her heart swelled almost to bursting. It cut her like a knife to be forced to part with the two favorites who were her pride and delight, and whom she loved like human beings. They were her own property. Her father had given her Pattercake as a birthday present, two years ago, and we already know how she acquired Tiny Tim. Alas! in her present position she could not afford to keep them. They were both sound, young valuable animals, as fresh on their legs as the day they were foaled, and having earned reputations, the one as a trapper, the other as a hunter, were sure to fetch a lot of money.

After a bit she passed on to Tiny Tim's box, and the

beautiful beast gave a whinny of recognition at sight of his mistress. He would have known her amongst a thousand, and though lively enough in the field, was as gentle as a lamb in the stable. Kitty could do what she liked with him—pull his ears, stroke his quarters, handle each leg in turn. He put up his soft muzzle as she approached, in anticipation of the sugar which she never failed to give him. He gobbled up three or four lumps with desperate avidity, and when he found no more was forthcoming stood slobbering and licking his lips like a great baby, rolling his long red tongue round the iron bars of his box. Kitty eyed him meanwhile with love and admiration. He was in the pink of condition, and a real picture. At a time of year when other horses begin to look rough in their coats and require frequent clipping, his remained smooth and shiny as satin. There was a ruddy sheen on his round bay body which made the good roan mare who stood next him appear quite a commoner. Although still somewhat on the big side, he was hard and full of muscle. His clear, prominent eye betokened health and high courage, and perhaps a spice of the devil when its owner was roused. His broad, level forehead testified to a more than ordinary share of intelligence. No real lover of horseflesh could have passed him by. He was so finely proportioned and truly put together. The flat, big-boned legs, the roomy feet, sloping shoulders, slender yet powerful neck, lean, varmint-looking head, short back, wide hips, strong loins, long quarters, muscular thighs, and great clean hocks, were all points which, when found combined with character, render a hunter worth his weight in gold. A rush of sorrow swept over Kitty's spirit as she gazed at him and felt that she must part with her pet and treasure. Knowing his peculiarities as she did, perhaps it was a pardonable pride which made her think that no matter into whose hands he passed he would never find any one to love, and consequently to understand him, like herself. She knew his character as well as if he were her most intimate friend, and she had won him by kindness, and by kindness alone.

With all Tiny Tim's good qualities, he was not fault-
less. He had a temper, and could be as obstinate as a
mule on occasion. Even with Kitty, sometimes when
the hounds had thrown up—he never misbehaved when
they really ran hard—if she wanted to jump one fence
he would take it into his head to jump another, or else
make for a gate if he happened to spy one handy. From
the first, she discovered that whipping and spurring rendered him a demon. She never fought with him, therefore. If she could not gain by coaxing and subterfuge
what she was able to obtain by force, then rather than
battle it out she let him have his own way. In argument, when a person gets heated and unreasonable,
the wisest course is, generally, to smilingly put the
question by, and it was owing to these feminine tactics
that she contrived to master Tiny Tim. Men have their
own theories regarding their steeds, and the necessity
of contesting every point, but it is quite certain that
high-mettled animals with light mouths and somewhat
peculiar dispositions go better with ladies and guided
by silken threads rather by heavy curb and lash.

Anyhow, whether Kitty was right or wrong in her
management of Tiny Tim, the result was so successful
that it left little room for criticism, and few people who
saw the gallant bay's bang tail disappearing over one formidable fence after the other had an idea how much good
handling had to do with his extraordinary performances,
or that in spite of his speed, stoutness, and undeniable
merits, he was not everybody's horse. Kitty loved him
all the better on this account, and a certain mixture of
pride was blended with her affection. That was only
natural, however. As she stood and looked at the good
little animal, and thought sorrowfully how in all probability she had sat for the last time on his back, she
turned abruptly away, with a hard lump rising in her
throat which rendered speech impossible. Silently she
mounted into the pony cart, gave Pattercake a light flick
of the whip that made him start into his collar, and
drove out of the yard.

CHAPTER XXV.

MR. PETER RUDDLE was a considerable personage.
Quite a third of the hunters which appeared with the
Furrowdale and the neighboring packs of hounds were
purchased at his establishment. He was known far and
wide as *the dealer* of the shires, and the prices he obtained
were frequently fabulous. He had a large connection
all over the country, and one of the secrets of his success
was that he knew exactly where to place each particular
animal. Good horses never give any trouble. It
requires no great ability to get rid of them. There
are always a dozen customers ready to snap them up.
But there are others classed between the rank brutes
and real high-class performers, which by judicious
management and knowledge of human nature can also
be planted so as to give satisfaction to the purchaser.
If a dealer wishes to make a name he must study the
individual requirements of his patrons as carefully as
he does the animals submitted for his inspection. One
man has no objection to a runaway-devil as long as he
can jump. Another does not care twopence about the
leaping capabilities of his steed if only he has good legs
and feet that will stand an amount of hard galloping on
the macadam. A third likes a quiet, lazy, good-natured
beast, who will let him eat his sandwiches in peace and
permit him to comfortably drain the contents of his
flask. A fourth goes in for speed, and nothing but a
racer will content him; whilst a fifth would not ride a
ready-made hunter at a gift, but cares only for four-
year-olds, and thinks no pleasure equal to the pleasure
of tumbling about and making them himself. So it

goes on. Every one has his or her particular hobby, and a successful horse-dealer must not only be a good judge of the equine, but also of the two-legged animal. He requires the kind of intuitive perception which, when a fresh customer enters the yard, enables him to say to himself at a glance, "Ah, I know the sort of cove you are."

Now, Mr. Ruddle possessed this art to perfection. He was a keen and close observer of his own species, and in addition possessed such a singularly candid countenance and natural, straightforward, manner that directly he opened his mouth he disarmed suspicion. He inspired people with trust at first sight. Every one liked and respected Mr. Ruddle—except, perhaps, Mrs. Ruddle, who, after the fashion of most wives, was lamentably deficient in the bump of veneration. She was ten years older than her spouse, and could not bring herself to realize that at the age of thirty-eight her Peter was no longer a boy requiring perpetual advice and supervision. Rumor said that she sat upon Mr. Ruddle disgracefully, but then Rumor is extremely fond of spreading such reports. Anyhow, if it were true, the fact did not prevent him from looking very jolly and prosperous.

To tell the truth, he owed a good deal to his wife. Had it not been for the fortune which she brought him, he never could have attained to his present position, and he bore this in mind whenever she tried his endurance more than usual. Peter started life as a stable-boy, and a proud lad was he when he obtained the situation of second horseman to Mr. Herrick. He remained in that capacity from the age of seventeen until he had passed his twenty-fifth birthday, when, wishing to better himself, he entered the bonds of matrimony. He was devoted to the Squire, and thought there was no one in the whole world to equal him, except, perhaps, Miss Kitty, for whom he entertained the profoundest admiration. During his years of service he had got into the habit of a Saturday night, when "stables were done," of smoking a pipe at Mr. Dumbleton's snug little public-house in the village, where he saw his friends and heard all the news. Mrs. Dumbleton—then in the flower of her beauty—was wont to charm a select company by the eloquence of her tongue, whilst Dumbleton, good fellow, sat mutely by, as husbands ought to do when they possess sparkling wives, and occasionally nodded his shaggy head as much as to say, "Just listen to her, isn't she a one-er to talk! There's not another woman in the county a patch on my missis when she rolls out them grand words."

He was a peaceable, steady-going chap, was Dumbleton, and did an excellent business. No one suspected, however, when he died quite suddenly of heart disease, that he would leave his widow such a nice, tidy bit of money. Three thousand two hundred pounds was the precise sum, as the village learned, and that three thousand two hundred pounds are not to be despised, most of the unmarried men very soon found out.

Mrs. Dumbleton had numerous offers of marriage. The poor thing was so hard beset by admirers that she never had a chance given her of remaining a widow. If only for the sake of peace and quiet, she was forced to marry again. So she began to look about for a rising, promising young man, and her eye fell on Peter Ruddle. "Slim" Peter Ruddle he was in those days, having the advantage of a very elegant figure. With his gentlemanly air, neat clothes, glib tongue, and tasteful compliments, he managed to eclipse all other rivals, and had the honor of conducting Mrs. Dumbleton to the altar.

To do Peter justice, he made an excellent husband, and the lady never had cause to regret her choice. Perhaps he could not say quite as much on his side; but, thanks to her capital, he was enabled to quit service and set up in the horse-dealing line, which had always been the secret ambition of his soul. Since then his career had been one of unbroken prosperity. Year by year the number of his customers, and his reputation as a fair, honest dealer, increased, until at last he was at his wit's end to find horses to supply the ever-growing demand. The cry was, "Something that can jump, gallop, and stay. All the rest is immaterial."

"I should think so indeed," Mr. Ruddle used to say, with a snort of derision, as he opened one letter after the other. "If folks aint satisfied with perfection—or as near perfection as the Almighty sees fit to turn out— they must be uncommonly hard to please."

As a consequence of the enormous demand for hunters, Mr. Ruddle's prices became very high; but he never forgot his old friends, or those who had been kind to him in his early days, and many a good-class animal had passed from his stable to Squire Herrick's at a purely nominal figure. When Mrs. Ruddle expostulated with her lord, and pointed out the folly of yielding to generous instincts which represented a sheer loss of £ s. d., he would reply apologetically, "Don't scold, Nancy, there's a dear soul. I wont say but what you are right in the main—you generally are. But if I'd never been horseman to Squire Herrick I should never have known you, and he has got that free, pleasant way about him, that I could give him all I possess for the mere asking. He's a gentleman, he is, and no mistake. And as for Miss Kitty, the very sight of her sweet smiling face does one good."

Mrs. Dumbleton curled up her lip at this, and responded disdainfully:

"You're a fool, Peter, that's what you are, and it's a mercy you've got me to look after you, else you'd very soon go to rack and ruin, and not have a decent house over your head. Business people has no right to sentiment. It's a luxury they can't afford to indulge in. A man like you shouldn't have favorites, or do more for one customer than for another. It ain't fair. Take my advice, Peter, keep impartial. Trade's trade, and feelings ought to have nothing to do with it. They're upsetting things at the best of times. If the Squire was a good master to you, you was a good servant to him, and so you're quits—leastways in my opinion; and as for making him a present of that roan mare—for letting her go for a hundred sovereigns was pretty much the same—why, I repeat, you're a fool."

Mr. Ruddle slapped the partner of his bosom jocosely on her broad back.

"If you want to get round a woman," he confided to his intimate friends, "never lose your temper, and throw in a touch of flattery whenever you can. It's astonishing how it smooths things."

"You are a wonderful person, Nancy," he said, in reply to Mrs. Ruddle's remarks, "and as you justly observe, I don't know where I should be were it not for your counsel; but you make one mistake—you don't take human nature sufficiently into account, and in my experience human nature is a thing which the majority of folk make a mighty poor fight against. It's all very well to *talk* about having no favor-ites, but a man can't help himself. Some people are so much nicer than others."

During the summer Mr. Ruddle had spent a portion of his profits in erecting a new yard and stabling for forty additional horses. His trusty foreman, David Frazer, was placed in charge of the establishment during his master's frequent absences to Ireland, Lincoln Fair, etc. David received high wages, and earned them well. A brilliant horseman, he knew how to display every animal he bestrode to full advantage. Directly he took the reins up in a firm, yet light grasp, you could see the quadruped champ at the bit in a playful, contented manner, and dropping his head and arching his neck, he would start off trotting or cantering, as the case might be, quite placidly and collectedly. It was a sight to see David pop over the show fences, which were in a field adjoining the stables. He rode up quietly and careless-like to within a few yards, then he gave his horse his head, and it all seemed so ridiculously easy, that nine times out of ten the customers went away perfectly satisfied after seeing David perform.

If the animal did not jump in quite the same form when they got on his back they very naturally attributed the fact to accident rather than to any inferior horsemanship on their part. Then David would say in his most artless manner—and he could be wonderfully artless when he chose—"That's it, sir. You've hit the right nail on the head. The truth is, our horses get to ken these fences after a bit, and jump them cunning; but you'll hae no cause to complain of this guid beastie in the hunting field. You may take my word for it." And they generally did.

A very canny Scot was David—discreet and cautious, knowing how to hold his tongue or to throw in a few impressive words just as the occasion seemed to demand. Mr. Ruddle had in him a most valuable auxiliary, and if it were necessary to try a new purchase in the hunting field, so as to ascertain what price to put on him, he knew that according to David's report—good, bad, or indifferent—the question might be safely settled. The two men worked wonderfully well together, and understood each other thoroughly. David concurred with his master in thinking honesty the best policy; only he put in a saving clause, "Whenever it was practicable." He never went out of his way to tell a falsehood. He looked upon such conduct as sheer folly; but, when absolutely imperative, he possessed a special gift in being able to invent a good thumping lie without moving so much as a muscle of his shrewd, hard-featured face.

The following is one of the anecdotes that went the round of the county:

David sold a valuable hunter to a gentleman, whose name it is not necessary to mention. The price was three hundred guineas. He was a fine upstanding animal, but David knew that his looks were the best part of him. In short, he was more than usually anxious to effect a deal.

"He is good at timber, I understood you to say?" said the customer interrogatively.

"First-rate," answered David.   "You cannot put him doon if you try ever so."

"And you can answer for his not shirking water? We have a great·many brooks in our part of the world."

"Sir," said David solemnly, "you may believe me or not as you like, but I've seen him tak water over and over again with my own eyes."

The gentleman bought the horse and went away perfectly satisfied.   David hoped he had seen the last both of him and of his three hundred guinea hunter. Imagine his annoyance when the purchaser reappeared a few days after the transaction in a vile temper, and bringing the horse back with him.

"You told me he was a water-jumper," he said indignantly.   "I particularly asked the question, and you ·swore he was."

"No, sir, never," answered David, with the utmost composure.

"What!   You deny your own words?   The brute stopped dead short at Burnside brook on Thursday last, and shot me clean over his head.   Pray, how do you account for that?"

"Insecurity of seat," murmured David, smiling blandly, "joost resulting in a voluntary."

"No such thing.   I don't believe the horse had ever seen a brook in his life.   What explanation have you to give?"

"A verra guid one," said David, in his quietest and most pacific voice; "I told you naething but the truth. What I did say was that I'd often seen him *tak* water. And so I have.   Here, Tom," calling to a stableman who happened to be passing by at the moment, "bring a boocket."

"—— your bucket," exclaimed the stranger, "you've done me clean."

"Sir," said David, very dignified, "gentlemen who come to Mr. Ruddle's yaird are welcome to every trial. It is na necessary for them to tak any one's word.   We

14

prefair their relying on their own judgment. If you hae been doon, you hae doon yourself."

The individual happened to be an unpopular man, and when the story got about in the county, as it did after a bit, the laugh was all on David's side. It was generally admitted that although he might have departed from the spirit, no one could allege that he had diverged from the letter of the truth, and the owner of the Water-taker—as the horse was promptly christened—received but little sympathy.

As may be gathered from the above specimen, it took a very sharp fellow to get the better of David. At first, Mr. Ruddle tried an occasional mild reproof, but he soon found out that the only way to manage his foreman was by giving him his head entirely. He went kindly enough if you let him alone, but he would not stand a touch of the curb.

CHAPTER XXVI.

A GALLANT GIRL.

No one had been more genuinely grieved by Squire Herrick's death than Mr. Ruddle. He felt as if he had lost a personal friend, and mourned truly for his decease. It so chanced that on the afternoon of Kitty's return from town he was standing in the yard nibbling a straw, and thinking sadly of the departed man, and what a gap his burly figure would leave in the hunting field, when he heard the sound of wheels. Looking up, he saw Kitty approaching, evidently with the purpose of paying him a visit.

"Why, Miss Herrick!" he exclaimed in surprise. "You don't mean to say it's you. I heard you had gone to London."

"I've been and come back again," said the girl, throwing the reins on Pattercake's quarters. "The fact is, Mr. Ruddle," and the blood rushed up to her face, "I want to have a talk with you. Are you busy?"

"No, miss, not for another hour."

Her eyes wandered in the direction of the house—a low, old-fashioned farm building.

"Perhaps you'd like to come in," said Peter. "It's more private-like."

"Thank you, Mr. Ruddle. I would rather not be seen just at present. I wont detain you long, but I've something very particular to say." And she jumped lightly down from the cart, before the gallant Peter could come to her assistance.

Mr. Ruddle preceded her into a low-roofed hall with heavy oaken rafters, and ceremoniously opened the parlor door. It was a room always kept very prim and polished, ready for the reception of visitors.

Kitty sat down on the nearest chair, and nervously twisted the fringe of its crochet antimaccassar round her forefinger.

"I have come, Mr. Ruddle, to ask a favor of you."

"If I can help you in any way, Miss Kitty," said Peter, "I shall be only too proud." He had known her since she was quite a little thing, and always called her Miss Kitty, except when he endeavored to appear extra polite. "Believe me," and he fumbled in his pocket until he found a large handkerchief with which he proceeded to blow his nose, "no one sympathizes with you in the loss you have sustained more than I. I would give half I am worth to bring the Squire back amongst us all again."

"Thank you, Mr. Ruddle," she said, trying hard to keep her voice steady. "I know you liked him. I should not have applied to you now had I not felt sure you would do my father's daughter a good turn if you could."

"Ay, that I would," he said emphatically.

"Perhaps you have heard," she continued, "that I have lost my fortune, and am penniless."

"I did hear a rumor to that effect, Miss Kitty, but I did not believe it."

"It is quite true, nevertheless. Henceforth I must work for my living. That is what I have come about. The fact is, Mr. Ruddle, I'm not suited for a governess, and I'm not clever enough to go on the stage, or write books, or do anything that brings in money. After thinking matters over very seriously, I have arrived at the conclusion that there is only one way in which I am really fitted to gain an honest livelihood. And so"— hesitating—"I have made up my mind to apply to you."

"To me!" exclaimed Mr. Ruddle in astonishment, not yet perceiving what she was driving at.

"Yes," returned Kitty, gaining courage now that she had broken the ice. "Do you remember, the very

last time my dear father and I were over here together,
your saying that you wished you could find a good lady
rider to show off your horses to your female customers?
It doesn't do for me to boast; but you have seen me
going to hounds, and know pretty well how I can ride.
If you think me good enough to fill the place I should ·
like to do so."

There, the murder was out at last, and she could
feel herself turning furiously red. Mr. Ruddle scratched
his head. To tell the truth, he was fairly startled by
the proposition. About the girl's capacity there could
be no doubt. She was the finest rider in the county,
but for his beloved master's daughter to turn horse-
breaker—a young lady who it was well known might
marry a duke's son, and who had always associated
with the best families in the place—appeared to him
such a terrible come-down that he could not reconcile
it to his ideas—at all events, not when first mooted.

"You are surely joking, Miss Kitty," he said disap-
provingly.

"Is it likely I should joke at such a time as this?"
she returned.

"But you do not know the hardships of the life. You
are not fit for it."

"I am fit for no other, and whether it be hard or easy
I must live. Besides," she added, blushing brightly,
"it may not last long."

"I will be quite frank with you, Miss Kitty," said Mr.
Ruddle, trying to dissuade her from a project which he
could not help regarding unfavorably. "It is true that
I am anxious to secure the services of a female horse-
breaker, but for many reasons I should prefer her not
being a lady by birth. It complicates matters very
considerably."

"In what way, Mr. Ruddle?"

"Let me set a few plain facts before you, Miss Kitty,
and name some of the duties such a person would have
to perform, then perhaps the question will answer itself.
To begin with, she would be called upon to get up at

five every morning of her life except Sundays, and go exercising at six. The work is monotonous in the extreme; the weather is often cold, wet, windy, and trying even to a strong constitution——"

"I am not the least afraid of my health breaking down," interrupted Kitty. "It is wonderfully good."

"When she came in," continued Mr. Ruddle, bent on painting the picture in its darkest colors, "she would have to superintend the stable where the light-weight hunters are lodged, see that the men feed and groom their charges properly, report all casualties, and keep account of the forage used. Afterwards there will probably be an invalid or two to take for an airing. By eleven everything has to be ready for the day. After that hour she must be prepared at any moment to jump on to some strange animal that a customer may happen to fancy, and show off his paces and fencing. There is always a certain amount of risk connected with the latter proceeding. Bad falls will occur now and again. Besides which, there are many times when I may consider it advantageous to the business to send her out hunting. In short, she would have to be a servant under my orders, just like any other, and expect but few privileges on account of her sex. However straight a dealer may be—and I do my best to give satisfaction—there are certain transactions inevitably attendant on the profession which would not prove exactly pleasant for a lady—a real lady, I mean—to be mixed up in."

"I am prepared not to find everything just to my liking," said Kitty.

"Then, too," went on Mr. Ruddle, steadily, "the men are sometimes rough, and might annoy you by unseemly language. I don't say they would, but they might, especially when they got a drop of liquor inside their skins. David is a queerish customer to deal with when once he gets put out. He does not always pause to choose his words, and you would have to be subject to his orders in my absence. The fact is, Miss Kitty," wound up Mr. Ruddle, with genuine distress, "I should not like you to undergo the discomforts and disagreeables of the situation."

She had listened very quietly to his remarks, and given them grave attention, but they failed to change her determination. Every objection which he brought forth had already presented itself to her mind, and taking the good and the bad together, she had decided that she could not do better just at present. Besides, to be near Cyril, and have the opportunity of seeing and talking to him every now and again, was an inducement for which she was prepared to sacrifice a great deal in the way of personal comfort. So in answer to Mr. Ruddle's attempts at dissuasion, she said:

"What you say is no doubt true, and I am genuinely obliged to you for the kind consideration you display on my behalf; but do you suppose that I have not already thought of all these things? The whole question is simply this: Beggars can't be choosers. If I were Miss Herrick of Herrington Hall still, with a handsome fortune and plenty to live on, I should not for one moment contemplate turning lady horse-breaker; but not having any income whatever, I must go into service of some sort. I know more about horses than about anything else, and would prefer being with you than with a complete stranger. No," she went on rapidly, as he made a gesture of dissent, "please hear me out. I know what you are thinking of. You think I am too much of a fine lady for the place; but my father always taught me that one of the truest attributes of a lady—in the real sense of the word—was to be able to turn her hand to anything. So, Mr. Ruddle, you need not be afraid of my not obeying orders, or forgetting that I am a paid servant. If you will only give me a trial you will see that I can be as good as my word. I will strive my utmost to please your customers, and endeavor in every way to earn the wages that you give me. I can't say more. Anything that a humbly born woman would do in the same situation I will do also. As I said before, I must live, and I have special reasons for not wishing to leave the county this winter. Therefore, you will let me have the place, yes or no? If you decide against me, I shall go to-morrow and offer my services to Mr. Hillyard, of Wrecester."

"Really, Miss Kitty," said Mr. Ruddle, feeling that he would have to give in, even against his better judgment, "I hardly know what reply to make. You place me in a very awkward position. It grieves me to refuse any request of yours, and yet——" stopping short.

"And yet," she interrupted, a trifle piqued at his reluctance, "you consider me too useless for the situation.".

"Indeed no, Miss Kitty. Please don't think that. You're the finest lady rider, bar none, I ever set eyes on, and I don't mind telling you so to your face; but you see the hunting season is at hand, and I shall want some one to go out, maybe two or three times a week, and ride the horses about for a couple of hours or so, just to catch the public eye. Now," he concluded, with considerable embarrassment, "I don't suppose you would like to appear in the field so soon after the Squire's death."

She thought for a moment, and as she sat facing the light a close observer might have seen that her upper lip and the muscles round her eyes quivered. Then she said in a subdued but decided voice:

"I have failed to make the situation clear, since you do not appear to understand that it is not a question of *liking*, but of necessity. It is imperative that for the next few months I should earn my bread in some manner. If papa is in heaven, he will know that I intend no disrespect to his memory, and the fact of my sitting on a saddle so many hours a day will not render it any the less dear. *He* would not think the worse of me for trying to gain a living in the only way that I can."

There was a touch of reproach in her tone which caused Mr. Ruddle to feel very uncomfortable, although he was conscious of the integrity of his motives, and that if he appeared stubborn it was only for her ultimate welfare according to his lights. He made one last effort, but without much hope of its proving successful.

"If it is merely to be a temporary arrangement, could you not put up with your friends for a while?" he suggested.

She tossed back her head, and a set expression hardened the lines of her pretty round face.

"No, Mr. Ruddle, I could not. I can't enter into my reasons, but I would rather work my fingers to the bone than place myself in a dependent position. Nobody possessing any proper pride would deliberately choose to be the recipient of a grudgingly-given charity sooner than make an effort to maintain him or her self. I have learned that in the last day or two." She spoke rather bitterly, but with such decision that Peter realized the fruitlessness of any further opposition.

Somehow, the sight of her seated there in her deep mourning garments, the graceful pose of her supple young figure, and the clear gaze of her bright appealing eyes, quite overcame the honest fellow. He felt ready to do anything in the world at her bidding. As he listened to her remarks, which showed such a mixture of girlish inexperience and delicate womanly spirit, a supreme pity and admiration filled his heart. She might be wrong in the resolve she had formed, but there was no denying her bravery and high courage. The majority of girls in her position would have wrung their white hands idly and bewailed their sad lot, without taking any steps to ameliorate it; whereas she, throughout their interview, had never uttered a complaint, nor breathed a single word of reproach against her father's name, but faced poverty and privation like a heroine. She was a gallant girl, and Mr. Ruddle felt as if he could have fallen down and kissed the hem of her garment.

CHAPTER XXVII.

No wonder Mrs. Ruddle called Mr. Ruddle a fool, and deemed it incumbent to engage none but the very ugliest maid-servants. He was impressionable; and, as she often declared, if she had not been there to look after it, that great soft heart of his would have been nothing better than an hotel, with people constantly walking in and out. Her principal wifely duty consisted in rigorously and faithfully guarding the weak organ of her spouse from all designing females, and it was astonishing how constantly she was kept employed.

Peter was vaguely aware that in yielding to Kitty's request he should probably call down the vials of Mrs. Ruddle's wrath on his devoted head. He foresaw the risk of introducing a young and pretty girl into the stable-yard, but he was no longer capable of offering further resistance to his visitor's wishes. She disarmed opposition, and even if a matrimonial quarrel were the result, he felt compelled to yield. Kitty's soft voice, star-like eyes, and sweet face were too much for him. They got the better of his common sense.

"Well," she said, a trifle impatiently, "time is passing, and I must not trespass too much on your good nature. What is your decision? Are you going to send me away depressed and despondent, or are you prepared to act the part of a true friend in my sore distress?"

Mr. Ruddle brought his great broad fist down with a thump on the table, and his throat swelled so that his voice was quite husky.

"God bless you, Miss Kitty," he said. "I can't bear

to think of your having to take to such a trade. It
don't seem the thing.   But right or wrong, I can't say
no, so let it be as you will."

She smiled, and putting out her hand, said, "Thank
you, Mr. Ruddle.   I felt sure I could depend on your
helping me in my trouble."

"A pound a week," he continued apologetically, "is
all I can afford to give, and five per cent. commission
on the horses sold out of your stable.   That mounts up
to something, but it's a mere drop in the ocean to a
lady like you."

"A lady like me doesn't take more to keep her than
a poor person," she answered brightly, "so please, Mr.
Ruddle, don't talk like that in the future.   Henceforth
you must forget who I am, and remember me only as
a friendless girl whom you are very kindly assisting.
And now," rising to her feet, "I will not detain you any
longer.   One question more before I go.   When shall
I enter on my new duties?"

"The sooner the better," he replied.   "I could do with
you at once.   We are likely to be very busy the next
few weeks."

"All right, then.   If convenient to you, I will come
the day after to-morrow.   By the bye, will you buy
Pattercake and Tiny Tim?   I must dispose of them
somehow, and should very much like them to pass into
good hands and have a comfortable home."

Mr. Ruddle pricked up his ears at this.   His business
instincts at once woke into life.   He knew, moreover,
that the chance of acquiring two such animals did not
often present itself.

"What's the price?" he inquired, coming to the main
point without beating about the bush.

She hesitated a moment before replying.   "I would
rather leave it to you, please, Mr. Ruddle.   I am afraid
I might ask too much.   The truth is, I think such a lot
of Tiny Tim that unless circumstances obliged me to
part with him I would not consider his value represented by a check for five hundred.   If any one were to

give me that sum to-morrow I should not know where to go to find his equal."

"That is always the way with favorites," said Mr. Ruddle, "and I agree with you—a better animal never was foaled. Nevertheless, he has two faults."

"What are they?" she demanded, with a touch of indignation.

"First and foremost, he doesn't stand much over fifteen-two; and secondly, although *you* can ride him it is not everybody who could. Put a fidgety, nervous woman on his back, and I question very much whether she would enjoy her day's hunting. He *will* be in the front rank."

"That's true," she said, with a smile. "Directly hounds run there's no keeping the good little horse back."

"May I make so bold as to offer a suggestion?" said Mr. Ruddle.

"Most certainly."

"Well, then, send the horses over here, and let me sell them for you for as much as I can get. They will make more money that way, and of course from you I shall not want any commission. I have a party in my eye at this very moment."

"Really! Mr. Ruddle."

"Yes, I received a letter yesterday morning from Mr. Van Agnew—the gentleman who has taken Gretton Grange—saying that he and his sister were on the lookout for horses, and would come over here next Wednesday. Report says they don't stick at price when they take a fancy to an animal, and it struck me if you were to ride Tiny Tim, and show him off yourself, we might get between two and three hundred for him."

Kitty approved highly of this idea, and arranged that Pattercake and the bay should change stables on the morrow. Then, having settled everything with Mr. Ruddle to her satisfaction, she shook hands with him and drove off, feeling very much more at ease respecting the future. It was quite a weight off her mind to

be able to look forward confidently to supporting herself throughout the winter without either having to beg
for or accept charity.   A pound a week was not much,
certainly, but it would enable her to subsist, especially
if she had three or four hundred pounds from the sale
of the horses to start with and to fall back upon in the
event of illness.

Directly she left Mr. Ruddle she went straight to
call on one Mrs. Perkins, who had been a laundry-maid
at Herrington Hall, and since then had removed to
Belfield, where she set up as a washerwoman.   Mrs.
Perkins was delighted to see her former mistress.   She
had a neat little cottage, not a hundred yards from Mr.
Ruddle's stables, and on hearing Kitty's story at once
offered to board and lodge her for the sum of fifteen
shillings weekly.   For this it was agreed the girl should
have the use of a tiny bedroom and a sitting-room.

"I shant be much at home, except in the evening," said Kitty, "so I hope you wont find me in the
way."

"I'm not likely ever to do that, Miss Herrick," came
the hearty response.   "But I can't a-bear to think of
your coming to live with the likes of me."

"I shall have five shillings over every week for
pocket-money," said Kitty to herself on the way home.
"Not so bad after all.   When the time comes"—and
a dimple showed in her round cheeks—"I shall be able
to buy quite a magnificent *trousseau*.   Heigho! I wonder what Cyril will say when he hears of the step I
have taken.   I do hope he wont be angry, and consider it *infra dig*.   If people would only recognize that
when one has to work it does not answer to be too particular, then they would not find so much fault with
their poorer brethren.   As it is," and she gave an
involuntary sigh, "I suppose I must look forward to a
perfect hurricane of abuse.   And yet, what could I do
better than I have done?   I wish to goodness my critics
would answer the question; for cut me up as they may,
I maintain that it is by no means an easy thing for a

girl reared as I have been, in the lap of luxury, to earn even a pound a week."

And she was right. If anybody doubts it, let them wait till they find themselves similarly situated, and then see if it be wiser to say, "I am too good for this—too fine for that," or to put their pride in their pocket and accept any employment rather than beg for grudgingly given alms from friends and relatives. There is no help like self-help; and it has this further advantage: it strengthens and ennobles the character. Instead of rendering people mere puppets in the hands of others, it enables them to stand alone.

Left to himself, Mr. Ruddle stole cautiously upstairs, intending to change his coat before going to the station. He had reason to believe that Mrs. Ruddle was busily engaged in the kitchen, superintending the salting of a pig newly killed; and wishing to think over his recent arrangement with Kitty, he was anxious not to disturb her. No sooner, however, had he reached the landing opposite his bedroom door than he heard a heavy step in his rear, and turning round with a guilty start, he espied the partner of his bosom immediately behind.

Now it must be known that at the precise moment when Kitty mounted into her pony trap, Mrs. Ruddle, happening to look out of the window, caught sight of a petticoat fluttering. A minute before she had heard the parlor door slam, and being an active-minded woman, she at once put two and two together. She was not jealous—not she; but she did not approve, on principle, of Peter receiving female visitors unbeknown to her. Consequently, she promptly withdrew her plump hands from the tub in which they were immersed, dried them hastily on a clean towel, and set off there and then in pursuit of her lord.

"Who was that, Peter?" she demanded, when she recovered breath enough to be able to speak.

He glanced at her with an air of well-simulated surprise.

"Who do you mean, my dear? There have been so

many people here to-day that, really, I get mixed among them all."

"Are your lady friends so numerous as all that?" she retorted. "You know perfectly well who I mean."

Mr. Ruddle brushed away a particle of dust from his shirt front. On principle he objected to being cross-examined, and familiarity with the process had not the effect of rendering him more partial to it. Nevertheless, there were many occasions on which, *nolens volens,* he was forced to resign himself to the inevitable; and this was one of them. So, seeing no help for it, he replied in his mildest and most conciliatory one:

"It was Miss Herrick, Nancy."

Mrs. Ruddle lifted up her coarse dark eyebrows in astonishment.

"Miss Herrick! and her father only dead a few days ago. What on earth did she want, pray?"

"It appears she is ruined," he answered, "and hasn't a penny in the world."

"No, Peter! You don't say so? That is news."

"It's true though—true as gospel. She told me so with her own lips, and mighty sorry I felt for the poor thing."

"So I suppose. You always do feel sorry for good-looking young women in distress. They can get round you in a minute. And what call had Miss Herrick to come here and confide her affairs to you without ever having the civility to ask to see your wife?"

"It was a pure matter of business, Nancy," he said soothingly—"a pure matter of business."

"In that case," said Mrs. Ruddle incredulously, for she had a firm belief in the fascinations of her Peter, and should not have thought it odd if a duchess had fallen in love with him, "I presume you have no objection to stating its nature?"

"Miss Herrick wished to sell her horses, and——" stopping short, undecided whether to make a confession which sooner or later must be told, or to withhold it as long as possible. But that temporary hesitation was fatal, and roused Mrs. Ruddle's suspicions to a fiery flame. There was a reserve and reluctance about Peter's manner which caused her to scent a mystery.

"And what?" she queried, bent on finding out the whole truth.

"Nothing, my dear, nothing," he answered evasively.

She fixed her cold green eye sternly upon him, and Peter changed countenance under its gaze.

"Yes, there is something," she said impressively. "I can tell that by your shuffly way of speaking. It aint natural to you. Now, Mr. Ruddle,"—she always called him Mr. Ruddle when she wished to be more than commonly dignified,—"I'm your wife, and it's not a bit of good your trying to hide anything from me. You know I always find you out in the long run."

This was true enough, as he acknowledged with a suppressed groan. Concealment, under the circumstances, was manifestly impossible without disturbing the domestic harmony.

"The fact is," he said, somewhat sheepishly, "Miss Herrick came to-day to beg me to engage her as a lady rider."

The color mounted to Mrs. Ruddle's face. She knew very little of Kitty, but she cherished an instinctive antagonism against her, for was not this the girl whom her susceptible Peter was always lauding up to the skies and quoting as a paragon of perfection? To have her perpetually hanging about the stable-yard, with him in constant attendance, was a prospect which by no means commended itself to Mrs. Ruddle.

"Well, I never!" she gasped. "It only shows what the world's coming to. You haven't gone and said you'd take her, Peter. You may be a fool, but surely you've never been such an idiot as all that?"

Her words provoked him.

"And why shouldn't I, pray? What have you to say against it, Mrs. Ruddle?" he returned, with considerable warmth.

"What have I to say against it? Everything. Any

one in their senses would tell you that if you want to
turn the yard topsy-turvy, and set all the men at sixes
and sevens, the way to do it is to introduce a female in
their midst.   You'll have David falling in love with
her to begin with."

Mr. Ruddle laughed out loud.   The idea tickled him
immensely, and struck him as being exquisitely ludi-
crous and far-fetched.

"David!" he exclaimed.   "What nonsense, Nancy!
You are such a one for fancying things."

"Am I, Mr. Ruddle?   Thank you, Mr. Ruddle.   You
take care, or you'll be the next to follow suit.   Lady
horse-breaker indeed!" and she shrugged her fat shoulders angrily.   "Lady Mischief would be a better name
for her.   You may laugh now, but you mark my words,
Peter; you'll live to rue this day's work."

"Come, come," he said impatiently, "that's enough.
I must be off, else I shall miss the train."   And he
slammed his bedroom door.   It is noteworthy that
whenever Benedict commits an action of whose wisdom
he is secretly doubtful nothing irritates him so much
as to be rated by his wife.   And wives possess such a
marvellous talent for attack.   It is useless saying to
them, "My dear, I am a man, and as a result of that
fact, your superior.   It is your duty to love, honor, and
obey."   They decline most decidedly to do anything of
the sort.   And why?   Because with almost impish faculties of perception they soon discover that with all
their talk they are very weak in reality, and each of one's
foibles is as patent as if printed in a book.   This is
what gives a married woman so much power, and makes
even a Samson quail before the sharp eye and incisive
tongue of a four-foot-high woman.

15

CHAPTER XXVIII.

IN THE LIGHT-WEIGHT STABLE.

On the appointed day Kitty transferred herself and her belongings to Belfield. To her surprise, she had not heard from Cyril since leaving town, and his silence caused her to feel extremely uneasy. Could it be that his mother's influence had prevailed directly her back was turned? She could account in no other way for not receiving a letter from him, and it was perhaps fortunate that during her short stay at Herrington she was so busy as to have little time for thought.

To her no small relief, Lord Algy did not come to see her again. To tell the truth, she rather dreaded what he would say when he learned that she had engaged herself to Mr. Ruddle as a horse-breaker, and was secretly thankful to get installed in her new situation without any of her friends making a fuss, or damping her spirits by their opposition. So when she received a note from Lord Algy intimating that he was unexpectedly forced to go away for a couple of days on business, and that he had arranged with Mr. Morgan that she might stay on at Herrington until the place was sold by auction a month hence, quite a weight of apprehension was removed from her mind. The step once taken past recall, then it would not matter so much what people said—she believed she could bear their criticisms better. So when she had unpacked her trunk, and succeeded in stowing away her various possessions in Mrs. Perkins's two diminutive apartments, she put on her habit, and at once went over to Mr. Ruddle's. That gentleman was in the yard when she arrived, and lost no time in showing her round the premises and giving *her his* instructions. There were about a dozen or fourteen horses standing in the light-weight stable, over which he proposed she should preside. They had just been dressed and groomed, and looked a very smart, useful lot. The one that took Kitty's fancy most was a sporting gray mare about three parts bred, with tremendous quarters, a lean, varmint-like head and neck, and beautiful shoulders. She was on the point of going up to her when Mr. Ruddle said warningly, " Be careful, Miss Kitty. She's a sweet creature out, but a regular devil in the stable—bites and lets fly without the slightest provocation."

Kitty drew back a step or two, and gazed attentively at the mare.

"She ought not to be a bad-tempered animal," she said, after a tolerably long scrutiny. "Her eye is not really wicked. She gives me rather the idea of having a naturally nervous temperament, rendered still more so by ill-usage. How long have you had her?"

"Some little time," answered Mr. Ruddle. "The fact is, she met with a serious accident in the summer, and has only just come round to be what you might call herself again. Do you see that blemish there?" and he pointed to a newly healed scar on her off fore fetlock, which was permanently enlarged. "She got it over wire."

"What a pity," ejaculated Kitty. "How was the injury done?"

"The party who owned her," resumed Mr. Ruddle, "turned her out with about half a dozen other horses— always a risky thing to do. It appears they took to chevvying each other round the field, and this mare tried her level best to jump a wire poultry netting between six and seven feet high. I happened to see her shortly afterwards. She was in a very bad way then, and her owner thought she'd never be fit for anything again. I held a contrary opinion, and made him an offer which he saw reason to accept, and here she is," he concluded, keeping a respectful distance from the gray's heels, which she was shifting uneasily.

"She looks an uncommonly nice mount, blemish not-withstanding," said Kitty, struck by the mare's good points.

"She's a regular nailer across country," said Mr. Ruddle. "I don't think I ever saw a much finer performer for her size. Since she came round, I let David take her over our fences, just to see if she had lost her form or not."

"The big or the little fences?" asked Kitty, with a smile, for she knew that customers were never favored to the former unless Mr. Ruddle were tolerably sure of his animal. "There is a considerable difference between them, if you will excuse my saying so."

He laughed a hearty laugh.

"Right you are, Miss Kitty. I see you know all about it. But I mean the big course this time, and it takes a real good hunter to jump those fences. This mare never so much as touched a twig. She cleared everything like a bird, and although she was out of practice and had no lead, did not offer to refuse. That's the sort for a lady. They want something free. No woman ought ever to ride a slug that requires whipping and spurring. For my part, I always say it's bad enough to have to make up your own mind without having to make up your gee's into the bargain."

"Is she a very high-priced one?" inquired Kitty, still scrutinizing the mare.

"Well, you see," he answered confidently, "it's like this. I bought her cheap, and as she has that unfortunate blemish, which, of course, takes something off her value, I can afford to sell her at a reasonable figure. Somewhere about a hundred and forty was the price I put upon her. That reminds me," pulling out his watch, "I've got Miss Bretby coming over here this morning to look at the little gray. I told her I thought I had one that would suit. Perhaps you wouldn't mind giving her a show, Miss Kitty?"

"Not in the least," said the girl, brightening up at the prospect of a ride. "What else am I here for?"

"The mare has got a very light mouth," said Mr. Ruddle, "and goes best when you let her head alone. She only wants good hands, however, and as far as jumping goes, you need not be afraid to set her at a house."

"Am I to take her over the big course?" inquired Kitty innocently.

"I don't know, yet. That depends upon how things shape. But if Miss Bretby seems sweet, and really like buying, I'll give you the word. When I put up my hand so "—and Mr. Ruddle raised his right arm—"you'll understand it's always the signal to stop."

"All right," said Kitty, "I'll do my best to obey instructions."

"By the bye," said Mr. Ruddle, "if at any time a customer should call whilst I am out of the way, I may as well tell you how we generally proceed. As a rule, we don't begin by showing the animal we intend to sell. You may very naturally ask why. The reason is, that with nine purchasers out of ten they prefer having a look round first. Coming into a dealer's yard is much like going shopping. Folks wont make up their minds all at once, and almost invariably require a little gentle humoring and persuasion from the vender. Consequently, I call attention first to one or two horses that I feel pretty confident wont suit. Customers dearly love displaying their knowledge by finding fault, and it's wonderful the remarks they pass sometimes. I often think to myself that if they only knew how they expose their ignorance—of course, I'm speaking of the generality—they would hold their tongues. There was a party in the other day who actually found fault with that mare's shoulders," pointing to the gray, "and called them loaded."

"He must have been an ignoramus," said Kitty, laughing. "Her shoulders are precisely her strongest point."

"So one would have thought. After we have wasted ten or fifteen minutes at this sort of game," proceeded

Mr. Rudd. , "we gradually work round to the right animal, introducing him as something very special. Then, when we have had a bit of a jaw, the horse is brought out of the stable, along with any others that may happen to have taken the customer's eye. Lots of people are quite content if they see the nag they fancy popped over one or two little cock fences, and in that case we don't go out of our way to recommend the big course, where the fences take some doing. If, however, the customer does not appear satisfied—and the knowing cards very often don't—and we feel sure of our animal, then we give a real good show which nearly always ends in a satisfactory deal, unless any unforeseen mishap takes place."

A roguish smile lit up Kitty's face. It was extremely amusing being given a peep behind the scenes.

"No doubt I shall learn discretion after a while," she said. "But I may as well confess, Mr. Ruddle, that I had an inkling of all this before. I have not paid you repeated visits without making use of my eyes."

The conversation was here interrupted by David Frazer, who came to tell Mr. Ruddle that Miss Bretby had arrived.

"Put the best clothing on to the gray mare and the little brown horse with the hogged mane," he said to a sulky-looking helper in whose charge the two animals apparently were. "We shall be round in two or three minutes, so look sharp." Then to Kitty:

"You know Miss Bretby, of course?"

"Yes," she said, with a shrug of the shoulders. "Who does not? In four and-twenty hours from now every one all over the county will be acquainted with the startling intelligence that Miss Herrick, of Herrington Hall, has turned horse-breaker. It's just like my luck, her coming here in search of a horse the very day that I enter upon my new duties."

Alicia Bretby was a maiden lady possessing an income of about two thousand a year, whose father and mother were both dead. She was at that indefinite

. time of a spinster's life when she never alludes to her age, and the older she grows the younger and more child-like she tries to appear. In the main, she was an empty, good-natured soul, hail fellow well met with everybody who gave her an inch, and with a fine capacity for ignoring a snub, which useful quality enabled her to exist on excellent terms with herself and on fairly good terms with her friends and neighbors. She had one fault, however, which caused the hypercritical to fight shy of her. She was a most inveterate gossip, and knew people's affairs rather better than they did themselves. The latest scandal was always at her fingers' ends, whilst if she could not manage to amass some choice story she would generally contrive to make one up to meet the exigency of the moment. No wonder, then, if she was the last person whom Kitty would have elected to see. She fancied she could hear her going about from one to the other saying, "What do you think? Kitty Herrick has gone in for horse-breaking, and is actually showing off hunters in Mr. Ruddle's yard. Did you ever know of a lady doing such a thing?"

Miss Bretby was an ardent sportswoman, and although by no means an accomplished equestrienne, possessed one great qualification—plenty of pluck. She was not at all afraid of bundling over the fences out hunting. Nevertheless, she required to be warmed up, and did not appear to full advantage until her elderly blood was aglow. Then she would shove and bustle and push with the best. At the beginning of the present season she had had the bad luck to stake her favorite horse— a wonderfully good animal whom she had hunted for eight winters. Such a loss is not easily repaired, and after scouring the county in hopes of picking up a bargain, she found herself compelled to apply to Mr. Ruddle. Hence her visit.

When Kitty heard the fair Alicia's voice—it was a remarkably squeaky one—in the distance, and perceived her and Mr. Ruddle approaching the light-weight stable, a nervous tremor passed through her frame. The color flamed up to her face, and her heart beat with loud, rapid pulsations. She would have given a great deal to avoid the coming encounter. There was nothing for it, however, but to stand her ground and carry off matters with a high hand. After a time, no doubt, she would get accustomed to meeting her former friends. It was only at first that the sight of an acquaintance made her feel so awkward and uncomfortable. She had done nothing to be ashamed of really. Well! and she gave her nicely poised head a defiant toss, if she wasn't good enough for them she didn't care. They were quite welcome to cut her if they liked. It was in this mood that she awaited Miss Bretby.

"What!" exclaimed that lady, giving a start of surprise as Mr. Ruddle pushed open the stable door and she perceived Kitty. "You here, of all people in the world, and," glancing at the girl's apparel, "in your riding habit too. What on earth are you doing?"

Kitty's eyes flashed under their long lashes. She was ready to fight on very small provocation.

"I am here as Mr. Ruddle's servant," she said, with a composure too exaggerated to be real.

"Are you mad, child? I suppose your troubles have turned your head," said Miss Bretby, thoroughly astonished.

Then, in spite of all Kitty's efforts at self-control, her voice trembled as she said, "Haven't you heard?"

"Heard! No, heard what?" said Miss Bretby, pricking up her ears.

"That I am ruined. I thought everybody knew it by this time. You can tell them if you like," she went on proudly, "that I am left penniless, and have to support myself. That is why I am here, not—" and her eyes filled, "because I have forgotten dear papa."

"You poor lamb," exclaimed Miss Bretby, who was by no means a bad-hearted woman. "I don't know whether to be more shocked or surprised."

"On reflection, you will probably be most shocked,"

said Kitty sarcastically. "I don't pretend that I have accepted my present position from choice, but since I *am* here the greatest kindness you can do me is to withhold your criticism. Abuse me as much as you like behind my back, but be merciful enough not to lecture me to my face."

CHAPTER XXIX.

KITTY could not have disarmed Miss Bretby more thoroughly than by this speech. Moreover, there was a pathos in her voice and a dignity in her manner which impressed the elder lady in spite of herself. But Miss Bretby's curiosity quickly triumphed over her tact. The thought of having such a wonderful story to tell stimulated her, and she was proceeding to ply poor Kitty with no end of questions when Mr. Ruddle, with an innate fineness and delicacy of feeling which would have done credit to a gentleman, came to the rescue.

"Excuse me, Miss Bretby," he said, "but I have another appointment at twelve o'clock. What do you say to having a look round the stable, and then if you wish to talk to Miss Herrick you can do so afterwards? There is a nice, snug saddle-room close by, which I hope she wont hesitate to use when she wishes to receive her friends."

The remark in itself was kind, and served the purpose of creating a diversion. Nevertheless, the blood crimsoned Kitty's face as she listened to it. The saddle-room indeed! See her friends in the saddle-room! Somehow it made her realize the change in her circumstances more than all that had gone before. Hitherto she had been sustained by a sense of novelty and adventure—a feeling that she was doing a plucky, even an unusual, thing; but Miss Bretby's ill-concealed surprise and openly expressed commiseration produced a revolution in her ideas. She began to see matters in a different light, and suffered from a secret shame at having reduced herself to the level of a groom. Nothing would

234

have induced her, however, to own to the fact. It might
be pride, or it might be obstinacy, but from the
moment her opinions underwent a change she was prepared to vindicate her actions with redoubled energy.
The person who ought to have helped her had failed
·her in her need—she could not refrain from acknowledging this—and so she had been thrown entirely on her
own resources. Cyril might easily have stuck up for
her. Now that she had had time to think over his conduct, she admitted with pain and bitterness that his
adherence was but lukewarm. He need not have let
her travel back to the country all alone; but even had
he done so he ought certainly to have written. She
would not have treated him as he had treated her.

She dismissed these dismal thoughts, however, when
the mare was saddled and brought out and Mr. Ruddle
politely requested her to put her through her paces.
The mere pleasure of sitting on a good, springy animal's back and cantering sharply through the autumnal
air sufficed to dispel all morbid fancies. Mr. Ruddle's
praise of the gray did not prove exaggerated. She
moved wonderfully well out-of-doors, and bounded over
the ridge and furrow with the elasticity of an india-
rubber ball. She pulled just enough to be pleasant,
although at the same time her mouth was so fine that
the rider could control her at will. Kitty and she
formed a pretty picture, both fresh, young, and full of
vitality. Even Miss Bretby expressed her admiration.

"How beautifully Miss Herrick rides," she observed
to Mr. Ruddle. "I don't think I ever saw any one sit
so straight and square on a horse in my life. And then
she has such hands! But, oh! dear, what a terrible
come down for the poor child." Then remembering
suddenly whom she was addressing, she got very red
and confused, and mumbled, "I beg your pardon. I
was forgetting."

"No offence, Miss Bretby," said Mr. Ruddle. "No
offence whatever. I quite agree with you, and pray
don't think it pleases me any more than it does you to

see Miss Herrick here. She is far away too good for
the place. But what could I do? She came to me as
her father's old servant, and vowed that if I wouldn't
engage her she'd go straight off and offer her services to
Mr. Hillyard, of Wrecester. I knew I could make it a
bit easier for her, in all probability, than he. By Jove!"
he exclaimed, "the gray is doing well now," as at a
sign from headquarters Kitty increased the speed to a fair
hand gallop. "Miss Herrick is sending her along.
She'd suit you, Miss Bretby, that mare would. Believe
me, I would not tell you so if it were not the case."

Miss Bretby vouchsafed no reply to this remark, but
gazed critically at the mare with the disparaging eye of
an undecided purchaser, until Kitty pulled up close to
where they were standing, her eyes sparkling, her fair
face all warm and flushed with the exercise.

"Well," she said, in a voice not intended for Mr.
Ruddle's ears, "how do you like the mare, Kitty? Tell
me the truth."

"Immensely," was the enthusiastic rejoinder. "If
she only jumps as well as she gets over the ground I
should strongly recommend you to buy her. She has
the most charming paces, and although she is powerful
behind the saddle, she is not the least tiring to ride."

"What sort of a mouth has she got?" inquired Miss
Bretby.

"Perfect, so far as I can judge just from cantering
her round the field. With hounds she might, perhaps,
pull a trifle from eagerness, but she answered to the
least touch of the curb, and I could have stopped her
with my little finger at any moment."

"Perhaps you would like to see the mare popped over
a fence or two," suggested Mr. Ruddle, mindful of the
flight of time.

"I should, most certainly," returned Miss Bretby.

Upon this Mr. Ruddle nodded his head, and Kitty
started off on the home circuit, which consisted of three
or four easy fences, laid out in a couple of fields. The
first was a natural hedge cut very low, with an innocent

little ditch on the far side. A horse could either brush through or jump it at his will. Then came a flight of brushed-up hurdles, and another fence higher than the preceding one, but minus the ditch, finishing up with a low flight of rails between three and four feet high, which brought one neatly back to the starting-point without having encountered any very formidable obstacle.

David Frazer had come out, partly in the event of his services being required, and partly to see how the new lady rider would acquit herself. Although he had often witnessed Kitty's performances in the hunting field, and entertained a high opinion of her prowess with hounds, he had been inclined to pooh-pooh the idea of a female horse-breaker invading what he considered his particular department. But when he saw the graceful and artistic way in which she handled the gray he was forced to admit that where feminine customers were concerned it no doubt would assist business letting them see with their own eyes how the horses for sale carried a side-saddle. A clumsy, nervous rider with a bad figure would have been practically useless, but Miss Herrick was an ornament to any steed.

"By jingo!" he muttered to himself, as, shortening her reins, and holding her hands low on either side of the gray's withers, Kitty set her straight at the fence, giving the mare her head in the last stride, and picking her up cleverly on the other side. "She can ride, and no mistake. I don't know but what the Guvnor was right after all. Guid Laird! how the gray jumps with her," as the gay little animal bounded lightly over the hurdles with at least a foot to spare. "It's a pleasure to see the pair of them."

It may be gathered that Kitty was fortunate enough to gain Mr. Frazer's approval—a circumstance calculated to smooth her path very considerably, since those who incurred his disapprobation promptly found it convenient to quit Mr. Ruddle's establishment. When Kitty once more came to a halt he condescended to walk up to the mare's head, and putting his strong hairy hand on the bridle, said to the rider:

"You rode her joost beautiful, miss. I could na hae done it better myself."

After this genuine compliment Kitty felt as proud as a queen, and forgot for a space the humiliation of her position. Miss Bretby expressed herself as quite satisfied with the mare's performances, and intimated her intention of mounting her. The gray did not jump quite so clean with her as with Kitty—she had heavy hands, and hung on to the curb; still she went creditably enough to induce the fair purchaser to buy her, after a great deal of haggling. She tried very hard to beat Mr. Ruddle down, but that gentleman, knowing the lady with whom he had to deal, stood his ground firmly.

"She's a bargain at £140, Miss Bretby, I do assure you," he said. "Take her or leave her, as you like; it's all one to me. She's a mare that wont remain long in my stable; but I can't accept a penny less than I am asking. In fact, from any one but you I should want another twenty pounds."

The price being at last settled, all would have gone well had not Miss Bretby elected to walk back to the stable and see the mare, whom she now regarded as her property, safely housed. The sulky-looking helper before referred to snatched the bridle from Kitty's hand in a very rude manner, and roughly pulled the mare, whose blood was up, into the box. He was a surly, ill-conditioned fellow of medium height, with low brow, cruel eyes, and a sinister expression. The hue of his ugly, fleshy nose cast a decided slur on his sobriety. It was easy to see at a glance that he had not the slightest love for horses, and consequently was quite unsuited to have anything to do with them. The mare evidently held this opinion, for, as he gave her a thump on the ribs with his bony fist so as to make her move over to one side, she flew at him open-mouthed, caught him by the arm, and in an instant had bitten into its flesh.

The man gave a yell of pain, and directly she loosed her hold fled from the box, muttering imprecations.

"Oh! what a brute!" exclaimed Miss Bretby. "Really, Mr. Ruddle, after seeing how she behaves in the stable I would not have her at a gift. If there is one thing I like more than another it is to make pets of my horses, and to be able to go up to them without fear of my life. You must let me off the bargain."

"Oh, certainly," said Mr. Ruddle rather stiffly, for he felt she was treating him a bit shabbily. He was accustomed, however, to the vagaries of lady customers, and, as he often patheticaly observed, would rather deal with twenty men than one woman; for, apart from never knowing their own minds, they seemed to think they had a perfect right to back out of a transaction at pleasure, no matter how legitimately it had been concluded.

"I am sure you are making a mistake in not taking the mare," said Kitty, who had seen enough to suspect that she was a victim of ill-usage. "No vicious animal would go so kindly. They often take dislikes to particular people, just as we do ourselves, and there are some horses," glancing at the helper, "who, if they have once been roughly handled, never forget the person who has treated them unkindly."

"Bravo, Miss Kitty," murmured Mr. Ruddle in her ear. "That was capitally done. You are a born horse-dealer."

The compliment, like David's, was genuine, but it did not afford the same pleasure. She felt it to be a clumsy one, and colored with vexation. Was she, indeed, showing a natural capacity for the profession, and taking kindly to "coping"? Devoted to horses as she was, would it be possible for her to lead the life without doing so? Nothing had been further from her intention when she spoke than to persuade Miss Bretby to buy; yet that was evidently how Mr. Ruddle construed the speech. He fancied she was deliberately playing into his hands, and trying to gain her five per cent. commis-

sion.   He was an excellent, estimable man.   She
respected him sincerely, but there were shades and
gradations of thought betwixt him and her which could
not fail to produce an occasional jar.   It was a pity that
Mrs. Ruddle did not know how little real cause for
anxiety she had.   It would have set her mind at rest
could she have been brought to believe that her Peter
was neither making love nor being made love to.

Meanwhile Miss Bretby remained firm in her determination not to buy the gray after the exhibition of vice
which she had recently witnessed.   She was notorious
for not liking to part with her money, and she had no
great difficulty in persuading herself that a hundred
and forty was more than the mare's real worth.   It
would have been more straightforward had she said
so openly, but she preferred to attribute it to the gray's
temper.

Mr. Ruddle listened to all she had to say with a polite
smile on his countenance but secret irritability.

"You are losing a nailing good hunter, Miss Bretby,
and one that would have carried you safely and well, bar
accidents, for years to come," he said, wishing to ter-
minate the interview.   "However, please yourself.
"It's not for me to persuade you."

"Perhaps you have something else," said the lady
uneasily, "a—a little cheaper."

"I don't keep screws," said Mr. Ruddle loftily.   "All
the same, you are welcome to take another look round."

After having half a dozen horses out which she had
not the least intention of buying, giving no end of
trouble, and keeping two excellent customers waiting,
Miss Bretby finally took leave, condescendingly saying
she would look in some other day when Mr. Ruddle
had a better lot more to her liking.

"That's what she always does," he exclaimed irately
to Kitty, gazing with strong disapprobation after Miss
Bretby's retreating form.   "She's the hardest lady in
the county to sell a horse to.   She's that close and
suspicious.   There's no pleasing her nohow, for she

has got it in her mind all the time that you want to rob her."

"It is to be hoped there are not many like her," said Kitty; "I don't envy you particularly if there are."

"You'll forgive me for saying so, miss, but I never feel sure of the ladies."

16

CHAPTER XXX.

THE SADDLE-ROOM.

MR. RUDDLE had confided the key of the corn bin to Kitty's care, and that afternoon, a little before four o'clock, she went into the stable to measure out the oats. The men were busy in the various boxes tossing up the straw with their pitchforks. Almost insensibly Kitty's eyes travelled in the direction of the one where the gray mare was housed. As her helper went about his duties she appeared very uneasy, and kept laying back her ears and making hurried snatches at space with her strong, yellow teeth that were adorned by sundry black marks which testified to her youth. Now and again as the straw tickled her heels she seemed on the point of kicking, and once when the man approached too familiarly she let fly in earnest, her iron-shod hoofs resounding against the wooden boards with a thud.

"You devil, you!" he exclaimed. "I'll teach you to do that again. I haven't paid you out yet for the bite you gave me this morning. My arm is black and blue." And so saying, he raised his pitchfork and deliberately prodded the mare in the fleshy part of the quarter with its sharp prongs. She gave a shrill squeak and reared straight up, pawing the air with her forelegs, and then, making a great plunge, began to lash out furiously. It so chanced that Kitty had seen exactly what took place, and her blood literally boiled with indignation. It made every vein in her body tingle to stand by and see a good horse ill-used. Without a moment's hesitation she marched straight up to the man and said hotly; "What on earth do you mean by hitting that mare with your pitchfork? She may well have a bad temper, poor thing, if this is the treatment she is accustomed to receive."

He looked at her, and over his sullen countenance there stole an impudent leer.

"It's no business of yourn," he answered surlily. "You leave me alone, and I'll leave you."

"I shant do anything of the sort," she retorted, with spirit. "Mr. Ruddle has placed me in charge over the horses, and I'm responsible for them to him."

He raised a great guffaw of derision. "You, indeed! And who are you, pray? We don't want a slip of a girl poking her nose into the stable and giving orders to people who know a great deal better what they're about than she does. Get along with you, miss."

Kitty flushed crimson to the temples, but she was too much of a lady to bandy words with such a rude, ill-bred fellow.

"I shall report your conduct to Mr. Ruddle," she said haughtily, moving towards the door.

"Oh! that's your little game, is it?" he shouted after her. "Want to get me dismissed, do you? I'll see you blowed first. The Guv'nor aint quite so big a fool as to listen to a woman's tales. He's master in the yard, whatever he may be in the 'ouse."

Kitty took no notice of this parting shot, but went off in search of her employer without loss of time.

It so happened that Peter and Mrs. Peter had just sat down to tea when the maid-servant interrupted their *tête-à-tête* by stating that Miss Herrick was waiting outside, and wished "very pertiklar" to know if she could speak a few words to the master.

"By all means, Jane," said Mr. Ruddle. "Show her in—show her in at once. You should never keep a lady standing."

Mrs. Ruddle drew herself up at this speech.

"You've turned very perlite all of a sudden," she observed sarcastically. "Many's the time you've kept *me* standing without making any apology. I wonder what Miss Herrick wants coming interrupting you of your meals."

And she put down her cup with a clatter.

"I'm sure I don't know, my dear," answered Mr. Ruddle mildly.

"I knew how it would be," resumed his spouse, her nostrils expanding like a war horse. "You'll have no peace. She'll always be running after you on some excuse or other. That's a way the designing creatures have."

"What nonsense you are talking, Nancy," he said good-humoredly. "You forget that Miss Herrick is a lady born and bred."

"Well, Peter, and are ladies made of different flesh and blood from other folk? A woman's a woman whether she comes from a palace or a cottage, and you may take one thing for granted, they all like the men."

"Hush!" he said warningly. "Not so loud, or she will hear you. Well, Miss Herrick," he continued in a higher key, courteously addressing Kitty, who at this moment entered the room, "I hope nothing has gone wrong?"

"I am sorry to trouble you, Mr. Ruddle," said the girl, "but I have come to tell you that that helper who looks after the gray mare ill-uses her most shamefully. It is my belief he is the sole cause of the temper she shows in the stable. Ten minutes ago I saw him deliberately prod her in the quarter with his pitchfork. He said he would pay her out for the bite she gave him this morning, and I shouldn't be the least surprised if she were dead lame by to-morrow."

"The deuce he did!" ejaculated Mr. Ruddle wrathfully.

"Although I particularly dislike finding fault the very first day of my arrival," went on Kitty, "I can't help telling you of the man's conduct, and also of his impertinence to me. When I remonstrated with him, and said he had no business to treat any animal in such a manner, he only jeered, and said he did not want the likes of me coming and finding fault and interfering in his affairs."

"It's that Job Lawson again, for a monkey," said Mr. Ruddle, rising hastily from his seat. "A low-looking ruffian with black hair?"

"Yes," said Kitty, "that's the man. He looks after the gray, the chestnut mare, and the bay horse with the hogged mane."

"He's a real lazy scoundrel," said Mr. Ruddle, "and I've been on the point of sacking him once or twice already. Now I'll do it."

"Not on my account, please, Mr. Ruddle. Only I felt I must make a stand, for if the men are to answer back whenever I give an order or have occasion to rebuke them, I can't be expected to keep proper authority over the stable."

"No, of course not," he said. "I'll precious soon put that all right."

"Peter," said Mrs. Ruddle impressively, breaking in on the conversation, "you had much better leave matters alone. Let Miss Herrick and Lawson settle their own difficulties. If you put the men out they are quite capable of striking in a body."

"I don't care a —— if they do," he retorted warmly. "I wont have Miss Herrick insulted if I can help it."

Mrs. Ruddle looked at Kitty with an ill-disguised animosity which seemed to say, "There, you see what mischief you are making."

"I have not the least doubt," she said coldly, "that Miss Herrick is quite capable of fighting her own battles, without your going out of your way to act as her champion. Sit down, Peter, and finish your tea, instead of buzzing about the room like a blue-bottle."

"My dear," said Mr. Ruddle, coloring with vexation at the covert impertinence of his better half's remarks, "this is a purely business matter. Oblige me by not interfering. Miss Herrick and I will arrange it between us."

Mrs. Ruddle burst into an hysterical laugh.

"Oh, of course. Pray don't mind me. I'm nobody. I'm used to being shoved into the background for the sake of the first pretty face that happens to turn up. Perhaps you would prefer having a private conversation together. If so, I will retire."

"Mrs. Ruddle," said Kitty, bewildered both by her words and her strange, stand-off manner, "what have I done to displease you?"

"Nothing, miss—nothing. Please don't mention it. I am accustomed to being sat upon in my own house."

"I am afraid I have called at an inopportune time," went on the girl, in great distress. "I had no idea you and Mr. Ruddle were at tea. It was stupid of me not to look at my watch, but the fact was I felt so indignant when I saw a valuable mare being knocked about that I considered it my duty to let your husband know what went on behind his back."

"I wish you were half as particular about what goes on behind my back," sneered Mrs. Ruddle.

"Let us come, Miss Herrick," said Peter, frowning darkly at his irate spouse. "You must not mind what my wife says. She is a trifle—ahem!—a trifle upset to-day. She has these bad turns every now and again." And so saying he hurried Kitty out of the room before Mrs. Ruddle had time to recover from the astonishment created by her Peter's audacity.

The helpers were still at work in the light-weight stable when they entered it.

"Look here, my men," Mr. Ruddle called out in a firm, determined voice, "I've something to say to you. Miss Herrick has been placed in charge here by me, and any one who refuses to obey her orders refuses to obey mine. Let that be distinctly understood once for all. Job Lawson," turning to Kitty's adversary, "here are your wages paid up to date. You need not show your ugly face inside my yard any more. After to-day I have done with your services, and you can go and hit somebody else's horses, not mine."

The fellow was so taken aback that he had not a word to say; for the rest, remonstrance was useless. He happened to be extremely unpopular amongst the other helpers, and they were glad to get rid of him.

"There!" said Mr. Ruddle, as he left the stable and returned to the house to allay the greater storm within doors, "that will be a lesson to them."

Kitty could not help feeling grateful to him for his loyal and manly conduct. Nevertheless, the episode was an unpleasant one. It left a disagreeable impression on her mind, and she wished it had never occurred. She felt that for some unknown reason she had made an enemy of Mrs. Ruddle, and taxed her brains to think what cause she could have given for offence. Such a fit of low spirits came over her that she retired to the saddle-room, and sitting down in a wooden arm-chair before the fire, reviewed the events of the day one by one. From the horses she had received unqualified pleasure; from the human beings, nothing but pain. How strange it seemed that the latter should hurt one so, and that those little tongues of theirs should possess the power of probing into the innermost depths of one's being.

Poor Kitty! It was the first day of roughing it in all her young life. Hitherto she had known nothing of the seamy side, and now, in addition to a certain amount of physical fatigue, she suffered from an excessive depression. In this condition, the warm fire, with its cheerful, flickering light, felt like a familiar friend, and proved a source of comfort. By degrees its glowing heat soothed her nervous system. Twilight was rapidly setting in out-of-doors — the evenings were shortening daily—and she fell into a doze. The saddle-room looked cosey and bright, and although she had despised it in the morning, there were many worse places to which to retire when one wanted a quiet half-hour. The leaping flames illumined the various bits, girths, saddles, and stirrups with which its walls were liberally hung. They darted from one to another, now resting on some polished curb chain, again evoking prismatic flashes from a straight steel snaffle.

Kitty sat forward on her chair. Her head rested wearily on her hands and her feet on the iron fender. Presently the door behind her opened suddenly. She gave a start, and looking up, saw Lord Algy standing by her side, with a face full of concern. The blood rushed to her cheeks.

"Kitty!" he said, in an agitated voice. "I have but this moment heard where you were. I met Miss Bretby as I was driving home from the station, and she simply horrified me by saying that you had accepted a situation as rough rider to Mr. Ruddle."

Her heart beat with great measured strokes. Its pulsations rang in her ears. As her eyes drooped before his a feeling came borne in upon her that it only needed his and Cyril's disapproval to fill her cup of bitterness to the brim. Just as if she had not enough to bear already without the two people whose opinion she most valued in the world censuring her conduct. The reproach which she fancied she discerned written on Lord Algy's countenance rendered her unjust. Cyril, possibly, had a right to lecture her, but not this other. The more humiliated she felt by her present position, the more resolved was she not to admit the fact.

Therefore, in answer to his speech, she said coldly, "You are very kind, Algy, to pay me a formal call in my new quarters. To tell the truth, I scarcely expected such condescension on your part."

He looked at her in surprise.

"Good heavens, Kitty, what makes you talk such nonsense? You must, indeed, think poorly of me."

"I—I thought," and her voice quivered in spite of every effort to keep it steady, "that—that your *horror* would have kept you away."

"Foolish girl, I expressed myself badly. I meant I was distressed beyond measure at your having recourse to such an occupation as this. Why did you not tell me what you were thinking of doing? At least we might have talked matters over together."

She shook her head in a dismal, melancholy fashion.

"That would not have done any good. You would only have tried to prevent me from putting my project into execution."

And she glanced at him with eyes which, though dim, yet had a touch of defiance in them.

CHAPTER XXXI.

LORD ALGY REMONSTRATES WITH KITTY, AND GETS SNUBBED FOR HIS PAINS.

Lord Algy took up a position with his back to the fire. He looked very tall and straight, and there was an air of strength about the square muscular set of his shoulders. She had always been accustomed to rule him, but to-day he awed her a little, and strange to say, she liked him none the less on that account, although she feared him more.

"I should certainly have done my best to induce you to reconsider your determination," he said, after a brief pause. "May I ask if Captain Mordaunt knows of the step you have seen fit to take?"

She hung her head. The question sounded somewhat judicial in its nature.

"Not as yet," she answered reluctantly. "I expect him every day, and then I shall tell him, of course. One can talk so much better than one can write."

"Then he did not give his sanction to the proceedings? I am glad to hear that."

"No," she said, a trifle bitterly. "I told Cyril that I should be obliged to earn my bread somehow, and as he either could not or would not offer me any advice on the subject, I felt at liberty to act according to the best of my judgment."

A very tender and sorrowful expression stole over Lord Algy's face as he listened to these words. She did not realize how much they confessed to a man of his age and experience.

"Poor little soul!" he exclaimed simply and spontaneously.

Somehow the ejaculation touched her to the quick,

250

and she was within an ace of breaking down and making a fool of herself.   Had he continued to pity her, and said more in the same strain, she must have done so.   His next observation, however, created a reaction which threw her back upon her pride, and again made her take refuge in it as in a fortress.

"One thing is certain," he said.   "You can't stay here.   It is quite out of the question."

"And why is it out of the question?" she demanded defiantly.

"For a hundred reasons.   To begin with, you are much too young to lead this sort of life——"

"My youth is a fault which Time will soon cure," she interrupted.

"Not until your name has been bandied about all over the county.   What do you think your future husband's friends will say when they hear that before your marriage you were earning your livelihood as a horse-breaker?"

"I don't much care what they say.   Of course, I know I shall have to face a certain amount of tattle."

"It is all very well talking," he rejoined.   "But you will find that you can't avoid caring for public opinion. No girl under twenty is strong enough to withstand it. And even if you could bear the remarks of your neighbors philosophically, some one else wont.   You may make up your mind to that."

"Whom do you mean—yourself?"

"No.   Captain Mordaunt."

"In that case," she retorted spiritedly, "let Cyril tell me so himself.   Everybody leaves me in the lurch, and then they find fault because I try to help myself."

Lord Algy bit his lip.

"I think that accusation is hardly fair, Kitty.   Your frends would have been only too glad to assist you had you given them the chance."

"There was nothing for me to do," she continued, her color deepening, "but to turn governess or to take to my present trade."

"I don't quite see that. You might easily have paid visits until—well, until you marry."

"And supposing my marriage were never to come off?"

A gleam of hope flashed in his eyes.

"Have you any reason for such a supposition?" And he tried hard to prevent his voice from sounding too eager.

"No—o—o. But it is impossible to tell what may happen."

"Has it occurred to you that by accepting a situation under Mr. Ruddle you might be placing an obstacle between yourself and Captain Mordaunt? A man has generally some pride for the woman he is engaged to, even if he has none for himself."

She turned furiously red at this question. It had already presented itself, and she had thrust it studiously into the background.

"I refuse to recognize what right you have to cross-examine me, or to criticise my actions," she answered angrily.

"I have no right. None whatever," he said. "I know that well enough, without your going out of the way to remind me of the fact. Nevertheless, as an old friend, and one who takes an active interest in your welfare, I deemed it my duty to protest against your mixing with the class of people you must necessarily meet here."

"You are very kind, Lord Algernon," she said, her nose slightly elevated. "But fortunately or unfortunately for myself, I have not your aristocratic prejudices. Blue blood is an excellent thing, no doubt, but it has its drawbacks."

Her tone and manner wounded him deeply, but he was determined not to lose his temper.

"I do not think we need enter into a fruitless discussion," he said quietly. "I cannot help my birth any more than you can help yours. Perhaps I have inherited a few prejudices. It may well be; but that has nothing to do with the main point."

"Is there a main point?" she asked flippantly. "After five minutes' most animated conversation it has not yet dawned upon me that there was one. May I venture to suggest that we should arrive at it?"

"Kitty, Kitty, what has come to you? You are not a bit like the girl you were a week ago."

"Indeed! I am delighted to hear it. Changed circumstances, changed girl. What could you have more correct or desirable?"

"You will get hard," he predicted.

"All the better. I shant feel the ignominy of my position so much, or be affected by the good-natured remarks of my friends."

"In time," he continued, "you might even grow horsy and vulgar."

"Thank you, my lord. May I ask if you have come here for the purpose of insulting me?"

"No," he answered resolutely. "But whether you like it or not, I have come to take you away."

She laughed, a cold, clear, mirthless laugh.

"A case of the Middle Ages. A mighty baron and an unwilling maiden. Really, this is quite romantic. Will you condescend to tell me where you intend taking the poor captive?"

"To Furrowdale Castle, for the present. Of course, when Captain Mordaunt arrives, you and he will be able to settle your plans."

"Your lordship is a most indulgent jailer." she said sarcastically. "Allow me to express my heartiest thanks for so magnanimous a permission."

"For heaven's sake, Kitty, drop that sneering tone. I can't stand it. Perhaps I express myself badly. If so, I apologize humbly. I always was a clumsy devil who said the wrong thing at the wrong time, but I think you must know that I mean well, and if I have not a polished manner like—like some people—Captain Mordaunt, for instance—it is my misfortune rather than my fault. But your father had sufficient confidence in me to make me one of your trustees, and I am more or less bound to take care of you."

"And you show your care," she said hotly, "by coming here and saying nasty, horrid things to me that put me out. Why can't you leave me alone? I am no longer a child to be lectured, and once for all, I refuse to go to Furrowdale."

"I shall not be there," he said, with a flush of annoyance. "I told you before that you need not be bored by my company."

"Thanks, but there is no occasion for you to leave your hunting and home comforts on my account."

"Why are you so infernally ceremonious?" he asked, beginning to feel his blood tingle.

"Because I prefer to stay where I am, and would a hundred thousand times sooner grow *hard* and *vulgar* and *horsy* than eat the bread of dependence. Must I forever go on saying the same thing?" And she made an impatient gesture.

"But, Kitty," he remonstrated, "you are so young and inexperienced. You do not know how people will talk."

"May I venture to remind you that you have already made that remark, and that there would be an agreeable freshness of sensation about an original one?"

He sighed. This cold, ironical vein baffled him altogether, and made him feel an utter fool, although he was conscious of the integrity of his intentions. He had come to her in all friendship and good-will, and she seemed determined to treat him like an enemy. It was very hard, and very puzzling. Still, he resolved to make yet one more attempt before retiring from the field. He felt angry, too, and sore at his reception. She might have talked matters over reasonably and quietly, instead of refusing to listen to a word.

"At the risk of being accused of repetition, I maintain that you cannot possibly stay on here," he said, after a somewhat hostile pause.

"And I say, I can and shall. You need not look so shocked," she added lightly. "I am quite comfortable, and have at last discovered my vocation. To use a slang expression, the life suits me down to the ground. Mr. Ruddle is a most kind and thoughtful master. I want for nothing—not even a reception-room." And she glanced at the shining bits and stirrups, and waved her hand airily.

"It is not the place for a lady," he said doggedly.

"Those who are ashamed of my occupation can stay away," she retorted.

"I suppose you mean that for me," he said, the blood reddening his cheek.

"You know best whether the cap fits. We have squabbled enough. All I want to impress on your mind is that I am my own mistress and decline to be dictated to."

"God knows I had not the least intention of hurting your feelings," he said in self-defence.

"You *have* hurt them," she rejoined passionately. "You have hurt them very much indeed. Why can't you keep quiet? It is not necessary to tell me all you think and what other people will think. I would far rather hear nothing."

"But you can't help hearing disagreeable remarks, Kitty."

"I don't see why I should, if it were not for my friends. But I suppose that is one of the prerogatives of friendship. Do you know," and she gave a forced laugh, "that you are standing there looking at me exactly as if I had committed a crime?"

"I am not responsible for my looks," he said.

"Yes, you are," she rejoined, with the unreasonableness of a woman who knows she is fighting in a wrong cause. "You talk a great deal about your interest in me, but do you imagine that a visit such as yours is cal-

culated to raise my spirits or make me feel more
cheerful than I do already? You seem to forget that it
is not all *couleur de rose.*"

"Nothing I do or say to-day is right, apparently," he
said, infinitely distressed. "Must I go back alone?"

"Yes. Henceforth I am Kitty Herrick, horse-breaker,
with the agreeable prospect of becoming hard, vulgar,
and horsy."

"Those expressions seem to have displeased you.
And yet I only spoke the truth."

"No doubt. The truth is always biting, and severe,
and—and good for one." .

"And you consider this life a fitting preparation for
your approaching marriage?"

She turned white with passion.

"Oh, for goodness' sake go away and don't torture me
any more with your questions. Can't you see that all I
want for the next few months is to be quit of my friends
and their advice?"

It was a hastily spoken speech, the result of brooding
shame, perplexity, and humiliation. Hurt by her mood,
which he did not understand, he turned short on his
heel, and said in a pained voice, "All right, Kitty,
your wish shall be respected as far as I am concerned."
And he strode out at the door.

She started to her feet, once she realized he was fairly
gone, and called aloud, "Algy, Algy, come back. I did
not mean what I was saying. You are so kind, and I—
I am so unhappy."

But either he did not hear or else she had offended
him past forgiveness. Anyhow, he took no notice, and
for very shame's sake she could not run across the yard
after him. She watched his tall form disappear, then
she shut the saddle-room door with a bang and burst into
tears. What a horrid, ungrateful wretch she had been,
to be sure. And all because he had had the courage to
tell her to her face what every one would say behind her
back.

It was no good trying to bolster herself up with the

consolation that she did not care.   She knew very well
in her heart of hearts that she *did* care, not only a little,
but desperately—vitally.   As Lord Algy's past kind-
nesses recurred one by one to her memory, she laid her
head down on the table and sobbed like a child.   Oh!
where was Cyril?   Why did he not come to comfort her
and restore her to self-respect?

17

CHAPTER XXXII.

NOT TO BE BEATEN.

FORTUNATELY, youth and fatigue prevailed over sorrow, and in spite of her troubles Kitty slept soundly. She awoke with a start, to find the little alarm-clock which she had brought from Herrington ringing violently. It was five o'clock, and nearly as dark as night. Her bed felt cosey and warm, and she would fain have lingered there another hour or two, but late rising was a luxury she could no longer indulge in, and with a yawn, followed by a sigh of reluctance, she got up and groped about until she found the match-box. Her eyes were heavy, and the atmosphere struck cold. Not wishing to disturb Mrs. Perkins at so early an hour, she had told that good woman the night before that she could dispense with hot water until her return from exercising, and would wait till then for breakfast. In order to stay the pangs of hunger, she had carried up a glass of milk and a slice of thick bread-and-butter. Altogether, it was very different from being called by a confidential maid, dressing at leisure, and descending to find nice hot fires in all the rooms and a substantial meal awaiting one. Comparisons, however, were useless, and she fully realized that it was not wise to dwell upon them. She therefore made a hasty toilet by the light of one flickering tallow candle, put on a thick covert coat over her habit to keep herself warm, gulped down the milk, bolted the bread, and then repaired noiselessly to Mr. Ruddle's yard over the way.

The morning was inclined to be wet, with a boisterous wind and occasional cold, driving showers. A few faint streaks of gray were just beginning to appear in

258

the horizon, and the outlines of the trees might be vaguely discerned against them. The birds were still at roost, and a great quietude prevailed everywhere. Kitty shivered as she entered the stable. Here the men were already busily engaged giving the horses a hurried rub down, and raking out the straw which had served as beds overnight. A little before six the inmates of the various stalls and boxes were led forth and marshalled into procession, each man leading an unmounted animal by the side of the one he bestrode. In all, there might have been some forty or fifty nags of different descriptions, and the string presented quite a formidable appearance when mustered.

Everything being now in readiness for a start, David Frazer appeared, and taking off his hat to Kitty said, " Guid morning, Miss Herrick. I was a-thinking that it might be as well for ye to ride the gray mare—that is to say, if ye hae nae objection."

"I shall be delighted to have such a good mount," answered the girl. " But is she sound?"

" Fairly so. I thocht she moved a leetle stiff behind as they led her out, but it's naething to speak of."

"I am very pleased to hear she's no worse," said Kitty. " After the treatment she received yesterday I quite expected to hear of her being on the sick list today." So saying, she mounted by the stone steps in the yard, and David gallantly arranged her habit.

" Maybe ye had better gae first and set the pace," he said. " For my ain pairt, I usually bring up the rear, and then I can keep my eye on the quadroopeds, and see whether they all gae briskly and weel."

Kitty did as desired, and put herself at the head of the procession, after first receiving orders from David to " shuck along " steadily by the sides of the roads as soon as they were clear of the village. Now this same " shucking along " may be a very convenient mode of progression to men, horses, and hounds, but it certainly is not to women. Nothing tires them so much as that slow jog-trot, which rarely permits of their rising in the

stirrup, and yet is productive of jolt after jolt if they
attempt to sit perfectly still.   It causes the feminine
back and muscles to ache most violently.   Kitty had
always prided herself on being able to jog from covert
to covert with less fatigue than the majority of her sex ;
but when it came to twelve or fourteen miles at a stretch,
with scarcely an interlude, she found the exertion exceedingly trying.   It had this good effect, however:
Before they had been out half an hour she got rid of the
sensation of chilliness which she had at first experienced
from the morning air and became thoroughly warmed
up.   The gray mare's quarter had filled somewhat from
the blow received on the previous day, and although not
actually lame, her action was scarcely true.   After a
while the day grew lighter, and a few country carts
passed by, rumbling slowly and heavily along the roads.
David kept the horses out for about two hours, and
although Kitty had turned such a deaf ear to all Lord
Algy's remonstrances, and had almost quarrelled with
him in consequence, she admitted inwardly that it was a
great relief not encountering any of her acquaintances.
She should not have liked them to see her riding in the
small hours of the morning, going exercising at the
head of a lot of stablemen just like a common groom,
and dressed in her oldest and most unbecoming garments.   Even she felt a little ashamed of the situation.
As they neared the village the horses began to prick
their ears and quicken their step, whilst David left his
position in the rear and ranged alongside of the girl.

"I am afraid ye're a bit tired, Miss Herrick," he said,
looking at her fair flushed face with eyes which betrayed
decided admiration.   "It's haird wark when one is nae
accustomed to it."

She smiled courageously.

"I shall revive when I have had a good breakfast, Mr.
Frazer.   It is astonishing what an appetite this exercising develops."

David shook his head solemnly.

'You must nae over-fatigue yerself," he said in a

grave voice. "After all, ye are but a wee bit slip of a girl, and I'm thinking that ye're speerit is just stronger than ye're flesh."

"Are we likely to, have a busy day?" she inquired, anxious to lead the conversation into a less personal channel.

"Yes, very. We hae got Mr. and Miss Van Agnew coming this afternoon, and the master will be wanting ye to show off the nags again, I reckon. I tell ye frankly, Miss Herrick," he continued confidentially, " I never was gin to set much store on female riding, but when I saw ye ride over thae fences yesterday I could nae help admitting that a purty young leddy makes a difference and satisfies the eye on horseback."

Kitty laughed. The seriousness of her companion's manner and the complimentary nature of his speech were so totally at variance. She was tickled also by the vein of patronage which colored all his remarks, but was sharp enough to see that he would be much pleasanter as a friend than as an enemy. Therefore, she pretended to be highly flattered, and said:

"Thank you, Mr. Frazer. I value your good opinion extremely, and only hope that I may prove fortunate enough to retain it."

"Ye are sure to do that," he responded graciously. "When I tak to a person once, I tak to them always. I'm not ain of the chop and change sort, and if ever I can do ye a guid turn, don't ye be afraid to apply to David Frazer."

This expression of exceeding good-will was rather overpowering Kitty might have been somewhat at a loss for an answer had not they at this moment re-entered the yard, where Mr. Frazer's attention became directed to two or three lively animals who began jumping about in their eagerness to return to their stable. After dismounting, Kitty saw her charges fed, and then repaired to Mrs. Perkins's, where she plunged into a bath, braided her hair up neatly, re-dressed, and partook of a plain but hearty meal. When she had finished eating she walked to the looking-glass and looked critically at her reflection.

"I wonder whether it is true that I shall grow hard, and horsy, and vulgar," she mused bitterly. "I wonder he did not add coarse and common into the bargain. He might just as well have made use of a few more pleasing adjectives while he was about it. I was very angry at the time, and yet there is a good deal of truth in what he said. I feel that it is quite possible one might degenerate, after a bit, into a regular female horse-coper." She clinched her hand and added passionately, "I wish Algy had held his tongue. I shouldn't have half as many uncomfortable ideas if he had not put them into my head. It was too bad of him—too bad of him altogether, for until he took to pitying and scolding me by turns I was perfectly resigned to the situation. However," shrugging her shoulders, "I've done the deed, and it's too late now to repent." Thus thinking, she returned to her duties.

About ten o'clock Mr. Ruddle looked into the light-weight stable to ask if she would mind trying a young four-year-old which he had recently purchased from a farmer with a view to offering him to Miss Van Agnew.

"He only came home the day before yesterday," said the dealer, "and I would rather like to see if he has any real notion of jumping. The owner, of course, swore that nothing could pound him; but one has to receive such statements with a certain amount of reserve. When a man has a horse to sell it's impossible to believe a word he says."

"Such a remark coming from you carries great weight," said Kitty archly.

Mr. Ruddle laughed, and led the way to a separate box, where the last arrival was usually housed in solitary confinement. The new four-year-old was a showy-looking brown thoroughbred, long and narrow, with a good forehand, but slack behind the saddle, and standing decidedly high on the leg. Although he carried a beautiful coat, and had pretty shooting action, calcu-

lated to take the eye, Kitty did not much fancy him.
There had been no better judge of horseflesh than the
Squire, and from her father she had learned to know the
points requisite in a hunter. The brown appeared lacking in several very essential particulars, but it was not
her place to criticise unless requested, so she wisely
said nothing.

"Do you mind riding a young, untried horse?" inquired Mr. Ruddle, misconstruing the expression of her
face.

"Not I," she replied. "I delight in it."

"I have had a couple of fences so arranged that even
if the animal runs right through them no harm can
come either to you or him," he said.

"I am not afraid," she answered confidently. "Thank
goodness, my nerve is good, and I have never had a
really bad fall to shake it."

"I hope you wont whilst in my service," he responded. "I should never forgive myself if you got
hurt."

Kitty now mounted the brown horse, and soon discovered that he was quite unused to carrying a lady.
He was remarkably green about the mouth, answered
with difficulty to the bridle, and kept turning his head
round to the off side as much as to say, "Why, where on
earth is your leg?" He seemed but half broken, for he
walked in a slovenly, lazy manner, catching his toes
against every little tuft of grass, and trotting roughly
and unevenly. When he cantered he held his head
low, hanging heavily on the bit, and from time to time
yawing in a most unpleasant fashion. In fact, he was
by no means an agreeable mount; but having a grand
pedigree tacked on to his name, it covered a multitude
of sins, especially as he came of a racing family several of whose members had run creditably enough on
the flat. After Mr. Ruddle had looked on for five minutes or so, and obtained a tolerably correct estimate of
his new purchase's form, he said to Kitty:

"Try him over a fence, please, Miss Herrick. He

is green enough in all conscience, still he may be able to jump a bit for all that."

But at the mere sight of a fence, Sir Moses, by High Priest, out of Sacrifice, showed unmistakable signs of temper. He snorted and sidled, and when Kitty tried to induce him to face the obstacle reared straight up on end. The girl loosed his head and flung herself on his neck. She then endeavored to soothe his alarm by caresses and reassuring words, but in vain. The brown plunged, backed, and lashed out in the most obstinate way. Finding gentle persuasion of no avail, she took him a rousing gallop round the field, so as to put him on his mettle and instil courage into his craven heart. But when she brought Sir Moses back to the fence again he evinced no greater inclination to approach it than hitherto, and reared so frequently and dangerously, that fearing he would fall over backwards, Mr. Ruddle begged Kitty to dismount. But if the brown's blood was now fairly up, so also was hers, and if there was one thing she hated more than another, it was being beaten.

"I'll have the brute cavessoned," said Mr. Ruddle, "and take some of the devil out of him. I don't believe he has ever seen a fence."

"Let me have another try," said Kitty eagerly. "We shall ruin him if we allow him to think he is master." And before Mr. Ruddle could give his permission, she raised her cutting whip aloft and brought it smartly down three or four times on Sir Moses's sleek side, at the same moment giving him a vigorous touch of her spurred heel. The effect was instantaneous. He stood up on his hind legs, then gave a plunge which almost tore her out of the saddle, and rushed wildly at the fence. About three yards before he came to it he took off, and making a huge spasmodic bound, landed all abroad with almost an equal distance to spare on the other side. Kitty sat like a rock, and throwing her weight on his quarters, managed to right him and keep him on his legs. She looked back at Mr. Ruddle with a smile of exultation. The will of the strong brute had succumbed to the will of the weak girl, and she was satisfied.

CHAPTER XXXIII.

RIDING FOR SALE.

"Hooray!" she called out. "He can jump if he chooses, although he is evidently new to the game; but he has got it in him, and only requires practice."

Mr. Ruddle hurried up and took hold of the hot and trembling animal by the bridle.

"Well done, Miss Herrick," he said. "You rode him like a Centaur, and stuck to him gallantly; but enough is as good as a feast, and you are now fairly entitled to rest on your laurels for to-day. The horse has got a nasty temper of his own, which will take some time to conquer, but as you have managed him so well already I shall leave him in your hands, and I have not the slightest doubt that he will soon improve. It is a rum thing," he continued meditatively, "but those High Priests are all the same. They never take kindly to jumping, no matter how much you school them, and in my experience they can seldom be depended on."

"Very likely Sir Moses might behave better in the hunting field," said Kitty. "It is not every young horse who will jump in cold blood, and very often the ones who show the most temper at first turn out best in the long run. Perhaps you will allow me later on to try him with hounds, Mr. Ruddle?"

"Most certainly," he replied. "But I can't have you endangering your limbs, Miss Herrick. Please bear that fact in mind. David is as tough as shoe leather, and the real brutes can always be relegated to him. Halloo!" he exclaimed, as they strolled back to the stable-yard, "here are Mr. and Miss Van Agnew, I declare. I did not expect them for another hour."

The arrival of this brother and sister, reported to possess twenty thousand a year each, had created a considerable amount of excitement in the county. Mammas with daughters and favorite sons were all on the *qui vive*, and were determined not to let such prizes escape in a state of single bliss. Kitty had heard so much about their wealth that she was curious to see them, especially as during her stay in town Lady Mordaunt had let fall various hints as to what a desirable bride the lady would have been for Cyril, had not his affections been already fixed in another quarter.

Instinctively, therefore, her eyes turned first to Miss Van Agnew. It was a great relief, somehow, to find that she was not at all pretty, and indeed had no pretensions to good looks. Nature had not favored the heiress. She was short and plain, with a square, clumsy, flat-waisted, round-shouldered figure. In addition, she possessed a curiously sallow complexion, a fleshy nose beneath which sprouted a very decided mustache, and a mouth filled with large, uneven teeth from which the gums receded. Her small, piercing eyes were overshadowed by a pair of dark, bushy eyebrows that gave a masculine appearance to her countenance.

In short, there was nothing fair or lovable about her when divested of the golden halo of money. Her brother was a curious fac-simile of herself on a slightly larger scale, and being a year or two younger, he appeared to defer to his sister's will. Old Mr. Van Agnew had originally made his fortune as a horticulturist and dealer in bulbs and orchids. He was Dutch by birth, but having married an English wife, he settled in London, where both his children were born. During his lifetime, being a gentleman of miserly propensities, he kept them remarkably tight. The consequence was, when he died the young people bore his loss philosophically, and testified a great desire to make up for back spans in the way of enjoyment. Curiously enough, although they knew next to nothing about

sport, they both had sporting tastes, and after learning
to ride a little they pronounced strongly in favor of a
hunting-box.

Gretton Grange happened to be empty, and on the
books of a well-known house agent. It possessed good
accommodation, and stabling for five-and-twenty horses,
so they took it for a year on trial, with the option of a
long lease. They then set to work to buy hunters, and
being comparatively ignorant, their purchases proved
so eminently unsatisfactory that at length, acting on
the advice of a friend, they determined to place themselves in the hands of Mr. Ruddle. Money being no
object, such customers were naturally extremely desirable ones for a dealer to secure, and Mr. Ruddle was
prepared to pay Mr. and Miss Van Agnew every attention. After a few minutes' preliminary conversation,
he flung open the stable door as an invitation to proceed
to business. The brother and sister peeped in at the
horses through the iron bars of their boxes, making
funny little remarks meanwhile, and looking at each
other in a would-be knowing manner destined to impress
Mr. Ruddle with their cuteness. Those glances seemed
to say, "We may be rich, but we don't intend to be
done, and we like to get our money's worth just as
much as other people."

"That's a pretty creature," said Miss Van Agnew,
pointing to a chestnut mare, the greatest screw of the
lot. "I like *him*. He has such a nice, shining coat,
and carries his tail so high. Pray, what might you
want for him, Mr. Ruddle?"

"Two hundred guineas," answered that gentleman,
promptly, who, having had considerable trouble with a
doubtful back sinew, would have been glad to accept
half the sum. "She's a beautiful mare, and worth
double the money."

"Then why don't you ask it?" inquired the young
lady with a direct shrewdness that was decidedly disconcerting.

"Hallo!" exclaimed Mr. Van Agnew, who was a

lively, impatient youth, and had gone on in advance.
"What have you got here? I rather like the look of
this little bay," pointing to the box where Tiny Tim
was located. "I suppose," and he laughed facetiously,
"you want four hundred pounds for him, eh?"

"Yes," said Mr. Ruddle gravely, "that's exactly
what I *do* want. You're a wonderful good judge of
horseflesh, Mr. Van Agnew, to have picked him out,
for he is the finest hunter without exception that ever
looked through a bridle." As a matter of fact, Mr.
Ruddle had fixed Tiny Tim's price in his own mind at
two hundred and fifty, but seeing the ingenious people
with whom he had to deal, and that they evidently only
valued an animal by the amount demanded, he at once
jumped to the conclusion that in order to insure Mr.
and Miss Van Agnew's respect, he must ask a high sum.

"Yes," simpered Mr. Van Agnew, greatly gratified
by the adroit compliment paid him by Mr. Ruddle, "I
flatter myself I do know a decent quad when I see him.
Do you think the bay would carry my sister to hounds?
Mind you, she requires something very perfect."

"He's the cleverest hunter in Great Britain," said Mr.
Ruddle, "and this young lady will vouch for the truth
of what I say." And he pointed to Kitty, who, having
dismounted from the brown, was clandestinely caressing
her favorite. "She can tell you all about him."

Mr. Van Agnew's eyes wandered to Kitty's face, and
rested there as if unable to withdraw themselves.
"Uncommonly pretty girl," he murmured in a loud
aside to Mr. Ruddle. "One of the neatest fillies I've
seen for a long time. Where does she hail from?"

"Allow me to introduce you to Miss Herrick, of
Herrington Hall," said Mr. Ruddle, with dignity.

Little Daniel Van Agnew's first impulse was to
address Kitty familiarly, but something in her attitude
and the proud carriage of her head made him pause,
and betrayed that whatever her present occupation
might be, she was a lady by birth. Like most undersized
men, he cherished a great opinion of his own powers

of fascination. This had been increased when he came into his kingdom, until he believed himself irresistible. So he smiled benignantly at Kitty, and going close up to her, said, "Mr. Ruddle refers me to you, Miss Herrick. I fancy the look of this little bay horse. Tell me, honestly, do you think he would carry my sister?"

"Can she ride?" asked the girl abruptly, for the boldness of his stare displeased her.

"Oh! of course. Why, she paid Mason, of London, thirty guineas only the other day, for lessons which she had been taking in his riding-school. After that, she ought to be quite slap up."

Kitty's lip curled. She knew that it took something more than thirty guineas' worth of tuition to ride Tiny Tim. "If your sister is a good horsewoman," she said, "there is not a better hunter to be found anywhere, but he wont stand being knocked about, and requires light handling. Nothing but necessity makes me part with him." And her eyes filled with tears which threatened to overflow.

"Can we see him out?" asked Mr. Van Agnew of Mr. Ruddle.

"Certainly," answered our friend Peter. "Miss Herrick shall ride him if you like. Tom," shouting to a stable-helper, "put the side-saddle on the bay horse at once, and look sharp about it."

"I should like to see him jumped," said Miss Van Agnew, in a loud voice. "Will you tell that pretty little horse-breaker of yours, Mr. Ruddle, to go at some fences—good big ones, too, such as you get out hunting."

The remark was quite audible, and the color mounted in a hot wave to Kitty's face as she heard it. "That pretty little horse-breaker," indeed! For a moment she felt as if she could have throttled the speaker. Then the hot blood fled from her cheeks, leaving them quite pale. After all, what right had she to resent such a speech? She was nothing but a horse-breaker, and if people were good enough to add the prefix of pretty, she ought to feel obliged to them rather than indignant.

" I am so sorry," Mr. Ruddle whispered, as Tiny Tim was led forth. " They have no more manners than a bear."

" Pray don't apologize," she said. " It sounds a little strange just at first, but I shall soon get used to this sort of thing."

So saying, she sprung into the saddle and took up the reins, which hung loosely on Tiny Tim's firm arched neck. He was very fresh, and gave a whinny of delight as she leaned forward and patted him on the shoulder. Her features quivered with emotion. The thought that she sat on him for the last time, and might never again feel his long sweeping stride beneath her as he galloped after the hounds, well-nigh overcame her fortitude. As she cantered round the field her heart was sorrowful, and it seemed as if her cup of bitterness were indeed full. Tiny Tim's beautiful level action and strong propelling power were quite thrown away upon the Van Agnews, who did not know a horse from a cow, but as he was very dear they considered it their duty to admire him, whilst Master Daniel was quite enthusiastic in his praise of the rider.

" Reduced circumstances, you say, Ruddle?" he chuckled, giving Peter a dig in the ribs. " Aha! Sly dog. Know what you're about. He, he, he!"

Mr. Ruddle resented this conduct as much as he dared, but he was anxious to effect a good sale, and so contrived to conceal the irritation which he felt.

" —— little puppy," he murmured under his breath. " I should like to give him a good hiding."

" Now for the fences," said Miss Van Agnew, impatiently, when Kitty, having put Tiny Tim through his paces, came to a halt. " This is slow sort of work, and we have had about enough of it."

" The big course?" inquired Kitty of Mr. Ruddle, in an undertone.

"Yes," he responded, "if you like. I suppose it's all right."

She gave a little tearful smile, and passed her hand down Tiny Tim's glossy neck.

"Never fear. Only"— two great drops rolled slowly from beneath her eyelids—"it breaks my heart to part with him, and especially to people like these, who evidently do not know the value of a good horse. That woman wont half appreciate such a treasure."

"Money is money," said Mr. Ruddle, trying to cheer her up, "and four hundred pounds is a tidy sum."

"Yes," she said sadly, "I know; but I would not take four thousand for the dear little horse if I could afford to keep him." So saying, she lightly shook her bridle hand, and set Tiny Tim at the nearest fence. It was a fair, honest one, with a wide ditch on the take-off side and a drop on landing. He quickened his stride, collected himself, and flew over like a bird. It was a sight to see the pair of them. They were so well matched and suited each other so admirably. There were some good big obstacles in the far course, including a double which could be flown at a pinch but required being taken steadily to clear in right form. As Kitty approached it Tiny Tim was clearly pulling hard, and tried to fly the whole thing, but the girl had got him well in hand, though the curb chain hung quite loose, and she made him go at it at a slow canter, hardly faster than a trot. The consequence was, he changed his legs on the top of the bank, and quick as lightning sprang over the far ditch with the activity of a cat. Nothing could have been better done. Both rider and steed seemed to have measured the distance to an inch and to be in perfect unison.

"Bravo!" exclaimed Mr. Ruddle. "That was neat, wasn't it?" addressing the brother and sister.

"She's a one-er to ride," said Van Agnew, enthusiastically, his eyes glued on Kitty's graceful upright form. "I say, Judith," turning to his sister, "I wish to goodness you could stick on like that instead of tumbling about all over the place."

"I am not a horse-breaker by profession," returned that young lady contemptuously. "If I'd lived in the stable all my life, like Miss Herrick, no doubt I should jump as well as she does."

"Pardon me," said Mr. Ruddle, "but Miss Herrick has not lived in the stable all her life. You labor under a misapprehension there. She belongs to one of the best old families in the county."

CHAPTER XXXIV.

A GOOD SHOW.

"Look, look," cried Mr. Van Agnew, excitedly. "Miss Herrick is going at another fence. By Jove, the bay is a clipper and no mistake. He jumps in such rare form."

The encomium was fully deserved, for the obstacle which Tiny Tim had just flung behind him with apparently supreme ease was a formidable one for any animal to charge in cold blood. The hedge stood nearly five feet high and had very strong growers running all along the top, which could not be brushed through carelessly; but what made it really awkward was a rise in the ground on the near side. To clear the entire fence necessitated great jumping powers, for the ditch on landing was both very wide and also slightly uphill. Many a good hunter had Mr. Ruddle seen either peck badly or else come to grief there in his time, and he knew that any horse who jumped it well might be safely trusted to perform satisfactorily in the hunting field. Kitty had already been round the course on foot, in order to become thoroughly familiar with the impediments she would be called upon to encounter. She therefore changed the tactics employed at the double, and this time drove Tiny Tim along in earnest, just steadying him, however, a trifle in the last few strides, so as to make him jump high as well as wide. The gallant little bay appeared to quite understand what was required of him. He cocked his pretty game ears, set his head in a resolute fashion, and launched himself into the air with a bold bound, such as none but a highcouraged hunter, confident both in his rider and his own powers, will make. He cleared the fence without touching a twig, then, finding the ditch rather wider than he had expected, he twisted his quarters round, and by bringing his hind feet down almost in the tracks of his fore, landed handsomely, and with plenty to spare. Although he must have been difficult to sit, Kitty maintained her equilibrium admirably, and did not budge an inch from the saddle.

"That little horse will suit me, Mr. Ruddle," said Miss Van Agnew decidedly. "What did you say the price was?"

"Four hundred, and he's worth every penny," replied Peter. "Such animals are not often to be met with in the market."

"Guineas or pounds?" she inquired laconically.

"Guineas. But wont you have a ride first, miss, just to feel how he moves under you?"

"No," she answered carelessly. "It's too much bother, and I'm quite satisfied after what I've seen. And now, what else have you got? If I remember rightly there was a gray mare you were telling me about. Is she really something tiptop?"

"Yes, I believe her to be almost as good as the bay. You can see her next if you like. I thoroughly recommend her to carry a lady."

"All right. Will you let Miss Herrick ride, and tell her to go over the same fences, if you please."

"They are rather big," he began.

"All the better," she interrupted. Then she laughed and added, "If the fences are large they match your prices, Mr. Ruddle, and the least you can do is to give customers like us a good trial." Miss Van Agnew was sharp enough in her way, and had a great idea of her own importance. She was quite aware that Mr. Ruddle did not get people to give four hundred guineas for a hunter every day of his life.

"You are welcome to every trial," he responded, "but you appear to forget that Miss Herrick has just been riding an animal she knows thoroughly. It makes a difference when you are an old favorite."

"I thought you told me the gray was as good," retorted Miss Van Agnew sharply.

"I believe her to be so, but since you wish to see her put over the big course, perhaps you will allow my foreman to do showman."

"Indeed no," returned the heiress vivaciously. "As I want the animal for myself, I greatly prefer her being ridden by a lady. One gets such a much better idea of their capabilities. I say, Miss Herrick," she called out to Kitty, who brought Tiny Tim back as gay as a lark "I have bought that horse, so you may as well get off him; and now I want you to jump the gray mare, but Mr. Ruddle is making all sorts of objections, and seems to think you might be afraid."

This speech roused Kitty's spirit.

"Did Mr. Ruddle really believe I was such a coward?" she inquired, glancing reproachfully at her employer.

"Well, perhaps not exactly," said Miss Van Agnew, "but he insinuated it." Then she paused, and added insolently, "I always thought people belonging to your profession had nerves of iron and were quite accustomed to tumbling about."

"So they are," rejoined Kitty sarcastically. "When our customers entertain such notions we should be very badly off without good nerve. I am only here for the purpose of 'tumbling about' in order to save purchasers such a risk, so I will ride the gray with pleasure."

Mr. Ruddle being in a minority, was unable to protest any more. His anxiety about Kitty was due to the knowledge that the mare was not quite herself, and in all probability would fail to perform as well as usual. But he yielded the point, being anxious to propitiate Miss Van Agnew. Having sold Tiny Tim so well, he not unnaturally looked forward to doing a deal on his own account. So the gray mare was brought out, and Kitty mounted her without delay. The girl had not been on her back five minutes before she became aware of the fact that the stiffness in her quarter had increased considerably.   Thereupon, she went up to Mr. Ruddle, and calling him aside, said:

"The mare is hardly fit to be shown.   Her action behind is far from true."

"I know it," he responded; "but Miss Van Agnew is bent on seeing her perform to day.   What am I to do?"

"I am not the least afraid," said Kitty, flushing up. "But I doubt whether the mare is sound enough to go the big course."

"Miss Van Agnew is so keen on jumping," he rejoined. "She turns up her nose at the small fences, and appears to have no idea of danger."

"That is the result of ignorance," said Kitty.   "When she has had one or two good falls out hunting she'll soon grow more cautious—at least where she herself is concerned.   If you are willing to run the risk of laming your horse, however, I am prepared to give a show."

"I'm ready enough to take the risk, Miss Kitty, and only objected on your account.   Every now and again one is obliged to go out of one's way in order to satisfy buyers."

She gave a short laugh which sounded somewhat hard and metallic.

"You must give up thinking me so precious, Mr. Ruddle.   Other people don't.   Why not take a leaf out of your customer's book?"

"Well, well," he said undecidedly, "I leave it to you. On the one hand, I should like to please Miss Van Agnew; on the other, I don't want anything untoward to happen.   By the by, I am asking three hundred for the gray.   Don't let out that Miss Bretby might have had her for precisely half the sum."   And he pulled out his pocket-handkerchief in an airy fashion, and lifting his hat, wiped his forehead.

Kitty opened her eyes wide.

"Of course I shall say nothing; but is it—is it quite

right, Mr. Ruddle, to ask double the price just because people are rich?"

He turned very red, and stared hard at the grass springing up round his boots.

"Don't look at me so reproachfully, Miss Herrick. I try my very best to be honest, but when you have been a little longer in the profession you will begin to see that as often as not it is the purchaser himself who determines the price of an animal. Look at Tiny Tim, for instance. I had made up my mind to ask two-fifty for him, but Mr. Van Agnew said out pat, ' I suppose you want four hundred for this little horse?' and I answered ' Yes.' I saw from the first that he and his sister think nothing of a hunter unless you lump it on. They don't judge by merit, but by money."

"You are right there," said Kitty thoughtfully. "It seems a funny way of buying, doesn't it?"

"It does to you and me; but there are a good many folk like Mr. and Miss Van Agnew, though I am bound to say the stingy sort are more common. What I was going to observe," he continued, buckling up the gray's girths, "was, that if you succeed in selling this little mare for three hundred, I will make your commission ten, instead of five, per cent."

Kitty shook her head.

"No," she said, "it is very good of you, but I can't accept such an offer. I am quite ready to do my best and study your interest in every way without being bribed. Let me feel that my wages are honestly earned. I ask for nothing more."

So saying, she moved off, whilst Mr. Ruddle looked after her with mingled feelings of admiration and shame.

"Dash it all," he said to himself. "I'm always putting my foot in it, even when I try to act most handsomely by her. Bless her dear heart! What a thorough little lady she is, to be sure. But she's right about the commission, of course. I must make it up to her in some other way — some way that wont interfere with her scruples." Thus resolving, he returned to Mr. and Miss Van Agnew, and launched out into a little judicious praise of the gray.

"I don't like her so much as the bay," said Miss Judith, cutting his panegyric short. "She is not such a nice color."

"Don't you think so, miss?" he returned, diplomatically. "It's odd how people's tastes differ. Now, for my part, I never consider a lady who rides well shows to such advantage as when mounted on a gray horse. To begin with, everybody notices her out hunting."

"There's something in that," said Miss Van Agnew reflectively. Her secret ambition was to shine in the field.

"You're never so well known, or so much observed, as when on a grey," pursued Mr. Ruddle, following up his advantage. "Take all the studs one can mention. If there happens to be a good gray among the number, his fame is established. The Duke of Furrowdale's huntsman rode one for many years. When he went to the hammer he was eighteen years old, and had hardly a leg to stand on. If you would believe it, that horse sold for three hundred and sixty guineas at his Grace's sale."

"I might waive my objection to the color," said Miss Van Agnew, "if your mare jumps well. After all, jumping is the main thing."

"She is a brilliant hunter," rejoined Mr. Ruddle. "Unfortunately, she met with a slight accident in the stable yesterday afternoon, and goes stiff behind, so that she may not acquit herself as well as usual to-day. You may take my word for it, however, that she's a bad 'un to beat across country."

"Excuse me," said Miss Van Agnew coolly, "but I make it a rule never to take any one's word for anything in this world. I find it preferable to rely upon the evidence of my own eyesight."

Mr. Ruddle bridled up at this speech, and responded stiffly, "Oh, certainly." Miss Van Agnew rather baffled him She was such a curious mixture of ignorance and shrewdness. The brother was easily classified as "pure fool and snob," but she did not exactly come under the same head, and possessed a considerable amount of individuality, if not of an altogether pleasant kind. He thought it best to conduct the conversation back to Miss Herrick.

"Bravo! Well over," he exclaimed, as the gray popped lightly over the first fence. "Not much fault to be found with that, eh?"

In spite of his expressed satisfaction, a close observer might have seen some anxiety depicted on Mr. Ruddle's features as Kitty went at the double, but the mare knew her business, and moreover had come from a country where doubles were numerous. She jumped on and off cleverly, if not with quite the same lightness and agility as displayed by Tiny Tim. Nevertheless, Mr. Ruddle noticed that she dragged her near hind leg, and landed with rather a lurch. Now came the big uphill fence. Knowing that pace was wanted to get over it, Kitty took her steed resolutely by the head and sent her along. But the pain in the gray's quarter apparently prevented her from getting up the requisite steam. She seemed to stop and half hesitate as she approached within a few yards of the fence; then her courage conquering her physical uneasiness, she made a fair spring at the hedge. But although she cleared it after a fashion, she jumped short and landed with both hind legs well in the ditch. The next moment she toppled on to her head and floundered into the field, slithering along a distance of several feet, and it was just touch and go whether she would roll over or not.

"She's down—down for a monkey!" shouted Mr. Van Agnew, in a desperate state of excitement. "By George! No, she's up again. Hooray! Miss Herrick recovered her splendidly!" as Kitty, by dint of sitting still, managed to stick on while the mare sprawled to her legs.

CHAPTER XXXV.

MR. RUDDLE followed the gray's movements with close attention, and when she arose without a fall he said in his ordinary voice:

"There's a yawning big ditch at that fence, and the mare made a bit of a peck. Miss Herrick might have sent her a trifle faster. The best of riders are apt to make errors of judgment at times." He said this because, as every dealer knows, when anything goes wrong it is essential to find fault with the horseman rather than the horse. It is so easy to say, "He rode too fast or too slow," in order to account for the deficiencies of an animal offered for sale, and as Kitty was out of earshot there could be no harm in converting her into the scapegoat. Miss Van Agnew was willing enough to accept this explanation. Her feelings had been rather ruffled by the comparisons instituted by her brother between Miss Herrick's equestrian powers and her own, and she was by no means displeased to hear Mr. Ruddle make the above criticism.

"Yes," she said, "I quite agree with you. I thought Miss Herrick went much too slowly at the fence. It was not a bit the mare's fault dropping her hind legs. She wanted 'hoorooshing.' Halloo!" she ejaculated suddenly. "What's the matter now? Miss Herrick is getting off and walking home through the gate."

In effect, the mare had fallen so lame that Kitty dismounted and led her back hobbling painfully on three legs.

"Poor little woman," said the girl, caressing her steed's smooth muzzle. "You were not the least to blame." Then she turned to Mr. Ruddle and said, "I'm dreadfully sorry, but it was as I expected. The quarter hurt her and prevented her jumping in her usual form. I hope it's nothing very bad, but I fear she will take a week or ten days to come round."

"If it had not been for your good riding," he responded, "the mare would have fallen outright. I saw her hesitate just as she took off. I knew you would have a squeak to get over the ditch. Luckily, there is no great harm done."

Kitty heaved a sigh of relief.

"I am glad you do not take a more serious view of the matter, Mr. Ruddle. I was so afraid it might spoil your sale."

"No, I think not. Miss Van Agnew seems rather sweet on the mare, and of course this is only a temporary affair."

The heiress's imagination had been so inflamed by Mr. Ruddle's adroit observations anent gray hunters being conspicuous objects in the field, and she was so firmly imbued with the idea, moreover, that the mishap had proceeded entirely from defective horsemanship on Kitty's part, that after a tolerably lengthy palaver she agreed to take the mare directly she came sound, subject to Mr. Ruddle finding her another should she not suit. Having arrived at this decision, Mr. Van Agnew mildly hinted that it was his turn to be attended to, and a variety of horses of one sort and another were brought out for his inspection. After a long but profitable morning's work, Mr. Ruddle proposed an adjournment to the house, where prices could be better adjusted over glasses of sherry and biscuits. Accordingly, they retraced their footsteps leisurely, Kitty going on ahead, when suddenly she uttered a little cry of pleasure and darted forward to meet a tall, good-looking young man who had evidently but just arrived on the scene.

"Oh, Cyril!" she exclaimed. "How glad I am to see you! But why have you never written me a line since I left town? It has been such a disappointment, looking

for a letter every morning, but now that you are here
it is all right." And she stretched out her hands
towards him. But he pretended not to see them, and
she looked up at him with a sense of blank dismay, all
her joy checked by the coldness of his manner.

"What — what is the matter?" she faltered. She
withered like a flower in the frost as she noticed the
dark, stern expression of his face.

"I wonder you deem it necessary to ask," he said
harshly. "What in the name of goodness are you doing
here? A report reached my ears before I left London
that you had turned horse-breaker and entered Mr.
Ruddle's service, but I did not believe you could have
demeaned yourself so utterly—you who, whatever your
faults might have been, I always considered had the
instincts of a lady."

It was a cruel speech, devoid of any kindly feeling,
and Kitty realized this, but she was too much crushed
to make a bold defence, and, glancing apprehensively
towards Mr. and Miss Van Agnew, said in a beseech-
ing tone, "Hush, please don't talk so loud."

"I demand an explanation of your most extraordinary
conduct," he said, taking no pains to comply with her
request.

"You shall have it, but not now. Oh! Cyril, Cyril,"
she continued, with extreme agitation, "for God's sake
don't make a scene before strangers. At least have the
decency to wait until they are gone, when I will answer
any question you choose to put."

"What good will that do? The thing is done. I am
ashamed of you, Kitty—yes, thoroughly ashamed; and
what my mother will say I don't know."

A crowd of rebellious thoughts surged up into her
mind. It seemed to her that his love was of a very
different sort from her own, and for the second time
she found that the actual man did not come up to the
ideal she had entertained of him. It gave her a kind
of shock, but she was too proud or too humble to retort,

and strove hard not to let him see that his words wounded her to the quick.

"Who are these dreadful people with Mr. Ruddle?" said Cyril, after a slight pause, looking with ill-concealed disfavor at the heiress and her brother.

"Mr. and Miss Van Agnew," answered Kitty shortly.

His countenance underwent a very decided alteration, and from being full of animosity his glance became benignantly interested.

"You don't say so! Do you know them, Kitty?"

"Yes, in a sort of way. Miss Van Agnew has just been good enough to buy Tiny Tim." And she shaded her eyes with her hand.

"The devil she has! Why on earth did you not let me know he was for sale? The little horse would have suited me down to the ground."

There was a frank egotism about this observation which struck a painful chord. It did not enter his head, apparently, that he might have bought him for his wife to ride. He thought only of himself, and displayed very little regard for her feelings.

"Could you have afforded to give four hundred?" she inquired, a trifle sarcastically. "If so, you must be better off than you make out."

Cyril colored. The reproof was well merited, and he resented it accordingly.

"You don't mean to say you got that for him?" he exclaimed incredulously. "He is not worth half."

"That is a matter of opinion. Miss Van Agnew apparently thought otherwise."

"By George!" he ejaculated, "she must be made of money to throw it away in this reckless fashion. She and her brother aint beauties, but as they are neighbors and we are likely to meet out hunting, you may as well introduce me."

There was no particular reason why Kitty should have resented this speech, but she did. It struck her as a personal insult. Why should he be so eager to make Miss Van Agnew's acquaintance? Only because she was rich. The sting of poverty entered there and then into the girl's soul, and she said to herself, "He liked me too when I was well-off. Now he does nothing but grumble and find fault."

"Did you hear what I said," he repeated. "Introduce me to the Van Agnews." There was a touch of imperiousness in his tone which roused her spirit.

"I shall do nothing of the sort. Ask Mr. Ruddle. You forget," and she smiled bitterly, "I am not in a position to put myself forward. Good-by for the present. When you have done doing the agreeable to the heiress you will find me in the saddle-room." So saying, she walked off, but had only gone a few paces when Miss Van Agnew fumbled in her pocket and ran after her.

"I may not see you again before I go," she said to Kitty. "And I am so much obliged, and—and——" a little awkwardly, slipping a small round substance into the girl's hand. "Here is something for you. I always make it a rule to pay my way, so you mustn't mind."

But Kitty *did* mind. She opened her hand, looked at its contents, and turned as scarlet as a peony. A shining half-sovereign lay on her palm, and seemed to burn a hole in it. Tipped like a common servant! And by a vulgar, noisy, purse-proud woman. She felt ready to sink into the bowels of the earth.

"Take back your money," she cried fiercely. "I don't want it—I wont have it."

"Oh, but you must," insisted Miss Van Agnew, with mistaken good nature.

"I tell you I wont; I'd rather die."

And thus declaring, Kitty, acting on a sudden impulse, flung the coin passionately to the ground. The astonishment and consternation depicted on Miss Van Agnew's countenance caused her to regret the action a moment afterwards, and, turning swiftly on her heel, she fled to the saddle-room. There she threw herself into a chair and waited with painful anxiety for Cyril to join her. After a long wait she at length heard his footsteps approaching. The sound made her heart beat violently. Had he followed her at once the probabilities are he would have found her tearful and submissive, but that quarter of an hour during which he kept her waiting for the purpose of ingratiating himself in the good graces of Miss Van Agnew created a curious revolution, and rendered her mood aggressive.

"Well!" she said, lifting her head defiantly as he entered, "I hope you have succeeded in making a favorable impression on the heiress."

The remark was too much in accord with his secret aspirations not to produce an irritating effect.

"Drop that," he said angrily. "I have come to talk about your doings, not about Miss Van Agnew."

She settled herself in her seat with a little air of well-simulated resignation, and crossing her hands, said:

"The subject is deeply interesting. One always enjoys being lectured. Pray proceed."

"There is only one way in which I can account for your conduct," he said, rather disconcerted by her composure."

"Be good enough to name it."

"You must be mad—stark, staring mad."

She laughed discordantly.

"You quite ignore the simple fact that I had to live. My lunacy is nothing more nor less than a struggle for existence."

"Not at all," he retorted. "You might easily have found some more respectable means of maintaining yourself."

"So every one tells me, now that it is too late. May I ask what profession you would deem *respectable* for a penniless girl born in the lap of luxury to adopt?"

He hesitated before replying, and then said vaguely, "Oh! there are plenty."

"Possibly, but perhaps you will kindly enumerate those by which I could earn the large sum of a pound a week. I am not a very enormous eater, but I cannot manage on less."

"Pooh! Kitty, you know what I mean."

"Pardon me, that's exactly what I don't know."

"You might have lived with your friends," he said somewhat lamely.

"Indefinitely?" she asked pointedly, drumming on the table with her fingers.

He made no answer to this query, which indeed was an awkward one. His silence roused her to a fuller sense of her wrongs, and with gathering warmth she continued. "What right have you to come here and blame me? You knew before I left London that I was without money, and must earn some at once, in order to subsist. Did you give me any advice? Did you offer to help me? No. On the contrary, you evaded the question and I was thrown back on my own resources. The only counsel you tendered was that I should quarter myself on the Duke and Duchess of Furrowdale because they were people worth cultivating, quite forgetting that a few days previously you had issued your lordly command for me to cut their son without rhyme or reason. From that moment, Cyril, I realized it was useless to count on you for assistance."

"But Kitty——" he began.

She interrupted him hastily.

"No, hear me out. Rightly or wrongly, I resolved from the hour I left your mother's house to be indebted to nobody. I told you I was willing to work and wait, and so I am. But," and her voice shook, "since you— you are ashamed of me, and the beautiful Miss Van Agnew is still unmarried, and therefore to be wooed, everything had better be at an end between us."

Perhaps in his heart Cyril acknowledged the wisdom of taking her at her word, but he happened to look at her and their glances met. There was a magnetism about her glistening eyes, her flushed cheeks, and trembling lips which appealed to all the passion of which his cold, calculating nature was capable. Involuntarily almost he stretched out his arms. The mere action was sufficient to disarm her wrath. With a little glad cry she flew into them and nestled her head against his breast. He pushed back the rebellious ringlets from her brow and kissed it. The touch of his lips sent a thrill through her whole frame, and she sighed softly with content.

"Well, Miss Spitfire," he said playfully, "do you feel in a better humor now?"

"Yes, much. Oh, Cyril, darling!" and her little soft hands wandered round his neck and clutched it tightly, "don't let us ever quarrel again. It is so horrid. You did not write, and then I got miserable and suspicious, and ready to believe all sorts of odious things."

"What was the matter with, you Kitty? I put off writing because I hoped every day to get away from town."

She blushed and looked away, but was too honest not to answer the question truthfully.

"I—I—think I was jealous of Miss Van Agnew."

"Little goose! Why, she's as ugly as sin."

And so they made up their quarrel, and for a few minutes the saddle-room was converted into a Garden of Eden.

CHAPTER XXXVI.

THE SPIDER AND THE FLY.

ONE of the peculiar characteristics of Cyril's love was, that from the moment he was no longer subject to Kitty's personal influence he uneasily questioned its wisdom. On the present occasion he had not left the saddle-room five minutes before he began to feel dissatisfied and blame himself for having yielded to temptation. Since his lady-love's departure from Sloane Street he had not had altogether a good time of it. His mother used every argument she could think of to prevent him from following Kitty into the country. He was dying to get back to the hunting, but Lady Mordaunt declared he would leave her absolutely miserable unless he first promised to break off the match. So he lingered on a few days, hesitating and undecided.

Now, a man may profess to be ever so independent, but anybody acquainted with the elementary rules of hypnotism knows how great an effect suggestion produces on the human brain. The consequence was that after her ladyship had suggested to her son a few hundred times that Miss Herrick was the last woman in the world he ought to think of marrying, and that she was bent on ruining his prospects merely to secure herself a home, his mind, which had begun by rejecting the idea, ended by assimilating and accepting it.

"Miss Herrick was all very well," said Lady Mordaunt, "when we believed her to have five-and-twenty thousand pounds and expectations into the bargain, but the circumstances are so completely altered now that it seems to me as if she were a right-thinking young *woman she* would perceive the selfishness of her conduct in wishing to continue the engagement, and refuse to let you sacrifice yourself utterly for her sake."

"At the same time," he replied, "if she doesn't—and I don't believe she will—you must see that I am in rather an awkward fix."

"Yes, if you go corresponding and making all sorts of foolish promises on paper; but not if you take my advice."

"And pray what is it, mother?" he inquired, although he knew quite well, having had it repeatedly dinned into his ears.

"Why, simply this. Don't write, and if you *must* go back to hunt——"

"My horses are at Furrowdale," he interrupted, "and I can't kick my heels about town all winter."

"Very well, then," she continued, "as I was about to observe, if you insist on going, for goodness' sake let things slide, and don't commit yourself by any foolish endearments. The girl is bound to cool off when she finds you are no longer keen."

"It's all very well for you to talk and lay down the law," he said, "but there are difficulties in the way, say what you like to the contrary. And as for not being keen, I should be keen enough still had not Kitty had the misfortune to lose her money. I like her better than any girl I have ever seen."

"Marry her, then, by all means," said Lady Mordaunt satirically, "and try how you like giving up your horses and your comforts, and living on twopence-halfpenny a year, with a couple of slatternly maid-servants to wait on you."

"I shouldn't like it at all," he said gloomily. "In fact, there are few things I should hate much more."

She gave a hard laugh of derision.

"I am quite aware of that fact, my dear boy. If there is one person in the whole world unsuited to domestic bliss on slender means, it is yourself. Dear little Tom, Dick, or Harry's wants would never seem half as *important* as your own, and I question greatly

19

whether you would be prepared to give up many luxuries on account of your wife and children. In short, you want the best of everything to keep you happy and in a good temper."

"I am not singular there," he said, wincing at the severe candor of her speech. "Nine men out of ten are the same nowadays."

"I don't say that you are not right, Cyril. They are a selfish lot at best; but why voluntarily doom yourself to a state of misery? There are more girls than one, and it is not difficult to find consolation. For my part," and she shrugged her shoulders, "I would not take Miss Kitty Herrick at a gift. Her tongue and her temper combined are quite enough to make any man wretched."

"She has always been niceness itself to me," he said, with a certain loyalty to his absent love.

"Oh! I dare say. So is every young woman who sets her cap at an eligible young man and makes up her mind to marry him. They are all on their best behavior before matrimony. You would think butter would not melt in their mouths. They are so sweet, and so innocent and adoring. But that does not last, and I feel convinced that in six months after the ceremony Miss H. would develop into a regular termagant. I'm a pretty good judge of my own sex, and seldom make a mistake."

"What am I to do?" he said, impressed by the force of her opposition, and soliciting her advice just as if she had not already given it times out of number.

"There are two courses open to you," she replied. "Either tell Miss Herrick straight out that in the altered position of affairs you are unable to fulfil your engagement, or—if you have not the nerve to do this—sheer off by degrees. The best plan, if you adopt the latter alternative, is to make her jealous."

"I don't know that I can. She's too sensible."

"Bah! there never was a woman yet who did not fall victim to the green-eyed monster."

"But, mother, even if I should succeed, what would be the good?"

"What good! Really, Cyril, you are extraordinarily dense. Miss Herrick will either sulk or fly into a passion. In either case, sooner or later she will shower reproaches upon your head. You reply warmly, and the inevitable result is a quarrel, during which one party or the other puts an end to the engagement without loss of credit on either side."

"There is an objection to your scheme," he said. "Supposing I find nobody decent at Furrowdale for me to flirt with?"

Lady Mordaunt smiled, pursed up her lips, and looked mysterious.

"I know one person at any rate who I am sure will feel flattered by the attentions of a handsome young guardsman."

"Whom do you mean, mother?" he inquired, not repudiating the idea.

"Why, Miss Van Agnew, of course. There's a girl worth looking after, if you like. Twenty thousand a year, and the father and mother both lying safely in Kensal Green. She and her brother have just gone to Gretton Grange. Mrs. Marshbank told me so yesterday, and you will have every opportunity of getting friendly. Now is the time. She has only come into her fortune recently, and therefore as yet is not much run after. But some kind, charitable, disinterested soul is sure to take her up before long, and then she will have every impecunious lord in the kingdom at her feet."

Lady Mordaunt said no more on this occasion, but she brought the conversation round so often to Miss Van Agnew and Miss Van Agnew's wealth that at length Cyril became fairly imbued with the notion of captivating the heiress. He knew that he should not have the moral courage to throw Kitty over all at once, but he did not shrink from the prospect of doing so by degrees. In short, after two or three days spent in his mother's society, her influence triumphed over the memory of

Kitty's pretty face, with its bright eyes and sparkling smile. . Acting on Lady Mordaunt's advice, he refrained from writing any missive of a tender and incriminating nature.

It so happened, moreover, that during Cyril's stay in town her ladyship received help from an unlooked-for quarter. A gentleman named Isaacs called to see Cyril, and by a piece of gross carelessness on the part of the butler was admitted to his master's presence. Mr. Isaacs was a little old man with a hooked nose, a humped back, and a yellow wrinkled face, framed by long wisps of thin gray hair. He wore a shabby black coat, threadbare at the seams, and at first sight one might have imagined him to be a most humble and un-assuming individual, possessed of no importance whatever. But appearances were deceptive, and in reality he wielded immense power. When it is stated that he did an enormous business in fashionable circles as a money-lender, it is needless to say more. All the young sparks about town went to him when distressed for that convenient commodity, R. M. D. He was a nice old man, for he never made any difficulties, and was always prepared to advance any sum in reason; but he demanded the modest interest of forty per cent., and report had it that very few flies ever escaped from the spider's net when once they had incautiously flown into it. He was an adept at sucking them dry.

Cyril was lounging about in the study, smoking a cigar and glancing casually at the morning paper, when this individual happened to be announced. The sound of Mr. Isaacs's name made him sit up and ejaculate, "The devil!" in a tone of intense irritation. The next moment he forced a smile to his face, and advancing a step towards the door, said, with a thin veneer of polite-ness, "Good morning, Mr. Isaacs. This is a most unex-pected pleasure."

"Indeed, Captain," responded the Jew, seating him-self in a comfortable arm-chair and removing his hat, as much much as to say he felt perfectly at home.

"Perhaps you have forgotten that little bill of mine which fell due the day before yesterday?"

Cyril frowned heavily.

"Are such documents easily forgotten?" he inquired, striving to conceal the perturbation created by the query.

Mr. Isaacs brushed his hat with his sleeve until the nap shone.

"All gentlemen are not so thoughtful as you, Captain," he said, in an unctuous voice. "The majority are inflicted with such bad memories that I find it absolutely necessary to give them a little reminder every now and again. It is good of you to save me the trouble."

"What is the amount?" said Cyril abruptly. "You can reserve your soft sawder for some bigger flat."

Mr. Isaacs pretended to be extremely amused by this remark.

"Ha, ha, ha!" he laughed. "What a pretty vein of humor the Almighty has been pleased to bless you with! It is most gratifying to find such unusual powers of discernment in one so young and so unversed in the ways of the world's wickedness. The amount, did you say, my dear sir! The amount is a mere trifle, hardly worth speaking about." Whereupon he drew a blue document from his pocket, and slipped a pair of spectacles over his beaky nose, where they rested in a furrow caused by long usage.

"Well!" said Cyril impatiently. "What does the darned thing come to?"

"The interest or the principal?" inquired Mr. Isaacs innocently.

"The interest, of course."

"It only comes to three hundred and fifty pounds," responded Mr. Isaacs, in accents full of regret. "But perhaps you may prefer to pay off the whole sum rather than renew?"

Cyril groaned. Unless he married Miss Van Agnew, or some one possessing a handsome fortune, he saw no prospect of getting out of his friend Solomon's hands.

"Six months more," continued Mr. Isaacs suavely, "will bring the interest up to five hundred and fifty. It's wonderful how slowly it accumulates."

This concluding remark was too much for Cyril's equanimity. He lost his temper entirely.

"You old thief, you!" he exclaimed, brandishing his fist so close to Mr. Isaacs's nose that that gentleman pushed back his chair in alarm. "If you had not got me so infernally tight I would kick you downstairs, and never set eyes on your ugly parchment-like face again."

"Softly, softly," said Mr. Isaacs. "Your humor is becoming personal. Kicking may relieve your feelings, but it wont help your purse."

"Forty per cent. is a monstrous rate of interest," continued Cyril excitedly. "The government should pass a law making it illegal for such skinflints as you to extort more than ten, or fifteen at most. They put a poor beggar in prison for robbing his neighbor of a loaf of bread, and yet you fellows are allowed to go about untouched. Not content with getting rich at our expense, you actually have the audacity to complain that you do not make money fast enough."

"Go on, Captain," said Mr. Isaacs sarcastically. "I dare say this gentlemanly abuse acts as a safety-valve to your feelings, and it don't hurt me as long as I get my bill settled. Am I laboring under a mistake in supposing," and he showed two or three yellow fangs which did duty for a smile, "that you entertain a natural objection to appearing in the Bankruptcy Court? It might interfere with your matrimonial prospects, eh?"

"What the dickens do you know about my matrimonial prospects?" said Cyril, taken aback by the man's cool impudence.

"Calm yourself, my dear young friend. Perhaps you are not aware that irascibility of temper produces apoplexy. As for me—I know everything. A money-lender's profession is regarded with contempt, and yet it is the finest one in the world. You young swells may profess to look down upon us, but we play upon human passions just as a white-fingered lady does on the keys of her piano. Our little den is an arena where Greed, Avarice, Shame, Despair, stalk rampant. One visit, and we gauge you thoroughly. You go in and you go out—curs, cowards, bullies, boasters, spendthrifts, snobs, idiots, gentlemen—and you are all so many open books to us whose pages we read with the greatest of ease. Don't flatter yourself for one moment that I am not acquainted with the programme you have drawn up for yourself." And Mr. Isaacs, whose spirit also seemed roused, riveted his small, gimlet-like eyes on Cyril's face. In spite of their size, they were wonderful eyes, bright as a ferret's, and full of penetration.

"W—what do you mean?" faltered the young man, thoroughly disconcerted by this bold attack. He had always found Mr. Isaacs cringing and subservient, and the sudden change in that individual's tactics proved most disagreeable. He failed to realize that he was responsible for it.

"You are a pretty fellow, Captain Mordaunt," continued the money-lender, a tinge of color showing through his sallow cheeks. "I'll give you your due, and your six feet, and your swagger manner, blue eyes, and silky mustache are good stock-in-trade where the fair sex are concerned. Women are like moths, easily attracted by a glittering surface. On the other hand, you're selfish—very selfish—and will always be fonder of yourself than of anybody else."

CHAPTER XXXVII.

DIFFICULTIES.

"D— your impertinence," cried Cyril furiously. "If you think you may come here and insult me to my face on account of your beastly bill you're very much mistaken."

"If insults have been passed on either side," retorted Mr. Isaacs, the blood mounting to his forehead, "may I ask who first set the example? You called me an old thief, and I said you were selfish. I scarcely think you are in a position, Captain, to accuse me of want of courtesy." Then, with an effort at self-control, he continued in his usual voice, "What I was going to remark is, that you like to live on the fat of the land and sail down-stream in good company. Consequently you have but two courses open to you. One is to apply to your old friend, Solomon Isaacs, who is always willing to oblige; the other is to profit by the favors of nature and snap up an heiress. Am I not right?" And he deliberately conveyed a pinch of snuff to his hairy nostrils.

"Look here," said Cyril, starting to his feet, beside himself with rage, "if you don't shut up this minute I'll—I'll——"

"Show me the door," suggested his visitor. "Believe me, I am quite ready to find my own way out without giving you the trouble of acting as guide, as soon as you will kindly settle my little account. Come, now," he added persuasively, "it can't signify much to a fine gentleman like yourself."

"I cannot settle it," cried the unfortunate guardsman. "You know quite well that I cannot, or you would

never dare to use such language to me. It's as much
as ever I am able to rub along at all."

"In that case," said Mr. Isaacs, with a chuckle, "I
presume we renew?"

Cyril nodded his head, and Mr. Isaacs took up a pen,
wrote a few words on the blue document, then handed
it to his companion. When the necessary signatures
were affixed he put on his hat, which by this time had
acquired a superlative gloss, and with a benevolent
relaxation of the facial muscles, said, "Good day, Captain Mordaunt—good day. I am sorry there should have
been any little unpleasantness between us, but have no
doubt that on reflecting you will acknowledge it was
more your fault than mine." And so saying he shambled out of the room, leaving Cyril sunk in the depths
of despair.

Some heavy losses on the turf and at cards had forced
him a year ago to apply to Mr. Isaacs, and since then
he felt as if a cloud were constantly gathering and
deepening over his head. In spite of Solomon's asser-
tions to the contrary, the rate at which the interest
mounted up was something alarming. He foresaw that
before long his embarrassments would increase, and
the constant need for ready money must end by involv-
ing his affairs hopelessly. If he persisted in marrying
Kitty, he perceived nothing but ruin ahead—or at least
what represented ruin for a man of his tastes and inclinations—namely, economy of a severe kind, and living
in a humble way, without hunters, shooting, racing and
gambling. The few hundreds which he had won during
the autumn were nearly expended—buying horses had
proved a costly affair—and he did not know where to
turn for a further supply when they disappeared. The
outlook was anything but promising. When he reviewed
the situation calmly he was forced to admit that a
wealthy marriage was his only chance.

After all, one soon got tired of any particular woman,
and a few years hence it would make very little difference whether he yielded to the proclivities of his heart

or not. Love was an ephemeral passion, when you came to analyze it, and depended almost entirely on the imagination. It could not compare with the stability and solid advantages presented by its great rival, money. Moreover, it was supremely selfish, and entailed untold misery on posterity. For when you came to think of it, what could be more cruel than to bring a lot of helpless, penniless brats into the world? People were bound to look ahead, and consider the consequences of a rash union founded on affection without sufficient means. Novels alone held up to admiration romance versus common sense. In real life folk termed such conduct rank folly and rank egotism. There was very little sympathy for poor lovers nowadays. Society was getting too provident to countenance couples who in all probability would not prove self-supporting.

Thus Cyril reasoned, and before he left for Furrowdale he had almost promised his mother that he would act in accordance with her wishes. When he first met Kitty at Mr. Ruddle's, he quite intended to provoke a quarrel, but somehow he failed in his part, and her pretty face upset previous calculations. When she flew into his arms, he could not refrain from kissing her—it would have seemed so unkind if he hadn't; and to do him justice, for a few minutes he almost brought himself to believe that he would be happier poor, and with her for his wife, than mated to an heiress. But the belief was only temporary, and other thoughts soon prevailed. As he walked along the road which led from Belfield to Furrowdale he felt conscious of having committed an egregious error, and bitterly regretted the lover-like termination to his interview with Kitty, which was in direct contradiction to the parting admonitions showered upon him by Lady Mordaunt.

"I've muffed it," he mused, "as I knew I should." Then he took heart and murmured, "Fortunately, there is no particular hurry. I've all the winter before me, and it's better to do these things by degrees. Of course, women don't understand. They're differently

constituted. It's precious hard lines on a fellow to be
expected to repulse a pretty girl when she is head over
ears in love with him and takes no pains to disguise
her passion."

There was a manliness and chivalry about his reflections which no doubt would have delighted their object
had she been aware of them. Strangely enough, after
Cyril left Kitty was not satisfied either. She tried to
imagine that she was perfectly happy, but in her heart
of hearts a secret voice whispered that his love was not
genuine.

"He went away and never said a word about our
meeting again," she soliloquized. "I had it in my
mind all the time to lead up to the subject, but I did
not like to. The proposition was one that ought to
have come from his side, not mine. Heigho!" and her
mouth drooped with a pathetic curve. "I wonder if I
am very exacting and expect too much. I wish I knew
what other girls would feel or say in my place. One
thing is quite clear. It's no good judging Cyril as
I judge myself. We see things differently."

This was a very sorrowful conclusion for a young
lady only recently engaged to arrive at; and Kitty
apparently entertained the same opinion, for she sighed
heavily once or twice, and remained for a long while
lost in thought. At last she started up, as if determined to dismiss all unpleasant subjects, and repaired
to the stable, where she found Mr. Ruddle had ordered
warm fomentations to be applied to the gray mare's
quarter, a treatment which was already producing a
favorable effect.

A few days passed away without any event of importance, except that during the matutinal exercise prome-
nade Mr. Frazer became increasingly gracious and condescending, and joined the fair leader at the head of
the string a trifle sooner every morning in order to
indulge in the pleasures of conversation. Kitty took
but little notice of the fact. She fully understood that
it was to her interest to keep on good terms with

David, and therefore listened attentively to all that he had to say, occasionally making some observation which sufficed to convince him of her appreciation. Neither did she perceive that the worthy foreman began to smarten himself up in the matter of dress and bestow an extra amount of soap and water on his hard-featured but not unkindly visage. These little external signs were lost upon her. At any other time, no doubt, they would have tickled her sense of humor, but just now she felt in exceedingly low spirits.

The first novelty of her situation was wearing off, and she began to realize a few of its hardships. Rising so early every day, and going through the operation of dressing by a tallow candle, required an immense effort, and when she got back to Mrs. Perkins's at night she often felt so thoroughly tired out that after having had something to eat she went straight to bed. Except on Sunday, she never had time to take up a book, to practise her music, or cultivate her mind. The life she led might be healthy, but it certainly was not an intellectual one, and already she began to suspect that it neither could nor would satisfy her aspirations. No one loved horses and hunting more than she did, but they were not the be-all and end-all of existence. She could even conceive of higher forms of amusement. Yet if anybody had asked her in these days to define the cause of her unhappiness, and to state her wishes, the probabilities are she would have failed to put them into words. Her thoughts were so vague and chaotic, and were tinged with so strong an element of sadness, that she shrunk from analyzing them. Nevertheless, when she did cross-examine herself as to the reason of the restlessness and depression from which she suffered, the answer was always the same. Cyril's lukewarmness. She had heard of his being out hunting, and therefore knew that nothing ailed him, but although Furrowdale was within walking distance of Belfield he had not come to see her again, neither had he written. Surely such conduct was strange.

A week went by anxiously and feverishly, and at the end of it the gray mare recovered from the lameness which had temporarily disabled her. Mr. Ruddle, therefore, gave orders for her to be taken over to Gretton Grange. Kitty happened to be by at the time, and formed a sudden resolution. The truth was, ever since she had scorned Miss Van Agnew's offering, and tossed it so indignantly to the ground, she had been a prey to sundry distressing pangs of conscience. She felt that she had acted rudely, not to say unlike a lady, and owed the heiress an apology. So she said to Mr. Ruddle:

"Would you have any objection to my riding the mare over?"

"None whatever," he responded. "The only thing is, Miss Herrick, how will you get back?"

"I can walk. I should quite enjoy a walk if you can spare me for an hour or two."

"But the saddle and bridle?" he objected.

"We will call for them to-morrow morning at exercise—that is, if you don't mind."

"Of course not," he replied. "By the way, you may as well ask to see Miss Agnew, and tell her not to work the mare too hard for a day or two, and also inquire if she has any message she would like to send back. It will be a polite method of conveying that a check would prove acceptable. Ladies," he continued explanatorily, "are such bad payers, as a rule, that I frequently find it necessary to give a delicate hint as a means of reminding them that the buying and selling of horses is a ready-money transaction."

"I think you will find Miss Van Agnew all right," said Kitty, with a smile.

"I have not the least doubt of it, but in a first deal payment on delivery is always satisfactory to the seller. One has so many losses to contend with that it does not do to be too easy-going and confiding. Experience has taught me that, consequently I go on the co-operative system—small profits, quick returns, and cash down. It's much the best plan."

Kitty laughed.

" I dare say you are wise, Mr. Ruddle. And now, with your permission, I'll make a start." Whereupon the gray mare was led out, and the side-saddle was strapped over her rug, in real rough-rider style. A pair of knee-caps were buckled round her knees, her head enveloped in a hood, and when all was in readiness Kitty mounted and rode out of the stable-yard. It did not take her long to reach Gretton Grange. She knew the house and its approaches well, having visited there in former days. Making straight for the stable-yard, she handed the mare over to the stud-groom, who gazed at her disdain-fully, the purchase having been effected without his aid, and said, " Can you tell me if Miss Van Agnew is at home?"

" I believe so, miss," was the response. " I 'ope you don't mean to say she 'as bought this 'ere screw."

" You had better question your mistress yourself on that point," answered Kitty haughtily. " My orders are to see her."

" Oh! all right," he said sulkily. " What name shall I say?"

" Herrick—Miss Herrick."

Upon this the man dived into the house through some back passages, leaving Kitty to admire a brand-new set of stable pails, brilliant with blue paint and large yellow monograms, which were ranged in a row against the wall.

Presently the stud-groom returned and said, " Miss Van Agnew's compliments, and will you walk this way, if you please?"

Kitty was now transmitted to the care of a tall, pow-dered-haired footman, dressed in a gorgeous livery of ultramarine and canary, who eyed her with an insolent familiarity which made her blood tingle. Finally, this offensive personage ushered her into the heiress's pres-ence. Miss Van Agnew was sitting before the fire reading a fashionable paper and studying the move-ments of the aristocracy. It was a wonder what interest

she could find in such twaddle as "The Duke and
Duchess of Apely passed through town yesterday on
their way to Neederham Court, their beautiful seat in
Devonshire," or in "Lady Janet Snookham has left her
residence in Belgrave Square for Homburg, where her
ladyship, who is in indifferent health, proposes drinking
the waters," or "Rumor avers that the youngest daughter of the Heir to the Crown will shortly be publicly
betrothed to the eldest son of one of our wealthiest Ducal families," but she did. She never tired of conning
over the doings of the so-called "great world," and had
an inborn veneration for a title. She was happily engaged scanning a list of the wedding presents given to
Lord Langmore and the Honorable Constance Fitzjack,
on the occasion of their marriage in St. Peter's Church,
Eaton Square; and had already learned how Her Gracious
Majesty the Queen had presented the bride with a cash-
mere shawl, how the Duke and Duchess of Weeds con-
tributed a magnificent diamond tiara, and the bride-
groom's elder sister, the Countess of Mufti, gave an oil
painting, painted by herself, when her further perusal
of this agreeable and instructive literature was interrupted by the announcement of Miss Herrick.

Kitty was proud, as we already know, and when the
door closed after her she stood on the threshold with her
head held very erect, as much as to say, "If you don't
consider me good enough to come in I'm sure I don't
want to."

CHAPTER XXXVIII.

IT so chanced that Miss Van Agnew had not been offended by Kitty's rejection of her half-sovereign. On the contrary, she rather approved of her action than otherwise, and considered it showed a fine, independent spirit. In her experience, people were all ready enough to grab money. It was quite a relief to meet with somebody who scorned a "tip." She had not any false shame, and being old Van Agnew's daughter, directly Kitty's back was turned made no bones about picking up the neglected coin and restoring it to her purse.

"I can give her some little present instead," she murmured. "She may like that better."

Since her visit to Mr. Ruddle's yard she had heard certain rumors anent Kitty and Lord Algernon Loddington in consequence of which her estimation of the girl had increased considerably. A young woman who could succeed in gaining the affections of a real live lord was not a person to be slighted, in Miss Van Agnew's opinion, however much she might give rise to envy. So she got up from her arm-chair, held out her hand, and said, "How do you do, Miss Herrick? Don't stand there. Come and sit down by the fire and warm yourself."

"Thank you," said Kitty, feeling relieved by this kindly reception, although it augmented her feelings of compunction. "I have ridden the gray mare over. She goes quite sound now, and I am sure will carry you well to hounds this season. I came myself," she went on, blushing very red, "because I—I—well, I wished to apologize to you for my behavior the other day. It was very wrong of me to act as I did. My only excuse is that I am not quite used to my place yet."

"Pray don't trouble your head about the incident, Miss Herrick," answered Miss Van Agnew good-naturedly—and she could be very good-natured when there were no men present before whom she desired to shine. "On thinking the matter over afterwards, I came to the conclusion that I was entirely to blame. I ought to have seen that you were a lady, and were not accustomed to be recompensed like a common person."

"That only makes my conduct the worse," said Kitty persistently. "I was horribly rude, and—and I am sorry. Will you forgive me?"

This frank appeal fairly conquered Miss Van Agnew.

"Don't let us discuss the subject any more," she said. "As for me, I have nothing to forgive. So you have brought the gray mare, have you?"

"Yes. Mr. Ruddle desired me to ask if there was any message in return."

"Ha, ha! He wants his check, I suppose. Well, he may as well have it. If I send it by hand it will save a penny stamp." And she laughed at her own prudence as she went to a side-table and, taking her checkbook from a drawer, wrote off the required amount. "There," she continued, returning to Kitty, "you can give him that, and tell him, with my compliments, that next time I want a horse he need not be afraid to trust me."

"It is only Mr. Ruddle's way of doing business," said Kitty explanatorily. "He says there are so many losses in the profession."

"No doubt. Don't go yet, Miss Herrick," as Kitty, considering the objects of her visit achieved, rose to take leave.

"I feared I might be intruding, Miss Van Agnew."

"Not in the least. I should quite enjoy a little chat about things in general."

Kitty waited for her to proceed, but as the heiress

20

suddenly became silent, and a lengthy pause ensued, she broke it by inquiring after Tiny Tim.

"Have you ridden the little bay horse yet?" she asked.

Miss Van Agnew gave a start, and said absently, "No, I am sorry to say he is coughing, and our groom seems to think he is in for an attack of influenza. Anyhow, he's doctoring him."

"I'm truly sorry to hear that," said Kitty. "May I be allowed to have a peep at the dear old fellow before I leave?"

"Most certainly." Then she gave one or two preliminary coughs, and seeing her visitor again showed symptoms of rising, said abruptly, "What about Captain Mordaunt? You two are great friends, are you not?"

The question took Kitty utterly by surprise.

"Who told you so?" she demanded, almost fiercely.

"Oh! nobody. Only I thought you and he seemed on pretty intimate terms the other day."

"We know each other fairly well," said Kitty coldly. "Captain Mordaunt has been hunting here ever since the beginning of the cub-hunting season."

"It's so nice getting hold of somebody who can tell me all about the good people in these parts," said Miss Van Agnew. "I'm not pretty, but of course I know I shall have every man in the place running after me before long, so it's just as well to make inquiries."

"Are you much accustomed to admiration?" said Kitty sarcastically.

Miss Van Agnew looked at her with sharp brown eyes.

"Don't be a fool. You know quite well that admiration has nothing to do with it. The men will come buzzing and swarming after my money, just like so many wasps round a treacle-pot. It's not all jam being an heiress, let me tell you, although perhaps you may think so. You feel as if you could never trust anybody. Since my father died I have thought over the situation a good deal, and have arrived at one definite conclusion."

"What is that?" inquired Kitty, who began to find the conversation extremely interesting.

"I mean to get married. I shall be twenty-five next birthday, and I don't intend to wait until I'm a confirmed old spinster with no ideas in my head beyond knitting and tea parties. The only thing is, I can't quite make up my mind on one point."

"Indeed," said Kitty, smiling.

"No, I can't decide whether to marry for love or for a title."

"Why not unite both?" suggested Kitty. "That strikes me as being the wisest solution of the problem."

"It's not easy. What's this Lord Algernon Loddington like? I hear, though, that he's devoted to you."

"Pray, don't consider me, if you have the least fancy for his lordship," said Kitty saucily. "He's quite available as a husband, as far as I am concerned."

"You are very kind, but I fear he wont smile upon poor me. Report says he's too far gone on somebody else, otherwise I should be perfectly willing."

"I should certainly make the experiment of laying siege to Lord Algy's affections," said Kitty, laughing.

"You only give that advice because you are sure of them. You can't blind me, Miss Herrick. After all," she went on, meditatively, "I've a great fancy for love. It always reads so nice in books, and if we went abroad we might buy a title from the Pope, or somebody or other with one to spare." Miss Van Agnew's notions on this subject were vague, but she had a fixed idea, in which she was not far wrong, that money could do anything.

"Who is the fortunate individual?" asked Kitty. "I presume there is one."

The fair Judith blushed, and looked pensively down at her foot. It was broad and flat, but was beautified by a gold-embroidered slipper.

"Oh, I'm only prospecting as yet. That's one reason

why I told Daniel I intended to go in for hunting. One meets such good men. By the by, that Captain Mordaunt seems a very nice gentlemanly fellow. I call him awfully good-looking in the lardy-dardy style, don't you?"

"Yes," said Kitty guardedly, "I suppose I do."

"He has the most lovely blue eyes I ever saw," went on Miss Van Agnew, who appeared to feel the need of a confidante. "I don't know what there is about them, but they seem to go right through one. They are so clear and bright and attractive. And then his mustache! My word, isn't it a duck?"

"I never considered it in that light," said Kitty, not altogether pleased by her companion's enthusiastic praise of Cyril's personal charms.

"Perhaps you have not noticed it?" continued Miss Van Agnew. "But I did particularly the other morning when the sun was shining on it. Do you know, it's as fine and silky as the hair which grows on a woman's head. And the way he twists it is adorable. You can tell at once that he is a soldier."

"Captain Mordaunt ought to feel very much flattered," said Kitty wearily. "He seems to have made quite a conquest."

"I'm only prospecting, as I said before," returned Miss Van Agnew. "But there is no harm in making inquiries. In fact, in my position I am more or less bound to do so."

"Are there any further questions you wish to ask?" said Kitty, with veiled satire. "I regret not being more capable of answering them."

"Oh! any amount, if you weren't fidgeting to be off. Has the gentleman under discussion any fortune? But I suppose not. He is too nice."

"Captain Mordaunt is not rich," answered Kitty constrainedly, beginning to find this cross-examination unendurable. "I know that for a fact."

"And who are his people?"

"His father was connected with the City, I believe,

and got knighted, but he has been dead many years, and his mother, Lady Mordaunt, lives in London."

"Oh! his mother is Lady Mordaunt. What a pity the son is not a baronet, or a lord, or a something."

"Would it make him any the nicer?" inquired Kitty, oscillating between sorrow and embarrassment.

"No, perhaps not. Still, titles count for so much in this world. I always think Captain sounds well, though, don't you? and of course being in the guards gives a person a certain amount of distinction. Guardsmen generally move in a smart set, and have all the women ready to worship them."

"It strikes me," said Kitty, "you know so much about Captain Mordaunt already that it is a work of supererogation your asking me for any details concerning him."

"I flatter myself we shall be tolerably good friends before long," said Miss Van Agnew complacently. "I met him out hunting yesterday, and asked him to look in to lunch to-day if he had nothing better to do. In fact, he had only been gone about half an hour when you came." And Miss Van Agnew smiled blandly, quite unconscious of the pain she was administering.

"Cy—Captain Mordaunt was here to-day?" said Kitty, almost inaudibly.

"Yes, and made himself most agreeable. I shall tell Daniel to ask him to dinner, in a friendly way, the next time they meet out hunting."

A pang shot through Kitty's heart. This, then, was what he had been about. Whilst she wondered day after day why he did not come to see her at Mr. Ruddle's, he was lunching with Miss Van Agnew, and could find plenty of time to make up to a new acquaintance, although apparently he was too busy to visit the old. She turned quite pale, her limbs began to tremble, so that when she endeavored to rise from her seat she was obliged to sit down again. · Her silence and pallor attracted Miss Van Agnew's attention.

"What is the matter?" she asked. "Are you ill?"

"No," answered Kitty, forcing herself to reply. "But

I have had a great deal of trouble lately, and my work tires me. It is nothing, only sometimes I feel rather faint."

"Let me ring for a glass of wine," said Miss Van Agnew, stretching her hand out towards the bell.

' Thanks, I would rather not. ' If you wont think it rude, I will say good-by. The fresh air soon puts me right again. The fire is delightful to look at, but it strikes a little hot when you first come indoors." Murmuring incoherent excuses, Kitty effected her departure, thankful to escape from the torture unwittingly inflicted by the heiress. If she could have spoken out the truth and said, "I am engaged to Cyril Mordaunt. He is my affianced husband, so you need not turn your thoughts his way. His blue eyes and silky mustache are mine," the situation would have been simple enough. She might even have laughed at Miss Van Agnew's admiration of Cyril, and in a degree have felt pleased by it; but her mouth was sealed, and she did not reveal her engagement for fear of incurring his anger, although for her own part she failed to see the reason for any mystery or concealment. Every day it placed her in a false position, and as she walked homewards she determined to take the first opportunity of begging him to proclaim to the world how matters stood between them.

She shambled along the road like one in a dream, her faculties deadened by the blow received at Miss Van Agnew's hands. From the numb misery of her mind one thought stood out with startling prominence. Cyril Mordaunt did not love her. He could not love her, or he would never have left her solitary and neglected at Belfield whilst he made advances to the heiress occupying Gretton Grange. Why should he run after Miss Van Agnew? The answer was, for her money, and she—Kitty—had lost hers. It made her feel as if there were nothing true and genuine in the world—as if man's affection resolved itself into a mere question of pounds, shillings, and pence.

When she returned to the stable-yard the first person she encountered was Mr. Ruddle, and the sight of him caused her to remember the check. She handed it to him mechanically, and he put the envelope in his pocket with a contented smile.

"Lord Algernon has been here since you were away," he said. "And a fine blowing up he has given me."

"What about?" she inquired listlessly.

"Some one told him that Miss Van Agnew had bought your bay horse, and I never saw his lordship so upset. He abused me for not letting him know he was for sale, said he would have given £500 for him, or anything I liked to ask, and marched into the stable and bought Pattercake for a hundred and fifty straight away."

"What use would Tiny Tim have been to Lord Algy?" said Kitty. "He rides over fourteen stone, and never could have hunted the little horse."

"He did not want to. He said he should have given him a good home, and not allowed any person to sit on his back except yourself. I can't tell you how wild he was when he found Miss Van Agnew intended appearing in the hunting field on the bay."

Kitty smiled faintly. It was a little grain of comfort to feel that there was some one who thought kindly of her still, in spite of her loss of fortune. She wished she could recall those hasty words spoken in the saddle-room.

"Did Lord Algy ask to see me?" she queried, with a pretence of indifference.

"No," answered Mr. Ruddle. "He inquired a great deal after you, and wanted to know how you were getting on, but he did not actually ask to see you."

Kitty sighed. Yet what could she expect? She had told him to leave her alone, and not to bother her, and he was simply obeying orders. It was like Algy to take her at her word. But, of course, she never meant him to put such a literal construction on one foolish speech.

Well, Pattercake was in good hands at any rate. She only wished Tiny Tim were in the same. Then she would have been quite at ease as to the gallant little horse's future.

CHAPTER XXXIX.

THE FALL OF THE MAN-GOD.

WHEN her day's work was done, instead of retiring early to rest, according to her usual habit, Kitty sat up writing to Cyril. But to compose a satisfactory letter was no easy task, and after various attempts she came to the conclusion that she said either too much or too little. She found that it was impossible to commit to paper all that was in her mind, and therefore finally determined to stick to the main facts, and avoid sentimental digressions. So she began anew, and ended by writing an epistle, which, although it did not satisfy her, was the best she could achieve under the circumstances. It ran as follows:—

My Dear Cyril,—I saw Miss Van Agnew to-day, and heard from her that you had been lunching there. I make no complaints. I do not think you can honestly accuse me of being jealous, or of expecting you to pay me too much attention. There was a time when you used to seek me out, and took pleasure in my society, but it apparently is past. Nevertheless, I wish to remark in a calm and friendly spirit that if you can find sufficient leisure to spend several hours in the company of a comparative stranger, it is rather odd your being unable to devote a few minutes to me. Miss Van Agnew asked a great many questions concerning you this afternoon which placed me in a most embarrassing position. Now, dear Cyril, what I have to beg is this: Release me from my promise of silence, and let our engagement be made public. There is no real reason for any mystery or concealment, and complications will inevitably result. It is unnecessary for me to repeat that I am perfectly willing to work and wait until you see your way to our marriage taking place, but meanwhile I think I have a right to demand that this very uncomfortable secrecy should cease. It obliges me to act like a hypocrite. I am conscious of not expressing myself well. Indeed, since my return from London a barrier has sprung up between us which God knows is none of my making. Cyril, if you are tired of me—if my altered fortunes have induced you to change your mind—it is not too late to draw back. It would give me less pain if you admitted the truth rather than pretend to an affection which is not genuine. For your neglect renders me very miserable. How could it be otherwise? At present, the uncertainty of my position as regards yourself creates all sorts of cruel suspicions in my mind, which one word from you can set at rest. Will you not speak it, dear? Either we are engaged or we are not. Which is it to be? I hope you will not feel angry with me for writing to you in this strain. And now good-by. Come and see me soon, or else write a line, for your silence simply kills me. Ever your loving

KATHERINE HERRICK.

Cyril received this letter on the following morning, just as he was sitting down to breakfast in the cosey little sitting-room belonging to his lodgings. It happened to be a hunting day, and the meet being some distance from Furrowdale he was up betimes. When the landlady brought in the square white envelope and laid it by his plate he glanced carelessly at the superscription, but a flush rose to his cheek on recognizing the clear feminine handwriting.

"Ahem! A note from Kitty," he soliloquized, not without a certain little nervous tremor, for in his heart of hearts he was well aware of the fact that he was treating her like a thorough blackguard. "What is her news, I wonder?" And tearing open the envelope he proceeded to read its contents.

At first he frowned darkly, but by degrees a slow smile overspread his features, and the expression of his countenance relaxed.

"Wonderful clever woman, my mother," he muttered. "Her knowledge of human nature is quite

extraordinary. Who could have thought that within a
week her predictions would come to pass. Here's
Kitty jealous already. It's as clear as the nose on one's
face." And he stroked his mustache complacently,
and looked admiringly at an elongated reflection of
himself presented by the pewter teapot opposite.
" Poor little Kitty! I wish I weren't so infernally fond
of her. It makes a rupture much more difficult. As
matters stand, I can't bring myself to break with her all
at once. She has had hard lines lately, one way and
another, and although she's as plucky as she can hang
together the blow would pretty well knock her down.
She is so tremendously in love that it would be positively wicked to chuck her without a fair amount of
preparation. Meanwhile I had better write a temporizing letter of a pacific character. I always find that
when you haven't exactly got right on your side there's ·
nothing like carrying off matters with a high hand,
and treating the injured party as if he, or she, were in
the wrong. But there's no time now to sit down and
write a long rigmarole. It will do when ˚ come in
from hunting."

Thus determining, he ate a remarkably hearty breakfast, after which he proceeded to put a few embellish-
ing touches to his toilet. When he had tied and re-tied
the bows of his leather breeches until at last they were
to his satisfaction, buckled on his spurs, and settled his
neckcloth, he sallied forth to the livery stable hard by
where he kept his hunters, and there mounted a favorite
steed. Being rather late, he trotted out to covert at a
steady pace, only pulling up into a walk when he came
to a hill, and he arrived just as hounds were moving
off. As he joined the rear of the procession he saw a
little squat, short-waisted figure ahead, perched on the
back of a gray mare. He eyed it critically for a few
minutes, and could not help instituting comparisons
between Kitty and Miss Van Agnew in the saddle.
The one sat straight and square, with shoulders back,
elbows in, and her whole body beautifully balanced,

whilst the other reminded him of nothing so much as a round pudding loosely tied up in a cloth. There could be no doubt about the fact that the heiress did not appear to advantage on horseback. A habit scarcely suited her style of beauty. Her stumpy little legs dangled helplessly, in a manner which proclaimed that they had no grip of the pommels whatever, her skirt rucked up from the convulsive wriggles she gave in her endeavors to rise, and her sallow face took on a greasy shine owing to the unwonted efforts to retain her seat. The gray mare was fresh, and once when a bird flew out of the hedge she gave a playful buck which very nearly unseated her rider altogether, and enabled Cyril to perceive a vast amount of daylight. Was he really going to give up slim, trim, pretty Kitty for this creature? A shudder went through his frame, but the next moment a mocking voice seemed to whisper, "Twenty thousand a year, my lad. Think of that. What do a good figure and a bright complexion signify in comparison? Shut your eyes and go in and win when you have a chance." So, after he had fully studied Miss Van Agnew's back he forced his way through the crowd until he reached her side, and raising his hat with a propitiatory smile, said, "Good morning. This is quite an unexpected pleasure. You told me yesterday that your horse was coughing and you saw no prospect of getting out to-day."

"Neither did I," she responded, "but as good luck would have it Miss Herrick came over after you had gone, and brought my last purchase. What do you think of her? Is she the right sort?"

Cyril looked the gray over with the eye of a connoisseur.

"Very much so," he said, "bar the blemish, which is a pity. Did you give a long price?"

"Oh! no," she answered carelessly. "She was quite cheap as horses go. Only three hundred."

"*Only* three hundred!" ejaculated Cyril, but he prudently refrained from saying more.

"I bought her from Mr. Ruddle," continued Miss Van Agnew. "Miss Herrick rode her the day we were introduced. Don't you remember?"

"I remember the pleasure of making your acquaintance," he rejoined gallantly.

She looked pleased and glanced at him kindly. He was goodly to look at in his scarlet coat and snowy breeches.

"I rather like Miss Herrick," she said presently. "She's a nice little thing in her way; but what a dreadful pity for her to have gone and turned herself into a common rough-rider."

"So all her friends think," he said dryly. "I, for one, am quite of your opinion."

"What made her do it?"

"*They* say obstinacy. *She* says necessity. You know when her father died the other day she lost all her money."

"Yes, poor girl. I heard something to that effect."

"The old man was a regular scoundrel," continued Cyril warmly, "and after his death it appeared he had been systematically robbing his own daughter. She is a nailer to hounds, and mad about horses and hunting, so when she found herself left without a penny she took to the stable-yard."

"I rather admire her pluck," said Miss Van Agnew. "But, of course, she will go down in the world. One can't associate with grooms and helpers without losing caste. Do people call upon her still, and ask her out?"

"I don't know, I'm sure. Her father has been dead such a very short time that I don't suppose she would accept their invitations even if they did."

"She has just missed being really pretty," said Miss Van Agnew, with generous meditation. "Her coloring is good, but those little baby features don't last. In a year or two she will be quite insignificant-looking."

"Do you think so," he said, rather relieved to find her remarks a justification for his own line of conduct

"Yes, I am sure of it. At five-and-twenty all the

bloom will be off; but I suppose in her case it wont
much signify."

"How do you mean?" he inquired.

"Why, she's going to marry Lord Algernon Loddington, is she not? Lucky girl. She'll be a duchess one of
these days."

"Who told you so?" he asked jealously.

"Oh, everybody says that his lordship is madly in
love. I taxed her with it myself."

"Well, and what answer did she give?"

"She laughed, but did not deny the charge. Thank
goodness! here we are at the covert. My poor back
is positively broken. Woa, mare, woa; now do keep
quiet, there's a darling." And Miss Van Agnew clutched
hold of the pommel with her right hand. The gray demanded so much attention that the fair rider found it
impossibe to continue the conversation, but the mare's
friskiness afforded Cyril an excellent opportunity of
soothing and encouraging her mistress.

Sport proved exceptionally bad. They came upon a
succession of ringy foxes who never ran more than a
field or two away from home. Scent also appeared exceedingly deficient. The consequence was, Cyril spent
the greater part of the day in Miss Van Agnew's society,
and when he left her that susceptible virgin had quite
settled in her own mind that he was the finest gentleman and nicest companion she had ever come across.
Daniel was made to invite him to dinner, and they
parted the best of friends, to meet again that evening.
Cyril rode back to his lodgings in a contented frame
of mind, firmly persuaded that he was a very irresistible
individual where the fair sex were concerned. He flung
himself into an arm-chair, devoured a couple of poached
eggs and a rackful of toast, and then scrawled off a
letter to Kitty:

What a little goose you are, to be sure! Is it possible
for me to lunch with you in Mr. Ruddle's saddle-room? If
not, what objection can there be to my lunching somewhere else? The austere privacy of Mrs. Perkins's cottage

equally prevents me from visiting you there.   To be quite
frank, I dislike the idea of a crowd of stablemen listening
to our conversation, and standing grinning by whilst we
exchange salutations.   You may not be sensitive on this
score, but I am, and when you talk of a barrier, I confess
that the ill-advised step which you have chosen to take
places considerable difficulties in my way.   Although I am
quite willing personally to make our engagement public,
surely you have not considered the disastrous effect it
would produce on my mother, whose opposition I trusted by
keeping quiet to soften.   If she once heard that you were
gaining your livelihood as a common horse-breaker I feel
sure she would insist on everything coming to an end between us.   You talk of being in a false position.   I fail to
see it, except by your own act.   Anyhow, if I accede to your
wish I estrange my mother.   I thought all this was clear,
but as apparently you either cannot or will not perceive
the importance of keeping our engagement secret for a
time, perhaps you will kindly appoint some place of meeting, other than Mr. Ruddle's saddle-room, where we can
have a quiet chat, removed from the stench of the stable.
Believe me, yours lovingly,   CYRIL MORDAUNT.

If Kitty had been unhappy before the receipt of this
letter, it rendered her a hundred thousand times more
so.   Its cold, cynical tone wounded her to the quick,
and then the impertinence of asking her to appoint
some place of meeting removed from the stench of the
stable!   It was a direct insult, and she resented it accordingly.   Her first impulse was to write back an
angry reply, couched in the same vein as his own, but
she was so indignant that she feared to yield to her immediate inclinations, and after a sharp struggle decided
to sleep on the matter.   Morning brought calmer, and
probably wiser, thoughts, as it generally does, and she
settled to treat his letter with the contempt it deserved,
and take no notice of it whatever.   One thing was certain,
she would not seek him.   If he were ashamed to visit
her openly at Mr. Ruddle's, then she would not imperil
her fair name by meeting him secretly in by-lanes.
He must come to her.   When he wanted to, no doubt

he could do so fast enough. In the interim she must accustom herself to the heartache and to expecting nothing at his hands. It was a poor lookout. But the worst feature of the whole business was, that her ideal was sorely shaken. Strive as she might against every disloyal thought, her man-god was no longer perched on the same sublime heights as formerly. She had loved him so truly that the pain of finding out his faults was intense. To know him weak and unstable, and to suspect him shifty and false, made insidious encroaches on the esteem without which that love could not exist. He had failed her again when she appealed to him for protection. Lucky are the women who have never undergone a similar experience. It is a dreadful ordeal for a woman to be thrown back upon herself, and to feel that she must stand alone against the world, without sympathy or support.

CHAPTER XL.

THE Duchess of Furrowdale was not only a great lady, but also a very superior woman. Looking down on the outside world from the high altitude of her position, she saw clearly that kindness of heart and goodness of disposition were much more likely to make Lord Algy happy than was mere rank.

Her eldest son, the Earl of Daleford, would never perpetuate the family name. For many years past he had suffered from a spinal complaint, brought on originally by a fall met out hunting. This led to a complication of diseases which were slowly but surely killing him. One of the most eminent London physicians had recently assured his afflicted parents that he could not possibly live for more than a couple of years. It was a very sad case, and the sympathy felt for the invalid was universal. But he himself never complained, and seemed in a measure resigned to his lot. Perhaps he realized that it was better to go whilst he was still beloved and not regarded as a burden, rather than live a miserable life of inaction and suffering, entirely dependent on other people. His mother nursed him assiduously, and was his constant companion. When his poor head ached she was always by to shake up the pillows, and, putting her arms gently round his attenuated frame, would give relief to his position. Often, when alone, the tears sprung to his eyes as he recalled her maternal devotion. She gave up going into society, and rarely left the castle for more than an hour or two at a time.

Lord Daleford's illness had lasted so long that almost

unconsciously the duke and duchess came to look upon
Lord Algy as their heir and successor to the strawberry
leaves. When they mapped out the future, their first-
born was no longer included in their calculations. For
many months past they had both agreed that it was high
time for Lord Algy to marry, and with this object in
view her grace was artfully inviting a series of desirable young ladies to Furrowdale. But although—taken
as a body—they were perfectly willing to fall in with
her wishes, and gave his lordship every possible encouragement compatible with maidenly modesty, he proved
singularly unresponsive and distractingly hard to please.
He found fault with them all. Either they were too
pretty or too plain, too fat or too slow, too townified or
too rural to suit his critical taste. They, on their part,
found him so steady and sober, so curiously formal and
polite, that they gave him up as a bad job, and bestowed
their attentions elsewhere.

Meantime the duchess became slowly aware of the
fact that whilst she had been scouring the country in
search of a bride, and brought dozens of cousins, twice,
thrice, and four times removed, for Lord Algy's inspection, he had calmly been at work in his quiet way and
had set his affections on some one close at home. Having made this remarkable discovery, she promptly communicated it to the duke, and finding he rather approved
of Algy's choice than otherwise, took to watching Kitty
narrowly. She wanted to ascertain what kind of girl
she really was, and if her character were as pleasing as
her appearance. Consequently, the Squire and his
pretty young daughter were frequently invited to Furrowdale, and whilst Mr. Herrick and the duke held animated conversations about the stable and the kennel,
the two ladies had many a confidential chat, during
which the clever woman of the world dissected her
unconscious guest, and obtained a considerable insight
into her thoughts and idiosyncrasies. It is to be pre-
sumed that her researches were satisfactory, for from
day to day she showed Kitty more favor, and beamed

21

benevolently on Lord Algy whenever he diffidently mentioned her name.

For a time, all had apparently gone well, and the course of true love ran with unusual smoothness, if somewhat slowly. The young man was happy and hopeful, and if Kitty treated him with cool, sisterly indifference rather than with warm affection, the duchess considered such conduct quite right and fitting in the circumstances. She did not approve of the modern fashion of young ladies running after young men and regularly hunting them to the altar. She held the antiquated opinion that the male should seek the female, not *vice versa*. So she thought none the worse of Kitty for standing a little aloof during the preliminary stages of courtship. But lately a change had come over the spirit of the dream, and the duchess found herself sorely baffled. Her darling Algy was evidently in low spirits, and went about the house with a face as sober as a judge. Now it so happened that almost immediately after Mr. Herrick's death she and the duke had talked matters over, and they both came to the conclusion that, although the young couple could not decently be married before the spring, now was the time of all others for Lord Algy to make known his intentions.

"Perhaps he does not like to speak positively to dear Kitty," said the duchess, "fearing we might withhold our consent. I think it would be as well to tell him openly that as far as we are concerned there are no obstacles in the way."

"Most certainly," said the duke. "I should like to see Algy's children playing about me before I die. For my own part, I think he has made a wise choice. The girl is a nice girl—none of your artificial painted-up things. Her roses are not the result of rouge. Besides which, she is a lady by birth, and the daughter of an old friend. I really don't see what more one could want."

"She has no fortune," hinted the duchess; "and of course people might think he ought to make a better match."

"That does not signify one jot," returned the duke. "Algy is fairly well off as it is, and some day he will have plenty of money. His wife will be raised to the position occupied by her husband, and a year hence nobody will care if Lord Algernon Loddington married the daughter of a country squire or of an earl."

"That is true," said the duchess, "and I have nothing to say against Kitty. I like her extremely. She is perfectly honest, natural, and unaffected, and in my belief will make a most excellent wife."

"Anyhow, he has chosen her," said the duke, "and we are both anxious to see him comfortably settled."

So the good couple decided to smile on their son's suit, in spite of Kitty's being left penniless, and the duchess undertook to let him know that they were prepared to receive the girl as their daughter-in-law. But to her grace's no small surprise, when she imparted this cheering piece of intelligence to Lord Algy it produced no inspiriting effect. He heaved a sigh, which seemed to emanate from the very soles of his boots, and said rather chokily, "It is awfully good of you and the governor, mother. Believe me, I feel your kindness deeply, but," and he averted his head, "it—it—cannot be."

"Cannot be!" echoed the duchess in surprise. "Why not? For what reason?"

"I am not at liberty to tell you the reason, but there is a most conclusive one."

A sudden suspicion ran through her mind.

"Do you mean that Kitty Herrick has refused you, Algy?"

He blushed a vivid crimson.

"No," he answered reluctantly. "I have never exactly proposed." Then he hesitated, and added, "It would be no good."

"Nonsense, boy. How can you tell till you try?"

"It's not that, mother. You don't understand."

"Am I to infer that she is aware of your affection and does not reciprocate it?"

"Yes," he said gloomily. "That's about the state of the case. It's useless proposing when you know you haven't got a chance."

This information took the duchess completely aback, and for a moment or two she pondered over his answer. Then her quick, womanly perceptions came to her aid, and hitting the right nail on the head, she said decidedly:

"If what you say is true, and you are not making a mistake, there is only one deduction possible. Kitty cares for somebody else. Tell me, Algy, is it so?" And she looked at him inquiringly.

He made no answer, and tried hard to preserve an impassive demeanor.

"Is it so?" she repeated more urgently.

"I am not able to give you any details, mother, but I have every cause to believe that your surmise is correct."

She stole to his side and laid her fine white hand tenderly upon his arm.

"Poor Algy," she said softly. "I am so sorry. It grieves me to the heart that you should have met with such a disappointment."

He stooped, and pushing back her hair, in which a gleam of silver was visible near the temples, kissed her on the forehead. His eyes glistened, and there was a suspicious tremor in his voice as he said:

"Thank you, mother darling. But don't pity me or look at me so sorrowfully. I—I can bear it best alone, and in time, no doubt, I shall forget. But it comes hard, just at first, when you have been in love with a girl for years."

"Years! Oh, Algy! Your father and I never knew this."

"Yes," he continued, with concentrated emotion. "I have been fond of her ever since she was quite a little thing. She always seemed to me different from any other girl; but there," breaking off suddenly, "it's no use talking."

"Kitty is very young," said the duchess hopefully.

"I can't believe that she has formed any serious attach-
ment.   This is probably some childish fancy from
which she will recover in a month or two."

He shook his head.

"No," he said, "she is not that sort.   I have tried
my very best to make her care for me, but I suppose
I'm not smart enough or good-looking enough.   Anyhow," and he shrugged his shoulders in a melancholy
fashion, "I have failed signally."

"Nonsense, Algy," said his mother indignantly.
"Just as if half the girls in the kingdom would not
jump at you if they had the chance."

"Yes," he said bitterly.   "On account of my title
and position   If I were plain Mr. Loddington, without
any money, they would not look at me.   No, no,
mother, it's useless deceiving one's-self.   That is why I
like Kitty.   She is too genuine to sell herself for mere
worldly advantage, and if she took a fellow at all she
would take him for his own sake, and not for what he
had got.   Do you think I couldn't see through all these
young women you were good enough to invite for my
edification?   There was not one among their number
who, as you say, would not have jumped at me, and
yet not a single girl cared twopence about me in
reality."

The duchess could not gainsay the truth of his words,
and did not attempt to argue the matter further.

"Is there nothing to be done, Algy?" she said sadly,
impressed by the sincerity of his passion.

"No, nothing," he rejoined, "unless you will persuade
the governor to do me a favor."

"What is it, my poor, dear boy?"

"I—I promised *her*," he said, a trifle unsteadily, for
his mother's tenderness touched him to the quick, "not
to let Herrington pass into strange hands   It is going
up to auction next month   I don't know how much it
will fetch, but probably between fifty and sixty thousand pounds   I can contribute half the price, and I want
the governor to give the rest   The land is good, and

adjoins our own, and its purchase would render the Furrowdale property complete."

"How strange!" she exclaimed, "that you should have mentioned this. It only shows how one's thoughts meet. Your father and I had already decided to buy Herrington, if it went reasonably, in order to present it to you and Kitty as a wedding gift."

His face lit up for a moment. It was easy to see what intense pleasure the prospect afforded. Then the shadow returned which had rested for so many days past on his countenance, and clouded out all the brightness and joy.

CHAPTER XLI.

THE DUCHESS OF FURROWDALE VISITS KITTY.

"Mother," said Lord Algy despondently, "I really do believe you are the best woman in the world; but it's really no use trying to encourage false hopes. Kitty wont have anything do with me—that's the long and short of the matter; so it is useless to dwell upon what might have been. I can fancy Kitty's delight when she found the old home would still be hers. However, even as things are, I should dearly like the governor to buy Herrington, if only for the sake of the associations."

"I will speak to your father on the subject," said the duchess. "Time will soften this blow, Algy dear, and if you can't take one bride there you might take another. You know how much we both desire your marriage."

"Don't urge it, mother," he responded, greatly agitated, "at all events for the present. Some day—perhaps—to please you and the dear old governor; but not for a long while—a long, long while."

"I consider Kitty has behaved abominably," said the duchess, indignantly. "What right had she to trifle with your affections?"

A mournful smile flitted over his features as he thought of the slender basis on which the accusation was founded.

"Mother," he said, "you must not let your disappointment render you unjust. Kitty has come here by your invitation, and we have seen a great deal of each other, but she has never given me any encouragement. She could not very well say to you in so many words, especially when I had not proposed, 'I do not care for your son in the way he wishes, and only entertain a sisterly regard for him.' You would have been the first to find fault had she done so; whilst, as far as I am concerned, she has tried everything in her power to prevent my reaching a climax. In fairness to her I deny that she has behaved badly." So saying, he marched out of the room, leaving his mother still furious with Kitty, in spite of his chivalrous defence of her conduct.

The duchess's anger was slightly tempered, however, by an imperious curiosity to discover who the favored individual was whom Miss Herrick had the bad taste to prefer to her paragon of an Algy. She could not realize his being a rejected suitor, for although he distinctly stated that he had not proposed, it practically came to the same thing.

"The little fool," she said to herself, when the first whirlwind of her wrath had subsided, and she was able to review the state of affairs more dispassionately. "She'll never get such another chance if she lives to be a hundred. Very few men are as good and kind and unselfish as Algy, and whoever his wife may be she is a lucky woman. Poor, dear old fellow! it goes to my heart to see him so downcast, and all on account of one silly chit of a girl. I must try what I can do to put matters on a more satisfactory footing, for, say what he likes, I can't believe that she does not care for him."

The duchess was lost in deep thought when Lord Algy returned and popped his head in at the door.

"By the way, mother," he said, with an assumption of carelessness, "it has come to my ears the last day or two that people are talking rather unkindly of Kitty, and wondering whether, in her present position, they will continue to visit her. What do you say to going to call? Folks are such snobs that if they once heard you had set the example they would follow suit in a flock. It seems rather a shame to show her the cold shoulder just because she is trying to earn her own living."

To his no small satisfaction, the duchess received this

proposition with favor, and removed a load from his mind by saying:

"I was just thinking I would like to have a little private chat with Kitty. I quite agree with you as to not deserting friends in misfortune."

"You wont talk about me, will you?" he said eagerly. "I must beg you not to mention anything that I have said."

"Of course not, you old goose," she answered playfully. "You may trust me to uphold Lord Algernon Loddington's dignity. I shall certainly not lead Miss Herrick to suppose that you are broken-hearted, or that I go to her as a suppliant. I know my boy's worth too well for that, and if she does not, all I can say is, she's less sensible than I gave her credit for being."

"You might just mention about Herrington," he said, "and ascertain if she has any objection to the place falling into my hands."

"Objection, Algy! Why, what objection could she possibly have? It seems to me you are over-sensitive where Kitty is concerned."

He colored. "One can't help being so, when—when one thinks very much about a person; and I shouldn't like to hurt her feelings in any way."

"She does not appear so scrupulous about hurting yours, else she never could have behaved as she has done."

"She had a perfect right to a free choice, mother. Because it has not fallen on me, that is no reason why we should censure her. When will you go to Belfield?"

"Did I not hear your father saying he intended to walk over to Mr. Ruddle's next Sunday, to see about getting two or three extra horses for the hunt servants? If so, I will accompany him, and pay Kitty a visit whilst he is at the yard. I expect she is busy on a week day."

"You will remember your promise not to talk about me, wont you, mother? It's no use trying to coerce her affections."

"I couldn't even if I would," answered the duchess practically. "There is no creature on the face of this earth so stubborn as a girl who fancies herself in love."

"And quite right too," he responded. "Her love is not worth anything if it can be blown about by every word, like a feather. I respect such stubbornness." He upheld Kitty at all costs, the more so because he felt inwardly alarmed as to what his mother might say and do on the occasion of her intended visit. His pride shrunk from her pleading his cause, either directly or indirectly; on the other hand, he knew that it would give Kitty a lift socially to be called upon by the duchess.

The fact of the girl having gone in for horse-breaking, and to a certain extent outraging the conventionalities prescribed by a respectable set of county dowagers, had caused a considerable number of her acquaintances to doubt the expediency of remaining on friendly terms. Of course, they did not intend actually to cut her — that would have been unkind; but they hesitated about asking her to their houses, and decided in their own minds not to exceed a few civil words when they met. The conviction that this feeling was abroad annoyed Lord Algy intensely, especially as he was debarred from showing his contempt for it by making frequent calls at Mrs. Perkins's. Such being the case, the next best thing in his estimation was to induce his mother to show the forsaken girl favor. Under the circumstances, he anticipated a good deal of opposition, and therefore was both surprised and relieved by her ready assent. In addition to the above reason, he longed to hear some authentic news of Kitty. He wanted to know how she looked, how she stood the work, if she were comfortable in her little cottage, and a hundred other things which a woman could report upon It is true that Mr. Ruddle had assured him incidentally of her well-being; but then, that was several days ago, and when one is in love and unable to constantly see the object of one's affections it is astonishing how one yearns for the least intelligence.

After this conversation with his mother, Lord Algy's spirits improved a trifle, and against his better judgment he even began to hope that her intervention might aid his cause. Since Captain Mordaunt's reappearance in the hunting field he had kept a sharp lookout upon him, and that gentleman's attentions to Miss Van Agnew had not escaped his observation. He drew his own conclusions from them. From the very first he had taken an instinctive dislike to Cyril, and suspected him of being what in his blunt phraseology he termed a "suck-up." Now his suspicions were confirmed, and he regarded him as a pure fortune-hunter, ready to throw a penniless girl over at any moment if he could but succeed in gaining a richer bride. Men judge each other pretty accurately, as a rule, and we have reason to know that Lord Algy was not far wrong in his estimation of Captain Mordaunt's character. The result of the mental notes which he made at Cyril's expense was undoubtedly cheering, for he could not help thinking that if Kitty's eyes were only opened to the real nature of the individual on whom she had bestowed her heart, he might still have a chance. When once this thought presented itself to his mind, he was powerless to dismiss it. Yet he despised himself for the joy it afforded, since the realization of his wishes could only be brought about by acute suffering inflicted on Kitty. He did not question the sincerity of her love. He had seen it revealed in every glance and gesture. Nevertheless, so great was his distrust of Cyril that he firmly believed if she once took the irrevocable step of marrying him she would be miserable for the remainder of her days.

Events must take their course, however. After the words she had spoken to him in the saddle-room he could not stir hand or foot. He had borne a good deal at her hands; but if she were proud, so also was he, and when she begged him to leave her alone he obstinately resolved to obey the behest, no matter what it cost him. Had he consulted his own inclinations at this period he would have abandoned the season's hunting and gone abroad for the winter, so as to be out of the way. But there were other considerations which rendered such a course impossible. His brother's health demanded his presence, besides which he virtually managed the hounds. The duke had practically retired from the mastership, and in all matters connected both with the pack and the estate he was his father's right-hand man. He could not desert his post without causing inconvenience to others, therefore he stuck to it manfully and kept his troubles pretty well to himself. And if he were a little graver and a little sadder than in the olden days, if his step were less buoyant and his smile of rarer occurrence, nobody took much notice of the fact except his mother.

But the duchess's heart was sore for her youngest born, and she resolved to find out if his suit were really as hopeless as he represented. She secretly believed that he exaggerated matters, but then it is a maternal failing to regard your geese as swans, and to imagine that everybody else must necessarily hold the same opinion. Her grace was no exception to the rule.

Sunday afternoon found Kitty sitting in her little room. The apartment was so small that, when a fire was lit, it became intolerably hot and stuffy, and although she kept the window open, a fusty odor of disused furniture pervaded it, in spite of two or three pots of sweet-smelling flowers which ornamented the window-sill. Owing to various causes, she felt unusually tired and dispirited. She was rapidly beginning to realize that, battle as bravely as one may against sordid and uncongenial surroundings, one can't help being influenced by them, and she asked herself in all seriousness what would become of her if she were forced to lead this life for a number of years. She did not exactly repent her choice of a profession, because she entertained so humble an opinion of her abilities that she fully believed herself to be unfit to follow any other. But she foresaw loss of friends, accompanied by a gradual sinking in the social scale, personal and mental deterioration, and possibly impaired health. She had never known until lately what it was to feel really fatigued—so tired that when she went to bed at night she could not sleep for the aching of her limbs, which state, curiously enough, was almost always accompanied by an abnormal activity of the brain. Hard labor did not suit her nervous system, and rendered her in turns irritable and despondent. She lost the cheerful serenity which had hitherto been one of her chief characteristics, and became thoughtful and absent, given to rare speech and frequent pondering. The future preyed continually on her mind. If Cyril were not to marry her after all, and she were to fall ill, the workhouse would constitute her only refuge. But even if he remained faithful, and the engagement proved one of those long, hopeless affairs, which drag on indefinitely, she saw herself growing older and plainer, losing her smartness and girlish bloom—in short, everything that had first attracted her lover, and gradually losing what little hold she already possessed over him. Her imagination ran so far ahead that she actually tried to picture her position as a jilted, forlorn old maid, robbed of illusion, cheated out of affection, and hopelessly disgusted with the male sex.

Suddenly her meditations were interrupted by a knock at the door, and her heart gave a leap. She had stayed at home on purpose, hoping that in spite of the offensive language he had seen fit to employ in his letter, Cyril would appear. And now he was here. How she had wronged him in her thoughts, and how ready she had been to judge him harshly. But he should see that she was equally ready to forgive, and that a single kindly word from him sufficed to dissipate every trace of resentment. With a joyous ring in her voice she called out·

"Come in, Cyril. How good of you to pay me a visit."

"It's not Cyril, whoever he may be. It's me, and if I'm a disappointment, I apologize humbly." And so saying, to Kitty's unutterable astonishment, in walked the Duchess of Furrowdale.

Her grace was very plainly dressed in a short walking skirt, a black cloth tailor-made jacket, and a little felt hat ornamented by a black cock's wing. Nothing could have been more simple or unpretentious than her attire; nevertheless, the graceful carriage of her head, the poise of her long white neck, and the elegant lines of her tall, commanding figure, lent an air of distinction, and infallibly proclaimed their owner's birth and breeding. Her first instinct, as we know, had been to seek Kitty in anger, but reflection brought more moderate views. She now kissed her on the brow, and pretended not to notice the hot wave of color which rushed to the girl's cheeks when she discovered her mistake. As for Kitty, she was bitterly disappointed, and although sensible of the kindness of the duchess's visit, she was in mortal terror of having unwittingly betrayed her secret.

"I—I—beg your pardon," she stammered, all rosy and confused. "I thought it was some one else."

The duchess laughed.

"So I gathered. Pray who did you take me for? A fascinating young man seeking to enliven your solitude?"

"Nobody," replied Kitty mendaciously.

"Is nobody called 'Cyril'?" asked the duchess, with playful archness. "My curiosity is aroused. What is Cyril's surname?"

Kitty made no reply. She was so angry at having inadvertently mentioned him that she could have bitten out her tongue.

CHAPTER XLII.

THE DUCHESS'S VISIT—CONTINUED.

"WELL, well, " said the duchess, after a pause, "I must not force your confidence, especially as it is quite clear that you prefer to keep your own counsel. And now, my dear, tell me, how are you?"

"Thank you," said Kitty, relieved at the conversation taking a different turn, "I'm pretty well."

"You don't look so," said the duchess, eying her critically. "You look tired and worried and out of sorts."

The girl gave a little nervous laugh, and to hide a certain amount of self-pity stooped down and smashed a lump of coal with the poker.

"I have to work harder than I ever did before," she said, "and am finding that it is one thing riding for pleasure, another being forced to do so from necessity."

"Yes," said the duchess, "it must be a great change living in this sort of way." And she took a comprehensive glance round the room.

Kitty reddened. "Beggars can't be choosers," she said briefly.

"No, indeed, poor child," said the duchess, whose kind heart was touched by the alteration in her young friend's circumstances. "I wonder what your father would say if he could see you here, and reduced to this, after all the comforts of Herrington. I think it would break his heart. Don't you feel dreadfully lonely?"

"Yes, sometimes. It seems so strange having nobody to talk to, especially at meals. One gets to hate them."

The duchess seated herself on a chair near the fire and unbuttoned the buttons of her jacket.

"I should be very much inclined to lecture you for having taken up such a profession, Kitty, did I not understand that it is unlikely to prove permanent." And so saying, she fixed her eyes on her companion's face.

Kitty's white eyelids drooped until their long lashes swept her cheeks. She felt they were approaching dangerous ground.

"It is a comfort to think that you will soon have a house of your own again," continued her visitor. "Of course, there's a certain spice of novelty about a lady turning rough-rider, but that will soon wear off, if it has not done so already."

Form the significant way in which the duchess spoke, Kitty jumped at the conclusion that Lord Algy had told of her engagement.

"You have evidently heard the news," she said, coloring deeply.

"Naturally," returned the duchess. "It is impossible to keep these happy events secret for long."

"I shall never trust anybody again," said Kitty indignantly. "Lord Algy promised me faithfully that he would respect my desire for silence."

"Hush, child. Don't blame Algy. He has not betrayed you. Quite the contrary. But it is not difficult to put two and two together."

"Captain Mordaunt will be dreadfully angry," murmured Kitty, in great distress. "He will think I am to blame. Pray do not mention the matter to any one. May I beg of you to do me this service?"

"Of course," said the duchess, inwardly elated at the success which was attending her tactics. "When is the happy event to take place?"

"I—I don't know," mumbled Kitty reluctantly, ashamed of the confession. "Nothing is settled as yet. Cyril says we must wait."

"Wait! What for? No state tries a young woman's patience, temper, and endurance so highly as a long engagement. If I had a daughter I would not countenance any suitor who either could not or would not marry her within a reasonable period."

"No doubt the principle is right," said poor Kitty, who felt its force peculiarly, "but where there are difficulties to contend with it is not always easy to carry it out. Some people are lucky, and everything is fair sailing for them; others are not. We belong to the latter division."

"Captain Mordaunt knows how you are gaining your livelihood, I presume?"

"Yes," answered Kitty, speaking as if the admission were being dragged from her by force, "he knows."

"It is not for me to criticise his conduct," said the duchess severely, "but all I can say is, if you and he are really engaged it is perfectly monstrous of him allowing you to remain in this miserable little place for one minute, or of your being in the service of Mr. Ruddle. I am certain that such would be the opinion of all right-thinking people. . In fact," she added conclusively, "there can be no two opinions on the subject."

This declaration, coming from the exalted personage it did, carried a good deal of weight, the more so as it had been Kitty's own feeling all along. But pride came to her rescue, and she sought to justify her lover's conduct before a stranger.

"I don't think Cyril is to blame," she said. "He is not at all well off."

"Nonsense, my dear. He's well enough off to keep horses and go hunting, and spend money on amusements, and surely he might spend some on the girl he intends to make his wife, and not leave her to do the work of a common stable-helper. If Algy were to behave so I should be ashamed to own him as my son."

And again the duchess fixed an attentive gaze on her companion.

"Algy never would," said Kitty impulsively. "He would deprive himself of everything he possessed for the sake of any one he liked. But then," stopping

22

abruptly and suppressing a sigh, "all men are not alike. It does not do to judge one by another."

"Perhaps not," assented the duchess. "But there are certain rules of right and wrong, honor and dis-honor, and I maintain that it is a mean and despicable thing for a man to enjoy every comfort and luxury whilst he leaves the woman he is engaged to to live on the wages of a groom."

Kitty winced. Every word went quivering into her heart like a sharp barb.

"Dear duchess," she said tearfully, "I know your indignation is kindly meant, but please—please let us refrain from discussing Cyril's conduct."

Her grace patted Kitty on the cheek, with an effusive show of approbation.

"Bravo! child; you are right to stick up for him through thick and thin, and you must excuse me if I speak my mind too freely. The fact is," and she inclined her head confidentially, "I had other hopes, and will not attempt to disguise from you what they were. I really did think at one time that you and Algy had a fancy for each other, but of course that was all a mistake."

Without any apparent cause, Kitty began to tremble.

"Yes," she assented mechanically, "all a mistake."

"Just so," pursued the duchess. "I dare say you are aware that the duke and I are exceedingly anxious for him to marry, and we look forward to attending his wedding before long. Algy was a bit smitten with you, you naughty little puss, I verily do believe; but you know what men are. They very soon console themselves, and I have reason to think that Algy will shortly follow your example and get engaged."

This was indeed news to Kitty. She could not ima-gine who the lady was, however, who had so quickly superseded herself in his affections.

"I—I—hope so," she faltered. "I sincerely hope so—for—h—his sake. Please tell him how g—glad I am." And she laughed hysterically.

"Thanks, my dear, you look so. By the way, the duke is talking of buying Herrington, so that when Algy marries he and his bride may settle there. Algy had some absurd idea that you might object; but you don't, do you, love?"

"Am I in a position to object to anything?" said Kitty bitterly, inwardly condemning the duchess's taste for entering into these details. To tell the truth, what with the unexpected intelligence of her rejected suitor's forgetfulness of Miss Katherine Herrick, and her visitor's calm, confident tone, she felt completely disconcerted. When the duchess had first entered the room she was prepared to receive a shower of reproaches. Instead, however, of showing the smallest symptoms of displeasure, here was her grace talking quite cheerfully of Lord Algy's marriage as an almost immediate event.

She did not like it. It semed too sudden, although the prospect of his becoming the proprietor of Herrington was not in itself displeasing. Since the place must be sold, she would rather it passed into his hands than into the possession of an absolute stranger. But somehow or other she could not fancy an unknown woman occupying the familiar rooms, and making herself at home in them. Like a flash of lightning it came borne in upon her mind that Lord Algy's wife was not only a new but a distinctly disagreeable idea. She felt convinced beforehand of one thing: she should never like her, no matter how nice she might be. She was sure to rob her of her old friend and playfellow and alter the relations existing between them. Lady Algy would always appear like an interloper. Her breath came fast and slow, and she felt so queer at the thought that she pressed her hand to her bosom.

"What is the matter?" inquired the duchess, who had been watching the girl's expressive face attentively. "Are you indisposed?"

"No—it is no—nothing," stammered Kitty in reply. "Did you say Al—Lord Algernon, I mean—was to be married soon?"

"Ah!" exclaimed the duchess playfully. "Now you want to know too much. We must be allowed to have our little secrets as well as you. I only told you what our hopes were, because I knew what pleasure the news would occasion."

"You wont forget to tell Lord Algernon that—that I am very glad," said Kitty, unsteadily.

"You shall tell him so yourself when you are both married and done for," rejoined the duchess, whose persistent gayety formed a striking contrast to the gravity of her companion. "At present, congratulations are premature, precisely as I gather they are in your case."

"Yes," said Kitty soberly. "Mine is likely to prove a very long affair."

"Take my advice, my dear; don't let it linger. You hinted before at impediments. May I ask what they are?"

"The old story," said Kitty. "Want of money. My lack of fortune is a stumbling-block. Everything went smoothly until then."

"Has Captain Mordaunt no income of his own?" inquired the duchess. "He surely possesses some means to live as he does."

"He has about eight hundred a year, I believe."

"And he declines to commit matrimony upon that? Why! if I loved a girl and owned as much I would marry her to-morrow. Bless my soul!" And the duchess made an indignant gesticulation. "What is the world coming to? It seems to me that young people grow more selfish and mercenary every day. Keep a sharp lookout on this fine lover of yours, my dear Kitty, for from all I hear it strikes me he is far fonder of Number One than of anybody else. The idea of his leaving you here when he has eight hundred a year."

"Indeed, duchess," said Kitty, "you judge Cyril too harshly. He has a great many expenses already, without my adding to them."

"Well," rejoined her grace, in an unconvinced tone, "we shall see. But I maintain he has no business to let you slave at work unfit for a lady whilst he goes out hunting, and probably flirts with every young woman he comes across, just as if you did not exist."

Tears sprung to Kitty's eyes. "What am I to do?" she said piteously.

"Make him marry you at once," rejoined the duchess, with energy. "That's the right and proper thing."

Kitty turned her head aside. Two great drops were rolling down her cheeks, and she could not bear her companion to see them.

"I—I can't," she said faintly. "I've tried my best, but Cyril says it's impossible, and that we must wait for something to turn up."

"Has he expectations?"

"None, until his mother's death, and she is comparatively a young woman, likely to live for twenty or thirty years." The duchess shrugged her shoulders. "Well," she said, "I suppose you know your own affairs best, but were I in your place I should consider matters extremely unsatisfactory, and I would insist on a definite time being appointed. From what I make out you may wait forever, and then wake up one fine day to find that Captain Mordaunt has changed his mind, or run off with an heiress." Kitty smothered a sob. This thought was not unfamiliar. It had already presented itself. In the last few minutes she began to suspect that she had made a great—a fatal mistake. And Algy, whom she believed so constant, whose affections she had more or less played fast and loose with! His turn had come at last, and in forgetting so soon and so easily, he punished with a vengeance. All the little conceit and girlish pride at having a man entirely devoted, ready to follow and obey like a dog, was knocked out of her at one blow. What a vain fool she had been to imagine for a single moment that he loved her too well to think of anybody else! She felt crushed, humiliated.

The duchess rose from her seat with a smiling countenance. In her heart of hearts she was genuinely sorry for Kitty, and regretted the pain she had inflicted.

"Good-by, my dear," she said affectionately. "I must be going now, and trust when we meet next to find you in better spirits. If you ever have any spare time on your hands, you must walk up to the castle and take tea with me and Arthur. He will be pleased to see you, I am sure."

"How is Lord Daleford?" inquired Kitty, remembering for the first time to ask after the invalid. "Is he better?"

The duchess shook her head and sighed. "He will never be any better. The end draws slowly nearer, and sometimes I almost wish it were at hand, so that his sufferings might cease. It is terrible to see him cut off from everything in the flower of his manhood. And now I must make haste home, for I do not like to leave the poor fellow for long. Mind and come soon." So saying, she descended the narrow stairs, accompanied by Kitty, who saw her safely off the premises, and then returned to the sitting-room, feeling intensely depressed and despondent. A voice seemed to ring in her ears, "Algy is going to be married. Algy is going to be married. He has quite got over his fancy for you." And then the old proverb about falling between two stools recurred to her mind, and she smiled a melancholy smile. She sat there brooding by the fire until twilight drew in and deepened into darkness. She never stirred even when Mrs. Perkins appeared bearing a teapot, a boiled egg, and a plate of bread-and-butter, which sumptuous fare constituted her evening meal.

Lonely! Yes, indeed she was lonely, so lonely that the mere sound of the landlady's voice came as a relief. She put one or two idle questions, just so as to detain her. Any company seemed better than none in her present mood, for when alone her thoughts were distracting. The duchess's scathing remarks about Cyril had put her to the torture, for alas! alas! it was impossible to gainsay their truth, and her heart corroborated every word. His so-called love was a poor, unstable reed to rest upon.

CHAPTER XLIII.

GOING OUT TO COVERT.

THE duchess walked quickly home, unaccompanied by the duke, whose business at Mr. Ruddle's took longer than anticipated. The keen wintry air brought a color to her cheeks in spite of her fifty-five years, and when she marched into the study usually occupied by Lord Algy she looked quite youthful and radiant. Her son was at a writing-table, going over some papers connected with the estate. His mother went up to him and kissed him so affectionately that before a word had been exchanged between them he knew that she brought good tidings. There was something indescribably encouraging in her tender, smiling countenance.

"Well?" he said interrogatively, endeavoring to maintain an appearance of unconcern. "So you are back again?"

"Yes," she replied, "and you will be pleased to hear that I have seen Kitty and had a long talk with her."

"What did she say, mother?" he inquired, throwing off his mask of indifference, and looking up at her eagerly.

"It's not so much what she said as what I gathered. My impression is that this marriage will never come off. Captain Mordaunt is shilly-shallying already."

He gave a start of pleasure.

"What makes you think so, mother? I have a great respect for your opinion, but in the present instance you may be mistaken."

"It is possible, of course, especially as I can't give any reasons. Nevertheless, I am sure of what I say. To begin with, the man's a rascal——"

"There I am entirely with you," interrupted Lord Algy. "A cold-blooded, calculating, mercenary rascal, if ever there was one."

"As for Kitty," went on the duchess, "she's perfectly honest, and was and still believes herself to be very much in love; but he has treated her so badly one way and another that she is pretty well cured of her passion, and only cherishes the lingering remnant of an outraged sentiment."

"I can hardly believe this possible," said Lord Algy. "A fortnight ago she was simply infatuated about Captain Mordaunt."

"That stage is past," replied the duchess. "But time will show whether my surmises are correct or incorrect. Kitty has begun to awake from her illusions, and is in that painful condition, poor child, when a woman sees a flaw in her deity. The disenchantment has set in, and she does not find the process particularly pleasant."

"Would to Heaven she had never set eyes on the brute!" exclaimed Lord Algy vehemently. "We were as jolly as sand-boys until he appeared on the scenes, and took to paying her compliments and sucking-up to her for the sake of her fortune."

"Softly, softly," said the duchess, restraining his vehemence. "Captain Mordaunt no doubt has his faults, but still Kitty accepted him of her own free will, and against her father's wishes. We cannot get over that fact. At the same time, she is very young—a mere child in point of years—and young girls frequently don't know their own minds. They believe the first man who tells them they are charming and captivating, and it never enters their foolish little heads to imagine that he has probably said the same thing to dozens of others. To do Captain Mordaunt justice, his appearance is good, and he is a specious, pleasant enough sort of person when he chooses. We may presume that in Kitty's case, and seeing five-and-twenty thousand pounds looming in the distance, he put forth all his powers of attraction. As long as he made up to her and professed abject devotion, it was natural for her to deem him perfection; but now he is cooling off, and consequently the scales are falling from her eyes. She sees him as he actually is. Meanwhile somebody else, whom she has been foolish enough to flout, rises in her estimation precisely as the false idol descends. One does not live to fifty-five without knowing something about one's own sex."

"Mother," said Lord Algy, turning very pale, "pray don't give me hope unless you have some good cause for what you say."

"My dear boy," she returned, "I have. Kitty is a great deal fonder of you than she herself is aware of, and depend upon it she institutes comparisons between you and Captain Mordaunt not altogether to that gentleman's advantage."

"Even if such were the case," said Lord Algy, with a kindling countenance, "I don't see that there is anything to be done."

"Not at present. She must make the first move, by breaking off her engagement; but you mark my words, Algy: before the winter is over we shall hear of Captain Mordaunt proving faithless. He could marry her now if he chose, but he doesn't. They would not be well off; still, he could afford to keep a wife in a small way were he so disposed. Instead of taking care of her, however, he allows her to gain her daily bread in a horse-dealer's yard. What can one think of such a lover, except that he is not very much in earnest?"

"It is a blackguardly thing for him to do, certainly," said Lord Algy.

"Of course it is, and in her heart of hearts Kitty thinks the same. She has pride and intelligence and spirit. They will come to her assistance, and teach her that she has been on the point of making a fatal mistake."

"You were not cross to her, were you?" he asked.

"Cross! I was kindness itself. I invited her to come to tea whenever she liked, and by way of consolation gave her to understand that you were not altogether heart-broken, but contemplated turning benedict at no very distant date."

"You didn't say that, surely?" he exclaimed in alarm.

"Yes, I did; and what's more, it did Kitty a lot of good, and brought her to her bearings in the most extraordinary manner."

"Well," he said resignedly, "I don't suppose she cared two straws. I might marry Jezebel for all it affected her."

"Wouldn't it, though?" cried the duchess, in a triumphant voice. "She was as put out as she could be, and turned quite pale."

"Really, mother? Truly?"

"Yes, and her voice regularly shook when she said that she was very glad to hear the news for your sake. Algy, darling," giving him a hug, "have patience. Look on at the game for only a little while longer, and all will come right in the end."

"Shall I say anything to her?" he asked, his big frame trembling with emotion. "I can't bear to think of her being in trouble."

"On no account. Leave her entirely alone. Don't seek her in any way. If you can contrive to make her believe that you're quite happy talking to some other fascinating young lady, so much the better. Jealousy is a wonderful quickener of love."

"I couldn't do it, mother. I couldn't play the hypocrite, or do violence to my own feelings."

"Well, then, just go on as you are doing. You have given up running after Kitty this last week or two, and until her engagement ceases you are more or less bound to preserve a policy of masterly inactivity. And now I must go and look after Arthur."

So saying, the duchess departed, leaving Lord Algy in a flutter of excitement. A chance still—a chance of winning the bride on whom his heart had so long been set. Ah! how different the world looked all of a sudden. Away with morbid thought. The goddess Hope once more smiled upon him, and he felt himself a new man.

He walked to the window and looked out at the green park and the vista of undulating fields beyond. The world was not such a bad place to live in after all. Suddenly he broke out into bird-like whistling. Joyous and musical were the notes, as they rose higher and higher, like the song of a lark. And his mother, hearing them as she took off her hat and jacket in the bedroom overhead, laughed softly to herself. She felt somehow as if she had been instrumental in bringing two loving hearts together, and in preventing a catastrophe which might have embittered their owners' lives.

Up to Christmas the season proved so mild that Mr. Ruddle's yard was never free from purchasers, and business throve apace. Horses were constantly coming and going. Kitty and David Frazer were kept so actively employed that they had no opportunity of going hunting. But towards the close of the year a frost set in, which afforded a little breathing space, although the arrears of work which had accumulated gave plenty to do. A great deal of clipping went on, accompanied by a general washing and mending of rugs, whilst bits and bridles received an extra amount of polishing.

Snow had fallen first, and then it took to freezing hard, in consequence of which the roads were so slippery as to be no longer safe for valuable animals. Therefore, the men set to work and constructed a straw ring in Mr. Ruddle's home paddock, and here, every morning when it was almost pitch dark, and so cold that her numbed hands could hardly feel the reins, Kitty went exercising with her stable companions. Apart from the darkness, and coldness, and dreariness of these wintry dawns, it was weary work jogging round the same perpetual circle, with precisely the same objects on which to rest the eye. The horses appeared to hate it as much as their riders, and in spite of the sharp, brisk air, they moved mechanically and without gayety or freedom. Every now and then a playful young one might give a buck, but he very soon subsided. The straw was heavy going. They sunk above their fetlocks at each step, and although it might improve their action, it quickly damped their ardor.

As usual, the hunting men had all rushed up to town at the first sign of frost. They could not stand the country directly they were debarred from pursuing their favorite sport. Cyril followed the general example, but his absence did not affect Kitty materially. Of late she had seen next to nothing of him, and they seemed to have drifted further and further apart. Occasionally Miss Bretby called to look at a horse—she was not yet suited, nor likely to be—and Kitty gleaned various scraps of information from her which did not contribute to raise her spirits. She learned thus indirectly that Captain Mordaunt's attentions to Miss Van Agnew in the field were beginning to be very much commented upon, and a general belief prevailed that the heiress was head over ears in love with him. Kitty refused to credit quite all she heard. She could not believe him guilty of such gross perfidy, and tried to console herself with the notion that Miss Bretby's love of gossip led her to exaggerate matters. Nevertheless, she gathered quite sufficient to render her extremely anxious to go hunting at some early date, in order to form her own conclusions. With this object in view, she contrived to ride Sir Moses for an hour or so every day, and got him fairly handy. He carried his head better, and was no longer so green about the mouth. He had also improved considerably in his jumping, although he still took off uncertainly, and one never could be quite sure whether he would get too near his fences or spring at them yards away. Kitty held the opinion that his performances with hounds would probably be an improvement on those at home, and for some time past she had been anxious to give the brown thoroughbred a trial.

On the 28th of December the frost broke up as suddenly as it had set in, and on the morning of the 30th a post-card arrived from the kennels intimating that, weather permitting, the hounds would meet at Dallington, a village two miles beyond Furrowdale, at twelve o'clock. This was joyful intelligence, and the fixture being close to Belfield, Mr. Ruddle was tempted by the mildness of the day and the comparative slackness of business to mount his favorite confidential cob, with the intention of having a look at the hounds. He also gave Kitty permission to take Sir Moses for an airing, and told David Frazer to bestride a high-mettled steed who was to be inspected by a customer on the morrow, and who would prove none the worse for a preliminary sobering. It was so long since Kitty had been out hunting that she was quite excited at the prospect, though she felt rather shy of greeting her acquaintances at the meet escorted on one side by Mr. Ruddle and on the other side by David Frazer. However, they had both been kind to her after their respective fashions, and she was determined not to let any false pride stand in her way, or give them reason to suppose that she was ashamed of their company. So, when the hour came for starting the trio rode forth together and proceeded leisurely in the direction of Dallington.

The frost had regularly got into the ground, and the roads were still in a very bad condition, with patches of sodden, slippery snow lying thawing in the faint morning sunshine. Although the "going" would improve every hour, it was evident that jumping could only be conducted under difficulties. The shady side of the hedges was as hard as iron in many places, and when our little party got into the fields they could hear their horses' hoofs rattling under them. Mr. Ruddle cautioned Kitty against being over-venturesome, and she promised to keep the warning in mind and do nothing rash.

"There will be no harm in showing Sir Moses off a bit before Miss Van Agnew, if you get the chance," said Mr. Ruddle, who, although on pleasure bent, had still an eye to business. "It is quite possible that he may suit her when he has had a bit more schooling, and her fancy evidently inclines towards a peacocky, showy-looking animal. Or that brother of hers might buy him if the horse were brought under his notice. He doesn't know a good hunter from a calf."

"They neither of them do," said Kitty. "But they might not be out to-day. I understood from Miss Bretby that both Mr. and Miss Van Agnew had gone up to town." As she finished speaking, Mr. Ruddle went on a few paces in advance, in order to open a bridle gate which led to the Dallington road, and all of a sudden a lady and two gentlemen came galloping up from behind. Kitty turned furiously, painfully red as she recognized them, for there was Miss Van Agnew riding her own darling, Tiny Tim, and looking very uncomfortable as he frisked about—that was one tiny crumb of comfort—and on either side of the heiress rode her brother and Captain Mordaunt.

CHAPTER XLIV.

AT THE MEET.

HAD it been possible to avoid the new-comers Kitty would gladly have done so, for she felt ready to sink into the ground with shame. That Cyril, of all people in the world, should see her going out to covert with Mr. Ruddle and David Frazer, was mortifying in the extreme. If it had been Lord Algy she would not have minded so much. He did not set such store on appearances; but Cyril—well! nothing could have happened more unfortunately. Their eyes met, and taking off his hat with an exaggerated politeness which secretly irritated her he said in a cold, distinct voice, "Good morning, Miss Herrick. I hope you are enjoying your ride to the meet."

She fancied she saw a sarcastic curl of the lip under his blonde mustache as he uttered these words, and retorted with spirit, "Yes, as much as I trust you are enjoying yours." And she glanced significantly at Miss Van Agnew, who, being nearly bucked off by Tiny Tim, was too intent on retaining her seat to give Kitty more than a passing nod of recognition. "Take care," cried Kitty, in alarm, "get his head up when he bucks like that. It's fatal to let him have it down."

"He's a brute, a regular brute," said poor Judith, almost in tears, and conscious of making an indifferent display before her admirer.

"Indeed he is not," answered Kitty, keen in defence of her pet. "Wait till you get him in a run. He's only fresh, that's all."

"Every lady does not have Miss Herrick's practice on horseback," said Cyril. "What's only fresh to her is a good deal to other people. Come, let us have a

canter. He'll soon settle down then." So saying, he
shook up his horse and rode off at a hand gallop, Miss
Van Agnew following suit. As Kitty gazed after their
receding forms she turned white to the very lips. Did
he intend to deliberately insult her in the presence of
another woman? In no other way could she account
for his conduct. It was rude, ungentlemanly, inhuman!
Without any provocation he had attacked her. She was
hot with righteous anger—so hot that she never noticed
little Daniel Van Agnew until his squeaky voice close
at her side restored her to a sense of what was going on.

"Ha, ha," he sniggered, "two's company and three's
none. Don't you think so, Miss Herrick?"

"I don't think anything at all about it," she answered
coldly. "My thoughts are otherwise engaged."

"He, he! very good, very good. Best thing that
I've heard for a long time. May I take it as a personal
compliment?"

"Take what?" and she looked at him with an air of
surprise.

"Come now, that wont do. You aint as innocent
as all that. I'll be bound you know a pair of turtle
doves when you see them, as well as most people.
Aint it a joke? Judith, too, of all women in the world,
to go falling in love. I say, Miss Herrick, I'm tired of
playing gooseberry. It aint good enough. Why
shouldn't you and I get up an opposition, just to show
we're not going to be left out in the cold, eh?" and he
winked at Kitty in a manner which set the crowning
seal on her wrath.

"I presume because I'm in a humble position you
think you can say anything you choose to me, Mr.
Van Agnew," she retorted indignantly. "Pray understand once for all that you are very much mistaken.
Mr. Ruddle," turning to her employer, "shall we trot
on to the meet?" And upon receiving an assent from
that gentleman she forged ahead, leaving Mr. Van
Agnew discomfited by his non-success, and murmuring
disconsolately that she was a high-stepper, don't you

know—a deuced high-stepper. None of your tame, pretty fillies, who come and nibble at the corn sieve directly it is held out as a lure to catch them, but a real out-and-out flyer.

The meet that day at Dallington proved unusally small. Owing to the suddenness of the thaw, a considerable number of the ordinary *habitués* of the hunt had not yet returned. Some few had posted back by an overnight train, but the majority were still absent. Kitty felt secretly relieved at finding so select a company assembled, and the gap left by many familiar forms occasioned little regret. She had no desire to greet her acquaintances, and in order to avoid them as much as possible took refuge behind a barn until the hounds were ready to move off. Here, although unseen herself, she was able to command a general survey of the field, and she quickly espied Cyril and Miss Van Agnew standing side by side and chatting away in confidential whispers which proclaimed that they were on the best of terms.

In one minute the girl knew all she had come out to discover. It was a revelation, and as she watched them from her hiding-place a feeling of unutterable scorn and contempt for him stole over her. For once, Miss Bretby had related the truth, and nothing but the truth, and there, before her very eyes, she saw her lover that had been making up to a plain, fat, commonplace girl, devoid of every recommendation save that of money. If Miss Van Agnew had possessed the least pretensions to good looks, or had been in any way attractive, Kitty told herself she could have forgiven his perfidy. But as matters stood, the mercenary spirit which actuated his conduct was so patent that a sentiment bordering on disgust filled her whole being. Was this the man to whom she had given her heart—this mean, despicable creature whose sole aim and object was to feather his own nest regardless of every consideration of honor and decency? He had never cared for her, any more than he cared now for Miss Van Agnew. All he did value

23

was wealth. The thing was so self-evident that she wondered at the blindness which had closed her eyes.

They were beginning to see clearly again, however, and her gaze grew more and more critical. When she saw him gaze into Judith's face and incline his head towards her as he spoke, Kitty felt as if she could have struck him to the ground. Then, yielding to a novel law of attraction, almost involuntarily her glance travelled in the direction of Lord Algy Loddington. He, whom her thoughts had so often spurned—the man whom she had considered too steady and slow-going, not smart or brisk enough to suit her taste—was sitting on a powerful blood-hunter, surrounded by the hounds, who leaped around him in recognition of a well-known friend. By some mental revolution the characteristics which formerly she had viewed with indifference now gave rise to a sense of admiration. How quiet and strong and manly he looked! What a good, kind face his was when you came to examine it narrowly. Yes, the beauty of expression certainly beat the beauty of form.

Thus thinking, she again turned her eyes on Cyril. Strange that she should not have seen it before! His handsome features were certainly spoiled by an impress of falseness and insincerity. The flash of his white teeth beneath his fair mustache reminded her of some sly, cunning, wolfish creature. All-unconscious that he was being watched, Cyril did his utmost to render himself agreeable to Miss Van Agnew, and apparently succeeded well, for her sallow face beamed with pleasure and gratified vanity. He was the handsomest man in the hunting field, and entirely devoted to her. She gave him back smile for smile. The only difference was that hers were genuine whilst his were not. She was playing the game of love seriously; he trifled at it hypocritically for the sake of the stakes. Curiously enough, Kitty's resentment did not extend to Miss Van Agnew. Her rival aroused sentiments of the profoundest pity. She looked upon her as a dupe, and knew that many a heartache, many a bitter tear, would be her portion in the future.

"Fools, fools," she muttered, gripping Sir Moses's reins tight in her small left hand. "We are all alike. Any specious, good-looking man can turn us round his little finger, and we never discover until it is too late that he only uses us as so many tools or stepping-stones that enable him to rise. What is a woman to men? Nothing. A toy, an incident, a mere passing diversion. They swear devotion to one, then to another, with equal ease. It makes no difference. Love is a pastime—a temporary amusement. Constancy, a thing to be ridiculed. And we break our hearts for such as these! Fools, ay, fools indeed!" Thus meditating, a haze rose up and obstructed Kitty's vision, which necessitated the surreptitious application of her handkerchief to her eyes. Fortunately, the friendly barn sheltered her, and no one witnessed this sign of weakness. .It did not last long. She thrust her handkerchief back into her pocket with a determined gesture, and her proud lip curled. She would let the traitor see that she knew him for what he was, and despised him now as much as she had loved him formerly. When the opportunity came she would turn upon him and pour forth all the contempt and scorn that made every vein in her body tingle.

At this juncture a stir was visible amongst the crowd, and the huntsman, putting himself at the head of the hounds, moved slowly off. And now came the worst ordeal of all to our heroine, for keep as she might in the background she could not avoid being recognized by her numerous friends. It may be that she was in a hypercritical, supersensitive condition, prone to imagine offence where none existed, but it certainly struck her that the women were either a trifle more patronizing or else more distant than their wont; and she resented the change either way. As for the men, the old ones were extra, extra paternal, full of sympathy and condolences, and the young ones accosted her with an unaccustomed familiarity which set her blood aflame.

Not a word, not a sign, not a look was lost upon her.
She was raw from a wound which everything made
bleed, and having settled in her mind that people would
show her the cold shoulder, she was determined not to
give them the chance of snubbing *her*, so she snubbed
them unmercifully.   Many of them went home saying
they could not think what had come to Kitty Herrick.
They had never seen a girl so altered for the worse in
their lives.   And they were unanimous in attributing
this deterioration to her profession.   "A woman who
turns horse-breaker, you know—what can you expect?
It must have a brutalizing effect.   By this time next
year she'll have gone to the dogs altogether, and probably end by marrying a groom."

There was one person out hunting, besides Cyril Mordaunt, with regard to whose conduct Kitty felt considerable interest.   This was Lord Algy.   An uncomfortable idea possessed her mind that he was offended, and
that she had sinned against him past forgiveness.   So
strong was the feeling upon her that she did not dare
take any notice of his presence, but waited timidly to
see if he would address her or not.   Apparently he had
no intention of renewing their friendship, for as he
passed close by where she was standing, shrinking back
for the procession to go on ahead, he merely lifted his
hat.   True, he turned very red, but for any other mark
of recognition she might have been a total stranger.
A sudden sense of despair assailed her.   She had
contrived to estrange her best friend, and no doubt he
also was ashamed to be seen speaking to her.   With a
brilliant smile she suddenly addressed David Frāzer,
and, conscious that many scrutinizing eyes were on her
flirted with him in a way which quite turned the sober
Scotchman's head.

"If I want a pilot to-day you will take care of me,
Mr. Frazer, won't you?" she said coaxingly.

"That I wull," he responded emphatically.   "But
don't ye gae flaring aboot here, there, and everywhere,
Miss Herrick.   It's mortal slippery."

"You keep by me," she laughed in reply, "and then I shall be all right and have some one to pick me up in case of misfortune."

"I'll do my best; but I'm just thinking it will na do to·bustle this young horse too much. Mister Ruddle wishes to pass him on to-morrow, and my orders was to guv him guid exercise but to run nae risks."

"Don't let me lead you into mischief, pray," said Kitty, in a tone of light banter.

He took off his hat and wiped his harsh, grizzled hair with a colored cotton handkerchief. Then he sighed deeply and said solemnly: "I'm a-feared ye hae done that already." There was something in his voice which alarmed Kitty so much—that suggested such an undesirable and perplexing possibility to her mind— that all at once she became silent, and devoted her attention to Lord Algy's back. She was most curious to ascertain if the lady who had superseded her in his affections was out, but came to the conclusion that she could not be, since he confined his conversation almost entirely to members of his own sex.

Feeling very bad all round, Kitty jogged humbly at the tail of the procession, among the grooms and the tradesmen and rough-riders, whilst Miss Van Agnew, mounted on her own dear Tiny Tim, with Captain Mordaunt sticking to her like a burr, bumped away in the front. Verily, in that moment did she loath the world—a world ready to fall and cringe at her feet as long as she was well-off and wanted for nothing, and which left her out in the cold directly Fortune's wheel made an adverse turn. There was one thing, however, which filled her cup of bitterness to the brim. And that was to find Lord Algy touched with the same snob- bishism which rendered Kitty Herrick, horse-breaker, a personage of no account from the moment she lost both money and position. She was not surprised at other people, but she was surprised at *him*.

During the morning she had been subjected to a series of mortifications, and if some of them existed

chiefly in her own fancy, they were none the less real
on that account.   In her father's time she had always
been accustomed to be petted and made much of.   The
ladies were friendly—if occasionally a little jealous;
and the gentlemen vied with each other in showing her
delicate attentions.   They had given her to understand
that she was a fascinating and attractive young person,
and if she wore her honors meekly it was not because
she was insensible to them.   But now everything was
changed, and she had begun to find out that when you
stand entirely on your own level, stripped bare of all
outward advantages except those conferred by nature,
folks trouble their heads mighty little about you.   You
cease to be lovable, you cease to be charming, save to
a very limited few.   There is nothing to be got out of
you; you have nothing to give, and so you are not
worth cultivating.

CHAPTER XLV.

A NATTY TOSS.

It would be wrong to suppose, however, that Kitty was wholly deserted. A variety of youths, mostly belonging to the Daniel Van Agnew type, sought her out with the amiable and gentlemanly intention of indulging in witticisms at her expense. They offered to come and see her in the yard; they suggested visits to Mrs. Perkins's, and volunteered mounts which, needless to say, she did not accept. She stood very much on her dignity, and plainly intimated to these juvenile Lotharios that, rough-rider and horse-breaker as she might be, she would not put up with any liberties, either of speech or conduct. Finding there was no fun to be got out of her, after a time they retired discomfited, the only effect of their notice being to make Kitty's wrath flare up fiercer than ever.

Everybody has bad hours in their lives, and she never spent much worse than on this particular morning, when she ran, so to speak, the gauntlet of the field. The covert once reached, the situation began to improve. As good luck would have it, reynard proved to be at home. He was none of your sneaking, twisting creatures, but a bold and gallant fellow, who at the first sight of the enemy set his mask straight for the open. The hounds quickly settled to the line, and in five minutes it became a case of every one for himself. Lord Algy had apparently issued orders to the hunt servants that they were not to jump unless absolutely compelled, and, as if aware of these instructions, the fox at first started most obligingly and led his pursuers through a

line of bridle gates of which they gladly availed themselves.

Little by little the mildness of the air, combined
with the smartness of the pace at which they travelled,
caused the blood to glow in Kitty's veins. She began
to think less of herself and her sorrows. The burdens
imposed by care, poverty, and anxiety, not to mention
disappointed love, seemed to drop away, until at length
her pretty, honest face beamed as in the days of yore,
illumined by the enthusiasm of the chase. Her cheeks
took on a soft pink hue, her eyes flashed and sparkled,
and insensibly her courage and her spirits rose higher
and higher. Horse-breaker or lady, what did it matter
when hounds were running?

Oh! glorious sport, that levels all social distinctions,
that renders the poor man equal with the rich, and puts
the humblest farmer on the same footing as the proud-
est gentleman. What true man or woman will dare to
decry thee? In a country full of snobs given to pros-
trating themselves before power, and wealth, and rank,
thou art indeed a blessed institution. My Lord Demi-
god, for all his title and rent-roll, bumps the ground
just as forcibly as plain John Smith who possesses but
a single broken-kneed screw. Hurrah! then, for the
chase, which enables the best man to go to the front, no
matter if he inhabit a palace or a cottage. On the
hunting field equality reigns supreme. The king is he
who has the quickest eye to detect the nearest way, the
steadiest nerve to lead over a nasty fence, and the
finest judgment in crossing a country. Put him on a
good horse, thrust his feet in the stirrups, gather the
reins in his hands, give him a fair start, and where do
riches, station, fame, stand then in comparison? For as
many hours as he sits in the saddle and a fox stands up
in front of the hounds he wears a crown of glory.

Some such thoughts as these flitted confusedly through
Kitty's brain as she gradually assumed her accustomed
place amongst the leading division. What a changed
being she felt! Now she could return her neighbors'

salutations without fearing they meant to avoid her. The speckled beauties ahead were responsible for this alteration.

For about ten minutes the hounds simply flew, and horse men and women were forced to gallop as hard as they could across the slippery fields and crush through the heavy gateways in hot haste. There was not a moment to be lost. He who hesitated soon got left behind. On the whole, Sir Moses behaved remarkably well, and went much more quietly than Kitty had antici-pated. Perhaps this was partly owing to the fact that, having naturally narrow feet, which periodically got balled with snow, the sense of insecurity thus produced prevented him from indulging in his usual vagaries. He galloped on with the rest, and his fine turn of speed quickly enabled him to assume a forward position. Kitty had the satisfaction of passing Miss Van Agnew, who seemed all abroad on Tiny Tim, and appeared afraid to let him extend himself, which deficiency of courage the bay resented by lowering his head, fixing his jaws, and pulling as hard as he knew how, thereby greatly increasing his rider's inward misgivings. She eyed the brown horse covetously as he swept by with a long raking stride, going kindly and comfortably.

"Halloo!" she shouted. "What's that you're on?"

"A young one," Kitty called back in reply. "I've just brought him out for an hour or two to see how he behaves with hounds."

"Why, didn't Mr. Ruddle show him to me?" said Judith. "I like him much better than this beast," giving Tiny Tim a job in the mouth.

"He is hardly fit to sell to a lady yet," answered Kitty, "although we hope he will come round in another fortnight or three weeks. Mr. Ruddle does intend to show him to you or Mr. Van Agnew later on, I know. But I think you had better leave it for a month or so, until I see how the horse progresses."

Lord Algy happened to be close by and heard this conversation. He turned round in the saddle, and took a steady look at Sir Moses. Kitty, impelled by some sudden impulse, immediately urged the brown to his speed, and racing by, sent a great clod of muddy snow flying past his lordship's face. It missed him by about the eighth of an inch. He gazed anxiously after her slender, upright figure, with its flat back, finely sloped shoulders, and small waist, and thought to himself how wonderfully well she looked in a habit, and what a marvellous seat she had on horseback. He longed to warn her against jumping an untried animal in the dangerous state of the ground, but could not summon up sufficient courage to address her after the interdiction which she had laid upon him at their last meeting.

For a few more minutes all continued to go safely and merrily, but then Pug seemed to discover that unless he altered his tactics loss of life would probably result. So, instead of playing at running away, he took to his heels in earnest. Doubling quickly back, so as to throw the hounds at fault, he struck out an entirely new line and headed for a country where the jump was imperative. Everybody knew what the orders anent leaping were. At the meet all had been unanimous in acknowledging their wisdom, and declared they would not imperil their own necks or their horses' fore-legs. But when hounds run, and a certain amount of preliminary galloping has warmed the blood, it is astonishing how caution flies to the winds. People talk no more, and think less of necks and fore-legs. The men cram down their hats, throw away cigar-ends, and with a grim resolve on every feature, say to themselves, "It can't be helped. We must chance it." All the forward riders of a hunt invariably arrive at the same conclusion, no matter how determinedly they may have expressed their intention beforehand of sticking to roads and gates. When it comes to the point they can't. The sight of the silvery pack streaming ahead is simply irresistible, and renders them temporarily defiant of danger. With a feeling of recklessness strong upon them, they abandon the safe path, and henceforth are prepared to do or die. "In for a penny, in for a pound," is the maxim that guides their footsteps.

A fence, not formidable under ordinary conditions, nevertheless of no mean size, now confronted the pursuers. It consisted of a stout blackthorn hedge, between four and five feet high, with a deep ditch half-filled with melting snow on the near side, and a nasty, greasy take-off. After a momentary hesitation, the huntsman charged it boldly, but his mare slipped about a yard before she came to the fence, and although she contrived to make a spring, landed right in the middle. Fortunately, the binders proved yielding, and tearing them away with her chest, she sprawled into the opposite field, leaving a very fair-sized gap in her wake, to which every one immediately crowded. The two men next in succession pulled their steeds up to a walk, and popped over at a stand. Kitty tried hard to follow suit, but Sir Moses, who hitherto had been as docile as a lamb, all at once exhibited signs of temper. Whether he had been alarmed at the crash made by the huntsman's horse, or whether instinct warned him against the slippery nature of the ground, nothing would induce him to face the gap, easy as it had now become. Kitty endeavored three or four times to bring him up to it, but as he took to rearing and lashing out with his hind heels she was forced to make way, though sorely against her will. While still battling with Sir Moses, who grew more and more fractious and obstinate, she became aware that Miss Van Agnew was close at hand and similarly employed. It was clear that Tiny Tim and his rider were having a very serious difference of opinion, in which the latter bid fair to be worsted. She was very flushed, panting and dishevelled, and altogether appeared exceedingly ill at ease. Knowing the little bay's idiosyncrasies, Kitty took a glance around, and immediately perceived the cause of his perverseness. The hounds had taken a sharp bend to the right, and Tiny Tim's eye was on them. He saw that by jumping another fence, which ran at right angles to the gap, he would avoid a considerable corner and make one leap do duty for two. Under these circumstances, Kitty knew the uselessness of battling with him. He would have his way, and it was sheer loss of time to attempt to oppose him. Perhaps his brain was larger than most of his species. Anyhow, it was as if he said to himself, "What! You think you know better than I? Not a bit of it. Leave me alone and I'll take you the shortest cut to hounds."

Not being as well acquainted with his peculiarities as Kitty, Miss Van Agnew found them extremely disagreeable, and began to lose her temper in exact proportion as the little horse lost his. She raised her whip aloft—it was a riding-school thing with a jewelled head—and was about to strike him, when Kitty called out hastily:

"For goodness' sake don't hit him. You'll drive him simply wild, and he'll be unmanageable for the rest of the day."

"He's not a horse, he's a devil," said Judith, tears of anger and vexation springing to her eyes. "I never rode such an animal. I can do nothing whatever with him."

"He only wants to get to the hounds," responded Kitty. "Pop him over that fence there and he'll be all right in an instant."

"Perhaps he wont jump," said Judith undecidedly. "He's brute enough for anything. Four pounds is more like his price than four hundred. Oh, dear! oh, dear!" and she groaned aloud. "What with his pulling and his bucking and his fidgeting I'm so stiff and sore I can hardly sit in the saddle."

"Give him his head," said Kitty, "and whatever you do don't hang on to the bridle as he jumps. There's not such another hunter in this county, so you need not be afraid."

Meantime Tiny Tim, growing impatient of the delay, took matters out of Miss Van Agnew's hands. He shook his lean head in a determined fashion, cocked his small game ears, and bounded forward before his unfortunate mistress fairly realized what he was about. As she neared the fence she retained just sufficient presence of mind to throw the reins on his neck and to grip convulsively hold of the pommel. The next moment she found herself jerked violently forward, and affectionately embracing his neck; but—oh! joy of joys—the fence was behind! By dint of a supreme effort she managed to regain her equilibrium and struggled back into the saddle. It was the first *bona fide* fence she had ever jumped, though she saw no occasion to proclaim that fact. The peril once passed, a thrill of triumph and elation ran like wildfire through her veins, and looking back at Kitty, she shouted out, "Come on. What are you waiting for? It's nothing of a place."

Kitty knew the difference between jumping a perfect hunter like Tiny Tim and an untrained animal like Sir Moses, but with such a challenge as this sounding in her ears she would have ridden an unbroken colt at the obstacle. It was the second occasion on which Miss Van Agnew had questioned her courage. She should see that she (Kitty) was not backward in following where another led. Therefore, she gave Sir Moses a sharpish touch of her spurred heel and galloped him at the fence. The ditch happened to be on the far side, and she knew that, if he jumped at all, he jumped better going fast than slow. Tiny Tim had apparently put heart into the timorous brown, for he went at the fence as if he meant having it. But he took off wildly, and very nearly a couple of yards too soon. The consequence was he landed with both hind legs well in the ditch, and pitching on to his head, rolled heavily over.

Just for a moment Kitty was stunned by the force of the fall. Then she saw a brown mass heave before her eyes, stretched out her hands to ward it off, and with a sudden sense of relief felt Sir Moses struggle to his legs again. She was not the least hurt, and was about to jump to her feet when she made the horrible discovery that she was not free. Her habit had caught over the pommel, and when Sir Moses took a step or two forward he dragged her after him. The position was dangerous

in the extreme. She realized this at once, for every
time he lifted his hind feet she could see his iron hoofs
flash close to her face. Once the off hoof hit her, and
broke in the crown of her pot hat. She was naturally
brave, but at this a terrible sensation of physical fear
took possession of her. She prayed inwardly, "Oh, if I
must be killed, let me be killed at once. Do not pro-
long the agony and keep me sensible whilst I am being
battered to pieces. Make the horse dash my brains out
with one kick!" As if in answer to her wish, Sir Moses
began to lash out irritably. He was by temperament a
nervous animal, and the fall and its consequences rendered him still more so. He broke from a walk to a
trot—a trot to a gallop. As his brown heels clattered
about her head, and she swayed helplessly to and fro,
Kitty thought that her last day had come. She gave
herself up for lost, and all her past life seemed to unfold
like a panorama before her vision.

How puerile one's hopes and desires appear at such
a time as this. What an insignificance even Love and
Marriage assume when Death stares one in the face.
The absolute triviality of all the things that recently
had engaged her attention, such as social position, the
slights and insults of the world, its apathy and coldness,
impressed itself upon her mind. Lately she had often
wished to die, but she had no idea the process was so
hard. The earth seems to grow very fair when you
believe you will never see it again. The sun gleams
brighter, the sky bluer, the fields greener. Ah! the
pity of it—the pity of it! Merciful heavens! What
was that striking her on the back again and again?
Why did not those cruel heels crush in her temples and
put an end to this awful suffering? She tried to scream,
but could not. An abject terror paralyzed her tongue
and prevented its muscles from working. And then,
what good could screaming do? It would not prevent
her dying—dying—dying in the flower of her youth and
beauty. Was it like this her poor father had felt? If
so, no need existed for man to judge him. A haze

obscured her eyesight, her senses were becoming enfee-
bled; a little more, just one or two more well-directed
blows, and unconsciousness would supervene and deaden
the frantic struggles of body and spirit. With her
whole soul she entreated God to hasten the moment.
Good-by, earth! Good-by, life! Good-by, Algy! Yes,
Algy; for she knew now what she might have known
all along. Good-by—good-by!

Suddenly she saw something red go by, and more
heels galloped over the ground. Faster they went—
faster than the remorseless ones which threatened her
so closely. She was dimly aware of a figure bending
over, snatching resolutely at the reins, checking Sir
Moses in his wild career, and jagging him again and
again in the mouth till he came to a halt. Then some
strong hand dexterously lifted up the hem of her habit,
and with a thud she fell to the ground; but free—free!
Although she lay motionless for a space, her arms outstretched, her face pressed against the moist grass, her
breath all faint and difficult, she knew that she was
saved, and thanked God for her escape. But what was
more wonderful still, after the first shock she began to
realize that she was comparatively unharmed.

"Kitty," said a well-known voice, rendered hoarse
by emotion, "are you hurt? Can you speak?"

She raised her head from the ground and looked at
the speaker. Lord Algy stood over her, his great limbs
trembling, his face whiter even than her own.

CHAPTER XLVI.

MISFORTUNES NEVER COME SINGLY.

SHE raised herself on one elbow and laughed hysterically. Something in the expression of Lord Algy's countenance made her heart beat thick and with quick pulsations. For a moment she was on the verge of betraying her feelings; then, just in time, she remembered the strange woman who was coming to inhabit Herrington, and at the thought she laughed again, even less naturally than before, and tottered to her feet. " Hurt!" she exclaimed. " No, nothing to mention. Only a bit bruised and shaken. I believe I'm more frightened than hurt."

" Thank God!" he ejaculated, handing her a pin with which she strove to repair a big rent in her habit. " I thought you were killed. It was the most awful sight I ever saw in my life!" And he shuddered at the recollection.

" Being dragged is not exactly a pleasant sensation," she said. " It makes one feel rather a coward. . I have to thank you for my life," looking up at him gratefully. " Had it not been for your promptitude I must have been killed."

" Don't talk of it, Kitty. The whole thing was appalling, and will haunt me like a nightmare for many a week to come. You were angry with me the other day for speaking the truth; but, say what you may, this work is not fit for a lady."

" Everybody takes a fall now and again," she rejoined with a touch of her old obstinacy.

" Frail, delicate women have no business to be exposed to these risks," he went on, unheeding the observation.

"Would you keep them under a glass case?" she inquired, beginning to revive. "You forget that when they are in the unpleasant position of having to gain their bread it is not so easy to wrap them up in cotton wool."

"Will you promise me something?" he asked. "Our opinions do not agree, so the best plan is to refrain from discussion."

"A rash promise frequently proves difficult to keep," she replied guardedly. "Tell me first what you wish."

"Simply this. Promise me faithfully never to get on the back of that shifty brown beggar again. I saw him sidling about at the meet, and knew then that he was only half broke and not fit for you to ride with hounds."

"I can't promise," she said after a moment's hesitation.

"May I not even make so slight a request as this?" he said, a shadow passing over his face.

"You misunderstand," she rejoined. "I am not my own mistress, and if a customer were to come into the yard, and Mr. Ruddle ordered me to show off Sir Moses, I should have to obey."

"Of course," he said ironically. "It was foolish of me to suppose that you would pay any attention to my words, especially as it has not been your habit to do so hitherto. However, perhaps if Captain Mordaunt adds his solicitations to mine——"

"They would produce no more effect," she interrupted. "Why should you display so much concern about me?"

"Because, Kitty," he began, but he checked himself suddenly, and she went on with a strange feeling of recklessness:

"I am an obstinate, wilful, unsexed young woman, who refuses to be guided or lectured even by her best friends, who has an unhappy knack of estranging the very people she likes most, who is her own worst enemy, and who has no brighter prospect in store than that of sinking lower and lower, and growing 'hard, and vulgar, and horsy.'"

24

He stared at her in amazement. "What on earth do you mean?"

"Oh, nothing—at least, nothing of any importance. Here is a second horseman," she added, with a sense of relief. "He wants to speak to you."

"What's the matter?" inquired Lord Algy, none the best pleased at the interruption, and turning impatiently towards the fresh arrival.

"Beg your parding, my lord, but the huntsman 'as met with a haccident. He's 'ad a fall, and his 'oss is a-bleeding to death."

"Confound it," exclaimed Lord Algy. "This comes of hunting when the ground is not fit to ride over. If Diana dies we shall lose one of the best mares in the stable. Do you know how it happened, my man?"

"I 'eard say, my lord, as how she got staked in the groin. She's lying there 'ard by." And he pointed to a distant field, where the forms of two or three men were visible bending over some dark object.

"I'll go at once," said Lord Algy. "Here, Kitty, let me put you up, and for goodness' sake take warning by the disasters of the morning. Don't attempt to ride over any more fences to-day." So saying, he hoisted her into the saddle, and placed her foot in the stirrup. In a hurry as he was to reach the scene of the disaster, he could not help lingering over that operation a minute, and she profited by the opportunity of his head being bent downwards to say, "Algy, I have not half thanked you properly, but"—and her voice trembled slightly— "I—I hope you wont think me ungrateful." Then a bright red flush rose to her face, and she added with an effort. "A little bird told me the news. I want to tell you how—how pleased I am. You k—know what I mean."

"The devil a bit." And he raised his eyes to hers in genuine bewilderment.

"Yes, yes, you must. I had it on the best authority. Your mother's."

All at once a broad smile illumined his countenance, *and he burst* out laughing.

"Thank you, awfully, Kitty. The time has not come yet for congratulations, but I hope it may soon, and I will be sure and let you know when it does." Whereupon he rode away, leaving her intensely unhappy. Up till now she had always clung to a belief that he would deny the truth of the duchess's information, but the manner in which he accepted her remarks left no doubt as to its veracity.

And yet, what did the white, scared face mean which she had seen but a few minutes ago? There was something puzzling and mysterious about the whole business which defied her comprehension. Why did he laugh and look at her so—in such a half-shy, half-uncertain, but wholly significant, way, which had the effect of contradicting his words and baffling her completely? Well! it was no use thinking. Things must take their course. She was powerless to contend against fate! With this conclusion, Kitty gathered up her reins and cantered off in pursuit of the hounds, who, left to their own resources, had come to a prolonged check within a couple of fields from where poor Diana lay stretched on the swand. Suddenly she met Lord Algy coming galloping back in a tremendous hurry.

"Can you tell me where David Frazer is?" he asked. "It is very important that I should find him at once."

"I haven't seen him quite lately, but he can't be far off," she responded. "Is not that him over there?" and after sweeping the country with her eye she pointed to a figure cautiously entering the next field by a gate.

"Hurrah!" he exclaimed, "so it is, and just in the very nick of time. The mare has cut an artery. Frazer is as good as a veterinary any day, and if he can only manage to pick it up we may save her yet; but there's not a moment to be lost." So saying, he clapped spurs to his horse and in almost less time than it takes to tell returned to the scene of the disaster, accompanied by David, Kitty following in their wake.

The shrewd Scotchman took in the situation at a glance. The mare had again slipped whilst in the act of jumping, and unfortunately was badly staked. She lay on her side a yard or two away from the fence where she had come to grief. Apparently, she did not suffer acute pain, for she was quite passive, and made no attempt to struggle. Her head and neck were outstretched in a manner suggestive of death, her eye was nearly closed, and only a slight blinking of the lid and an occasional twitching of the nostrils proclaimed that life had not yet altogether departed. The grass beneath her was red with blood—quite a great pool had collected—and the crimson fluid came gushing forth with a pump-like action from a jagged wound in the fleshy part of her left thigh. It was a horrible sight, and her rider stood over her in deep distress, unable to stanch the fatal stream which was rapidly destroying his favorite animal. For Diana was an old friend who had carried him brilliantly and with scarce a fall for over two seasons. If one of his children had died he could scarcely have felt its lost more. Tears stood in his keen eyes as he watched the poor thing gradually growing fainter and fainter.

In an instant David Frazer sprung from his horse, and produced a small case from his pocket in which were a pair of forceps and some strong, waxed thread. Then he stooped down and examined the wound critically. To his great satisfaction, after a minute scrutiny, he perceived a short stringy object protruding ever so slightly. He pounced upon it triumphantly with his forceps, nipping the ends hard. Then quickly, but neatly and firmly, he tied the severed vein tight with the thread, when the terrible loss of blood immediately ceased. His net care was to bring the lips of the wound together and secure them by means of some long pins, and this operation he performed so deftly that when completed the wound no longer presented a very formidable appearance.

"The stake hae nae gone in so far," he said, "but it will be a near thing. The femoral artery was sevaired, and if I had nae just happened to come up when I did she would have been dead as a door nail in another minute." And he proceeded to feel Diana's pulse. As

might be expected, it was very feeble. He could just
detect a flicker and no more, and he at once decided
that some strong restorative was necessary to prevent
collapse. So, looking round, he said, " Hae any o'·ye
gentlemen a drap o' brandy or guid Scotch whiskey to
spare. I'm a-thinking she'll be nane the worse for a
dram."

Half a dozen flasks were promptly tendered, and David
poured their contents one by one down the poor animal's
throat. Before long their effect became visible. She
groaned two or three times almost like a human being,
and opened and closed her eyes, whilst a tremulous motion agitated her ears.

"Give her plenty o' air," said David, peremptorily
waving back a crowd of useless by-standers with his
hand. " She is coming to foine, but there's nae occasion
to bustle the puir crittur, or to put her aboot, for she has
had a mortal close squeak for it." And he patted
Diana's sleek neck with a tenderness which one would
not have expected judging from his rugged appearance.
But though a canny Scot, David's heart was kind,
especially where women and horseflesh were concerned.

Five minutes or so elapsed, and the mare manifestly
began to revive. She raised her head from the ground,
and although it fell back with a flop, by degrees she
showed increasing signs of vitality. Her extremities,
however, were very cold. Lord Algy divested himself
of his coat, and threw it over her quarters, whilst the
huntsman rubbed her chilly little ears so assiduously
that at length he succeeded in imparting some warmth
to them. Whilst all this was going on, a number of
idle spectators gathered round the spot, who, the crisis
past, tendered their advice with great volubility and
freedom. But when it became evident that Diana was
slowly but surely recovering, the excitement gradually
subsided. Some left to rejoin the hounds, others returned to their agricultural employments. The mare
now made endeavors to rise from her recumbent position, efforts which were ably seconded by her human
friends, who were anxious to get her off the wet grass

as soon as possible. After several fruitless struggles,
she finally succeeded in regaining her legs, though she
could scarcely stand without support, being very faint
from loss of blood and partially numbed with the cold.
A sorry object she looked, her coat staring and be-
smeared with gore, her head drooping listlessly, her
limbs trembling beneath her, and the muscles of the
wounded thigh quivering spasmodically.

"We hae better get her into yon shed," said David,
pointing to one that fortunately happened to be close
by. "Has anybody sent for a vaiterinairy surgeon?"

"Yes," said Lord Algy, "I have. I told my second
horseman to ride as fast as he could to Furrowdale and
bring back Mr. Hesseltine."

"Ye hae done weel, my laird. I tak it that the mare
will just be requiring a deal of attention for the next
twa or three days. She should be kept warrim, and
hae plenty of licht, nourishing food given her to eat,
and a cordial every three or four hours."

"Thank you, David," said Lord Algy. "If her life
is saved, it will be entirely owing to you." And he
slipped a sovereign into Frazer's hand.

"Only too glad to render ye a sairvice, my laird, now
and all times," said David, consigning the coin to his
pocket.

Lord Algy's eye rested on Kitty, who had not yet
moved away. She was unusually pale, and he saw at
once that although she might refuse to admit the fact,
she had been considerably shaken by her fall. Her lips
were almost as white as her cheeks, and she sat her
horse as if in pain.

"Persuade Miss Herrick to go home," he said to
David. "The hounds have come to a check, and I
shall give strict orders that there is to be no more
jumping to-day."

"I'm afeared she'll nae be for coming awa so airly in
the day, my laird."

"She must. She has had a bad fall, and been
dragged. In fact, she was within an ace of losing her
life."

"Ye dinna mean it!" exclaimed David, moved out of his usual calm.

"I do, though," responded Lord Algy. "Whatever Mr. Ruddle is about, to send her out hunting on such a leggy, shifty, nervous, dangerous brute, I can't understand. All I know is, I shall have something to say to him on the subject."

"Miss Herrick has sich a foine, high speerit o' her ain," remarked David admiringly.

"That's no reason why she should be allowed to kill herself," rejoined Lord Algy, in unusually stern accents. "As long as she is in Mr. Ruddle's service it is his duty to take care of her and see that she comes to no harm."

"The maister will be terrible put aboot when he hears Miss Herrick has met with an accident," said David. "He thinks a powerful lot of her, as indeed we all do."

"Then why the dickens don't you get her to give up this trade," exclaimed Lord Algy impulsively. "She's far and away too good for it."

David looked at Lord Algy, then at Kitty, and back again at the speaker.

"I'm just thinking ye are nae sae far wrang in your remarks, my laird, and I'll do my verra best to induce her to abandon the profaisshon, for, to be quite candid, I hae held the same opinion as yourself ever since the first day she came to the yaird." So saying, David went up to Kitty, and with all the weight of his authority represented that it was high time for them to take their valuable steeds back to their stable.

"The hounds will do naething mair to-day," he said. "I hae it on his lairdship's ain word. He says the ground is nae in a fit state to hunt, and nae sensible body can deny that he is in the recht. People hae been tumbling about like ninepins, and I did hear a report that Mr. Martin, of Courthill, had slipped up and broken his leg. Tak my word for it, Miss Kitty, we're best at hame on sic a day as this, for it's nae safe for man nor beast."

CHAPTER XLVII.

LEAVING THE HOUNDS.

KITTY was not sorry when David Frazer suggested a retreat. After standing still for a while, she began to realize how very sore and stiff she was from her fall. Her back ached with a burning pain which could not have been much worse had a hot iron been applied to it, and she felt curiously faint and dizzy. She was fain to acknowledge that a quiet seat by the fireside offered superior attractions to remaining in the saddle— at all events, for that day. Nevertheless, she did not like to give in and go meekly home, just as a good little girl obeying orders might do. Lord Algy watched David's attempts at persuasion, and seeing a certain hesitation visible in Kitty's countenance, accosted her.

"I'm always asking favors of you, and laying myself open to rebuffs," he said, "but perhaps just for once you'll oblige me in a small thing which entails little or no sacrifice on your part."

"You are very ceremonious, my lord," she returned, striving to speak in a tone of flippant ease. "Pray express your wishes—or rather commands, for such extreme solemnity betrays that they belong to the latter category."

"Go home, Kitty. The hounds have about lost their fox, and we are not likely to have any sport. Will you do this to please me?"

She glanced at the pack, who, with noses down and waving sterns, were scattered in various directions, and then at his honest, anxious face. A lump rose in her throat. "Yes," she said, "I will."

He held out his hand and squeezed hers hard.

"Thank you. Although you won't admit it, I know you are not feeling quite up to the mark. And now good-by. I suppose," wistfully, "it will be ages before we meet again."

"I suppose so," she acquiesced. And then, without any more parting words, she turned from him abruptly, and said to David Frazer:

"Come, let us go. Since we have marching orders, it's no use standing about any longer and letting the horses get cold."

"By all means," he responded readily. Upon which they walked off side by side, making for the Belfield road by a series of bridle-gates which led through the fields. A wind had sprung up since the morning, which rendered some of the gates rather heavy, and the first one of all proved peculiarly troublesome. The latch was so stiff that David finally had to dismount in order to open it. Whilst thus engaged Miss Van Agnew came bustling up from behind. A tail of her hair had come undone, and hung down her back, her hat was blown to one side, and altogether she presented an extremely dishevelled appearance.

"Oh," she gasped, "I'm so glad I've caught you up. I never could get through these abominable gates by myself, especially with this horse; he's so fidgety and impatient, and wont stand still for a moment. May I come back with you, Miss Herrick?"

"Most certainly," answered Kitty. "Our road lies the same way for a couple of miles."

"I'm delighted to hear that. Perhaps you can tell me how far I am from Gretton Grange."

"Just five miles, Miss Van Agnew; so you have not a very long ride home."

"What a mercy! This is, without exception, the most horrid day I've ever been out hunting. As far as the riding part of the business went, I've simply hated it, haven't you?"

"The going certainly was not very grand," Kitty replied, "and in consequence there have been a good many accidents. Poor Diana! I'm so glad she did not lose her life. A valuable mare like that is not easy to replace at the beginning of the season. I presume, however," and she glanced significantly at her companion, "that if you have not enjoyed the actual hunting you have liked seeing your friends?"

Kitty had noticed with scorn that Cyril scarcely left the heiress's side for a second, hence this remark.

The fair Judith colored consciously.

"Now, Miss Herrick," she said, "don't go poking your fun at me. I know quite well what you mean. Of course I liked my friend's society. Why shouldn't I?"

"Oh!" said Kitty demurely. "For no reason whatever."

"I should have enjoyed myself much more, though," continued Miss Van Agnew irritably, "had I only been riding a nice, steady animal, but this celebrated hunter of yours is enough to drive one wild. When one is in mortal terror of being bucked off every instant it is impossible to talk comfortably."

"Conversation must certainly prove rather trying under such circumstances," said Kitty, with an indulgent smile.

"Trying! I should think it was. To begin with, I could not hear more than about half of what Captain Mordaunt was saying."

"That must have been a terrible deprivation," said Kitty, unable to refrain from satire.

"I felt it to be so," said Judith, in all good faith. "He is so extremely pleasant and agreeable. Be quiet, will you," as Tiny Tim, fresh as when he came out, shied at a wheelbarrow by the roadside. "Why can't you behave properly, instead of in that fiendish manner, exactly, too, when I wasn't expecting anything."

"You'll get to like him, after a bit, just as much as you dislike him now," said Kitty. "He only wants knowing."

"Humph!" growled Miss Van Agnew. "I have no desire to cultivate his acquaintance any further, and shall take precious good care never to get on his back again."

Kitty opened her eyes wide at this. To give four hundred guineas for a horse one day and discard him the next seemed rather extravagant. Besides, she did not like the idea of Tiny Tim being chopped and changed from one stable to another, and in all probability going from a good home to a bad. "What do you intend to do with the little horse?" she asked. "You wont keep him to look at, will you?"

"No, certainly not. I shall sell him. In fact, I have a customer in my eye at the present moment."

"I hope you wont think it impertinent, Miss Van Agnew, if I ask who he is?"

"Lord Algernon Loddington. He came up to me to-day whilst I was in difficulties, and said if ever I wanted to part with the horse he would take it as a particular favor if I gave him the first offer."

"And what did you say?"

"I said that Tiny Tim did not suit me, and probably would be for sale before long, in which case I would bear his request in mind. But," added Judith, with characteristic shrewdness, "I don't intend to lose any money over the transaction, if only to prove to Captain Mordaunt that I did not make such a bad bargain as he pretends. He declares four hundred was a ridiculous price for me to have given, and that the horse is not worth half."

"You seem to set great store by Captain Mordaunt's opinions, Miss Van Agnew. Are you quite sure of their disinterestedness?"

"How do you mean?" inquired Judith, struck by the bitter tone which her companion assumed.

"Only that I happen to know the gentleman in question was most anxious to secure Tiny Tim for his own riding, and probably would buy him to-morrow if he could persuade you to part at a reduced rate."

"Why do you put such a nasty, mean idea into my head?" said Miss Van Agnew, with a heightened color. "I wish *you* wouldn't."

"Because," began Kitty impetuously, but she checked herself just in time, and refrained from showing Cyril up in his true light.

"After all," she said to herself, "why should I spoil his little game? The necessity of his marrying money has been impressed upon me frequently, and Miss Van Agnew is old enough to take care of Number One. If she has fallen in love with Cyril Mordaunt, so much the better for him and so much the worse for her."

"I say, Miss Herrick," said Judith, after a somewhat prolonged pause, during which she had steadily scrutinized her companion's features, "what's your grudge against Captain Mordaunt? It's no use pretending you haven't got one, for I know better."

"You possess a lively imagination, Miss Van Agnew. I am afraid it runs away with you at times."

"Not in the present instance. You look as spiteful as possible whenever Cy—I mean Captain Mordaunt's— name is mentioned."

"I apologize for my looks. Unfortunately, I can't alter them even to please you. If I could I would."

"Now, don't be sarcastic. It aint your style. Do you know what has occurred to me?"

"No, how should I?"

"You wont be offended if I speak plainly?"

"No. I have already remarked that you are given that way. If spitefulness is one of my defects, plainness of speech is equally one of your attributes."

"Well, then, it has struck me—now, don't get cross— that you are just a trifle—ahem! jealous of the attentions Captain Mordaunt shows me."

Kitty laughed hysterically. "Jealous! Oh, dear no! How utterly absurd! Whatever made you fancy such a thing as that?"

"I don't know," said Miss Van Agnew, sucking her under lip thoughtfully; "but somebody told me that he had been very attentive to you before I appeared on the scene, and I thought—please don't frown so—I thought that you might not perhaps like being superseded in *his affections* by a comparative stranger."

" *His* affections!" echoed Kitty scornfully. She longed to tell her companion how little they were worth, and that he was only after her for the sake of her money; but the charge of jealousy effectually sealed her lips and prevented her from giving Judith any warning. Perhaps she realized, also, that it would be useless. Miss Van Agnew was evidently in a state of flattered vanity which rendered her temporarily impervious to the voice of common sense. So Kitty resolved to say nothing calculated to awake her from the fool's paradise where she was dreaming illusive dreams destined never to meet with realization.

"Once upon a time, Captain Mordaunt was condescending enough to take notice of your humble servant," she said satirically. "But when I lost my fortune, like a sensible youth he perceived the folly of his ways. As far as I am concerned, he is perfectly at liberty to address his attentions where he pleases. You can tell him so from me." Miss Van Agnew's countenance cleared, and she smiled with an air of relief.

"That's all right. Do you know, Miss Herrick, I had a kind of notion that there was something up between you and him, and although I don't mind admitting that I like him awfully, and consider him the handsomest and most agreeable man I have ever met, still, situated as I am, I should not deem it right to poach on another girl's ground. Money is a great power, and it gives me an advantage in the matrimonial race. You understand what I mean, don't you?"

"Yes," said Kitty, "perfectly. And your scruples do you honor. Not many women are such fair rivals or display so generous a regard for another person's feelings."

"Well," said Miss Van Agnew, "since we have got on the subject I am glad we have had this little explanation. It seems to clear the course somehow."

Kitty quite agreed with the sentiment. There was a blunt, if somewhat unrefined, honesty about her companion, together with a shrewdness and originality which were far from displeasing. She felt that in spite of many patent defects Judith Van Agnew's heart was in the right place, and wealth had not yet rendered it hard.

"If you have the least uneasiness with reference to Captain Mordaunt's civilities to me," she said, "take my advice, and ask him to tell you the whole story of our friendship with his own lips. But you may safely believe me when I affirm that any little liking or admiration he may once have entertained has long since passed away. As Miss Herrick, of Herrington Hall, he condescended to know me, but I am far beneath his notice nowadays." And she flicked away a clod of mud from Sir Moses's shoulder.

Miss Van Agnew looked at her sharply, as if not wholly convinced of the truth of this statement.

"I don't like you one bit," she said, "when you talk like that. You have a nice, pleasant open face naturally, and it doesn't suit to be bitter and say sarcastic things."

"One can't help being sarcastic sometimes," responded Kitty, with a sigh. "And now, Miss Van Agnew, we must part company, for this is your way. I don't think you can mistake the road," pointing to a grassy lane which branched off to the left. "It goes straight to Gretton Grange."

"Thanks, Miss Herrick. I am sorry to have to say good-by so soon, especially as we were having quite an interesting talk. By the way," and she reined Tiny Tim back a pace or two, "I want you to do me a favor."

"Willingly, if it be in my power," rejoined Kitty, who was beginning to conceive a certain liking for the heiress, mingled with compassion for a fellow-sufferer laboring in Cupid's toils. "What is it?"

"Captain Mordaunt," began Miss Van Agnew, "we, I mean, are talking of getting up a ladies' point-to-point race next month. Miss Bretby, Mrs. Douglas Morgan, and several others have already promised to enter their horses. I shall enter my gray mare, probably; but

Captain Mordaunt says Tiny Tim is much faster, and also a better stayer, and he thinks that provided you would consent to pilot him he is bound to win."

Kitty colored. "I am infinitely obliged to Captain Mordaunt for the flattering opinion he entertains of my equestrian powers. May I ask if he proposes that I should ride for hire?"

"Now, there you go again.. Really, Miss Herrick, you are too bad. Because I had so little tact as to hurt your feelings once, do you suppose that I am such a brute as deliberately to do so again?"

"I was not speaking of you, but of Captain Mordaunt," answered Kitty somewhat penitently.

"And I asked you to do me a favor, leaving money out of the question altogether. If we win, and it affords me pleasure to give you some little present as a memento of the occasion, surely even you cannot be so churlish as to refuse."

"I seem to have made a very bad impression, Miss Van Agnew."

"No, but you are horribly proud—as proud as Lucifer, and your pride is of a sort which hurts yourself without doing anybody else any good. Now, don't be angry with me for speaking the truth."

"You may be right," said Kitty reflectively. "I used to think it a fine thing to be proud and independent, but I'm beginning to alter my opinions. Certainly you present me to myself in a new and not wholly favorable light."

"I did not intend to do that," said Judith. "You must not think too much of my random remarks."

"They are aimed pretty straight," said Kitty. "At any rate, they hit the target. When I get home I promise to sit me down in an arm-chair and meditate seriously on all my sins of omission and commission."

"I would much rather you would give your mind to the race," rejoined Miss Van Agnew; "for you see if Tiny Tim won it I should be able to sell him well and get as much from Lord Algernon as I gave. The thing is, will you agree to ride?"

CHAPTER XLVIII.

KITTY thought a moment before making an immediate reply. It was torture to her to see Tiny Tim badly ridden and not done justice to. She could not bear watching his mouth being jagged at, and his temper destroyed, knowing all the while how differently he would go if properly handled. At Furrowdale he would have the best of homes, and literally be in clover, besides belonging to a master who, if unable to do more than hack him about, would never ill-use him. Yet she shrunk from the thought of appearing in a public race so soon after her father's death. Miss Van Agnew seemed to anticipate this latter objection, for she made haste to say, " It will be quite a private affair—no mob, or crowd, or anything of that sort. We intend to keep the race strictly among ourselves, and Mr. Cree—you know whom I mean, that nice red-headed farmer—has promised to find us a course over his land. So what do you say, Miss Herrick? Will you or wont you?"

" I will," answered Kitty firmly. " But," she went on, glancing at Tiny Tim, " the little horse is as fat as a bullock. If he is to have a chance he must be properly trained. At present I can see he is not in condition. What is the distance?"

".About three miles. At least, so Captain Mo——"

" So Captain Mordaunt says," interrupted Kitty mockingly. " I quite understand that his utterances are all-paramount, and am becoming accustomed to the phrase."

She was both surprised and relieved to find how great an alteration had taken place in her feelings. She was as a new being, a free creature recently escaped from slavery, for Cyril's desertion ceased to occasion regret. The bonds which had held her were loosened, the last link broken. Her love was dead—a thing of the past, which could not be recalled. And she rejoiced in her new-found liberty, and even wondered whether the sentiment she had entertained for Cyril had ever been a genuine passion, or merely some strange and passing infatuation.

"How would it answer for me to send Tiny Tim to Mr. Ruddle's, and then you could ride him yourself every day?" suggested Miss Van Agnew.

"The very thing," rejoined Kitty, "always provided that Mr. Ruddle agrees to such an arrangement."

"He's sure to do that," said Judith confidently. "I'll make it worth his while, and buy another horse from him."

"When is the race coming off?" asked Kitty. "You have forgotten to mention the date."

"For the excellent reason that it is not yet fixed. I will let you know as soon as it is." So saying, Miss Van Agnew waved her hand cordially and trotted off at a pace which made Kitty shudder for Tiny Tim's fore-legs.

"Poor little horse!" she mused. "In three or four years' time you'll be getting old, and will require kind treatment. I am glad I said Yes, for your sake." Then apparently, a disagreeable thought flashed across her brain, for she clinched her small fist resolutely, and added mentally, "I only hope to goodness he'll never mount Lady Algy on my poor, dear pet. If I thought that, nothing—no, nothing—would induce me to ride in the race. I'd sooner cut my head off."

Whilst the two ladies had been conversing, David Frazer very discreetly kept in the background, but directly Kitty was once more alone he came to her side, and regarded her with a scrutinizing glance so keen and penetrating that it considerably disconcerted its object.

"What are you looking at?" she demanded. "Is anything the matter?"

25

"Na, but I fear ye are nae feeing exactly weel, Miss Herrick. I watched ye trot the noo, and thought ye seemed to rise a bit uneasy in the saddle."

"I shall be all right after a night's rest," she said. "Sir Moses is excited and wont walk. His constant ambling is rather fatiguing, I admit."

"He's just a shuffly brute at best," said David, transferring his gaze to the brown. "If I had been by at the time I never would hae let the maister buy him. But we mak mistakes noo and again. For my ain part, I entirely agree with his lairdship's remarks."

"What did Lord Algernon say?" inquired Kitty, with a sudden flush.

"He was talking about ye, and mentioned it as his opinion that ye ought to give up your present profaishun."

"That's all very well," she said impatiently. "But how can I?"

David's countenance suddenly assumed a curious expression. On a visage less stern it would probably have been termed sentimental. If a closing of the eyes, an expansion of the nostrils, and a widening of the mouth are indicative of supreme tenderness, then Kitty might have had some inkling of what was coming. As it was, she happened to glance down at her knee, where she saw an incipient hole over the pommel which completely occupied her attention.

"There is a way," he said; "but to be quite plain with ye, Miss Herrick, I feel a delicacy in mentioning it."

Of course this was enough to arouse Kitty's curiosity, this and his odd mysterious manner.

"Please explain yourself, Mr. Frazer."

"Ay, but that's just what I dinna altogether like to do."

"Why not, pray?"

"I wad nae care to offend ye, Miss Kitty, and that's just the truth."

Even now she had not a suspicion what he was leading

up to, and replied fearlessly. "You could not possibly do that."

Thus emboldened, David hemmed and hawed, fixed his eyes on his horse's ears in order to prevent their straying to his companion's face, and with sundry stoppages and hesitations, most unusual to the laconic mode of speech which he adopted as a rule, began, "Weel, then, Miss Kitty, remember ye hae given me your wurrd not to be offended, and ye must nae think I mean this as an impairtenance."

"No, no," she interrupted. "Go on."

"Weel, then, I'm just a plain man, neither mair nor less."

"Do you mean plain in the sense of looks?" she broke in again. "If so, don't be so unkind to yourself."

Her playful and unconscious observations evidently rather balked him, but having once screwed up his courage to the point, he recommenced. "As I was remarking, I'm but a plain man, and hae nae pretensions to be in the same class o' life as yourself, but ain way and ainither I hae managed to lay by a guid bit o' money, and could afford to keep a wife pretty comfortable. Anyhow, she would na have to wairk so hard as in the yaird, and,"—turning very red,—"if ye wad tak me——"

He came to a sudden halt, for Kitty's eyes were directed to his with an expression of terrified appeal.

"Don't, don't—please don't say any more, Mr. Frazer, for both our sakes."

He set his lips firm. His was one of those slow, tenacious natures not easily daunted.

"I knew how it wad be," he said doggedly. "Ye do not think me guid enough. Ye want a fine gentleman."

"Indeed, Mr. Frazer, you are wrong. You have been a kind friend to me since I entered Mr. Ruddle's service, and God knows I have no pride; but——"

"But what?" he demanded eagerly. "Ye will obleege me by speaking straight oot all that is in ye're mind."

There was a ring in his voice, a look in his eye, which aroused her womanly pity.

"Oh," she cried. "Why do you persist in bringing this pain on yourself? I appreciate the goodness of heart which doubtless has prompted your offer. You are sorry for me, and think by making me your wife to save me from a hard and toilsome life; but you do not love me."

"I do," he interposed, in a tone which admitted of no misinterpretation.

"And," she exclaimed hastily, "I do not love you."

"Not noo, may be. But if I try verra hard ye might perhaps some day."

She shook her head, and glanced at his great knotted hands, rough with work, and at their broken black nails, then her eyes travelled upwards and rested on his coarse red throat enwrapped in a bird's-eye handkerchief, and on the homely face above. That glance rendered yet more distinct the gulf which necessarily exists between a refined and cultured lady and a comparatively uneducated man lacking the external marks of personal smartness and cleanliness which characterize a gentleman. She had heard of girls running away with grooms and even marrying them, but she could not conceive of the state of mind which rendered such an alliance possible. In the present conjunction, she felt that the truest kindness was to speak without reserve.

"Mr. Frazer," she said, "I do not know what first made you entertain the idea of addressing me as you have done, but it is only right to tell you straightforwardly that I cannot consider your proposition either now or at any future time. It will save us both a good deal if you will understand this once for all." He sighed and stared ahead more pertinaciously than ever. A long silence ensued. He broke it at length by saying, "Weel, weel, Miss Kitty, I scarcely expected ye wad say yes. It was nae in the nature o' things that ye should fancy me, but I promised Lord Algernon that I wad do my verra best to persuade ye to give up the profaisshun, and I could nae think of any better or more honorable way."

She turned upon him with eyes of fire and a face flushed red from throat to brow.

"Ah!" she cried indignantly, "now I have found out the reason of this strange conduct on your part. It was acting on Lord Algernon Loddington's advice, I suppose, that you proposed? *He* suggested that I would make you a suitable wife?" She was transformed. Her whole frame quivered with passion.

"Na, na, Miss Herrick," said David, feeling instinctively that he had committed an error in introducing his lordship's name. "I did na say that. Ye are making a mistake—quite a mistake. Lord Algernon had naething to do with the matter."

"I'm glad to hear it," she responded, quieting down, though her cheeks still flamed.

"It was my incleenations prompted the proposal," said David. "I hae had it in my mind for some time."

"Mr. Frazer, will you do me a service? Will you promise faithfully never to allude to this subject again? Let us forget it entirely."

"It is nae so easy to do that," he responded, lifting his hat and rubbing his fingers through his close-cropped hair.

"I think you can manage it if you try. And now, shall we trot on? I am cold and tired."

Ay, and humbled and heart-sore, she might have added. Was this what she had come to? Had she fallen so low that out of pure pity for her forlorn condition a common working-man asked her to be his wife in order to remove her from the hardships incidental to the profession which she had deliberately chosen? With shame and remorse it occurred to her that in the fancied security of birth, which from her point of view rendered all amatory feelings out of the question, she had chatted to David with a freedom and treated him in a friendly, familiar manner which doubtless had encouraged false hopes and were responsible for this humiliating climax, for humiliating she felt his proposal to be. It argued a want of reserve on her part which she now bitterly regretted. And yet she had acted in all innocence, never for one moment imagining that any tender passages were likely to arise between them. It was impossible to be angry with David; nevertheless, a secret voice whispered that the distance which separated them must appear smaller to him than it did to her, otherwise he never could have entertained the sentiments which he did. Altogether, it was a most unfortunate affair, and one which she heartily wished had never taken place. It rendered the situation so much more complicated, and must necessarily create constraint and embarrassment in their future intercourse. Her thoughts shrunk from the morning exercise and the daily meeting in the yard. How could she ever look him in the face or meet his eyes again, with the mortifying consciousness strong upon her that she had only to say the word in order to become Mrs. David Frazer?

Neither he nor she uttered another syllable until they reached Belfield. Then David lifted his head, and said:

" It has occurred to me, Miss Herrick, that it wull na be sae pleasant for us to meet in the future, and I hae made up my mind, therefore, to gae straight to the maister and gie him warning."

"For goodness' sake, don't do any such thing," she responded in alarm, knowing what store Mr. Ruddle set on David's services, and how such conduct would inevitably give rise to explanations. "There is no reason why we should not continue friends."

He shook his head obstinately.

"I dinna seem to fancy the auld place any longer. It is too small for both of us, and I can find anither situation easier than you. My mind is made up, so it's nae guid your trying to prevent me."

She dared not remonstrate. He looked so stern and decided. But this announcement rendered her thoroughly wretched, for she could not help realizing that things would never have reached such a crisis but for her advent in the yard. Acting on his intention, no sooner had David dismounted than he requested an interview with Mr. Ruddle, who had returned early. That gentleman again happened to be on the point of taking tea with his better half, and invited Frazer to join him in a cup of the refreshing beverage. But David was too perturbed in mind to accept the invitation. Love was a new experience, and it took away his desire for stimulants. After some hesitation, he blurted out that he wished to leave in a fortnight's time. As may be supposed, his employer was considerably taken aback by the intimation, and pressed him to declare his motive. David at first refused, but Mr. Ruddle became so urgent that finally he yielded to persuasion, and confessed the state of his affections. Poor Mr. Ruddle was in despair at the prospect of losing his right-hand man, but no offers of increased wages would induce David to reconsider his determination. He vowed that go he would and must. When he left the room, Mrs. Ruddle looked triumphantly at Peter and made use of the pithy but overwhelming remark so dreaded by faulty husbands. She did not attempt to sympathize with him in his misfortunes; she merely said, "Peter" (the voice very severe), "*I told you so.* You've nobody but yourself to thank for this."

CHAPTER XLIX.

KITTY SPEAKS HER MIND.

A COUPLE of days later, Kitty had occasion to go to the station in order to send off a telegram for Mr. Ruddle. She rode Sir Moses over, and whilst waiting for a porter to take the message inside a train came rushing along, and two or three minutes after it had been brought to a standstill Miss Van Agnew appeared, followed by a footman laden with parcels. Directly she perceived Kitty, she went up to her and said: ·

"How do you do, Miss Herrick? You are the very person I wanted to see."

"Indeed!" exclaimed Kitty, bending low over Sir Moses's neck so as to facilitate the process of conversation.

"Yes," responded Judith. "I've two pieces of news to tell you, and will begin with the least important."

Kitty could not help remarking how extremely pleased Miss Van Agnew appeared to be. Her face beamed with a joy which she took no pains to conceal, and happiness seemed to radiate from her whole person. For the time being it rendered her almost good-looking, and lent a glow of animation to her countenance which supplied the place of beauty. Looking at her, Kitty said to herself, "Why, dear me, you are not so plain after all. My first impressions were wrong, or else you have very much improved."

"To judge from your appearance," she said with a smile, "your news is good.".

Judith laughed a cheery laugh which effectually confirmed the supposition.

"I hope you wont be disappointed," she said, "but owing to various circumstances the race is given-up."

"Given up!" echoed Kitty in surprise.

"Yes. Somebody," and the heiress blushed a deep red, "did not like the idea of my riding and endangering my precious neck; and so we agreed, after some discussion, that it would be better to let the thing drop. Two or three ladies had promised us their support, but others were opposed to the notion, and nearly all the men, without exception, were down on a female point-to-point. So perhaps everything has turned out for the best. I only hope you don't mind our change of plans, Miss Herrick?"

"Not I," rejoined Kitty. "To tell the truth, the sole reason I agreed to pilot Tiny Tim was because, in the event of your selling him, I wished to secure him a really good home."

"Then you will be pleased to hear that he has one. I parted with him yesterday."

"To Lord Algernon Loddington?"

"Yes; he was always at me about the horse, and he gave me the price I paid, so that I have lost nothing by the transaction."

"In spite of Captain Mordaunt?" queried Kitty, with fine malice.

"Yes," continued Judith; "but if I had only known what was going to happen to-day I should have kept him and given him in a present to somebody else."

"To the gentleman named?" asked Kitty, with a feeling of relief that Tiny Tim had escaped this fate, for Cyril was not kind to his horses, and rode them like machines. She had often seen him bully them considerably.

"You make a good guess," responded Miss Van Agnew, the color again surging up to her cheeks. "And now for my second piece of news. I wonder if it will surprise you very much?"

"I fancy not," said Kitty, demurely. "Is it connected with matrimony?"

"Oh! you are a regular witch. However, to begin at the beginning. Be it known, then, that I ran up to town this morning by an early train to try on a habit. Imagine my astonishment when, just as the guard was shutting the door of my compartment, in jumped Captain Mordaunt, looking so handsome! You can't conceive how handsome he looked."

"I presume he had not the slightest idea you were going?" said Kitty with irrepressible sarcasm.

"I believe I did happen to mention it beforehand, but quite in a casual way, and I never thought for a single moment that he would make the supreme effort of rising at seven and breakfasting at eight in order to be my travelling companion."

"It wouldn't do him any harm to exert himself for once," remarked Kitty unsympathetically.

"Oh! now if you are going to be disagreeable I shant say another word."

"Vain threat," said Kitty with a smile. "As if you could keep your secret to yourself! Why, you are positively bursting with it!"

"We had the carriage all to ourselves," went on Judith, confidentially, "and I must say he was awfully nice—nicer even than usual. At first we talked about indifferent things, but after a while the conversation took a sentimental turn, and to cut a long story short he ended by proposing."

"And you—you accepted him? But the question is superfluous."

"I did." And Judith glanced apologetically at her companion. "Of course, I know that Daniel will call me a fool, and most people will be of the opinion that with my fortune I ought to have done a great deal better; and perhaps I ought. But the truth is, Cyril has won my heart—he's so awfully good-looking; and I don't mind telling you in confidence that I'm tremendously in love with him."

By an involuntary movement Kitty put out her hand and rested it on Miss Van Agnew's. The sentiment paramount in her breast was one of intense compassion mingled with individual relief.

"I hope you will be happy," she said gravely, unable to offer any warmer congratulations, though she felt the words sounded cold.

"Thanks.   I hope so too.   Marriage is a great lottery for a girl situated as I am, who never can make sure of any one caring for her for herself.   But I believe that I have chosen rightly.   Anyhow, my heart has decided the affair."

"Did you leave Captain Mordaunt in town?" inquired Kitty.

"Yes, we went straight off to see his mother, but he is coming down by an evening train, and we both intend to hunt to-morrow.   Now you understand why I regret having sold the bay.   He would have made Cyril such a lovely engagement present—so much better than jewelry, or anything of that sort.   By the way, I met Lord Algernon to-day in Bond Street, and tried hard to be let off my bargain."

"And did he agree?" inquired Kitty.

"No.   I had always looked upon him as a nice, good-natured fellow; but he refused my request most obstinately, and even when I went so far as to confide the reason, he still remained obdurate, which was really too bad."

"Then you told Lord Algy that you were engaged to Captain Mordaunt?"

"Yes.   After all, there is no occasion to make any mystery about the matter.   All the county will know in a day or two."

"And what did he say?   Did he seem as if he approved?"

"He behaved in the oddest fashion.   All of a sudden he seized hold of my hand and wrung it up and down as if it were a pump-handle.   Really, I felt quite affected by the warmth of his congratulations, and my knuckles have not got over it yet.   But now I must be going.   That reminds me—Daniel wants to have a look at the brown horse you were riding the other day. Will you tell Mr. Ruddle we shall come over on Friday morning?"

"What time?" demanded Kitty laconically.

"About twelve. Ta-ta." And with a gay wave of the hand Miss Van Agnew mounted into her carriage and drove briskly away.

When she was fairly out of sight, Kitty gathered Sir Moses's reins together and rode slowly home. A crowd of thoughts surged up in her mind. As before stated, she pitied the heiress sincerely, and harbored no ill-will against her; but for the man who worshipped at the shrine of Mammon, who made self his God, and was incapable of a true and serious passion, she had the deepest contempt. His conduct was inexcusable, and she bitterly regretted that she had not already done what for some time past she was resolved upon—namely, write and break off her engagement. Now he had taken the first step. But although every one would hear sooner or later that she was a jilted maiden—for it is impossible to keep these things secret—it was not too late to let him know what she thought of him. So as soon as she reached her lodgings she seized pen and paper and wrote the following:—

Captain Mordaunt,—I have just seen Miss Van Agnew, and she has informed me of the state of affairs. Why could you not have told me to my face that your so-called love disappeared simultaneously with my fortune? Such conduct might not have been kind, but at least it would have been straightforward and have saved me much cruel suspense and humiliation. Instead of which, you simulated a false passion, put me off with excuses which at first I was too infatuated to see through, and left me to find out by degrees that you did not care for me when my money was gone. Your behavior has been shameful. No honorable man could have acted as you have acted; but coward, traitor, as I now know you to be, I thank you,—yes, I thank you,—for setting me free. I loved you well and truly, far better than you deserved, but my eyes are thoroughly opened at last to your meanness and deceit. Miss Van

Agnew believes in you as I once did. Poor girl! You will make her as miserable as you made me. But your power over me has gone. I see you as you are, and so seeing, offer up prayers of thanks for the doom I have escaped. Good-by. In return for the wealth she bestows, the comforts and position she secures, I trust you will treat your wife better than you did the penniless

KATHERINE HERRICK.

Having finished this letter, she posted it, and felt as if a crushing load had been removed from her mind. But the following afternoon, to her unutterable surprise, who should come riding into the yard but Cyril Mordaunt. He had evidently been out hunting, and was splashed with mud from top to toe. She had not given him credit for possessing courage enough to court an interview.

"May I have a word with you?" he asked. His face was pale, and the muscles of his cheeks twitched as he spoke.

She arched her level eyebrows, and in the coldest and most provocative manner said, "Whence this honor?"

"I could not rest, Kitty," he responded, much agitated. "I got your letter this morning."

"So I suppose. The post seldom miscarries in these civilized times."

"For God's sake don't speak and look at me so. Do give me an opportunity of explanation."

"Have you a right to dictate my speech or control my looks, Captain Mordaunt? As for an explanation, if you can make one I am willing to listen."

"It was a cruel letter," he continued in tones of deep emotion. "I have not had a happy moment all day for thinking of it."

"Fie! in spite of the presence of your betrothed! Is she very dear to you? Are you very, very much in love?"

"Kitty," he cried desperately, "you make a great mistake if you fancy I am happy——"

"And are you not? You have everything to make

you so," she interrupted. "Twenty thousand a year! Surely the thought of such a fine income offers infinite attractions. You will be the envy and admiration of all your brother fortune-hunters."

"I am the most miserable man on the face of this earth," he responded gloomily. "You would not taunt me if you knew how wretched I am."

"Misery is good for some people," she retorted, quite unmoved by the confession. "A little of it wont do you any harm."

"Oh! Kitty, don't be so cold and hard. Surely there can be no need for me to tell you that I have only proposed to Miss Van Agnew from necessity."

"A very honorable motive, Captain Mordaunt," she said, with a sneer. "Might I recommend your imparting it to the lady?"

"What between my mother, on the one hand, and my creditors on the other," he went on bitterly, "I can hardly call my soul my own. I am hurried from pillar to post; but you must know that you are the only girl for whom I have ever cared really."

"One does not generally heap insult and neglect on the object of one's affections," she said coldly. Her heart was quite dead to him. Dead to his protestations, dead to his flattery, dead even to his personal beauty; but he could not realize the fact, and sought to take her hand. She drew it away as if a serpent had stung it, and exclaimed passionately, "How dare you?"

"Kitty," he said penitently, "forgive me. Let us be friends if we can't be anything else. I know I have behaved like a beast."

"Say, rather, like a coward and a hypocrite," she rejoined scornfully. "If you had come to me after my poor father's death, and said honestly, 'Kitty, I love you, but you are poor and I am poor, we cannot afford to marry,' I should have accepted the ultimatum without a murmur. But you did nothing of the sort. You temporized, made vague promises, and talked of something turning up, knowing quite well all the while that you had no prospects, and only awaited a convenient opportunity to throw me over without loss of credit to yourself. Of me you did not think—you did not care. If I had been a creature of stone you could not have treated me worse. I scarcely knew whether I was engaged or not. You never came near me. You hardly answered my letters, and paid attention to another girl before my very eyes. No, you need not appeal to my feelings," as he made a sign for her to forbear. " I. have none. You have killed them—at all events where you are concerned. My illusions are gone, and if you were the last man in the world, and had a hundred thousand a year, no earthly power would induce me now to become your wife. Yes, look at me—look at your own handiwork. Here I am, a lonely, forsaken, jilted girl, living on a pound a week; but I would rather—infinitely rather—be myself than you. I have said my say, now go." And she pointed to the road with a gesture of command which long pent-up passion rendered authoritative beyond description.

And he went. She exercised a mesmeric dominion over him which he was quite unable to resist. He sneaked off like a whipped hound, conscious that every word she spoke was true, and that he could offer no defence against her accusations. The recollection of her glowing, scornful young face was branded for all time on his memory, and as he rode dejectedly back to Furrow-dale her vibrant and contemptuous voice still rang in his ears. Indeed, he war not to be envied, for in spite of Miss Van Agnew, and the ease and affluence to which he looked forward, he realized at this moment that there are some stains on a man's honor, some dark blots on his manhood, which even money fails to gild.

CHAPTER L.

CONCLUSION.

THE Van Agnews were punctual to their appointment, and drove into Mr. Ruddle's yard a few minutes before twelve on Friday morning. The talk that had taken place concerning the ladies' point-to-point race had fired little Daniel Van Agnew's imagination, and he was now intent on picking up an animal likely to make a good steeplechaser and on entering him for some of the cross-country events which came off in the spring. Although fond of hunting, his nerves were somewhat defective, and he had arrived at the conclusion that jumping was nasty, dangerous work. But steeplechasing possessed this great advantage: you could always declare you were too heavy or too light—had no fear yourself, but must yield to the fond terrors of female relations, and so get somebody else to risk his neck— without the slightest imputation being cast on your courage. If the horse won, you got the credit. If he failed, the blame was invariably attributed to the jockey.

To a casual observer, Sir Moses presented the appearance of a fine racing-looking animal, and when Mr. Van Agnew saw Kitty riding him with hounds he was much struck with the brown. In fact, he pretty well made up his mind to purchase Sir Moses provided he could gallop. Not intending to act as pilot himself, speed was the essential point. He did not attach too much importance to manners, for in the event of his purchasing the thoroughbred he proposed sending him to a good training stable, where he could be thoroughly schooled.

After inspecting Sir Moses in his box he requested that he might be led out.

"Isn't Miss Herrick going to ride him?" he asked, as a helper flung a gentleman's saddle over the horse's loins.

"I thought you would prefer to see a man on his back," answered Mr. Ruddle, who, after a severe reprimand received from Lord Algy, was determined not to let Kitty run any risks.

But little Daniel was a great admirer of the fair sex, and half his pleasure in patronizing Mr. Ruddle's yard consisted in seeing Kitty and watching her lithe young figure sway gracefully to and fro in the saddle. So he rejoined, "Indeed I should not. In my opinion Miss Herrick sets a horse off far better than a great, ugly man, and I've come here to look at her quite as much as at the animal."

"You wont want her to go round the big course, will you, Mr. Van Agnew?" inquired Mr. Ruddle uneasily.

"No, no," responded Daniel, with impatience. "I quite understand that the horse is not a finished performer as yet. All I wish is to see him galloped, and perhaps popped over a hurdle, just so as to ascertain in what form he jumps."

Foreseeing no danger to the rider, Mr. Ruddle gave his consent. Mr. and Miss Van Agnew were too good customers to be lightly offended.

"In that case," he said, "we will go into the big meadow across the railway. It is nice and flat, and three-quarters of a mile round."

After a slight delay, they proceeded to the field in question, Kitty riding Sir Moses slightly in advance. The horse was fresh and well, and looked to advantage as with a light, peacocky step he walked along, arching his neck, whisking his tail, and champing playfully at the bit.

A connoisseur might have taken exception to his want of muscle, weak thighs and hocks, and long back; but Mr. Van Agnew knew little about the real points of a steeplechaser, and greatly admired Sir Moses's fine glossy coat, his air of breeding, and his generally

26

spirited appearance. No doubt, too, his admiration
was enhanced by the fact of a pretty girl being seated
in the saddle. Anyhow, he winked at Judith, and she
winked back at him, as much as to say, "Depend upon
it, this is the horse to carry off silver cups by the score."

When she came to the gate that led into the meadow,
Kitty stooped, and with a dexterous twist of her hunting
crop, threw it wide open. She stood for a moment
awaiting orders, and Mr. Ruddle went up to her and
said, "You need not trouble about any preliminaries.
Send him along at his best pace, and don't stop until I
hold up my hand. Then ease him at once. We must
not betray his weak point."

She nodded her head, and immediately started off at
a canter, which she gradually increased until Sir Moses
was fully extended. The turf was in beautiful condition, dry, yet not hard, and as elastic as a springboard.
This particular field happened to be almost as flat as a
billiard table, and offered no impediments to a leggy,
badly ribbed animal in the shape of ridge and furrow.
Consequently Sir Moses went at a rare pace, skimming
over the ground with a long, low stride as smooth as
machinery. Galloping was his chief accomplishment,
and for five furlongs he was almost fast enough to win
on the flat. But he could not stay. Both Kitty and
Mr. Ruddle knew this; but it was not their business to
proclaim the fact on the housetop. About the third
time round, Sir Moses's rider began to feel her steed
sob beneath her, and she therefore steadied him slightly,
glancing meanwhile expectantly in the direction of Mr.
Ruddle. He was a wonderful man on such occasions,
and knew exactly when to give the word. As if an
electric current had passed between him and the girl,
in a second up went his hand. Kitty pulled Sir Moses
back to a trot, and joined the little circle of spectators,
not noticing a well-known form walking behind a hedge
bordering the road close by, and whose owner was evidently making in their direction. The horse engaged
her full attention. He was inclined to be fidgety after

his gallop, and refused to stand docilely for further inspection.

"Bravo!" exclaimed Mr. Van Agnew, eying the brown approvingly. "He can slip along, and no mistake."

"He's the fastest animal we've had in our stable for many a year," observed Mr. Ruddle, who was anxious to pass Sir Moses on. "But then, just look at his pedigree. If breeding counts for anything he's bound to show a clean pair of heels between the flags to the cocktail division."

"Let's see him jump," interposed Judith, who considered galloping tame work in comparison, and never could perceive that there was any advantage in it.

"Get on the horse yourself, Mr. Van Agnew," urged Mr. Ruddle, "and pop him over those hurdles," indicating a flight within fifty yards.

But Daniel's modesty was such that it shrunk from a public display. He was not fond of jumping in cold blood, or indeed at any time, and infinitely preferred watching the performance to taking an active part in it.

"It is hardly worth while changing saddles," he said. "We must get back in time for luncheon." And he pulled out his watch.

"You don't object to giving Daniel a show, do you, Miss Herrick?" asked Judith laughingly. "His nerve is not exactly of the first order."

"Certainly," responded Kitty, with a broad smile. "No doubt it is well for him to be on the safe side."

She had not jumped Sir Moses since his fall, and was disagreeably surprised to find how great an impression it had made on his equine mind. Nothing would induce him to approach the hurdles. He declined them most obstinately, reared, plunged, and showed more temper than he had ever done before. Kitty tried all she knew to get him to face them, but in vain. He was regularly roused, and conducted himself like a perfect demon. Twice he reared so straight up on end that she had to throw herself on his neck in order to avoid slipping backwards.

"For God's sake get off the infernal brute, Kitty," cried a familiar voice from behind. "I thought you were never going to ride him again?"

She turned round, and perceived that Lord Algy had joined the group of bystanders. But she did not heed the injunction. She felt that in his presence nothing would induce her to show the white feather. It put her on her mettle. Clinching her teeth with grim resolve, she took Sir Moses short by the head, and gave him a sharp touch of the spur. He shook his ears and gave an angry snort. Up—up—up, then a horrible moment in which she struggled frantically to retain her equilibrium, followed by the vision of a great brown mass falling to earth—a crash, and—unconsciousness. . . . .

"You cur!" cried Lord Algy, turning furiously on Daniel. "You cowardly, contemptible cur, to let a woman ride a brute you are afraid to mount yourself. You have killed her." And before any one could say a word he rushed to the spot, dragged Sir Moses with herculean force from the girl's prostrate body, and lifted her in his arms as tenderly as if he had been a woman.

The weight removed, she sighed and opened her eyes. They met his, and slowly, as consciousness returned, a warm blush suffused her cheek. "Algy," she said faintly, "where—are—you—taking me?"

He pressed her to his heart. A wonderful sense of safety and protection stole over her spirit. She felt as if she could have lain there forever.

"I am taking you home, my darling—to Furrowdale Castle. Please God never to leave it except as my wife. We've had enough, and more than enough, of this tom-foolery."

She lay quite silent. A terror seized him—a terror lest, after all, things might go wrong. What if his mother had made a mistake?

"Kitty," he said hoarsely, "haven't you anything to say to me? Not a word? Wont you put me out of my agony?"

She averted her head, and by a supreme effort forced

herself to answer. She was ashamed, so horribly
ashamed of the past.

"Yes, I will; but I—I don't deserve your love. I am
like a butterfly whose wings are stained. Don't you understand?"

"I understand that I have been after the butterfly
ever since it was a chrysalis, and having captured it
with infinite trouble, shant let it go in a hurry."

"But, Algy, it looks as if I were only taking you
because I am poor and deserted, and not," shyly lifting
her eyes to his, "because I—love you."

Their glances met. His was honest and true, hers
full of remorse and embarrassment; and yet something
in the expression of her upturned face made his heart
beat with great, triumphant pulsations. He held her
tight. She could feel the muscles of his strong arms
swelling beneath his coat.

"Kitty," he whispered—"Kitty darling, is it possible!
Has it come at last, after all this weary waiting—these
mistakes?"

"Yes," she said softly; "I am ashamed to tell you so,
but it is true nevertheless. I have known it for some
time, and looking back, it seems to me that the feeling
was always there deep down in my heart. The other
was all a delusion."

"Are you sure you have recovered from your liking
for a third person?" he asked gayly, his countenance
grown suddenly bright.

"Yes, quite. I hate myself for ever having cared for
him. He is not worthy to tie your shoestrings. If you
only knew how different he is, Algy."

"Do you really love me, Kitty? Don't say so if you
do not; but I must know the truth one way or the
other."

"Algy, I do—I do—I do!" Her left hand seized his
and clutched it quite hard. She could not lift the right;
there was a curious dead pain in it. All at once he felt
her grasp relax, and became a prey to horrible fear;
but she had only fainted, and her face wore a smile of

such ineffable content that it touched him to the quick whilst it exercised a reassuring influence.

He would not allow any one to relieve him of his precious burden. He held her in his arms until a carriage was got ready, and then he drove straight to Furrowdale, where the duke and duchess welcomed her as a daughter.

Her right wrist was broken, but time and a good surgeon soon mended it, and three months afterwards she became Lady Algernon Loddington. The newly married couple made Herrington their home, and as the years passed a very happy one it proved. Children came and filled the old house with their sweet voices and the sound of their little pattering feet; and Algy—dear, kind, honest Algy—made as good a father as he did a husband. He and Kitty were devoted to each other, and effectually refuted the modern theory anent the misery and unnaturalness of marriage. They showed that the union of two pure and loving hearts is the highest form of existence possible on this faulty earth, and that there is such a thing as love after all. Many a laugh did they have together when her ladyship went forth to the chase mounted on Tiny Tim and she confided to her husband's ear how strong a dislike she had conceived for the future Lady Algy. They roared like children over that joke, and were never tired of repeating it.

David, after the fashion of old and valued servants, thought better of the warning he had given Mr. Ruddle, and owing to Miss Herrick abandoning the "profaishun," he remained in that gentleman's employ, and in course of time took unto himself a strapping lass of his own nationality. He still considers her ladyship, however, the most perfect specimen of womankind he has ever seen. Mrs. Ruddle makes great capital out of his affair with Kitty, and uses it as a lever against Peter whenever that excellent man exhibits a tendency to wander from the path of domestic virtue.

And Cyril, the egotist and fortune-hunter?

He, too, married, and obtained all the worldly advantages which wealth can bestow. But they could not give him a cheerful, contented disposition. Neither, as the years rolled by, did the possession of riches enlarge his aims or improve his character. Mrs. Mordaunt insisted on purchasing Gretton Grange, although he would have preferred to settle in another county; and it was gall and wormwood to him to see his wife and Lady Algy on the best of terms and to feel withered by her ladyship's contempt every time they met. He would have liked to make it up, and to carry on a *sub rosa* flirtation with his old flame; but Kitty showed him so plainly what she thought of him that he was forced to abandon the attempt. He and Judith quarrelled incessantly, but as his wife held the purse-strings, she had the upper hand; and he gradually sunk down into being a moody, dissatisfied man, forced to submit to a stronger will than his own. He had got what he wanted— money—but it failed signally to render him happy, and often he regretted the unfortunate circumstances which caused him to forsake "that pretty little horse-breaker" —the only girl who had ever made an impression on his cold and calculating heart.

THE END.

Printed in the United States
130393LV00005B/84/A